STUDIES IN THE CHRONOLOGY
OF THE DIVIDED MONARCHY
OF ISRAEL

HARVARD SEMITIC MUSEUM

HARVARD SEMITIC MONOGRAPHS

edited by
Frank Moore Cross

Number 48
Studies in the Chronology
of the Divided Monarchy
of Israel

by
William Hamilton Barnes

William Hamilton Barnes

STUDIES IN THE CHRONOLOGY OF THE DIVIDED MONARCHY OF ISRAEL

Scholars Press
Atlanta, Georgia

Studies in the Chronology
of the Divided Monarchy
# of Israel

by
William Hamilton Barnes

© 1991
Harvard University

Library of Congress Cataloging in Publication Data

Barnes, William Hamilton.
    Studies in the chronology of the divided monarchy of Israel /
William Hamilton Barnes.
    p. cm. — (Harvard Semitic monographs ; no. 48)
    Includes bibliographical references and indexes.
    ISBN 1-55540-527-4 (alk. paper)
    1. Bible. O.T. Kings—Chronology. 2. Jews—History—953-586
B.C.—Chronology. 3. Middle East—History—To 622—Chronology.
I. Title. II. Series.
BS1335.5.B37 1991
222'.5095—dc20   91-22768
                                          CIP

Printed in the United States of America
on acid-free paper

To my family,

in loving gratitude,

this book is dedicated.

(Joshua 24:15)

TABLE OF CONTENTS

LIST OF ABBREVIATIONS

ANEP *The Ancient Near East in Pictures.* James B. Pritchard, ed. Princeton: Princeton University Press, 1954.

ANET *Ancient Near Eastern Texts Relating to the Old Testament.* James B. Pritchard, ed. 2nd ed. Princeton: Princeton University Press, 1955.

ASAE *Annales du Service des Antiquités de l'Egypte.*

AUSS *Andrews University Seminary Studies.*

BA *The Biblical Archaeologist.*

BAR 2 *The Biblical Archaeologist Reader.* Vol. 2. Eds. David Noel Freedman and Edward F. Campbell, Jr. Garden City: Doubleday & Co., 1964.

BASOR *Bulletin of the American Schools of Oriental Research.*

BIFAO *Bulletin de l'Institut français d'archéologie orientale.*

BJRL *Bulletin of the John Rylands Library.*

CdÉ *Chronique d'Égypte.*

Dtr The Deuteronomistic History.

$\mathcal{G}^B$ Codex Vaticanus of the LXX.

$\mathcal{G}^L$ The (proto-)Lucianic recension of the LXX.

IDB *The Interpreter's Dictionary of the Bible.* Four vols. G. A. Buttrick, ed. Nashville: Abingdon Press, 1962.

IDBS *The Interpreter's Dictionary of the Bible.* Supplementary volume. Keith Crum, ed. Nashville: Abingdon Press, 1976.

IEJ	*Israel Exploration Journal.*
JANES	*Journal of the Ancient Near Eastern Society of Columbia University.*
JAOS	*Journal of the American Oriental Society.*
JARCE	*Journal of the American Research Center in Egypt.*
JBL	*Journal of Biblical Literature.*
JCS	*Journal of Cuneiform Studies.*
JEA	*Journal of Egyptian Archaeology.*
JNES	*Journal of Near Eastern Studies.*
JPOS	*Journal of the Palestinian Oriental Society.*
JQR	*Jewish Quarterly Review.*
JTS	*Journal of Theological Studies.*
LXX	The Septuagint.
MS(S)	Manuscript(s).
MT	The Massoretic Text.
PSBA	*Proceedings of the Society of Biblical Archaeology.*
RdÉ	*Revue d'Égyptologie.*
SJT	*Scottish Journal of Theology.*
VT	*Vetus Testamentum.*
ZÄS	*Zeitschrift für Ägyptische Sprache.*
ZAW	*Zeitschrift für die alttestamentliche Wissenschaft.*

LIST OF TABLES

PREFACE

One scholar, in a recent article on the subject of the chronology of the Divided Monarchy of Israel, after a brief and impatient survey of the subject, apparently had had enough: "Now the field of Biblical chronology is notoriously littered with scholars who have lost their heads," he declared.[1] After several years of study, the present writer is inclined to agree. There is something about all those mesmerizing numbers which are contained in the books of Kings and Chronicles--all those regnal totals, all those seemingly precise synchronisms--which both bedazzle and befuddle the would be chronographer who only longs to discover the key which would unlock the mystery, line up the kings, and straighten out the chronology for this important period of Israelite history.

Whether the present writer is in imminent danger of such capital impairment, the reader will no doubt soon decide. I can promise no alchemic elixir in the following pages, only an honest grappling with the various chronographic data from the several contemporary civilizations of the Ancient Near East. Nonetheless, it is hoped that some progress has been made, both in refuting some of the more extravagant suggestions which have been urged (often in surprisingly dogmatic language) as well as in formulating a chronology which has some chance of withstanding the test of time.

Acknowledging one's debt to previous scholarship may seem to be an expected task at this point: necessary, but performed in a perfunctory manner. However, in the area of chronology, such an acknowledgement is so overwhelmingly appropriate that I will gladly state the obvious: my reliance upon the work of others is evident on nearly every page of the present work. If I have made tangible progress in this subject, it is largely as the result of the work of my predecessors, and to them I am indeed grateful.

---

[1]Julian Reade, "Mesopotamian Guidelines for Biblical Chronology," *Syro-Mesopotamian Studies* 4 (1981) 3; see below, p. 128.

A number of individuals should be singled out for special thanks. Professor Frank Moore Cross originally suggested the topic; he has served as an unfailing source of encouragement and advice. It is also he who suggested that I publish this monograph, a revised version of my Harvard Th.D. thesis, in the Harvard Semitic Monograph series. Professors Hanson, Moran, and Strugnell have all proffered helpful suggestions as well. A special note of thanks must go to Professor Michael Coogan, whose comments, both literary and personal, have proved most valuable. I wish to thank as well Michael VanDoren, David Meppelink, and Stephen Stroup who have rendered hours of valuable technical assistance in generating this camera-ready document for Scholars Press. In addition, let me single out for special thanks my esteemed colleague, Rev. Steven Fettke, who proofread closely the final copy of the entire manuscript, ferreting out those pesky mistakes which seem to multiply in the night. Most of all, however, I must express my profound gratitude to my wife, Jan, and to my children. No doubt every graduate of a doctoral program can readily recall what a trying time the writing of the thesis is--but it was, in large measure, the result of the patient understanding and unfailing encouragement of my dear wife that this study has been completed, and my hours of research and writing were made far more bearable than I would have expected by the fresh perspective and good humor that only children can supply.

William H. Barnes

Southeastern College
Lakeland, Florida
March (Nisan), 1991

CHAPTER I

INTRODUCTION

In his brilliant essay on the structure of the Deuteronomistic History entitled *Überlieferungsgeschichtliche Studien*,[1] Martin Noth pointed to the importance of the chronological framework of the books of Kings:

> If we take even a superficial look at Dtr's work in Kings, we find that he is not exclusively interested in evaluating the individual kings and thus, indirectly, the monarchy *per se* (most scholars lay a one-sided stress on this aspect alone); rather, he is just as interested in constructing a definitive chronology, and for this purpose went to the trouble of taking over and reporting so many individual numbers from his sources.[2]

A closer examination of Dtr's chronological material in Kings presents us with an impressive variety of chronological data for the Divided Monarchy: all Judahite and Israelite kings are listed with their lengths of reign (and in the case of most of the Judahite kings, their ages at accession); synchronisms link the date of accession of nearly every king of either nation with the corresponding year of the current ruler of the other nation (until the fall of Samaria and the termination of the monarchy of the Northern Kingdom); and, not infrequently, various

---

[1]The essay was first published in 1943; second and third (unchanged) editions were published by Max Niemeyer Verlag, Tübingen, in 1957 and 1967; and an English translation entitled *The Deuteronomistic History* was published in 1981 as vol. 15 of the *Journal for the Study of the Old Testament Supplement Series*, David J. A. Clines, Philip R. Davies, and David M. Gunn, eds. (Sheffield, England: JSOT Press). For Noth, the term "Deuteronomistic" (Dtr) identified the work of the Exilic author/composer of the history of Israel found in the books of Joshua-Kings, as well as the framework of the book of Deuteronomy. More recently, F. M. Cross (*Canaanite Myth and Hebrew Epic* [Cambridge, Mass.: Harvard University Press, 1973], pp. 274-89) has argued persuasively for two editions of Dtr, a major programmatic document dating from the time of Josiah (Dtr 1) as well as the later Exilic edition (Dtr 2).

[2]Noth, *Deuteronomistic History*, p. 18.

historical events (some of which may now be dated from extant Assyrian or Babylonian annals) are linked to specific regnal years of the relevant king of Judah or Israel. Indeed, the overall Dtr framework of Kings, with its relentless, interlocking progression of Judahite and Israelite regnal notices and evaluations, itself emphasizes Dtr's concern with chronology.

Such an abundance of chronological data would normally be a source of delight to the historian of the Hebrew Bible, but the frequent inconsistencies and outright contradictions which exist among the various chronological notices in Kings have long perplexed biblical chronologists. The following example is all too typical: Amaziah of Judah, we are told, began to reign in the second year of Joash of Israel, and he reigned for a total of 29 years (2 Kgs 14:1-2). Elsewhere we are told that Joash reigned 16 years (2 Kgs 13:10), and was succeeded by his son Jeroboam II who reigned 41 years (2 Kgs 14:23). Simple arithmetic leads us to the following synchronism: Jeroboam's accession coincided with the 15th year of Amaziah's reign; and indeed we find such is the case according to the notice found in 2 Kgs 14:23. Again, we conclude from the Biblical data that Amaziah's son Azariah (Uzziah) became king in Jeroboam's 15th year, but this time we are told (in 2 Kgs 15:1) that Azariah became king in Jeroboam's 27th year! There is no accounting for the intervening 12 years in the biblical text; who (if anyone) reigned over Judah between Jeroboam's 15th and 27th year is unclear.[3]

Within the last century, as a secure Assyrian and Babylonian chronology of the first millennium B.C.E. has been established, resulting in some twenty external synchronisms for the period of the Divided Monarchy (with absolute dates in the Julian calendar),[4] further discrepancies in the biblical data have come to light. These external synchronisms serve as fixed "anchor points" to secure the chronology

---

[3]For a comprehensive discussion of the various types of chronological inconsistencies, see Edwin R. Thiele, *The Mysterious Numbers of the Hebrew Kings*, 1st ed. (Chicago: University of Chicago Press, 1951), pp. 5-9.

[4]The synchronisms are conveniently tabulated in Hayim Tadmor, "The Chronology of the First Temple Period: A Presentation and Evaluation of the Sources," *The World History of the Jewish People, First Series: Ancient Times, The Age of the Monarchies: Political History*, vol. 4, pt. 1, Abraham Malamat, ed. (Jerusalem: Massada Press, 1979), pp. 54-55.

of the Divided Monarchy at several key points (e.g., the fall of Samaria in 722/21, the siege of Jerusalem in 701 by Sennacherib, and the fall of Jerusalem in 587/86). However, these absolute dates also tend to complicate various reconstructions of the biblical chronology, as biblical scholars attempt to accommodate the already contradictory data to a fixed external chronology. A notorious example of this is the question of the dating of Hezekiah. The Dtr notices in Kings repeatedly and unequivocally maintain that he was already king of Judah before the fall of Samaria in 722/21 B.C.E. (2 Kgs 18:1-2; cf. vv 9-10 where the fall of Samaria is specifically dated to the sixth year of Hezekiah). However, we are later told (in v 13) that Sennacherib invaded Judah in the 14th year of Hezekiah (almost certainly corresponding to Sennacherib's Palestinian campaign in the summer of 701); as both external synchronisms are quite certain, some or all of the biblical data must be in error. A good number of scholars (including W. F. Albright) discount the biblical notices dating Hezekiah's accession to before the fall of Samaria, and, largely on the basis of the Sennacherib synchronism, suggest the year 715 as his actual accession year. Yet, as will be discussed at some length below in Chapter IV, one may indeed query the likelihood of the Dtr editor being so mistaken about the chronology of such an important Judahite king (especially so in Deuteronomistic terms, cf. 2 Kgs 18:3-7); would Israelite and Judahite tradition not have recalled correctly at least the identity of the king of Judah in power when the Northern Kingdom of Israel fell?

One major overall effect of these external synchronisms upon any effort to reconstruct the chronology of the Divided Monarchy is to cast considerable doubt upon the accuracy of the lengths of reign claimed for several of the Israelite and Judahite kings: the biblical numbers are simply too high. Either we must assume numerous co-regencies (i.e. a king designating his son as a coregent while he himself still remains on the throne, resulting in an actual chronological overlap in the regnal totals as given by Dtr for the two kings), or we must repeatedly question the soundness of the biblical data. At this point in the discussion, I merely point out the nature and extent of the problem; closer examinations of several of the biblical regnal totals will be found later in this chapter (also cf. the notes to my own tentative chronological reconstruction as found in the Appendix).

To be sure, modern biblical scholarship has not hesitated to grapple with the problem of the chronology of the Divided Monarchy.

In an important article in the *Encyclopedia Miqra'it*, Hayim Tadmor cited some fourteen different scholarly reconstructions (all proposed between 1884 and 1961) of the chronology of the Divided Monarchy;[5] and there have been several more proposals since.[6] For present purposes of introduction, it is hardly necessary to rehearse all these various proposals, several of which employ methodologically dubious procedures;[7] however, two of these proposals have proved to be quite influential, and therefore merit closer critical attention. To be specific, I refer to the contributions of W. F. Albright, and of E. R. Thiele. In the following paragraphs, I propose to summarize and analyze critically both of these important reconstructions, and in the process, formulate some methodological principles to guide my own subsequent chronological analysis. Thus, it is hoped, I will be able to avoid the *ad hoc* argumentation characteristic of all too much of the recent scholarly discussion.

W. F. Albright, in his 1945 *BASOR* article,[8] presented his own revised chronology of the Divided Monarchy of Israel. He acknowledged at the outset that his conclusions were tentative, "since we still lack a sufficiently large number of contemporary checks to warrant easy

---

[5]Hayim Tadmor, "Chronology" [Hebrew], *Encyclopedia Miqra'it*, vol. 4 (Jerusalem: Bialik Institute, 1962), cols. 261-63; see also Thiele, *Mysterious Numbers*, 1st ed., pp. 228-67, and especially his chart on pp. 254-55.

[6]Claus Schedl, "Textkritische Bemerkungen zu den Synchronismen der Könige von Israel und Juda," *VT* 12 (1962) 88-119; Walter R. Wifall, "The Chronology of the Divided Monarchy of Israel," *ZAW* 80 (1968) 319-37; K. T. Andersen, "Die Chronologie der Könige von Israel und Juda," *Studia Theologica* 23 (1969) 69-114 (a revised and updated version to be found in the *Scandinavian Journal of the Old Testament* [1/1989], 1-45); also cf. the brief article of Julian Reade, "Mesopotamian Guidelines for Biblical Chronology," *Syro-Mesopotamian Studies* 4/1 (May, 1981) 1-9.

[7]For an excellent discussion of earlier critical scholarship, see Joachim Begrich, *Die Chronologie der Könige von Israel und Juda* (Tübingen, 1929), pp. 1-54; for more recent work, cf. the articles cited above in n. 5.

[8]W. F. Albright, "The Chronology of the Divided Monarchy of Israel," *BASOR* 100 (1945) 16-22. Undoubtedly the single greatest influence on Albright's own efforts at chronological reconstruction for this period of Israelite history was the important study by Sigmund Mowinckel entitled "Die Chronologie der israelitischen und jüdischen Könige" (*Acta Orientalia* 10 [1932] 161-277); this especially proves to be the case in their striking accord (over against nearly every other chronological hypothesis then current) in dating Hezekiah's accession to c. 715 B.C.E.

dogmatism" and "the only date which is absolutely certain is that of the Fall of Samaria."[9] Nevertheless, he expressed confidence that most of his proposed dates were accurate to within five years or so.

Albright's approach to the biblical chronological data is worthy of close examination. Although retaining a healthy skepticism toward much of the biblical data ("it is incredible that all these numbers can have been handed down through so many editors and copyists without often becoming corrupt"),[10] he nevertheless placed special emphasis on the accuracy of the Judahite synchronisms (i.e. the synchronisms expressed in terms of the regnal years of the kings of Judah) such as those found in 2 Chr 15-16 (the reign of Asa of Judah). He argued that much of the independent material in Chronicles is of high historical value (as shown by recent archaeological discoveries); consequently, "we have no right to disregard the datings by regnal years of the kings of Judah which we find there, especially when they are as consistent and reasonable as, e.g., in the case of Asa."[11] Accordingly, Albright cited the synchronism found in 2 Chr 16:1 MT (which implies that Baasha was still king of Israel in the 36th year of Asa) as strong evidence for his proposed reduction of the Dtr regnal total for Rehoboam from 17 to 8 years, and for his surprisingly low date of 922 for the disruption of the United Monarchy.

Albright went on to suggest a more general application of this approach:

> It follows that we must take the synchronisms in which the accessions of kings of Israel are given in terms of the regnal years of kings of Judah seriously except when other data compel us to regard them as secondary. On the other hand, there is no evidence that there was any corresponding series of synchronisms in terms of Israelite regnal years available to the Deuteronomic editor of Kings; these synchronisms may then have been calculated secondarily by the latter (or a precursor).[12]

---

[9]*Ibid.*, p. 17.

[10]*Ibid.*

[11]*Ibid.*, pp. 18-19.

[12]*Ibid.*, p. 19. In support of this assertion, Albright cited Mesopotamian parallels, such as the Babylonian Chronicle and the various synchronistic lists of Assyrian and

Turning to the problem of the excessively high regnal totals in Kings, he pointed out:

> The tendency of ancient chronological numbers to increase with time is very well known; it is unfair, however, to the ancient scholar and scribe not to recognize that it was usually influenced (and often caused) by their efforts to do justice to variants by including them in a new total, either by direct addition or by selecting the higher of any two alternatives. . . . It is not surprising that the regnal years of the kings of Israel are rather more accurate [than] those of the kings of Judah, since there were presumably many more available variants of the latter than of the former.[13]

Consequently, Albright showed no hesitation in lowering the totals of the regnal years for a number of the Israelite, and especially of the Judahite, kings in the light of the (presumed) more original and accurate Judahite synchronisms.

The following example should make this method of calculation clear. Albright suggested reducing the regnal total of Amaziah of Judah to 18 years (from the Dtr figure of 29 years, as reported in 2 Kgs 14:2). His justification for this emendation is based on the Judahite synchronisms found in 2 Kgs 14:23a (in the 15th year of Amaziah, Jeroboam II of Israel began to reign) and in 2 Kgs 15:8 (in the 38th year of Azariah [the son of Amaziah], Zechariah, the son of Jeroboam II, began to reign), and on the accuracy of Jeroboam's traditional regnal total of 41 years (2 Kgs 14:23b). Thus reckoning by the antedating system,[14] we can make the following calculations:

15th of Amaziah = 1st of Jeroboam II (2 Kgs 14:23a); and 41st of Jeroboam II = 1st of Zechariah (2 Kgs 14:23b); but, 1st of

---

Babylonian kings.

[13]*Ibid.*, p. 19, n. 12.

[14]In the antedating system, the portion of the civil year in which a king was enthroned was reckoned as his first regnal year, whereas in the postdating system, it was reckoned as his "accession year," and the following (complete) year was reckoned as his first regnal year. The former system was generally used in Egypt, the latter in Mesopotamia. For a more detailed exposition of these two systems, see Tadmor, "First Temple Period," pp. 48-49.

Zechariah = 38th of Azariah (2 Kgs 15:8); hence, 41st of Jeroboam II = 38th of Azariah; and by simple subtraction, 1st of Azariah = 4th of Jeroboam II; therefore, 4th of Jeroboam II = 18th of Amaziah. From this we conclude that Amaziah actually reigned for only 18 years.

In this context, I should point out that Albright was very reluctant to assume any coregencies to account for the discrepancies in the biblical numbers, in clear (and conscious) contradistinction to E. R. Thiele;[15] only in the case of the "*attested* coregency" of Jotham of Judah with his father Azariah (Uzziah) did he allow for an 8 year coregency.[16]

As already noted, Albright did not claim certitude for his results, but rather general accuracy to within five years or so. His heavy reliance upon the comparative Ancient Near Eastern chronological data (and especially the external synchronisms provided by the Assyrian and Babylonian annals) is evident in the copious footnotes supporting his numerous emendations of the Dtr regnal totals; in general, the comparative material helped limit any excessive manipulation of the biblical data. In the next three chapters I will examine in some detail Albright's discussion of a number of these external synchronisms; my immediate concern is to analyze his approach toward the biblical data, and to evaluate his underlying methodological assumptions concerning those data.

First of all, Albright's heavy reliance upon the Judahite synchronisms was novel and venturesome. He was sensitive to the different redactional levels in the Dtr work, and was surely right to date

---

[15]Cf. Albright, "Chronology," p. 21, n. 21, where he defended his emended regnal total for Amaziah:

"To illustrate the fact that my approach yields intrinsically more reasonable results than, e.g., Thiele's, it should be noted that if we accept (as only reasonable) the biblical data with regard to the ages of the kings of Judah at their accessions, Amaziah would be (according to Thiele) 16 at the birth of his son Uzziah and the latter would be 32 at the birth of his son Jotham. According to my reconstruction these ages would be 27 and 22, respectively."

[16]*Ibid.*, p. 21, and n. 23, emphasis his; the attestation is presumably to be found in 2 Kgs 15:5.

the Judahite synchronisms earlier than the Dtr regnal totals as now extant. Nevertheless, the following caveats should be made:

1. Albright's too facile blurring of the different redactional levels for the various types of synchronisms is unfortunate. To be sure, synchronisms such as those found in the Asa narratives of 2 Chr 15-16 may well represent a very early and historically reliable tradition, and they almost certainly predate the final redaction of the book.[17] The same thing may well be argued about certain synchronisms found in the Dtr work such as 1 Kgs 22:1-2, or even 2 Kgs 15:30 (note the discrepancy with 17:1a). However, the Judahite synchronisms such as those I have cited above as support for emending Amaziah's regnal total clearly represent a later redactional level; they are found in the Dtr regnal formulae, and they most likely represent later calculations based on originally independent royal annalistic sources or king lists.[18] Again, it does not necessarily follow that the Judahite synchronisms found in the stereotyped Dtr regnal formulae need predate their Israelite counterparts; I would prefer to argue that the original Judahite *regnal totals* which were used to compile these synchronistic calculations may well have been more accurate than their Israelite counterparts. At least, the redactional situation is even more complex than Albright had envisioned.

2. Albright's virtually total repudiation of the possibility of coregencies (except in the one case of Azariah and his son Jotham) seems excessively doctrinaire. I suspect that E. R. Thiele's mechanical over-emphasis of this phenomenon (with its occasionally odd results)

---

[17]For a recent delineation of the redactional levels of the Chronicler's work, see F. M. Cross, Jr., "A Reconstruction of the Judean Restoration," *JBL* 94 (1975) 4-18, where he distinguished between three editions of the Chronicler's work: *Chr 1* comprises 1 Chr 10-2 Chr 34 plus the *Vorlage* of 1 Esdras 1:1-5:65 (= 2 Chr 34:1-Ezra 3:13), a propaganda work supporting the restoration of the Davidic kingdom under Zerubbabel; *Chr 2* adds the Aramaic source in Ezra 5:1-6:19 as the preface to the Ezra narrative proper beginning in Ezra 7:1 (whose original order is now found only in 1 Esdras); and *Chr 3* introduces the Nehemiah memoirs and the genealogies of 1 Chr 1-9. Cross dated Chr 1 around 520 B.C.E., Chr 2 after Ezra's mission in 458, and Chr 3 around 400 or shortly thereafter.

[18]This will be discussed more fully in Chapter V. For a cogent presentation of the hypothesis of two originally independent "king lists" underlying the Dtr regnal formulae, see Shoshana R. Bin-Nun, "Formulas from Royal Records of Israel and of Judah," *VT* 18 (1968) 421-25.

contributed significantly to Albright's evident distaste for the subject.[19]
A more balanced treatment may be found in Tadmor's discussion. He
noted that the Dtr narrative material points to a number of coregencies
in the Judahite monarchy: not only Jotham and Azariah, but also
Azariah and his father Amaziah (2 Kgs 14:17).[20] Tadmor concluded:

> Whether the [Dtr] chronologist knew about these and other co-
> regencies but decided to ignore them, or whether he did not know
> about them at all--as was more probably the case--it is clear that the
> method he chose has created serious discrepancies in the chrono-
> logical scheme of the book of Kings.
>   The assumption that there actually were co-regencies in both
> Judah and Israel--in itself logical and clearly alluded to in the
> sources--does much to solve a few of the more serious contra-
> dictions.[21]

I will return to the subject of coregencies, whether real or only con-
jectural, later in the chapter. At this juncture, I merely wish to point
out that at least some of the excessively large Dtr regnal totals may well
be the result of overlapping coregencies, unrecognized as such by the
Dtr editors.

    3. Finally, I note Albright's resort to what might be termed the
"pragmatic argument": i.e., the results of a hypothesis are probably
correct if they "work," if they fit reasonably well into a pre-assigned

---

[19]See, e.g., his comments cited above in n. 15. Also, cf. Albright, "Alternative
Chronology," *Interpretation* 6 (1952) 101-103 (his review of Thiele's *Mysterious
Numbers*, 1st ed,), where he declared:

> "In scaling it down [i.e. the date of the accessions of Jehu and Athaliah] we
> must depend either on assumed coregencies, as done by Thiele, or on reducing
> reigns in accord with the Israelite synchronisms (which appear to be original)
> as I do. One coregency is known, and there may have been others, but it is
> risky assuming them when the biblical text offers no warrant for the assump-
> tion" (p. 102).

[20]Tadmor, "First Temple Period," p. 53, and n. 27; cf. his chronological discussion
in "Amaziah" [Hebrew], *Encyclopedia Miqra'it*, vol. 1 (Jerusalem: Bialik Institute,
1950), col. 439, where he suggested a 15 year coregency between Amaziah and Azariah,
probably as an unintentional result of the former's ignominious defeat and capture at Beth
Shemesh by Joash of Israel (2 Kgs 14:11-14).

[21]Tadmor, "First Temple Period," p. 53.

chronological framework. This is only a minor feature in Albright's overall presentation (whereas, as I shall presently demonstrate, it provides the major justification for E. R. Thiele's approach), so I need not belabor the point here. Nonetheless, it is pertinent to point out that such appeals as the following are somewhat precarious:

> If we examine the chronological material for the century following Jehu's rebellion (which is fixed to within a year or two by Assyrian data), we note that the century between 842 and 742 B.C. is occupied in Kings by four Judahite reigns, totalling 128 years, from which 3-4 years must be [deducted] in accordance with antedating practice. The excess of some 24 years can be eliminated entirely by . . . basing our revised estimates of their reigns solely on the synchronisms with Israel (which throughout contradict the regnal totals of the kings of Judah). After one slight correction in the contemporary Israelite list has been made with the aid of the synchronisms, the total of the Israelite reigns is exactly right for the interval in question, so we are justified in treating it as at least approximately correct. By similar methods we are in a position to revise the chronology of the period which antedates the rebellion of Jehu.[22]

Again, one example should illustrate my point. As noted above, Albright wished to reduce Amaziah's regnal years from the Dtr total of 29 to 18 on the basis of the synchronisms with Israel. He then suggested dating these years to c. 800-783 B.C.E. Albright did accept the Dtr regnal total of 16 years for Joash of Israel, and he dated those years to c. 801-786.[23] However, I have just alluded to an important and probably original synchronism found in 2 Kgs 14:17, which states that Amaziah "lived" (*wayyĕḥî*) 15 years after the death of Joash of Israel. Admittedly, the root *ḥwy* is an unusual form to denote regnal activity; Tadmor and Aharoni may well be correct in interpreting the synchronism as indicating some sort of coregency.[24] At any rate,

---

[22]Albright, "Chronology," p. 19.

[23]*Ibid.*, p. 21.

[24]See above, n. 20, for a summary of Tadmor's approach. Yohanan Aharoni, in a brief but provocative article entitled "The Chronology of the Kings of Israel and Judah" [Hebrew] (*Tarbiz* 21 [1950] 92-100), proposed essentially the same kind of chronological

Albright's proposed regnal dating clearly precludes any sort of viable interpretation of this synchronism with an Israelite king; and, so far as I can tell, he has altogether ignored it (even though by his own reasoning it would have provided valuable evidence by which to straighten out the inflated Dtr totals). At least, such a synchronism should have been discussed in the notes supporting his emended regnal totals; a general appeal to the "pragmatic argument" that the totals are "exactly right" is at best insufficient.

These three caveats should not unduly detract, of course, from the overall brilliance of Albright's chronological investigations. He has set a valuable example of how to reconstruct biblical chronology, and the following represent some general principles implicitly endorsed by Albright which will inform my own subsequent efforts at chronological analysis:

1. One should be thoroughly familiar with every external synchronism which may shed light upon the biblical chronological period in question. This familiarity should include a general control of the various chronological procedures used by the Ancient Near Eastern cultures in question, as well as specific awareness of the current scholarly consensus (or lack of consensus) for each potential synchronism.
2. One should then allow the external synchronisms to determine, as far as it is possible, the parameters of variability among the conflicting biblical data.
3. One must then evaluate the various conflicting biblical chronological data, recalling their different redactional origins and levels of accuracy, in order to interpolate (as accurately as possible) between the relatively firm "anchor points" provided by the external synchronisms.
4. Finally, one should claim only the level of precision for one's conclusions which is clearly appropriate.

---

reconstruction (see especially his arguments on p. 95); a brief listing of his results may conveniently be found in Appendix 1 of his *The Land of the Bible: A Historical Geography*, revised ed., trans. and ed. by A. F. Rainey (Philadelphia: Westminster Press, 1979), pp. 424-28.

I next turn to the work of Edwin R. Thiele.[25] As will soon be quite evident, Thiele approached the biblical chronological material in a very different manner from that of Albright. Assuming the uncanny accuracy of virtually all of the chronological data in the books of Kings (at least as preserved in the MT), he posited an elaborate series of coregencies to account for all of the high numbers in the regnal totals, and he presupposed a complicated series of variations in calendar (with the regnal year beginning in the spring in Israel, and in the fall in Judah) and in mode of computing regnal years (antedating and post-dating) to account for most of the variations in the synchronisms.[26] Thus, Thiele concluded that the chronologists in Judah shifted from postdating to antedating at the time of Jehoram, then back to postdating at the time of Amaziah, at which time the chronologists in Israel also shifted from antedating to postdating; and all the various synchronisms are to be understood from the perspective of the system in local use.[27] Thiele was quite optimistic about the results of his approach:

> The best argument for the correctness of the above outline of chronological procedure among the Hebrews is that it works, giving us a chronological scheme of the kings of Israel and Judah in which there is internal harmony and which fits into the chronology of neighboring states. When these principles are applied to the Hebrew kings, it will be found that the irritating discrepancies that have so long baffled and perplexed students of Old Testament history will at last disappear.[28]

---

[25]E. R. Thiele, "The Chronology of the Kings of Judah and Israel," *JNES* 3 (1944) 137-86; see also his expanded discussion in *The Mysterious Numbers of the Hebrew Kings*, 1st ed. (Chicago, 1951), 2nd revised ed. (Grand Rapids: Eerdmans, 1965), 3rd re-revised ed. (Grand Rapids: Zondervan, 1983).

[26]Thiele, "Chronology," p. 143. For the antedating and postdating systems, see above, n. 14; Thiele employed the terms "nonaccession-year system" for antedating, and "accession-year system" for postdating.

[27]*Ibid.*, pp. 143-44.

[28]*Ibid.*, p. 144. In the second edition of his *Mysterious Numbers*, Thiele made even a stronger statement:
> "The original chronicles of the kings of Israel and Judah were contemporary productions, in full accord with the facts of the times. During the period of exile the records from North and South were brought together in a

Thiele adamantly opposed any adjustment or emendation of the chronological data:

> A change in the figure for a single length of reign may involve, as we have seen, many additional changes in figures all the way down the line, and the same is true with the synchronisms. These two sets of data fit so tightly together that no adjustment can be made in any single item without vitally affecting the whole composite structure of Hebrew chronology.[29]

The following example should illustrate Thiele's methodology. I have already noted the chronological problems surrounding the reigns of Amaziah and Azariah of Judah, and the reconstruction proposed by Albright.[30] Unlike Albright, however, Thiele did not emend any of the biblical chronological data, but posited a number of coregencies to explain the disparities in the biblical numbers.[31] More specifically, he suggested that Jeroboam II was coregent for 12 years with his father Joash of Israel (this explains the otherwise "missing" 12 years of 2 Kgs 15:1, cf. my above discussion, pp. 2-3), and Azariah first became coregent with his father Amaziah in the latter's 6th year (this is necessary in the light of the otherwise high figures found in the synchronisms of Zechariah, Shallum, and Menahem of Israel, 2 Kgs 15:8, 13, 17).[32] Hence, all the regnal totals and synchronisms line up without exception (even Amaziah outliving Joash of Israel by 15 years,

---

single book. The facts we have set forth here in the restoration of the chronological patterns of the individual reigns give evidence that the work, from beginning to end, was done with great devotion and almost unbelievable accuracy" (p. 197).

[29]Thiele, *Mysterious Numbers*, 1st ed., p. 256.

[30]See above, pp. 2, 6-7.

[31]For the period in question, both Israel and Judah used the postdating system (according to Thiele); this will simplify comparisons between the two regnal systems.

[32]Incidentally, the synchronisms of the 6 month reign of Zechariah (= 38th year of Azariah) and of the 1 month reign of Shallum (= 39th year of Azariah) illustrate Thiele's contention that the regnal year was reckoned in the spring in Israel and in the fall in Judah.

2 Kgs 14:17); in terms of an absolute chronology, Thiele's results are as follows:[33]

Israel		*Judah*	
Joash	798-782	Amaziah	796-767
Jeroboam II	793-753	Azariah	791-740
Zechariah	753-752		
Shallum	752		
Menahem	752-742		

A closer examination of Thiele's conclusions presents us with some curious results, however. To be sure, Amaziah is given his full 29 years of reign (2 Kgs 14:2), but in reality he was sole ruler for only 5 years (796-792), quite a different situation than what seems to be presupposed in the biblical narratives of 2 Kgs 14 and 2 Chr 25. In his discussion of Amaziah's chronology, Thiele suggested, reasonably enough, that Amaziah was forced to elevate his 16 year old son Azariah to coregency as a result of the former's disastrous defeat and capture by Joash of Israel;[34] but this must be dated by his own methodology to before the 6th year (of an alleged 29 year long reign). The biblical narrative in 2 Kgs 14:17-22 seems to recount a rather different sequence of events: Amaziah lived 15 years after the death of Joash of Israel (obviously, then, at least 15 years after his defeat and capture at Beth Shemesh by that rival king); he was eventually assassinated in Lachish, buried in Jerusalem, and then, presumably, his 16 year old son Azariah was proclaimed king by the people. Admittedly, the schematic nature of much of the Dtr regnal material in Kings cautions us against insisting

---

[33]For the clearest comparison between the various rulers and coregents, see Thiele's excellent charts in "Chronology," opposite p. 154, and in *Mysterious Numbers*, 1st ed., opposite p. 74. For the sake of simplicity I have ignored Thiele's distinction between the Israelite calendar year (beginning in the spring) and the Judahite calendar year (beginning in the fall); to be more exact, the absolute years cited here should be understood from that perspective (e.g., Jeroboam's first year was reckoned from the spring of 793 whereas Amaziah's first year dated from the fall of 796, etc.).

[34]See his discussion in "Chronology," pp. 153-54; *Mysterious Numbers*, 1st ed., pp. 71-72.

upon a strict chronological ordering of the narrative sections of 2 Kgs
14, but surely the Dtr editors give us no hint that they envisioned only
a 5 year *de facto* reign for King Amaziah.[35]

Thus, Thiele's general approach to the biblical chronological
data may be summed up as follows: he assumed the complete accuracy
of virtually all of the regnal data of Kings as now extant in the MT,
regardless of their original redactional levels or innate likelihood of
transmissional accuracy; he then allowed these seemingly conflicting
data to indicate the frequency and length of the (generally otherwise
unattested) coregencies. The only way we know of the 12 year coregency of Jeroboam II with his father Joash, for example, is as the
result of a comparison of his regnal total of 41 years (2 Kgs 14:23) with
the synchronism found in 15:1; there is *no other* biblical (or, so far as
I am aware, extra-biblical) evidence for this alleged coregency.[36] But
this is not an isolated example: Jehoram's alleged 5 year coregency
with his father Jehoshaphat, and Azariah's alleged 24 year coregency
with his father Amaziah are attested only by their regnal totals
compared with the corresponding synchronisms;[37] indeed, Jehosha-

---

[35]This point is essentially conceded by Thiele in his second edition of *Mysterious
Numbers*, pp. 180-82, where he discussed late editorial misunderstandings of the chronological data. It is worth noting that if all the biblical ages at accession are correct,
Amaziah would have been 15 at the birth of his son Azariah according to Thiele's reconstruction, whereas he would have been 38 at Azariah's birth according to the Dtr ordering
of the Amaziah narratives (as I have just discussed). Cf., however, Albright's comments
as cited above, n. 15 (Albright was apparently following Thiele's erroneous calculations
found on p. 284 of his first edition of *Mysterious Numbers*; contrast the corrected ages
found in his second edition, p. 206). Admittedly, on this point Thiele's reconstruction
seems more plausible than that apparently presupposed by the Dtr editors; however, that
of Albright seems yet more plausible. Interestingly enough, the resulting age of Amaziah
at Azariah's birth would have been 22 according to Aharoni's and Tadmor's reconstructions (see above, nn. 20, 24).

[36]Certainly the Dtr formulae (2 Kgs 13:10-13; 14:15-16, 23-29) give no hint of such
a coregency; cf. the Elisha narrative found in 2 Kgs 13:14-25. On the recurrence of a 12
year dislocation in some of the chronological data, see below.

[37]This may be most clearly seen in Thiele's charts illustrating his chronological
reconstruction (see above, n. 33, for references). In the case of Jehoram and Jehoshaphat,
the two varying synchronisms for Joram of Israel (2 Kgs 1:17; 3:1) attest the coregency;
in the case of Azariah and Amaziah the situation is more complex in that it involves the
synchronism linking Azariah and Jeroboam II (2 Kgs 15:1) and the latter's alleged 12 year
coregency with his father Joash.

phat's alleged 3 year coregency with his father Asa and Manasseh's alleged 10 year coregency with his father Hezekiah lack even this attestation.[38]

To be fair, I should point out that there are a few synchronisms found in Kings which Thiele acknowledged are in error: these synchronisms concern the reigns of Hoshea, Ahaz, and Hezekiah. I have already noted (see above, p. 3) the serious problems attending the synchronisms which link the early part of the reign of Hezekiah to that of Hoshea of Israel and the fall of Samaria; for my present purposes I merely point out that Thiele admitted that some four synchronisms connected with this period (i.e. the synchronisms found in 2 Kgs 17:1; 18:1, 9, 10) are about 12 years too low.[39] But, aside from these four synchronisms, Thiele did insist that every regnal total and synchronism now extant in the MT of the books of Kings is completely accurate, at least when understood within the framework of his chronological system.

The reader will recall Thiele's strong appeal to what I have termed the "pragmatic argument": in brief, his reconstruction should be accepted because "it works," it fits the seemingly diverse and contradictory biblical chronological data into a relatively simple system sensitive to the constraints of the external Assyrian and Babylonian synchronisms.[40] I must admit the seductive appeal of such an argument: W. F. Albright, for example, was forced to emend some 8 (out of 20) regnal totals for the rulers of Judah, and some 6 (out of 19) regnal totals for Israel (not to mention the number of synchronisms implicitly altered), yet his results were, on his own admission, only accurate to within five years or so; E. R. Thiele, on the other hand, claimed to be able to extract a remarkably precise chronology out of the biblical numbers (accurate to within a year or less), virtually without a single emendation. Indeed, it seems an impressive *tour de force*![41]

---

[38]Again, it is best to consult Thiele's charts for the details. In brief, as I will point out below, only Jehoshaphat's and Manasseh's regnal totals (as extant in the MT) give us any hint al all concerning these alleged coregencies.

[39]See Thiele, "Chronology," pp. 163-77; *Mysterious Numbers*, 1st ed., pp. 136-52.

[40]See above, pp. 12-13, and nn. 28-29.

[41]S. J. De Vries, for example, in his comments on the chronology of the Divided

The pragmatic argument, however attractive it may be initial-ly, is ultimately unconvincing. Whether it is Albright's occasional use (see above, pp. 9-11), or Thiele's bold emphasis, the likening of a chronological reconstruction, as it were, to the fitting together of a jigsaw puzzle, is at best precarious. To state the obvious--we do not have all the pieces, and the pieces we do have can fit in more than one way. Consider the following defense Thiele recently gave for his system:

> The combination of interlocking synchronisms and lengths of reign ties the years of Israel and Judah so tightly together as to make impossible any arbitrary adjustment of as much as a single year in the reign of any king, without introducing widespread disruption into an otherwise harmonious pattern. So rigid is the pattern of interlocked reigns that the assignment of a specific date to any year of any king, provides the dates for all the kings of both nations, from the beginning to the end of the divided monarchies.[42]

Here is indeed a strong appeal to the "pragmatic argument": Thiele's system and Thiele's system alone works; any adjustment of only a single year would introduce "widespread disruption into an otherwise harmonious pattern." But is this true? Let us examine Thiele's proposed coregency of Jehoshaphat with his father Asa.[43] According to Thiele we must posit a 3 year coregency between the two kings; the biblical data demand it. Actually, the only datum which compels such a coregency is Jehoshaphat's extant regnal total of 25 years (1 Kgs 22:42). Had the MT, for whatever reason, attested a different (and, for Thiele, necessarily incorrect) regnal total for this king, would that have

---

Monarchy found in "Chronology of the OT," *IDB*, 1:584-99, concurred almost entirely with Thiele's reconstruction; cf. also De Vries' comments in *IDBS*, pp. 162-64. In addition, John Gray, in his chronological reconstruction found in *I & II Kings: A Commentary*, The Old Testament Library (London: SCM Press, 1964), pp. 55-74, although differing from Thiele in a number of details, nevertheless agreed with nearly all of his suggested coregencies, and in fact posited two additional ones (Joahaz/Joash of Israel and Ahaz/Hezekiah of Judah).

[42]Thiele, "Coregencies and Overlapping Reigns among the Hebrew Kings," *JBL* 93 (1974) 175.

[43]See Thiele, "Chronology," p. 151; *Mysterious Numbers*, 1st ed., pp. 65-66; also cf. his charts (references found in n. 33 above).

introduced "widespread disruption into an otherwise harmonious pattern"? Not at all! If Jehoshaphat had reigned, according to the MT, for some 29 years, then Thiele need only posit a 7 year coregency with his father Asa; had the regnal total been only 24 years, then only a 2 year coregency need be presupposed, and so on. In short, a considerable leeway (from 22 up to about 64 regnal years) is permissible in Jehoshaphat's regnal total without requiring *any other element* in Thiele's system (besides the length of his alleged coregency with Asa) being altered in any way. A similar situation obtains with the alleged coregencies of Hezekiah and Manasseh, except that a somewhat smaller variation in the latter's regnal total is permissible before "widespread disruption" might occur.[44]

    Strong assertions, especially those which seem *prima facie* to be well supported, demand strong rebuttals. I have cited the above examples not to belittle the patient and ingenious work of a competent scholar, but to restore a sense of perspective to the murky business of biblical chronology. The following queries of Thiele's system, less dramatic perhaps, but no less urgent, are offered in a spirit of honest inquiry rather than one of hostile opposition. At this point in my discussion I will only be able to outline the basic problems; probable solutions (if there are any) must await more detailed analysis in the following chapters.

    1. Some of Thiele's proposed coregencies do "work" rather impressively: they fit the chronological data of the MT quite closely and the constraints of the external synchronisms reasonably well; and, indeed, they do not permit any arbitrary adjustment of even a single year in either a biblical synchronism or regnal total. One should not overemphasize this phenomenon (at best, less than half of the suggested coregencies fit into this category), but one need not minimize it either. Probably the most impressive "fit" is the double coregency of Amaziah/Azariah and Joash/Jeroboam II discussed earlier (pp. 13-14). Thiele is essentially right here: the arbitrary adjustment of a single year in any biblical synchronism or regnal total will indeed throw the entire reconstruction into chaos (to be exact, one might account for the shift of

---

[44]Thiele suggested a 10 year coregency between Manasseh and his father Hezekiah, almost wholly on the basis of the 10 year excess in the biblical regnal totals for this period; see "Chronology," pp. 178-79; *Mysterious Numbers*, 1st ed., pp. 153-57; also his charts (references in n. 33 above).

a single year in some of the data by adjusting the antedating/postdating mode of reckoning as Thiele has done in the earlier periods, but that is all).[45] Consequently, one does seem to be compelled to accept a 24 year coregency for Amaziah/Azariah and a 12 year coregency for Joash/ Jeroboam II if he or she takes the biblical chronological data at all seriously, even though these results seem quite out of line with the biblical narratives themselves. But is this indeed the case? Let us examine the chronological data once more. It soon becomes clear that one synchronism alone provides the crucial support for both alleged coregencies: the synchronism found in 2 Kgs 15:1. This synchronism links Azariah's succession to the 27th year of Jeroboam II, and it seems to be 12 years out of line (see above discussion, pp. 2, 15-16). In other words, by extrapolating from the biblical data found in 2 Kgs 13 and 14, and not assuming any coregencies, we would have expected Azariah's accession to be dated to Jeroboam's 15th year; the 27th year is some 12 years too late. But perhaps we should check whether or not the 27th year might be correct and the other biblical data 12 years too early; this suggestion seems not at all unreasonable when one recalls that (by Thiele's own admission) some four other synchronisms are also 12 years too early.[46] If four synchronisms found in 2 Kgs chapters 17 and 18 represent a variant chronological system 12 years earlier than the other biblical system, might not the synchronisms of chapters 13 and 14 also fit into the former system as well? Such a hypothesis would eliminate the need for a 12 year coregency between Joash and Jeroboam II, and cut the alleged 24 year coregency between Amaziah and Azariah in half, a much more likely situation in the light of the narrative material.[47] At least, such a hypothesis should be tested before one multiplies the number and length of hypothetical coregencies just to fit one otherwise aberrant synchronism.

---

[45]See Thiele, "Chronology," pp. 152-54; *Mysterious Numbers*, 1st ed., pp. 67-73; and his charts.

[46]See above discussion, p. 17; the synchronisms in question are found in 2 Kgs 17:1; 18:1, 9, 10. By "early" I merely denote the relative position of the Judahite monarchs to their Israelite counterparts; e.g., 2 Kgs 17:1 dates Ahaz of Judah 12 years too early (according to Thiele's reconstruction) in relation to Hoshea of Israel.

[47]See above discussion, pp. 14-15. I have already pointed out that Tadmor and Aharoni both preferred a 15 year coregency for Amaziah and Azariah (see nn. 20, 24 for references).

2. The above paragraph illustrates a more general problem with Thiele's methodology (one which he himself recognized to some extent): the need to disagree repeatedly with the Dtr editors' arrangement and interpretation of the narrative material concerning a number of the kings of both monarchies, while continuing to emphasize the remarkable accuracy of their transmission of the chronological data themselves. I have just alluded to the Amaziah material where (according to Thiele) the Dtr editors have misunderstood their own chronological data and have mistakenly placed Azariah's accession notice after the description of his father's assassination (when it in reality occurred some 24 years earlier).[48] But this is not an isolated phenomenon. The Dtr chronological order for Pekahiah, Pekah, and Jotham is also mistaken (according to Thiele); both Pekah and Jotham actually preceded the reign of Pekahiah even though the Dtr editors clearly thought otherwise. In other words, Thiele accepted as correct all the chronological data found in 2 Kgs 15 (even Jotham's accession in the 2nd year of Pekah, v 32),[49] but he totally rejected the clear import of the Dtr chronological ordering of the chapter, which put Pekahiah, then Pekah as kings of Israel, and finally Jotham as king of Judah (and whose accession is then dated to Pekah's 2nd year). One may indeed reject the Dtr editorial ordering of the kings in 2 Kgs 15 for whatever legitimate reason (such as the distinct possibility that the Dtr editors were unaware of Jotham's coregency with Azariah, 2 Kgs 15:5), but one must then explain how all the synchronisms (which accord with, and almost certainly resulted from, the Dtr editorial arrangement) nevertheless remain completely accurate, and consequently may be used to support a chronology clearly at odds with that of the Dtr editors.

A third example, and one which Thiele himself cited as evidence for a coregency,[50] may be found in 2 Kgs 8:16 MT, "In the fifth year of Joram the son of Ahab the king of Israel, and Jehoshaphat

---

[48]In his second edition of *Mysterious Numbers*, p. 182, Thiele acknowledged this late editorial misunderstanding of the chronological data.

[49]Of course, Thiele interpreted this synchronism to indicate Jotham's coregency with his father Azariah; see "Chronology," pp. 168-69; *Mysterious Numbers*, 1st ed., pp. 110-16.

[50]Thiele, *Mysterious Numbers*, 1st ed., p. 36; "Coregencies and Overlapping Reigns" (see above, n. 42), p. 174.

(being then) king of Judah, Jehoram the son of Jehoshaphat the king of Judah became king." Here it seems we do have biblical evidence for Thiele's suggested coregency between Jehoshaphat and Jehoram of Judah; but is this actually the case? Further inquiry indicates that such support is oblique at best; for as J. D. Shenkel has pointed out (and as Thiele himself later conceded), the phrase about Jehoshaphat is out of place in a synchronism which (according to Thiele) referred to Jehoshaphat's death and Jehoram's accession as sole ruler. Thus, rather than representing a valuable biblical attestation of Thiele's proposal of a coregency between Jehoshaphat and Jehoram, the synchronism in 2 Kgs 8:16 probably contains only a late editorial misunderstanding of the chronological data.[51] Again, the chronological data are accurate (when understood according to Thiele's system) but the Dtr editing is not.

Finally, I turn to the confusing chronological situation surrounding the reigns of Jotham and Ahaz. First, a brief review of Thiele's proposed reconstruction for this very confusing period is in order. Thiele posited a four year coregency between the two Judahite kings, Jotham and Ahaz, largely on the basis of the notice found in 2 Kgs 15:30 with its reference to the 20th year of Jotham, but also in light of the external Assyrian synchronisms.[52] According to the Dtr regnal formulae, however, both Jotham (15:33) and Ahaz (16:2) reigned only 16 years; this left (according to Thiele's reconstruction) a 4 year gap between the two kings. As I have just noted, his solution was to posit a coregency--but here he faced a unique situation. Heretofore he had been confronted by high regnal totals and the necessity for chronological overlap to account for the biblical numbers, but now for the first time there was a paucity in the regnal totals: neither Jotham nor Ahaz had been credited with the 4 regnal years in which they both supposedly ruled. As one might suspect, Thiele's discussion at this point becomes rather curious,[53] but the essential problem remains--the

---

[51]See J. D. Shenkel, *Chronology and Recensional Development in the Greek Text of Kings*, Harvard Semitic Monographs, vol. 1 (Cambridge: Harvard University Press, 1968), p. 81; also Thiele, *Mysterious Numbers*, 2nd ed., pp. 181-82.

[52]See Thiele, "Chronology," pp. 170-72; *Mysterious Numbers*, 1st ed., pp. 115-17.

[53]See Thiele, "Chronology," p. 172, and especially the following remarks from his discussion in *Mysterious Numbers*, 1st ed., pp. 117-18:

Dtr regnal totals give no hint of any four year coregency between the two kings, indeed, no hint of a missing four years at all. Only the passing reference to Jotham's 20th year in 15:30 gives Thiele any reason to suggest the alleged coregency. So again, the chronological data are "correct" in some sense, but the Dtr editors mistaken; for this time they implied that both Jotham and Ahaz only reigned for 16 years, whereas (according to Thiele's reconstruction) they both actually reigned for 20 years.[54]

But a further problem remains. When Jotham became coregent with Azariah (in Pekah's 2nd year, according to Thiele's reconstruction, cf. 15:32), in reality it was not the usurper Pekah who was on the throne at that time (according to Thiele he was not yet reckoned as king), but rather the official king Menahem. One would then have expected the synchronism 2nd year of Menahem = 1st year of Jotham, or the like, as Thiele himself pointed out:

> It will be noticed that the synchronism of Jotham's accession is expressed in terms of the years of Pekah rather than Menahem, although it was Menahem who was then upon the throne. We have here a clear indication that not all the synchronisms that have come down to us were immediately recorded in the form in which they now are found, at the time of a king's accession. It is entirely possible that at the time that Jotham took the throne in the second year of Menahem, his accession was synchronized with the years of that king and thus entered into the official records, and that later, when Pekah took it upon himself to appropriate the years of the house he

---

"The question would then arise, how long did Ahaz rule? Should his reign be reckoned from 736/35, when he was brought to power by this pro-Assyrian group, or from 732/31, when he began to rule in his own right? Had the pro-Assyrian group continued in power the answer would of course have been twenty years, and if that item had somewhere entered into the records, the difficulty of our task would have been lightened. . . .

"Whether the reign of Ahaz is reckoned as a twenty-year reign beginning in 735--the sixteenth year of Jotham when the latter relinquished control of national affairs--or whether it is reckoned as a sixteen-year reign beginning in 732/31, the twentieth and last year of Jotham, it would in either case terminate in 716/15 when Hezekiah came to the throne."

[54]This is clear from his chronological charts (references in n. 33 above); Thiele never actually stated this, however (cf. his comments quoted in the previous note; also cf. the comments in his second edition of *Mysterious Numbers*, pp. 127-28).

overthrew, an adjustment was made in harmony with a reign for
Pekah figured upon such an unusual basis. In such a case it would
be possible for vestiges of an earlier synchronism to come down to
a later period together with another synchronism from a later time.
Certainly the two synchronisms for Hoshea's accession, the one in II
Kings 15:30 and the other in II Kings 17:1 should raise a question as
to their exact significance.[55]

Now this is curious reasoning. A later editor replaced Menahem's name
with Pekah (thus, retaining the correct chronology since that latter king
reckoned himself as ruling at the same time as the former); nevertheless, the other variant synchronism remained (accession of Pekah =
52nd of Azariah, 2 Kgs 15:27); and such disparate synchronisms were
retained by the Dtr editors presumably for reasons similar to those
explaining the two variant synchronisms for Hoshea's accession (one of
which Thiele rejected as demonstrably wrong). Once more, we find,
according to Thiele, amazingly correct chronological data, but incorrect
(even incoherent) Dtr editing.[56]

    3. As I have briefly indicated above, Thiele's high regard for
the accuracy of the biblical chronological data is reserved exclusively
for the data as found in the MT. This assumption is also open to
question. In an impressive text-critical study of the Greek texts of the
books of Kings, J. D. Shenkel[57] has proposed the intriguing thesis that

---

[55]*Mysterious Numbers*, 1st ed., pp. 118-19. In the second edition of *Mysterious
Numbers*, p. 124, Thiele suggested a different possibility: a rival reign in Gilead by Pekah
beginning in Menahem's first year (cf. 2 Kgs 15:25, where a band of Gileadites later
helped Pekah eliminate Pekahiah); after Pekah took over the rule of all Israel, he reckoned
his years as king in Gilead as part of his regnal total of 20 years (and thus the
synchronism of 15:32).

[56]As I have already pointed out (see above, p. 20), the chronological data of
2 Kgs 15 accord well with the Dtr editorial arrangement of the chapter, and its resultant
chronological ordering of first Azariah, then Zechariah, Shallum, Menahem, Pekahiah,
then Pekah, and finally Jotham. Is it not far more likely that the corresponding synchronisms tying together the Dtr ordering of the monarchs are of Dtr provenance? If this
be the case, the basic question of the propriety of Thiele's utter reliance upon the accuracy
of the synchronisms, while denying the validity of the Dtr editorial arrangement itself, must again be raised.

[57]Shenkel, *Chronology and Recensional Development* (for full reference, see above,
n. 51).

significant remnants of a variant chronology may still be detected in the independent chronological data found in the Greek versions of Kings; this chronology both predates the MT chronology of Kings and proves to be more accurate, especially for the chronology of the period from Omri to Jehu. Shenkel argued strongly that a detailed analysis of the recensional development of the Greek text must precede any analysis of the Greek chronological data; only then can one clearly distinguish extant remnants of the chronological system of the earliest Greek versions (the so-called "Old Greek") from later secondary developments. Only Shenkel's central thesis need concern us at this point (I will examine his study and some recent critical reactions to it more closely in the Appendix);[58] Shenkel summarized it as follows:

> Viewed from the perspective of the historical development of the Greek text, it is now evident that the Old Greek chronology, far from being the artificial contrivance of late scribal activity, was the earliest chronology in the Greek textual tradition and was already present in the Hebrew *Vorlage* of the earliest translation of the Books of Kings.[59]

But Shenkel went even further than this. He concluded from an examination of the prophetic narratives of Kings that they implicitly supported the Old Greek chronological sequence over against that of the MT (the so-called "Hebrew" chronology). Thus, where the Old Greek chronology differs from the Hebrew chronology, the former should be preferred.

A good example of this is the question of the dating of the reign of Jehoshaphat. In particular, the Codex Vaticanus ($\mathfrak{G}^B$, cf. the Lucianic texts boe$_2$) differs from the MT as follows: in $\mathfrak{G}^B$, in 3 Reigns 16:28^{a-h}, Jehoshaphat's accession is dated to the 11th year of Omri, whereas in the MT, in 1 Kgs 22:41-50, his accession is dated to the 4th year of Ahab, a disparity of at least four years.[60] As usual, Shenkel

---

[58]For two important reviews of Shenkel's work, see D. W. Gooding, *JTS* 21 (1970) 118-31, and Thiele, "Coregencies and Overlapping Reigns" (see above, n. 42), pp. 176-91.

[59]Shenkel, *Chronology and Recensional Development*, p. 110.

[60]$\mathfrak{G}^B$ = MT in 1 Kgs 22:41-51; the Lucianic texts boc$_2$e$_2$ omit these verses entirely. Shenkel follows Thackeray in classifying the text of $\mathfrak{G}^B$ in 1 Kgs 22-2 Kgs as the so-called καίγε recension, which conforms more closely to the MT than that of the Lucianic texts (the so-called proto-Lucianic recension); cf. Shenkel, *Chronology and*

preferred the Old Greek chronology over that of the Hebrew, one implication of this being his suggestion that in the account of the military campaign against Moab found in 2 Kgs 3, the identification of the Judahite king as Jehoshaphat was secondary:

> Analysis of the narrative in II Kings 3 revealed that the kings of Judah and Israel in this story, as in similar stories in the same section of Kings, were originally anonymous. The discordant identification of Jehoshaphat as the king of Judah in the narrative of the Moabite campaign was an innovation of the proto-Masoretic text. Because the Hebrew chronology alone makes this identification possible and because the identification of Jehoshaphat conflicts with the original chronology implicit in the prophetic narratives, the only sound conclusion is that the Hebrew chronology was a secondary development.[61]

It is immediately apparent that Shenkel's conclusions contrast sharply with the conclusions of E. R. Thiele. I have already pointed out Thiele's exclusive reliance upon the chronological data of the MT for his reconstruction. He was, of course, quite aware of the divergent Greek data, but he basically dismissed them as secondary emendations to account for the apparent inconsistencies in the MT.[62] Such an approach, however, fails to grapple with Shenkel's entirely plausible suggestion of an early, independent Greek chronology which is still attested in some of the Greek data; indeed, I might add that such an approach fails to grapple convincingly with the divergent MT data themselves (e.g., with the two variant synchronisms for the accession of Joram of Israel, 2 Kgs 1:17 and 3:1). Boldly positing coregencies on the basis of such divergences in the MT, but dismissing as secondary any and all divergences in the Greek texts, is a precarious procedure at best; it becomes positively perverse when some of the Greek data are shown to be almost certainly more original, and very likely more accurate, than their Hebrew counterparts.

Recensional Development, pp. 8, 11-12.

[61]*Ibid.*, pp. 110-11.

[62]Thiele, *Mysterious Numbers*, 1st ed., pp. 167-203; cf. his comments in "Coregencies and Overlapping Reigns" (see above, n. 42), pp. 181-88.

The above discussion is not meant overly to diminish, however, the significant value of much of Thiele's work. Albright, for example, was quick to cite Thiele's careful analysis of the records of Tiglath-pileser III, especially in connection with the dating of Azariah of Judah.[63] Not least among Thiele's accomplishments in my opinion was his patient and persistent analysis of the interplay of biblical synchronisms and regnal totals, and his confidence that the extant numbers of the MT accurately represent the original chronological data (in this regard I suspect Albright's approach was somewhat too negative).[64] Certainly, Thiele was extreme in his approach to the biblical numbers; he too often resorted to *ad hoc* measures to explain away inconsistencies among the data.[65] I am not as confident as

---

[63]Albright, "Chronology," p. 18, and n. 8.

[64]*Ibid.*, p. 19, n. 12, which I have already quoted in part (see above, p. 6, and n. 13). The end of Albright's footnote, however, is worth quoting here:

"Once the numbers [i.e. the regnal totals of the kings of Judah and Israel] were included in the text of the great work of the Deuteronomist, they were transmitted by copyists with astonishing accuracy, as proved by confrontation of the versions."

[65]This type of argumentation, I suspect, resulted largely from an excess of enthusiasm for a method (the positing of coregencies) which seemed to straighten out in an amazing manner such disparate biblical chronological data as, e.g., those pertaining to the reigns of Amaziah and Azariah of Judah and Joash and Jeroboam II of Israel (see my above discussion, pp. 18-19). These *ad hoc* measures of Thiele are indeed to be deplored; but they do not, I feel, warrant criticism such as the following:

"To argue that one must postulate the existence of such a coregency [i.e. between Jehoshaphat and Jehoram] in order to reconcile the data of the MT and then that the data of the MT must be reconciled because the MT has a consistent and harmonious system of chronology and, further, to argue this reconciliation because it can be shown that all the data in the MT can be fitted into a consistent pattern, if, among other postulates, the existence of several coregencies is accepted--all these arguments are patently an example of circular reasoning and not arguments from indirect or implicit evidence in the Bible."

The quotation is from Shenkel, *Chronology and Recensional Development*, p. 75; the criticism is of Thiele.

It is true that Thiele's suggested Jehoshaphat/Jehoram coregency may be seen to be the result of "circular reasoning," but such a criticism may *not* be fairly leveled against his system as a whole. Thiele has suggested a hypothesis (that there were coregencies), and he has tested it by his attempts to accommodate the various biblical data (with the results I have already discussed at length). It is entirely possible that his hypothesis could have proved less tenable than it did; each of his alleged coregencies must be evaluated

Thiele was that the diverse biblical chronological data can (or even should) be pressed into a single harmonious chronological pattern; but I do nevertheless remain optimistic (partly as the result of the work of Thiele and Shenkel) that a number of biblical chronological systems can be isolated, and that such a process can and will contribute significantly to the goal of establishing an absolute chronological reconstruction for the Divided Monarchy of Israel.

In conclusion, it is fair to say that the chronological reconstructions of both W. F. Albright and E. R. Thiele, despite their faults, represent significant advances in the study of biblical chronology: the overall methodological rigor of Albright's investigations will continue to exert a profound influence upon my own chronological analysis, while his impressive control of the external synchronisms remain a valuable resource to which I will repeatedly turn in the next several chapters. And Thiele's suggestions, while not infrequently biased and contrived, will nevertheless continue to affect significantly my own eventual wrestling with the biblical numbers in the Appendix.

---

on its own merits. If the reader remains unconvinced by my comments, let him or her work out Thiele's hypothesis in detail, especially in regard to the above-mentioned Amaziah/Azariah and Joash/Jeroboam II double coregency--the results are indeed impressive. As will be recalled (see above, p. 19), I did disagree with Thiele concerning his suggested reconstruction of the chronology of these kings; nevertheless I am willing to concede the impressive "fit" which Thiele has succeeded in creating. Criticisms of "circular reasoning" such as that of Shenkel's clearly miss the mark; they are insufficient to account for Thiele's impressive, albeit flawed results.

CHAPTER II

THE TYRIAN KING LIST:
AN EXTERNAL SYNCHRONISM FROM PHOENICIA

Any reconstruction of the Divided Monarchy of Israel must ultimately depend upon the constraints imposed by the external synchronisms derived from the historical records of Phoenicia, Egypt, and especially Mesopotamia. Such external synchronisms serve a twofold purpose:

1. They establish absolute dates (in the Julian calendar) in which to date many of the Judahite and Israelite kings (e.g., the fall of Samaria in 722/21, which allows one decisively to date the end of the reign of Hoshea of Israel, as well as quite possibly the date of the accession of Hezekiah; cf. my discussion below in Chapter IV).

2. They clarify to some extent the biblical methods used to reckon the regnal chronological data (e.g., whether antedating or postdating was used in compiling the synchronisms from the regnal totals). This clarification actually encompasses two separate approaches: a) The implicit likelihood that the Dtr editors would have followed an approach similar to that attested elsewhere (e.g., by the Mesopotamian scribes who compiled the Babylonian Chronicle); and b) the specific links of the external synchronisms with the biblical chronological data which serve to confirm or deny the plausibility of various features of a biblical chronological reconstruction (e.g., whether a hypothetical coregency, posited as a result of the biblical data, is indeed likely, or for that matter, at all possible).

In general, of course, the external synchronisms also effectively attest the overall accuracy (or inaccuracy) of the biblical chronological data for the various periods of the Divided Monarchy; and, not least, they serve to restrain some of the originality and ingenuity of the various efforts at chronological reconstructions by biblical scholars. It will be immediately apparent in the light of the above comments why one must seek to determine, as far as possible, the identity and reliability of any potential external synchronism for the Divided Monarchy of Israel, especially for the tenth and early ninth centuries

B.C.E. where chronological precision has heretofore been notably lacking.

I have already noted the surprisingly low date of 922 proposed by W. F. Albright for the disruption of the United Monarchy (see above, pp. 4-5); this represents a relatively wide variation from the more commonly accepted date of 931 (preferred, e.g., by E. R. Thiele).[1] In his review of Thiele's first edition of *Mysterious Numbers*, Albright discussed their disagreement concerning the dating of the disruption of the monarchy, and he cited the "Tyrian chronology as transmitted to us from Menander of Ephesus by Josephus" which "seems to settle the matter in the reviewer's favor."[2] As additional supporting evidence, he noted M. B. Rowton's proposed date of 959 for the founding of Solomon's temple (based on the Tyrian chronology and Timaeus' date of 814 for the founding of Carthage);[3] as Albright pointed out, Rowton's conclusion, although derived from independent sources, accorded with Albright's chronology to the exact year.[4] In a later article, Albright again turned to the subject of the chronology of Tyre; he presented his proposed chronological reconstruction of the Tyrian kings in the light of a newly discovered Assyro-Tyrian synchronism, and he concluded as follows:

> In this paper we have shown that there is nothing in the new Assyrian synchronism with Tyre that conflicts with my low Israelite and Egyptian chronology in the tenth century B.C. The data of Menander and Timaeus remain fundamental and there does not appear to be any conflict between them and the now available chronological evidence from other sources.[5]

---

[1]Thiele, "The Chronology of the Kings of Judah and Israel," *JNES* 3 (1944) 147; cf. *The Mysterious Numbers of the Hebrew Kings*, 1st ed., (Chicago, 1951), pp. 55-56.

[2]Albright, "Alternative Chronology," *Interpretation* 6 (1951) 102-103.

[3]Rowton, "The Date of the Founding of Solomon's Temple," *BASOR* 119 (1950) 20-22.

[4]Albright, "Alternative Chronology," p. 103.

[5]Albright, "The New Assyro-Tyrian Synchronism and the Chronology of Tyre," *Annuaire de l'Institut de Philologie et Histoire Orientales et Slaves* 13 (1953) [*Mélanges Isadore Lévy* (Bruxelles, 1955)], p. 9.

More recently, however, F. M. Cross, Jr., in his article on the Nora Inscription, suggested a different reconstruction of the Tyrian chronology (although based on the same material of Menander as transmitted by Josephus, and utilizing the same Assyro-Tyrian synchronism).[6] Cross's proposal, in contrast with Albright's, accorded more closely with a higher date for the founding of Carthage, that of Pompeius Trogus (825). Cross then suggested the date of 968 for the founding of Solomon's temple and 971-932 for the reign of Solomon, thus implicitly confirming the date of 932 for the disruption of the monarchy.

Even this brief summary of the scholarly discussion clearly illustrates the need for a close re-examination of the Tyrian chronological material in order to delineate precisely any external synchronism(s) for the period of the Divided Monarchy of Israel. The following discussion represents such an analysis: first, of the Tyrian data as transmitted by Josephus from Menander of Ephesus, and secondly, of the various dates for the founding of Carthage attested in the classical literature. Such an undertaking, although seemingly quite tangential to the major purposes of the present thesis, should nevertheless prove worthwhile indeed if it succeeds in shedding light on the presently murky chronological situation obtaining in the tenth and early ninth centuries B.C.E.

The Tyrian chronological material consists of a few passages from a certain Menander of Ephesus quoted by Josephus (*Contra Apionem* 1:117-26; cf. *Antiquities* 8:144-46). One of these fragments comprises a list of Tyrian kings from Hiram (the contemporary of Solomon) to Pygmalion (in whose seventh year the founding of Carthage is attributed); the list includes the length of the life and of the reign for each king. Apparently still relying on Menander, Josephus then gives two additional chronological data of great significance for our purposes: the whole period from the accession of Hiram to the founding of Carthage amounts to 155 years and eight months, and the temple at Jerusalem was built in the 12th year of Hiram. Thus, if Josephus' data are trustworthy, we are able to compute the absolute date of the founding of Solomon's temple wholly independently of the disputed biblical chronological data of the Divided Monarchy of Israel, provided only that we can ascertain with precision one more

---

[6]Cross, "An Interpretation of the Nora Stone," *BASOR* 208 (1972) 17, n. 11.

chronological datum--the date of the founding of Carthage.[7]   In
addition, according to the chronological notice found in 1 Kgs 6:1, the
building of Solomon's temple was begun in the fourth year of the
king's reign; this notice permits us to calculate a date in absolute terms
for the beginning of Solomon's reign from the Tyrian chronological
data.   Finally if the 40 year length of reign attributed to Solomon
(1 Kgs 11:42) be an exact figure (rather than a round number), we may
ascertain (to within a year or so) the absolute date for the disruption of
the United Monarchy of Israel; once again, such a calculation remains
totally independent of the murky biblical chronological data for the
period of the Divided Monarchy.   It is therefore quite clear that the
Tyrian chronological data may well provide the valuable external
synchronism we seek to lend stability to the chronological period most
in need of it--the period of the United Monarchy of Israel and the
disruption of the kingdom after the death of Solomon.

However, the accuracy of Josephus' Tyrian data has been
repeatedly questioned.[8]   It is certainly evident that some textual
corruption is to be found in the extant MSS of Josephus, both in the
numerical figures for the regnal totals as well as in the transliterations
of the Phoenician names themselves.   Such corruption is only to be
expected when arcane data such as these are copied and recopied;
nevertheless it is true that, as Tadmor has pointed out,[9] none of the
extant MSS of Josephus attests regnal totals for the Tyrian kings (from
the accession of Hiram to the founding of Carthage in Pygmalion's
seventh year) which add up to 155 years and eight months, Josephus'
own total.   Nevertheless, few would dispute the basic authenticity of
Josephus' tradition, especially in the light of his own appeal to the
"public records" to corroborate his polemic against the enemies of the
Jews and his attempts to glorify the Jewish people:

---

[7]Actually, to be more exact, we must ascertain the date for the founding of Carthage
which Josephus (and/or his source[s]) considered to be most accurate; as I have already
noted in passing (and will soon discuss in some detail), the classical literature attests
several different traditions for the dating of the founding of Carthage.

[8]See, e.g., the comments made by Hayim Tadmor in his "Chronology" [Hebrew],
Encyclopedia Miqra'it, vol. 4 (Jerusalem: Bialik Institute, 1962), col. 300; also, E. R.
Thiele, "A Comparison of the Chronological Data of Israel and Judah," *VT* 4 (1954)
188-91.

[9]Tadmor, "Chronology," col. 300.

I therefore now propose to pass on to the allusions to our race in the Phoenician chronicles, and to produce the evidence which they afford. For very many years past the people of Tyre have kept public records, compiled and very carefully preserved by the state, of the memorable events in their internal history and in their relations with foreign nations. It is there recorded that the Temple at Jerusalem was built by King Solomon 143 years and eight months before the foundation of Carthage by the Tyrians. . . .

To prove that these assertions about the Tyrian archives are not of my own invention, I will call upon Dius, who is regarded as an accurate historian of Phoenicia, for his witness. . . .

I will, however, cite yet a further witness, Menander of Ephesus. This author has recorded the events of each reign, in Hellenic and non-Hellenic countries alike, and has taken the trouble to obtain his information in each case from the national records. . . . [Here follows a description of Hiram's reign, and then the list of Tyrian kings from Hiram to Pygmalion.] It was in the seventh year of his reign that his sister took flight, and built the city of Carthage in Libya.

The whole period from the accession of Hiram to the foundation of Carthage thus amounts to 155 years and eight months; and, since the temple at Jerusalem was built in the twelfth year of King Hiram's reign, 143 years and eight months elapsed between the erection of the temple and the foundation of Carthage.

What need is there to add further Phoenician evidence? The agreement of the witnesses, as will be seen, affords strong confirmation of their veracity.[10]

A further confirmation of the fundamental accuracy of the Tyrian chronological material lies in the fact that none of the numbers given for the life spans or regnal totals of the various Tyrian kings is

---

[10]Josephus, *Contra Apionem*, 1:106-27; translation by H. St. J. Thackeray, *Josephus*, vol. 1, The Loeb Classical Library (Cambridge: Harvard University Press, 1926), pp. 205-13. In *Antiquities* 8:144, Josephus again referred to Menander and described him as the one "who translated the Tyrian records from the Phoenician language into Greek." For an excellent discussion of the nature and accuracy of these Tyrian records as preserved by Josephus, see H. Jacob Katzenstein, *The History of Tyre* (Jerusalem: Goldberg's Press, 1973), pp. 77-85, 116-21; I would, however, disagree with his conclusion that "the reduction of the document to a mere list of names was the work of Josephus himself" (p. 117).

rounded off.[11] Indeed, the numbers appear to be taken directly from some sort of formulaic archival source or king list, which gave only the life span and regnal total for each king of Tyre plus brief remarks pertaining to his dynastic status (cf. the seemingly superfluous retention [at least for Josephus' purposes] of the numbers for the life spans of the various kings).[12]

I have already noted that the extant Tyrian regnal totals do not correspond with the overall total of 155 years and eight months given by Josephus (for the interval between the accession of Hiram and the founding of Carthage); as one might expect, this disparity has led to a number of scholarly conjectures to account for the discrepancies. It is beyond the scope of the present study to rehearse all these conjectures; however, the proposals of W. F. Albright, E. Lipiński, and F. M. Cross, Jr., do merit our close attention, not least because they all attempted to incorporate, in some form or other, the important Assyro-Tyrian synchronism contained in the then recently published annals of Shalmaneser III.[13]

First, however, a brief discussion of the Assyro-Tyrian synchronism itself is in order. In the 18th campaign of Shalmaneser III

---

[11]Katzenstein (*ibid.*, pp. 80-81), in his discussion of Josephus' Tyrian regnal material, pointed out:

> "The regnal years and the life-spans of the rulers are not given in round numbers, so there is no reason to doubt the veracity of this tradition. More-over, Josephus does not digress from listing the kings of Tyre even to comment on Ethbaal (Ithobal), the father-in-law of Ahab, although he is mentioned in the Bible."

This last point confirms the likelihood, in my opinion, that Josephus basically transmitted the Tyrian king list which he found in his sources, rather than that he himself edited his sources to produce such a list.

[12]For a discussion of the phenomenon of king lists in royal annalistic materials, see my discussion below in Chapter V; also cf. Shoshana R. Bin-Nun, "Formulas from Royal Records of Israel and of Judah," *VT* 18 (1968) 414-32.

[13]W. F. Albright, "The New Assyro-Tyrian Synchronism and the Chronology of Tyre," *Annuaire de l'Institut de Philologie et Histoire Orientales et Slaves* 13 (1953) [*Mélanges Isadore Lévy* (Bruxelles, 1955)], pp. 1-9; E. Lipiński, "Ba'li-Ma'zer II and the Chronology of Tyre," *Rivista degli studi orientali* 45 (1970) 59-65; F. M. Cross, Jr., "An Interpretation of the Nora Stone," *BASOR* 208 (1972) 17, n. 11. The Assyro-Tyrian synchronism in question was first published by Fuad Safar, "A Further Text of Shalmaneser III from Assur," *Sumer* 7 (1951) 3-21 + plates I-III; the reference to *Ba'li-manzer* is to be found in col. iv, l. 10.

(841 B.C.E.), reference is made to a certain ^{m}*Ba-a'-li-ma-an-zer*, "the Tyrian," who, along with Jehu of Israel,[14] paid tribute to the Assyrian king. The context of the notice, as Albright pointed out, makes it quite clear that *Ba'li-manzer* was king of Tyre at the time.[15] The Assyrian transcription most likely presupposes the Phoenician form *Ba'l-mazzer*.[16]

Such a closely dated Assyro-Tyrian synchronism would normally be expected either clearly to confirm the chronological data

---

[14]Akkadian transcription ^{m}*Ia-a-ú mār Ḫu-um-ri-i*; usually identified with Jehu of Israel. Recently, P. Kyle McCarter ("'Yaw, Son of 'Omri': A Philological Note on Israelite Chronology," *BASOR* 216 [1974] 5-7) suggested that inasmuch as the Akkadian ^{m}*Ia-a-ú* probably represents the hypocoristicon *Yaw*, a perfectly acceptable form for either Jehu (*Yaw-hū'*) or Jehoram (*Yaw-rām*), the reference may well have been to the latter since only he was in any real sense *mār Ḫumri*, "(grand)son of Omri." However, Manfred Weippert ("Jau[a] Mar Ḫumrî--Joram oder Jehu von Israel?" *VT* 28 [1978] 113-18) presented a powerful rebuttal to McCarter's thesis, pointing out that the Assyrians referred to Israel as "Beth Omri" for many years after the fall of the Omride dynasty; hence, it is not at all unlikely that Jehu would have been termed "son of Omri."

[15]Albright, "New Assyro-Tyrian Synchronism," p. 2, and n. 4; his translation of col. iv, ll. 7-15, is as follows:
"To Mount Ba'al-rōš [the South Canaanite pronunciation of the name of the promontory at Nahr el-Kelb near Beirut] which is a headland of the sea opposite the land of Tyre I went; my royal image I set up there. The tribute of Ba'al-manzer, the Tyrian, of Jehu of Beth-Omri I received. On my return I ascended Mount Lebanon; my royal image beside the image of Tiglath-pileser [I], the great king, my predecessor, I set up."

[16]*Mazzer* appears as a Punic name from the fourth-third century B.C.E. at Carthage; cf. Albright, *ibid.*, pp. 3-5. Albright also noted the Hebrew hapax legomenon *minzār* in Nah 3:17 where the plural form appears as the name of a class of Assyrian citizens and (according to Albright) should be translated "religious votaries" or the like (cf. the root *nzr*, "to vow"). Lipiński, "Chronology of Tyre," pp. 60-62, suggested a different possibility: inasmuch as the name *B'l-m'dr* is attested twice at Ugarit, he preferred reading *Ba'li-ma'ēr* (root '*zr*, "to help") as the Phoenician name underlying the Akkadian transcription. The Punic example cited by Albright seems to me to be more impressive, however; not only does it accord more closely with the Akkadian transcription, but it also provides a closer (chronological and linguistic) parallel with ninth century Tyre. (On the Akkadian tendency for dissimilation of doubled *z*, see Wolfram von Soden, *Grundriss der Akkadischen Grammatik* [Rome: Pontifical Biblical Institute, 1952] §§ 32b, 96j; cf. Sabatino Moscati, ed., *An Introduction to the Comparative Grammar of the Semitic Languages: Phonology and Morphology*, Porta Linguarum Orientalium [Wiesbaden: Otto Harrassowitz, 1969], § 9.10.)

found in the Tyrian king list, or clearly to contradict them; but, as will be presently demonstrated, the synchronism proved to be more ambiguous. The basic question, of course, is which (if any) of the kings in Josephus' list corresponds with *Ba'li-manzer* of the Assyrian annals. To answer this question we must first examine the extant Greek transcriptions (with variants) for the Tyrian kings as transmitted by Josephus. Table I is a list of these transcriptions (including significant variants) based upon Niese's edition of Josephus, *Contra Apionem*.[17]

---

[17]Benedictus Niese, ed., *Flavii Iosephi Opera*, vol. v (Berlin, 1889). The parallel evidence of Eusebius (cf. the various textual traditions listed in Table I, note c) and Theophilus were independently collated by myself.

TABLE I
THE TYRIAN KING LIST: THE NAMES OF THE KINGS[a]

Codex L[b]	Significant Variants[c]
1. Εἴρωμος	Σιρώμος Syn[e]
2. Βαλεάζερος	Βααλβάζερος Syn cf. Eus Arm (*Bahalbazerus*) *Balbazerus* Lat Βαλζάβερ Eus ex gr Βάζωρος Theo[f]
3. ᾽Αβδάστρατος	᾽Αβδάσταρτος Eus et Syn *Abdatratus* Lat om. Theo[g]
4. [μεθ᾽ οὓς] ῎Ασταρτος	[μεθ᾽ ὃν] ῎Ασταρτος Eus et Syn Μεθουάσταρτος Theo cf. Lat (*Metusastartus*)[h]
5. [ο] Δελαιαστάρτου	*Leastrati* Lat om. Theo ᾽Ελεαστάρτου Eus Arm et Syn ᾽Ελεστάρτος Eus ex gr[i]
6. ᾽Ασέρυμος	*Astirimus* Lat ᾽Ασθάρυμος Eus ex gr et Syn *Astharimus* Eus Arm ᾽Αθάρυμος Theo[j]
7. Φέλλητος	*Pellete* Lat *Phelite* Eus Arm ῎Ελλης Theo Φέλλης Syn[k]
8. Ειθώβαλος	᾽Ιθόβαλος Eus ex gr *Ithobalus* Eus Arm Ειθόβαλος Syn ᾽Ιουθώβαλος Theo
9. Βαδεζωρος	*Balezorus* Eus Arm Βαλίζωρος Eus ex gr Βαλέζερος Syn *Badezodus* Lat Βάζωρος Theo[l]
10. Μάττηνος	*Mettinus* Lat Μέτηνος Eus Μέτινος Syn Μέττηνος Theo
11. Φυσμαλίου	*Pigmalion* Lat *Physmanon* Eus Arm Μυγδαλίων Φυσμαλίωνος Eus ex gr Μυγδαλίων Φυσμανοῦν Syn ἐν Πυγμαλίων Φυγμαλίουμ Theo[m]

Notes to the Table will be found on the next several pages.

Suggested Greek Original[d]
1. Εἴρωμος
2. Βαλβάζερος
3. ᾿Αβδάσταρτος
4. ῎Ασταρτος
5. Δελαιάσταρτος
6. ᾿Αστάρυμος
7. Φελλης
8. ᾿Ιθόβαλος
9. Βαλέζερος
10. Μάττηνος
11. Πυγμαλίων

[a]Josephus, *Contra Apionem*, 1:117, 121-25.

[b]I.e. *Codex Laurentianus*, an 11th century MS, yet the earliest Greek MS extant for *Contra Apionem*; as will be readily seen from the transliterations, this MS is faulty in many respects. Hence, we are not infrequently dependent upon the evidence of Eusebius as well as the old Latin version of Cassiodorus; cf. the comments of Niese, pp. iv-xxiv; Thackeray, pp. xviii-xix.

[c]Key to the sigla:

L   *Codex Laurentianus, plut.* 69, *cod.* 22, as cited by Niese.

Lat   The Old Latin Version of Cassiodorus, as cited by Niese.

Eus   Eusebius, *Chronicle*, part 1 (commonly referred to as the *Chronography*). The *Chronography* is no longer extant in Greek; however, an Armenian translation (which probably dated originally to the 6th century) is extant for virtually the entire text, and Greek fragments (some of which are direct and explicit quotations of Eusebius by later Greek writers; others of which, though not expressly attributed to Eusebius, nevertheless correspond closely in content and phrasing to the Armenian translation) are extant for much of the work. These Greek fragments as well as a Latin translation of the Armenian version are printed together in parallel columns in A. Schoene, ed., *Eusebi Chronicorum Libri Duo*, vol. 1 (Berlin, 1875). Niese, in his critical edition of *Contra Apionem*, generally considered the evidence of Eusebius to be of high value in restoring the text of Josephus. For an excellent introduction to the textual problems of Eusebius' *Chronography*, see Timothy D. Barnes, *Constantine and Eusebius*, (Cambridge: Harvard University Press, 1981), pp. 111-13; also Alden A. Mosshammer, *The Chronicle of Eusebius and Greek Chronographic Tradition* (Lewisburg: Bucknell University Press, 1979), pp. 29-83.

Arm   The Armenian version of the *Chronography*, translated into Latin, as found in the edition of A. Schoene, *Eusebi Chronicorum Libri Duo*, vol. 1, cols. 117, 119.

ex gr   Greek excerpts of the *Chronography*, collected by Schoene, *ibid.*, cols. 118, 120; these excerpts were originally published by J. A. Cramer, ed., *Anecdota Graeca e Codd. Manuscriptis Bibliothecae Regiae Parisiensis* (Oxford, 1839), 2:186-87.

Syn   Greek excerpts of Eusebius as extant in the *Chronographia* of Georgius Syncellus, Guilielme Dindorfi, ed., vol. 1 [= *Corpus Scriptorum Byzantinae*, vol. 12], (Bonnae, 1829), p. 345.

Theo   Theophilus of Antioch, *Ad Autolycum*, 3:22; cf. J. C. T. Otto, ed., *Theophili Episcopi Antiocheni Ad Autolycum Libri Tres* [= *Corpus Apologetarum Christianorum Saeculi Secundi*, vol. 8] (Jena, 1861), pp. 244-48. For a convenient introduction, critical text, and English translation of *Ad Autolycum*, see Robert M. Grant, *Theophilus of Antioch: Ad Autolycum* (Oxford, 1970).

[d]The normal canons of textual criticism, especially *lectio difficilior* and *lectio brevior*, do not necessarily apply to the problem of reconstructing the original forms of the Greek transliterations of Phoenician names; cf. the rather strange proposals made by Niese, an otherwise competent text-critic. Crucial to any such reconstruction, of course, is a thorough awareness of Phoenician onomastica. The present treatment is heavily indebted to the proposals made by F. M. Cross, Jr. ("Nora Stone," pp. 17-18); see below, Table III, for his Phoenician equivalents for these names.

[e]A clear case of graphic confusion of the Greek uncials E and Σ (Ɛ and Ͼ). A number of similar examples of graphic confusion (not all of which are, however, as readily explainable) will be cited in the following notes.

[f]Theo has levelled through Βάζωρος for both name no. 2 and name no. 9 (see note 1 below). Confusion of the uncials A and Λ (Λ and ⅄) may have contributed to the variations in the spelling (Βα-, Βαλ-, Βααλ-) of the first syllable. Albright ("New Assyro-Tyrian Synchronism," p. 3, and n. 5) may well be right in suggesting that the Βαλβάζερος of Josephus was a cursive corruption of Βαλμάζερος (since Greek cursive β and μ [ʋ and ⅄] often closely resembled each other). Alternatively, assimilation of the second labial to the first may have occurred.

[g]Theo omits entirely the name and chronological data for this king, a haplography probably due to *homoeoarkton* (μετὰ δὲ τοῦτον . . .).

[h]As a comparison of the various textual traditions demonstrates, major textual corruption has occurred at this point. It is clear that there were originally four usurpers, all sons of *Abdastartos'* nurse (τροφός); but seemingly only three names have survived: according to L, first the anonymous elder brother (ὁ πρεσβύτερος), who reigned 12 years; then "after them" (μεθ᾽ οὕς) a certain *Astartos ho Delaiastartou* (the patronymic is unexpected at this point), who lived 54 years and (also) reigned 12 years; then *Aserumos*, who also lived 54 years, but reigned only 9 years; and finally *Phelletos*, who lived 50 years and reigned 8 months. Eus also mentions the anonymous eldest usurper, but he gives no regnal total for him. Syn does likewise, but inexplicably counts only "three" children of the nurse (τρεῖς παῖδες), although all four of the above candidates are still present. Theo, just after a major haplography, attests the name Μεθουάσταρτος, which Niese adopts for his critical text (cf. *Metusastartus* of Lat). Albright ("New Assyro-Tyrian Synchronism," p. 6, n. 2) disagreed: he suggested that the hypocoristic name *Astartos* (= *ʿAštart*) is far more likely to have been the original form (cf. the common Greek equivalent *Straton*). Also, the μεθ᾽ ὃν ᾿Ασταρτος of Eus (cf. Syn) is to be preferred over the plural reading μεθ᾽ οὕς ᾿Α. of L; the latter reading resulted from a misunderstanding of the connection between the following words and the immediately preceding υἱοὶ τέσσαρες.

[i]All textual traditions except Eus ex gr and Theo attest the patronymic in some form or other; nevertheless, as Cross ("Nora Stone," p. 17, n. 11) has pointed out, "we do not expect the second brother's patronymic." Theo, interestingly, omits the name altogether

(but, to be sure, Theo totally lacks any reference at all to the brothers' usurpation). The nominative form *Elestartos* of Eus ex gr, on the other hand, may well attest an earlier stage of textual transmission (cf. the comments in the previous note). As for the variation in the spelling of the initial syllable(s) (Δελαι-, 'Ελε-, Λε-), possible confusion of the uncials Δ and Λ (Δ and Λ), as well as the question of the presence or absence of the particle δέ in the *scriptio continua* (cf. the recurring μετὰ τοῦτον of L vs. the μετὰ δὲ τοῦτον of Theo) undoubtedly led to the extant spelling variations. Cross (*ibid.*) suggested the Phoenician form represented by the Greek transliteration was *Dalay-'Aštart* (root *dly*; cf. the Hebrew name *Dĕlāyāhû*).

ʲPossibly a confusion of cursive θ and ε (ϑ and Ɛ) led to the clearly corrupt 'Ασέρυμος of L. However, the name was probably originally spelled with a *tau* instead of a *theta* (cf. Lat *Astirimus*; also the spellings with *tau* found in the previous three names).

ᵏSyn, although a relatively late witness, here preserves most accurately the likely original Greek transcription *Phellēs* (= Phoenician *Pillēs*). The Phoenician name is a hypocoristicon according to Lipiński ("Chronology of Tyre," p. 64, and n. 1), and it is already attested in the *Corpus Inscriptionum Semiticarum*, 1:2890, 3662.

ˡAgain, Syn has probably preserved more accurately an earlier stage of textual transmission. Interestingly enough, as has already been noted (above, n. f), Theo reads Βάζωρος for both no. 2 and no. 9; although originally these two names may well have been identical (see below, Table III), the readings in Theo probably represent only a secondary assimilation (all the other witnesses attest an early divergence between name no. 2 and name no. 9 in the Greek textual tradition). L again attests confusion between the Greek uncials Δ and Λ (Δ and Λ), while Lat also attests confusion between the Latin capitals *D* and *R* (*D* and *R* in the so-called "rustic capital" script).

ᵐSeveral cases of conflation are to be found in these witnesses. Apparently, early confusion between the Greek uncials M and Π (M and Π) as well as between Γ and Σ (Γ and С) led to two significant variants in the textual tradition (Μυγδαλίων and Φυσμαλίων) which were then conflated in Theo, Syn, and Eus ex gr. The identification of the king himself is certain: he is the notorious Pygmalion of Tyre whose sister Elissa (or Dido) was forced to flee the city after he murdered her husband (Virgil, *Aeneid*, 1:343-64; cf. Justinus, *Epitome Pompei Trogi*, 18:4 [this Pygmalion is not to be confused with the Pygmalion of Cyprus who, according to legend, fashioned an ivory statue which eventually came to life]). The surprisingly wide orthographical divergences reflected in these witnesses should be noted: after all, Pygmalion was a reasonably well known king. Such orthographical variations lend strong plausibility to the argument that (*contra* Albright, "New Assyro-Tyrian Synchronism," pp. 2-5) *Balbazeros* son of *Eirōmos* and *Balezeros* son of *Ithobalos* actually represent variant Greek transliterations of originally the same Phoenician name, *Ba'l-mazzer* [I and II].

TABLE II
THE TYRIAN KING LIST: THE CHRONOLOGICAL DATA

	Name[a]	Length of Life[b]	Length of Reign
1.	Eirōmos	53	34
2.	Balbazeros	43	17 (7)[c]
3.	Abdastartos	39 (29, 20)[d]	9
4.	Astartos	[?][e]	[20][f]
5.	Delaiastartos	54 (53)[g]	12
6.	Astarumos	58 (54)[h]	9
7.	Phellēs	50	8 months[i]
8.	Ithobalos	48 (40, 68)[j]	32 (12)[k]
9.	Balezeros	45	6 (7, 8, 18)[l]
10.	Mattēnos	32	9 (25, 29)[m]
11.	Pygmaliōn	58 (56)[n]	47 (40, 7)[o]
		TOTAL[p]	155 years 8 months

[a]See Table I for textual and orthographic variants; the names found here correspond with those found in the last column of that table. For a key to the sigla of the textual witnesses, see Table I, note c.

[b]Figures for the life spans of all the kings (except *Eirōmos*) are lacking in Syn.

[c]17] Eus Arm Syn Theo: 7 L Lat Eus ex gr.

[d]39] Eus (Arm + ex gr): 29 L: 20 Lat: om. Theo (see Table I, note g). It should be noted, however, that if these numbers are indeed reliable, *Balbazeros* was only about 13 years old when he became a father, rather young even by ancient standards.

[e]See Table I, note h, for a discussion of the problem. L Lat Eus Theo do give figures for the life span and length of reign of *(Methou)astartos*, but their present position in these witnesses is probably secondary. It seems that all regnal data for the first usurper are now lost.

[f]Following the suggestion of Cross ("Nora Stone," p. 17, n. 11). See Table I, notes h and i, for a discussion of the textual problems and his proposed reconstruction.

[g]See above, note e, for the present location of these figures in the various witnesses. 54] L Eus (Arm + ex gr) Theo: 53 Lat.

[h]58] Eus (Arm + ex gr) Theo: 54 L Lat.

[i]Eus ex gr, oddly, reads 18 (ιη´) months.

[j]48] Eus (Arm + ex gr) Lat: 40 Theo: 68 L.

[k]32] L Lat Eus (Arm + ex gr) Syn: 12 Theo.

[l]6] L Lat: 7 Theo: 8 Eus Arm Syn: 18 Eus ex gr.

[m]9] L Lat: 25 Eus ex gr Syn: 29 Eus Arm Theo. The higher numbers are almost certainly secondary attempts to fill in the missing years (see below, note p). As Albright ("New Assyro-Tyrian Synchronism," p. 7, and n. 2) pointed out, *Mettēnos* would have been only three (or else seven) years old when he became king, "which is quite possible, but not too likely in those days of repeated dynastic upsets." J. Katzenstein (*The History of Tyre* [Jerusalem: Goldberg's Press, 1973], p. 119) concurred:

> ". . . otherwise Mettēn would have been only three years old upon his accession to the throne of Tyre. While this is possible, it certainly was not desirable from the Tyrian point of view, since this was a period of political turmoil, marked by two campaigns of Shalmaneser III against the nations of the west. To this we must add as a general consideration the continuity of Tyrian colonization, a phenomenon difficult to imagine under an unstable regime."

[n]58] Eus (Arm + ex gr): 56 L Lat Theo.

[o]47] L Eus (Arm + ex gr) Syn: 40 Lat: 7 Theo.

[p]This total includes only the first seven years of Pygmalion's reign, which corresponds with the date of the founding of Carthage according to Josephus or his source(s). It should be emphasized that this exact figure of "155 years and 8 months" from the accession of Hiram (*Eirōmos*) to the founding of Carthage is attested in virtually all of the textual witnesses (in Syn it is not explicit, but see below; Eus ex gr alone reads "155 years and 18 months," cf. above, note i). This textual unanimity is all the more striking when one considers that none of the regnal figures as now extant in the various texts add up to this figure (all except Eus Arm fall short). For further analysis of these regnal totals, see Niese's comments in his introduction to *Contra Apionem*, pp. xi-xiii; also the helpful tables found in J. M. Peñuela, "La Inscripción Asiria IM 55644 y la Cronología de los reyes de Tiro," *Sefarad* 14 (1954) 40-42. Syn does omit the 155 year, 8 month total reckoned from Hiram's accession but is nevertheless in full agreement with all the other texts (except Theo) in dating the founding of Solomon's temple to Hiram's 12th year and reckoning a period of 143 years and 8 months between that event and the founding of Carthage. Any reconstruction of the regnal years based upon this overall total of "155 years and 8 months" must remain hypothetical, of course, but the uniformity of

this tradition (especially in the light of its disparity with the individual regnal totals found in all the textual witnesses) greatly encourages all such efforts.

It is apparent that the only Greek transliterations of the Phoenician kings which correspond at all closely with the Akkadian *Ba'li-manzer* are *Balbazeros* (my no. 2) and *Balezeros* (my no. 9); chronological constraints, however, eliminate the first possibility inasmuch as his father (Hiram) was a contemporary of David and Solomon (1 Kgs 5:15).

The correspondence of *Balezeros* (my no. 9) with the Akkadian *Ba'li-manzer* is less exact, however, than one would expect; indeed, Albright denied the possibility of making such an identification at all (he proposed that Greek *Balezoros* [sic] = Phoenician *Ba'al-'azōr*; but Akkadian *Ba'li-manzer* = Phoenician *Ba'al-mazzer*, Greek *Balbazeros* [II]); and he suggested a haplography in the extant king list (the original *Balbazeros II*, successor [or possibly precursor] of *Balezoros*, having fallen out of the list, due to the similarity of the names [see Table III]). In support of this hypothesis, he noted that since the total of the individual regnal years as transmitted by Josephus is less than his own total for the overall interval, the suggestion of some sort of haplography is perfectly natural. Again, it would have been unlikely that a son of *Ithobalos*, born before the latter's usurpation of the throne, would have been given a dynastic name; whereas the grandson of *Ithobalos* might well have borne such a name.[18] Thus, according to Albright, the newly discovered Assyro-Tyrian synchronism actually corresponds with a lacuna in the Tyrian king list of Menander as transmitted by Josephus. Albright's conclusion to his study has already been cited (see above, p. 30).

E. Lipiński, in his own paper on the chronology of Tyre, disagreed: "The hypothesis that a king's name fell out of Menander's list could be accepted only as a desperate solution."[19] Lipiński suggested an original **Balmazeros > Bal<ba>zeros*, and that this king indeed did correspond with the Akkadian *Ba'li-manzer*; therefore, he

---

[18]Albright, "New Assyro-Tyrian Synchronism," pp. 3-5, and especially p. 5, n. 2. In reply to his argument concerning the dynastic name *Ba'l-mazzer*, would it not be possible to bestow such a throne-name (if such it be) upon a usurper's heir at (or soon after) his takeover?

[19]Lipiński, "Chronology of Tyre," p. 61.

may be dated with confidence to around 841 B.C.E.[20] I will return to his preference for the date of Pompeius Trogus for the founding of Carthage presently.

F. M. Cross, Jr., concurred with this suggested correspondence (see Table III).[21] His major contribution was the brilliant suggestion that the patronymic *ho Delaiastartou* of *Codex Laurentianus* (cf. Table I, line 5) actually represents a corrupted form of the name of the second brother of the four usurpers: "We do not expect the second brother's patronymic. None are given for other usurpers or founders of new dynasties in the entire king-list."[22] Indeed, it seems far more reasonable in my opinion to suggest such textual corruption (with the retention, albeit reinterpreted, of all the original names), than to have to explain why the name and chronological data of the eldest (and presumably most notorious) usurper are not lost, while the second usurper's name, chronological data, *and patronymic* are extant.

Cross's suggested regnal total of 20 years for *Astartos* (the first usurper), while of necessity hypothetical, remains entirely possible given the strong textual support underlying Josephus' own total of 155 years and eight months for the interval from the accession of Hiram to the founding of Carthage (see Table II, especially note p). While Lipiński was forced to conclude that this overall total of Josephus was "confused" and in error,[23] Cross was able to demonstrate its intrinsic accuracy, both in the light of the various extant names and regnal totals of the Tyrian king list as well as in the light of the new Assyro-Tyrian synchronism. Thus, we may conclude that there is indeed solid evidence for a *Ba'l-mazzer II* reigning in Tyre in 841 B.C.E.; and since he reigned for only six years or so (see Table II, line 9), we are able

---

[20]*Ibid.*, pp. 62-64. As I have already noted (see above, n. 16), Lipiński suggested *Ba'li-ma'zēr* as the original Phoenician name.

[21]Cross, "Nora Stone," p. 17, n. 11.

[22]*Ibid.* The textual situation is complex and in clear disarray in all the extant witnesses. For a brief description of the likely course of textual corruption (to the extent that it can be deciphered), see Table I, notes h and i.

[23]Lipiński, "Chronology of Tyre," p. 64. He suggested that Josephus mistakenly added the number given for Hiram's life span (53 years) instead of his actual length of reign (34 years).

then to date quite precisely both his reign and the reigns of his predecessors and successors.

TABLE III
THE TYRIAN KING LIST: THREE RECONSTRUCTIONS[a]

	Albright[b]		*Lipiński*[c]		*Cross*[d]	
1.	Ḥîrōm	34	Ḥīrōm	34	Ḥīrōm	34
2.	Ba'al-mazzer	17	Ba'li-ma'zer I	7	Ba'l-mazzer I	17
3.	'Abd-'Aštart	9	'Abdi-'Aštart	9	'Abd-'Aštart	9
4.	(Anonymous)[e]	?	(Anonymous)	12	'Aštart	[20]
5.	'Aštart	12	'Aštart	12	Dalay-'Aštart	12
6.	'Aštar-(?)	9	'Aštarōn	9	'Aštar-rōm	9
7.	(Phelles)[f]	8 mos	Pillēs	8 mos	Pillēs	8 mos
8.	'Ittō-ba'al	32	'Ittō-ba'l	32	'Itto-ba'l	32
9.	Ba'al-'azōr	6	Ba'li-ma'zēr II	6	Ba'l-mazzer II	6
	<Ba'al-mazzer II 20?>[g]					
10.	Mittin	9	Mattēn	9	Mattin	9
11.	Pu'm-yatōn	47	Pummayyōn	47	Pummay	47
TOTALS:[h]	155 yrs, 8 mos		137 yrs, 8 mos		155 yrs, 8 mos	

[a]For ease of comparison, only the reconstructed Phoenician names and the regnal totals are given for each king. Full references for each of the three reconstructions may be found above in n. 13 on p. 34.

[b]W. F. Albright, "New Assyro-Tyrian Synchronism," pp. 6-7. His suggested dates for these kings span c. 969-774.

[c]E. Lipiński, "Chronology of Tyre," pp. 63-64. His suggested dates for these kings span c. 962-785.

[d]F. M. Cross, Jr., "Nora Stone," p. 17, n. 11. His suggested dates for these kings span c. 980-785.

[e]Albright (p. 6, n. 1) suggested that "in all probability the eldest of the brothers reigned so briefly that his name was not recorded in the lists."

[f]Albright gave no Phoenician equivalent for the Greek name.

[g]See my above discussion, p. 46, for this addition to the list.

[h]All the totals include only the first seven years of Pygmalion's reign (= the date of the founding of Carthage, according to Josephus).

This conclusion, however, naturally leads to the question of the date for the founding of Carthage, or to be more exact, which (if any) of the various dates attested in the classical literature for the founding of Carthage are in accord with the relatively firm dates set by the Assyro-Tyrian synchronism and the regnal data of the Tyrian king list. There are essentially only two divergent dates for the founding of Carthage which are historically feasible, that of 814 B.C.E. according to Timaeus of Sicily,[24] and attested elsewhere;[25] and that of 825 B.C.E. according to the Roman historian Pompeius Trogus.[26] J. Liver, writing soon after Safar's initial publication of Shalmaneser's annals, first drew attention to the newly discovered Assyro-Tyrian synchronism; he pointed out that only the date of Pompeius Trogus for the founding of Carthage (825) would permit the successful reconciliation of both the Tyrian and the classical chronologies.[27] Liver concluded that Hiram's accession should be dated to 979/78, and that the disruption of the United Monarchy of Israel occurred in 931/30.[28]

At about the same time as Liver's paper, J. M. Peñuela published a lengthy study (in two parts) on the Tyrian chronological material.[29] Working independently of Liver, Peñuela also concluded that Josephus relied upon the date of Pompeius Trogus (825) for the founding of Carthage; but he suggested that the original text of Menander probably stated only that Elissa (also known as Dido) fled

---

[24]According to Timaeus (Dionysius of Halicarnassus, *Antiquitates Romanae*, 1:74), Carthage was founded 38 years before the first Olympiad (776 B.C.E.), i.e. in 814 B.C.E.

[25]According to Servius, *Ad Aeneam*, 1:12, Carthage was founded 60 years before the foundation of Rome (753 B.C.E.), i.e. in 813 B.C.E. Other classical writers agree with this date; cf. the detailed discussion of F. X. Kugler, *Von Moses bis Paulus* (Münster, 1922), p. 173; also Katzenstein, *History of Tyre*, pp. 119-20, and especially n. 27.

[26]According to Pompeius Trogus (Justinus, *Epitome Pompei Trogi*, 18:6, 9), Carthage was founded not 60 but 72 years before Rome, i.e. in 825 B.C.E.; cf. Katzenstein, *ibid.*, p. 120, n. 28.

[27]J. Liver, "The Chronology of Tyre at the Beginning of the First Millennium B.C." *IEJ* 3 (1953) 119-20.

[28]*Ibid.*, p. 120.

[29]J. M. Peñuela, "La Inscripción Asiria IM 55644 y la Cronología de los reyes de Tiro" [in two parts], *Sefarad* 13 (1953) 217-37 and 14 (1954) 1-39.

Tyre in the seventh year of Pygmalion's reign, not that she founded Carthage in that year. Nevertheless, Josephus himself, probably relying on Pompeius Trogus, did specifically date the founding of Carthage to the same year as Elissa's departure from Tyre, i.e. the seventh year of Pygmalion, or 825 B.C.E.[30]

Soon after seeing the first part of Peñuela's study, W. F. Albright wrote his own article on the chronology of Tyre.[31] He concluded that there was no reason to abandon the traditional date of Timaeus (814) for the founding of Carthage; indeed, he felt that his reconstruction of the Tyrian king list (see Table III) not only confirmed Timaeus' date for the founding of Carthage in the light of the new Assyro-Tyrian synchronism, but also confirmed his own low date for the disruption of the United Monarchy of Israel.[32] I have already discussed his hypothesis that there was a haplography in the Tyrian king list of Menander; however, it should be emphasized at this point that such an assumption is *required* in order to align Timaeus' (or Albright's) dates with the chronological evidence provided by the new Assyro-Tyrian synchronism.

More recently, E. Lipiński published his own reconstruction of the Tyrian king list (again, see Table III); he basically agreed with Peñuela that Josephus (and Pompeius Trogus) considered Pygmalion's seventh year as the year of the founding of Carthage.[33] I have already

---

[30]Peñuela, "Cronología," *Sefarad* 14 (1954), pp. 28-29, and nn. 164-67; he suggested that Menander may have reckoned a twelve year period of time as separating Elissa's flight from Tyre and her founding of Carthage (this would accord with Timaeus' date for the founding of the city). At least, as Peñuela has demonstrated quite conclusively, both of these events were not necessarily reckoned by classical authors to have taken place in the same calendar year.

[31]Albright, "New Assyro-Tyrian Synchronism," which was published in 1955; he apparently had not seen the second part of Peñuela's study (cf. his comments on pp. 1-2) and thus was unaware of the latter's chronological proposals.

[32]*Ibid.*, p. 5, and n. 3; also pp. 7-9. For a useful, although inconclusive, discussion of the problem of the dating of the founding of Carthage from the viewpoint of two classical scholars, see G. C. Picard and C. Picard, *The Life and Death of Carthage*, Dominique Collon, trans. (London: Thomas Nelson, 1968), pp. 28-35. Concerning Albright's low date for the disruption of the United Monarchy of Israel, see below, Chapter III.

[33]Lipiński, "Chronology of Tyre," p. 62, and n. 5.

noted (above, p. 46) his disagreement with Albright's assumed haplography in the Tyrian king list. Lipiński concluded his study by suggesting the date of c. 952 (= the eleventh year of Hiram) for the founding of Solomon's temple;[34] but since he considered the biblical figure of 40 years for Solomon's reign to be an "ideal" figure, he declined to give even an approximate date for the disruption of the Israelite monarchy.

F. M. Cross, Jr., as I have already noted (above, p. 31), also preferred the date of Pompeius Trogus for the founding of Carthage. His suggested dates for the Tyrian kings are as follows:

Name of King	Length of Reign	Dates
Hīrōm < 'Ahī-ram	34	980-947
Ba'l-mazzer	17	946-930
'Abd-'Aštart	9	929-921
'Aštart	[20]	920-901
Dalay-'Aštart	12	900-889
'Aštar-rōm	9	888-880
Pillēs	8 months	879
'Itto-ba'l	32	878-847
Ba'l-mazzer (II)	6	846-841
Mattin	9	840-832
Pummay < Pu'm-yatan	47	831-785

And as I have noted, Cross dated the founding of Solomon's temple to 968, and Solomon's overall reign to 971-932.[35]

---

[34]*Ibid.*, pp. 65-66. In *Antiquities*, 8:62, Josephus attributes the founding of Solomon's temple to Hiram's *eleventh* year, which Lipiński prefers over the "round figure" found in *Contra Apionem*, 1:126 (Hiram's twelfth year); see, however, my comments in n. 37, below.

[35]Cross, "Nora Stone," p. 17, and n. 11; cf. also his discussion of the etymology of the name Pygmalion on pp. 17-18.

Cross's reconstruction of the Tyrian king list remains the most convincing to the present writer. Any reconstruction of this nature, to be sure, requires a positive approach to the sources; one must assume the reasonable accuracy of the extant names and numbers unless evidence to the contrary is presented. Some adjustment of the regnal totals (or, less likely, of the names) of the Tyrian kings may be required as further evidence comes to light (especially from Mesopotamia), but for the present we may conclude quite confidently that the Tyrian king list of Menander as preserved in Josephus' *Contra Apionem*, 1:117-26, coupled with the dated reference in Shalmaneser's annals to the Tyrian king *Ba'li-manzer* and the date of Pompeius Trogus for the founding of Carthage,[36] provide a firm external synchronism for biblical chronology, and particularly for the dating of the founding of Solomon's temple in 968 (the twelfth year of Hiram of Tyre),[37] as well as the dating of Solomon's accession to 971. A variation of a year or two is possible, of course, especially in the light of our ignorance of Phoenician dating practices, but I seriously doubt that an error of more than two years either way is likely. Reckoning the date of the disruption of

---

[36]It should be emphasized that, as Peñuela and Lipiński have pointed out (see my above discussion, pp. 51-53), Josephus clearly identified the seventh year of Pygmalion not only with Elissa's departure from Tyre, but also with her founding of Carthage. In this identification he was probably dependent upon the first century B.C.E. Roman historian Pompeius Trogus. It should also be noted, however, that Josephus does not discuss the dating of the founding of Carthage; he is interested rather in the Phoenician evidence proving the extreme antiquity of the Solomonic temple. Therefore, it is only incidental that, by means of the recently discovered Assyro-Tyrian synchronism with its reference to the Tyrian king *Ba'li-manzer*, we are able to determine the date for the founding of Carthage which Josephus prefers. In other words, the Assyro-Tyrian synchronism merely demonstrates that Josephus and Pompeius Trogus were in probable agreement on the date for the founding of Carthage; it does not prove that they were necessarily correct in that agreement. One firm date does emerge from all this, however: it was in the seventh year of Pygmalion of Tyre when Elissa departed from the city, and this departure can be closely dated to the year 825 B.C.E.

[37]The ordinal number "twelfth" is clearly attested in *Contra Apionem*, 1:126 (cf. 1:108), and should not be rejected (as Lipiński does, cf. above, n. 34); although the transmission of numbers in classical sources is often problematic, both the general accuracy of the regnal totals for the Tyrian kings as well as the arithmetic precision of Josephus' own overall totals (155 years and 8 months from Hiram's accession to the founding of Carthage, and 143 years and 8 months from the founding of Solomon's temple to the founding of Carthage) greatly encourage one's confidence in the accuracy of the figure "twelfth year" (of Hiram) found in *Contra Apionem*, 1:126.

the United Monarchy is more problematic: Solomon's biblical 40 year reign is probably a round number (although unlikely to be far off from the exact figure); therefore the date of 932 (assuming ante-dating practice) should be reasonably accurate, although not to be understood as necessarily exact. I will return to this problem in the next chapter. At this juncture, it is sufficient to emphasize the following fact: extant extra-biblical sources point with a high degree of precision to the year 968 as the date of the founding of the Solomonic temple, and any future reconstruction of the biblical chronology of the Divided Monarchy must reckon seriously with this datum.

CHAPTER III

THE CHRONOLOGICAL EVIDENCE FROM EGYPT:
A. DATING THE INVASION OF SHISHAK

Biblical scholars have generally conceded that the chronological evidence from Egyptian sources is of little help in dating the
kings of the Divided Monarchy of Israel. There are two basic reasons
for this:

1. The biblical accounts contain only three (or possibly four)
references to Egyptian kings during this period which are specific
enough to serve as external chronological synchronisms. The three
clearest references are: a) the explicit dating of Shishak's invasion to
the fifth year of Rehoboam of Judah (1 Kgs 14:25); b) the reference to
"Tirhakah king of Ethiopia" in connection with the biblical account of
Sennacherib's invasion of Judah (2 Kgs 19:9); and c) the notice of
Pharaoh Neco's encounter with Josiah at Megiddo (2 Kgs 23:29-30),
almost certainly to be dated to Josiah's 31st year (2 Kgs 22:1).[1] A
fourth potential reference, that to Hoshea of Israel sending messengers
to "So, king of Egypt" (2 Kgs 17:4), is more problematic, as will be
discussed below.[2]

2. The Egyptian royal chronology itself for most of the period
corresponding to the Divided Monarchy of Israel is murky at best;
this is especially so for the Twenty-second to Twenty-fifth Dynasties
(which, e.g., Albright dated to c. 935-685/84 B.C.E.).[3] Indeed, the
question of the actual existence and identity of several of the pharaohs

---

[1]The reference to Shishak's invasion will be discussed in this chapter; the reference
to Tirhakah in Chapter IV. In contrast to the chronological uncertainties which attend
these first two references, the Neco reference in 2 Kgs 23:29-30 can be firmly dated on
the basis of the Babylonian evidence to the year 609 B.C.E. (see, e.g., Hayim Tadmor,
"Chronology of the Last Kings of Judah," *JNES* 15 [1956] 226-30).

[2]See Excursus II following Chapter IV, below.

[3]W. F. Albright, "New Light from Egypt on the Chronology and History of Israel
and Judah," *BASOR* 130 (1953) 10-11.

alleged to have ruled during this time is still unsettled, and a number of the extant regnal totals exhibit wide variations in the chronographic traditions (or else fail to accord with the monumental evidence).[4] It will be evident, therefore, that scant precision is likely to be gained from any analysis of the Egyptian chronological data; nevertheless, such an analysis remains necessary, not least to refute (or at least to call into question) the conclusions of several of the recent biblical chronographers who suggest that the Egyptian chronological evidence unequivocally supports their own particular chronographic system for the Divided Monarchy of Israel.

A detailed examination of the various issues and controversies surrounding the field of Egyptian chronology is, of course, far beyond the scope of the present inquiry (not to mention the expertise of the present writer). The following discussion concerns itself rather with the biblical evidence for specific points of contact between Egypt and monarchical Israel; the conclusions of recent Egyptian chronographers are then cited only as they tend to clarify (or contradict) the biblical synchronisms. I expect, however, that even this limited analysis will still advance the discussion significantly--not only to enable the critical evaluation of those proposals advanced by biblical scholars who cite Egyptian evidence, but also to act as a control over my own subsequent efforts at biblical chronological reconstruction.

At first glance, the biblical reference to Shishak's invasion of Jerusalem, dated specifically to Rehoboam's fifth year (1 Kgs 14:25), appears to be a potentially valuable external synchronism--one which could lend precision to the chronologically uncertain period immediately following the Disruption of the United Monarchy of Israel. Surely, one would assume, such an invasion would have been clearly attested in the Egyptian historical materials, with the result that one could calculate the absolute date of the invasion (and thus independently ascertain the date

---

[4]Cf., e.g., Alan Gardiner, *Egypt of the Pharaohs: An Introduction* (Oxford: Clarendon Press, 1961), pp. 333-34; for a useful introduction to the subject of Egyptian chronology, see pp. 46-71 of the same work. Probably the best discussion of calendrical calculations remains that of Richard A. Parker, *The Calendars of Ancient Egypt*, The Oriental Institute of the University of Chicago: Studies in Ancient Oriental Civilization, No. 26 (Chicago: University of Chicago Press, 1950). Extant excerpts of Manetho have been conveniently collated by W. G. Waddell, *Manetho*, The Loeb Classical Library (Cambridge: Harvard University Press, 1940).

of the disruption of the monarchy, and the accession of Rehoboam). A survey of the results of Egyptian chronographers demonstrates that such is, however, not the case: although Shishak (= Shoshenq I) is clearly attested as the founder of the Twenty-second (Bubastite) Dynasty, and there is abundant archaeological and epigraphic evidence that he invaded not only Jerusalem but most of Palestine (from the Negeb northward to the Esdraelon valley and eastward into parts of Trans-jordan);[5] unhappily, chronological precision is altogether lacking in the Egyptian materials, not only concerning the date of the invasion,[6] but

---

[5]John Bright, *A History of Israel*, 3rd ed. (Philadelphia: Westminster Press, 1981), pp. 233-34; cf. the extended discussion in Kenneth A. Kitchen, *The Third Intermediate Period in Egypt (1100-650 B.C.)* (Warminster: Aris & Phillips, 1973; 2nd ed. with supplement, *idem*, 1986), §§ 252-58; 398-415; and also the map on p. 297.

[6]Unfortunately, the great triumphal relief at Karnak which commemorates the invasion contains no date; however, most scholars suggest that the invasion probably occurred near the end of Shishak's reign inasmuch as the relief was seemingly never finished. In particular, the figure representing Shishak himself appears never to have been completed (cf. the discussion in W. F. Albright, "Further Light on Synchronisms between Egypt and Asia in the Period 935-685 B.C." *BASOR* 141 [1956] 26-27, and especially n. 18). However, in the preface to the official publication of the Shishak relief (University of Chicago Oriental Institute Publications No. 84: *Reliefs and Inscriptions at Karnak*, Vol. III, *The Bubastite Portal*, by the Epigraphic Survey [1954], pp. viii-ix), George R. Hughes offered a different explanation: he suggested that the figure of the king, though indeed not executed in incised relief like all the other elements of the relief which sur-round it, nonetheless had been completed:

"Close examination of the wall in retrieving the remaining outline traces of his [Shishak's] figure . . . has convinced us that the figure was neither left unfinished nor destroyed by human agency, but that it was more probably executed in some other manner than was the rest of the relief" (p. viii).

Hughes went on to conclude:

"It is our belief that the king's figure was very delicately modeled, at least in outline, in a thin coat of gypsum plaster applied to the stone and that at many points the modeling impinged upon the stone beneath. The details of dress, etc., were then painted in as usual. The purpose of this exceptional treatment is not apparent, but it would have resulted in the figure of the king assuming a striking contrast to the rest of the relief. Perhaps that effect was precisely the purpose" (*ibid.*).

More recently, Donald B. Redford, "Studies in Relations Between Palestine and Egypt during the First Millenium B.C.: II. The Twenty-second Dynasty," *JAOS* 93 (1973), p. 10 and n. 62, suggested that Shishak's Palestinian campaign was undertaken fairly early in his reign inasmuch as it was termed in the relief "his first victorious [campaign]"; however, as Edward F. Wente, in his review of K. A. Kitchen's *Third Intermediate Period*

even concerning when, and for how long, Shishak reigned as pharaoh.[7]

According to the biblical notice in 1 Kgs 11:40, Shishak was the pharaoh under whom Jeroboam had sought political asylum after his falling out with Solomon. A change in dynasty would help explain why Jeroboam would have fled to the vary nation which had previously allied itself with his nemesis Solomon (1 Kgs 3:1; cf. 9:16).[8] It is of interest, however, that the cryptic notice in 1 Kgs 11:14-22 attests a previous occasion when Egypt had sheltered an enemy of a Davidic king: when Joab the commander of David's army had sought to exterminate the Edomites, Hadad the Edomite prince (at the time only a little child) was able to flee to Egypt along with some of his royal retainers;

(*JNES* 35 [1976] 276), pointed out, Redford failed to note Jeroboam's presence as a refugee in Egypt under Shishak during the reign of Solomon in Israel, thus making it most unlikely that Shishak's later Palestinian campaign took place before his eighth regnal year (at the earliest).

[7]It is generally agreed that Shishak reigned for about 21 years (so most versions of Manetho); cf. also the date on the Silsilis Stela, "year 21, second month of *šmw*" (see Ricardo A. Caminos, "Gebel Es-Silsilah No. 100," *JEA* 38 [1952] 46-61). The stela commemorates Shishak's reopening of a quarry at Silsilis in order to obtain sandstone for the erection of two new structures in the great temple of Amun at Karnak (these additions to the temple include the triumphal relief discussed in the previous note). Hence, as a number of scholars have pointed out, if the figure representing Shishak in the Karnak relief indeed had not been completed before his death, the date on the Silsilis inscription would provide strong confirmation that Shishak's reign did not extend much beyond 21 years (cf., however, Hughes' alternate explanation, cited in the previous note, for the appearance of the king's figure in the relief). Wente, in his review of Kitchen's book (see previous note), disagreed with the suggestion that Shishak reigned only about 21 years; he preferred assigning 34 years to the king (in agreement with the Book of Sothis); see his discussion on pp. 276-78 of the review. Finally, not only is the evidence for the length of Shishak's reign somewhat ambiguous, but (as I will discuss at some length below), few (if any) firm external synchronisms exist by which his reign can be assigned absolute dates.

[8]Shishak was a Libyan nobleman who had served as commander-in-chief of the Libyan mercenaries; his family was related in marriage to at least one pharaoh of the preceding 21st Dynasty (for details, see Kitchen, *Third Intermediate Period*, §§ 239-40; also Redford, "Relations between Palestine and Egypt," pp. 7-9). The inscriptional evidence suggests that Shishak's takeover was relatively peaceful (Psusennes II, Shishak's predecessor, had apparently died without a male heir).

there he was graciously received by the (unnamed) pharaoh.[9] Our suspicions that the Egyptian hospitality was not altogether altruistic are confirmed by the notice (in v 19) that the pharaoh agreed to give him the sister of his own wife in marriage (thus promoting a diplomatic alliance analogous to the later one with Solomon?).[10] At any rate, the anonymous pharaoh undoubtedly appreciated any opportunity to undermine (or at least to counter) the growing Israelite military presence in Palestine. The story breaks off abruptly in the biblical text, leaving us in doubt as to the nature and extent of Hadad's later rebellion against Solomon,[11] but we are at least able to conclude that the subsequent pharaonic diplomatic alliances with Solomon need not have precluded Egyptian alliances with his adversaries as well.

Another brief notice in Kings deserves mention at this point. We are told in 1 Kgs 9:16 that the pharaoh who entered into diplomatic alliance with Solomon gave the town of Gezer as dowry to his daughter, Solomon's wife; the Egyptians had previously captured the town, which

---

[9]Presumably he was one of the pharaohs of the weak 21st Dynasty, although both the chronological imprecision of the biblical notice as well as the chronological uncertainties surrounding this period of Egyptian history make a specific identification impossible (cf., e.g., Gardiner, *Egypt of the Pharaohs*, p. 329).

[10]Again, specific identification is uncertain. The biblical notice purports to give the name of the Egyptian queen: *Tahpĕnês* (MT), or *Thekemeina* ($\mathcal{G}^B$). Albright (*BASOR* 140 [1955] 32) suggested that the Hebrew name (if not corrupt) may reflect an Egyptian *T_j-ḥn.t-p,'* (or *pr*) *-nsw*, "She Whom the King (or Palace) Protects"; the Greek name would probably reflect an Egyptian *T_j-k,'l-(n.t)-mn*, "The Female Attendant (or the like) of Min." John Gray (*I & II Kings: A Commentary*, 2nd ed., The Old Testament Library [Philadelphia: Westminster Press, 1970], p. 285) suggested that the Hebrew probably represents a corruption of *t,'-ḥmt-nsw*, "the wife of the king"; he gave no proposal for the Greek form. Kitchen (*Third Intermediate Period*, § 231, n. 183) inclined to a similar view: he suggested that the name in the MT reflected a "slightly-syncopated Hebrew transcription of the Egyptian phrase *t,'-ḥ(mt)-p,'-nsw*, 'wife of the king', i.e. 'queen'" (he likewise gave no proposal for the Greek form). Cf., however, the queries of E. P. Uphill in his review of Kitchen's book (*JEA* 61 [1975] 281).

[11]Although a detailed text-critical examination of this part of Kings is beyond the scope of the present study, even a cursory comparison of the MT over against the Greek versions (especially $\mathcal{G}^L$) demonstrates considerable disarray in its textual transmission; cf., e.g., the notes found in Gray, *I & II Kings*, 2nd ed., pp. 280-88.

was apparently still an independent Canaanite enclave on the Israelite-Philistine border (cf. Judg 1:29).[12] As John Bright commented:

> There is probably more in this brief notice than meets the eye. It is hard to imagine the Pharaoh undertaking such a long and arduous campaign just to capture a city for the Israelite king. It may be that the Pharaoh, now that David was dead, hoped to reestablish Egyptian control in Palestine and, to that end, had launched a campaign against the Philistine cities (over which he claimed suzerainty), in the course of which the frontier city of Gezer was taken, but that then, finding himself confronted by a stronger force than he had bargained for in the form of Solomon's army, thought it wiser (or was compelled) to yield territorial concessions and make peace. We do not know. In any event, the incident illustrates both the relative importance of Israel and the low estate to which Egypt had sunk: Pharaohs of the Empire did not give their daughters even to kings of Babylon or Mitanni![13]

Most scholars suggest that this event probably occurred quite early in

---

[12]The accuracy of the biblical notice (in 1 Kgs 9:16) was confirmed by the recent Hebrew Union College/Harvard Semitic Museum excavations at Gezer (1964-1971): see Bright, *History of Israel*, 3rd ed., p. 212, n. 62, and references given there (e.g., W. G. Dever, *et al.*, *BA* 34 (1971) 94-132 [especially p. 130]). Bright (*ibid.*) pointed out that other nearby cities were also destroyed at this time (mid-tenth century): Tell Mor, the port of Ashdod, and perhaps Beth-shemesh; very possibly in the course of the same Egyptian campaign. A number of years ago, before the HUC/HSM excavations at Gezer, Albright (*JPOS* 4 [1924] 142-44; also cf. *Archaeology and the Religion of Israel* [Baltimore: Johns Hopkins Press, 1942], pp. 213-14) had suggested reading *Gerar* (northwest of Beersheba) in place of *Gezer* in the Kings text in the light of the apparent absence of an appropriate destruction layer in Macalister's earlier excavation of Gezer as well as the seeming implausibility of David leaving undisturbed such a strategic Canaanite enclave. On this last point, cf. Bright, *History of Israel*, 3rd ed., pp. 198-99, where he followed A. Malamat and others in suggesting David's apparent reluctance to seize Gezer (as well as the Philistine coastal cities of Ashdod, Ashkelon, and Gaza) may have stemmed from his desire to avoid hostilities with Egypt (who still claimed suzerainty over the area).

[13]Bright, *History of Israel*, 3rd ed., p. 212. For a different interpretation of these events, see Redford, "Relations between Palestine and Egypt" (above, n. 6), p. 5, and n. 21a.

Solomon's reign, although again the biblical and Egyptian evidence is less than conclusive.[14]

W. F. Albright, in a 1953 *BASOR* article entitled "New Light from Egypt on the Chronology and History of Israel and Judah,"[15] discussed at some length the Egyptian chronological material (especially several recently published inscriptions), and suggested that the Egyptian evidence independently confirmed his low date of 922 for the disruption of the United Monarchy of Israel. It is appropriate at this point to examine his contentions, especially in the light of my recent conclusion that the Phoenician evidence (*contra* Albright) supports rather a date of c. 932 for the disruption of the monarchy. In brief, Albright argued as follows: a datable lunar eclipse[16] plus other recently published Egyptian inscriptions and chronological reconstructions[17] now permit us to determine the chronology of Shishak within considerably narrower limits than heretofore. Indeed, the problem of Shishak's dating can now be attacked from both directions: from the time of Takelot II (by means of Albright's suggested date of 822 for the lunar eclipse

---

[14]See, e.g., Gray, *I & II Kings*, 2nd ed., pp. 117-20, and references cited there. Bright, *History of Israel*, 3rd ed., p. 212, suggested that the pharaoh in question was probably Siamun, next to the last pharaoh of the 21st Dynasty; Kitchen, *Third Intermediate Period*, § 235, concurred with this, and he went on to suggest that the Egyptian conquest of Gezer and the alliance with Solomon probably occurred in the last decade of Siamun's reign (c. 978-959 B.C.E.). However, Redford, "Relations between Palestine and Egypt," p. 5, was more cautious, suggesting that the pharaoh in question could have been either Siamun or his successor Psusennes II.

[15]Albright, "New Light," *BASOR* 130 (1953) 4-11.

[16]*Ibid.*, pp. 4-6. The Karnak temple records of Osorkon mention a calamity (*nšny*) of some sort which was accompanied by "the sky not swallowing the moon" (*n 'm p.t i'h*); this event is dated to the 15th year of Takelot II, on the 25th day of the fourth month of the *šmw* season. According to Albright, the celestial phenomenon in question is to be identified as a lunar eclipse, which he explained as follows: "Though it was always feared that 'the sky might swallow the moon,' it never actually happened; in Egypt there is always a reddish glow around the periphery of the circular shadow cast by the earth" (p. 5). Therefore he suggested translating the phrase as follows: " . . . the sky not having swallowed the moon [completely], there was a *nšny* in this land."

[17]I.e. Caminos, "Silsilah" (see above, n. 7); also Richard A. Parker, "The Names of the Sixteenth Day of the Lunar Month," *JNES* 12 (1950) 50; and, finally, M. B. Rowton, "Manetho's Date for Ramesses II," *JEA* 34 (1948) 57-74.

attributed to Takelot's 15th year) on up to Shishak (by cautiously relying upon the Manethonian regnal data); and from the time of Ramesses II on down (by following M. B. Rowton's suggested chronology for the New Kingdom and later periods, and especially his suggested date of c. 1290 for the accession of Ramesses II). Albright concluded that Shishak's reign should be dated c. 935-914, and that his campaign in Palestine (= the fifth year of Rehoboam) probably took place in approximately the 18th year of his reign, i.e. in 918/17 B.C.E.[18] One will readily see that Albright's proposed dates accord well with his date of 922 for the disruption of the Israelite monarchy, but would not fit a date appreciably higher (such as 932).

These conclusions of Albright's, however, have not remained unchallenged. Ricardo A. Caminos, in a detailed analysis of the inscriptions of Osorkon on the Bubastite Gate at Karnak,[19] remained unconvinced that a lunar eclipse had even occurred in that fateful 15th year of Takelot II:

> The sentence in Osorkon's Chronicle 'the sky did not swallow up the moon' means, I am convinced, that there was no lunar eclipse. As aptly explained by Le Page Renouf as long ago as 1885, the sentence is concessive and suits admirably the statement that follows it, the point being that *although* there was no ominous sign like a lunar eclipse to give warning of a major disaster, yet a calamitous civil war broke out in the country nevertheless. To quote Le Page Renouf, 'the calamity occurred without any such previous notice as an eclipse or other natural portent might have yielded to the wise men of the period'.[20]

---

[18]Albright, "New Light," pp. 6-7, and n. 12; also cf. his chart on pp. 10-11.

[19]Caminos, *The Chronicle of Prince Osorkon*, Analecta Orientalia, Vol. 37 (Rome: Pontifical Biblical Institute, 1958).

[20]*Ibid.*, § 130 (p. 89); emphasis his. The quotation is from P. Le Page Renouf, "The Eclipse in Egyptian Texts," *PSBA* 7 (1885) 163-64. As Caminos expressly stated in a footnote (see pp. 89-90, n. 5), he had not seen Albright's article until after he had written his own comments on this passage; nevertheless, he felt there was no reason to change his opinion: "For my part, I continue to believe that Le Page Renouf's interpretation is correct, and have accordingly made no change in my comment on this controversial passage." More recently, Kitchen (*Third Intermediate Period*, § 148 [pp. 181-82]) also agreed that there had been no eclipse. Indeed, as Kitchen pointed out, it appears from a close reading of Albright's own comments (as found in "New Light," p. 5, n. 7a) that

Klaus Baer, in his own chronological reconstruction of this obscure period of Egyptian history,[21] agreed with Caminos that no eclipse had occurred on that date. However, he went on to suggest:

> On the other hand, references to eclipses are exceedingly rare from ancient Egypt, so the remark that ["the sky did not swallow the moon but a storm broke out in this land"] . . . cannot simply be ignored as meaningless; it is too unusual. The Egyptians knew that lunar eclipses only occur at full moon (Parker, *JNES* 12 [1953]: 50), and I would propose that the passage implies that the rebellion ("storm") broke out on a day when an appropriately inauspicious omen such as a lunar eclipse could have been anticipated, i.e., that the date was that of a full moon.[22]

After determining that there were only two possible dates (between 865-840 B.C.E.) for a full moon occurring on the specific calendrical date given in the inscription, Baer examined the plausibility of each of the two dates in the light of the other Egyptian chronological evidence. He concluded that the full moon of March 10-11 (Julian), 845 B.C.E. was definitely the more likely of the two possible dates; therefore he proposed dating the 15th year of Takelot II on astronomical grounds to 846/45 B.C.E. and his accession to c. 860 B.C.E.[23]

Parker himself had eventually come to a similar conclusion about the eclipse. (Note, however, that Parker in his original article, "Names of the Sixteenth Day" [see above, n. 17], had definitely posited a datable lunar eclipse in Takelot's 15th year; and this was the article which had heavily influenced Albright's subsequent conclusions.)

[21]Baer, "The Libyan and Nubian Kings of Egypt: Notes on the Chronology of Dynasties XXII to XXVI," *JNES* 32 (1973) 4-25.

[22]*Ibid.*, p. 8.

[23]*Ibid.*, pp. 10-11. As Baer pointed out, the full moon of March 10-11 (Julian), 845 B.C.E. occurred on what would normally have been reckoned as the 24th day of the Egyptian month; however, contemporary Egyptian calendrical calculations were sufficiently imprecise as to allow for such an error (cf. Parker's discussion in "The Lunar Dates of Thutmose III and Ramesses II," *JNES* 16 [1957] 39-40). Also, Baer's outer limits of 865-840 B.C.E. for Takelot's 15th year deserve some comment: as will be recalled, Albright proposed dating Takelot's 15th year to 822 B.C.E., a date which is not even within the overall range of dates considered by Baer. However, the Egyptian chronological evidence is sufficiently specific to indicate that Albright's low date for Takelot II is virtually impossible (e.g., it would require positing some very long life spans

Edward F. Wente, in his own articles about the chronology of this period,[24] emphasized the importance of this date, fixed as it is by astronomical calculation:

> Unfortunately there are still too many unknowns to make the accession of Shoshenq I [the biblical Shishak] one of the "certain" dates in Egyptian chronology. Baer's 860 B.C. for the accession of Takelot II appears to me to be the first "fixed" date after the accession of Ramesses II, as determined by a lunar date in his reign.[25]

Although the present scholarly consensus seems to favor a date c. 945 B.C.E. for the accession of Shishak,[26] Wente is surely correct in his caveat: apart from the biblical synchronism with Rehoboam (which as I have noted above remains problematic at best) there is no other

---

for a number of the royal officials). For a detailed discussion of this last point, see § 10 of Baer's article (pp. 9-10).

[24]Wente, Review of Kitchen's *Third Intermediate Period* (see above, n. 6), pp. 275-78; also cf. Edward F. Wente and Charles C. Van Siclen III, "A Chronology of the New Kingdom," *Studies in Honor of George R. Hughes*, The Oriental Institute of the University of Chicago: Studies in Ancient Oriental Civilization, No. 39 (Chicago: The Oriental Institute, 1976), p. 224.

[25]Wente, Review of Kitchen's *Third Intermediate Period*, p. 278. For a recent attempt to date the 15th year of Takelot II by means of the (partial) lunar eclipse of March, 850, see Winfried Barta, "Die Mondfinsternis Im 15. Regierungsjahr Takelots II. und die Chronologie der 22. bis 25. Dynastie," *RdÉ* 32 (1980) 3-17; but cf. the comments of K. A. Kitchen ("Further Thoughts on Egyptian Chronology in the Third Intermediate Period," *RdÉ* 34 [1982-83] 59-63; also *Third Intermediate Period*, 2nd ed., §§ 454-60).

[26]So, e.g., Gardiner, *Egypt of the Pharaohs*, p. 448; Kitchen, *Third Intermediate Period*, §§ 57-60 (pp. 72-76); and Erik Hornung, *Untersuchungen zur Chronologie und Geschichte des Neuen Reiches*, Ägyptologische Abhandlungen, Band II (Wiesbaden: Otto Harrassowitz, 1964), pp. 24-29. However, it should be noted that Kitchen and Hornung relied on the Rehoboam synchronism (and E. R. Thiele's reconstruction of the biblical chronology) to arrive at this date for Shishak. In contrast, Wente (in the articles cited above in n. 24) suggested dating Shishak's accession one year higher (c. 946 B.C.E.); and, as I have just pointed out, he preferred to rely upon Baer's date for Takelot II as the most securely "fixed" date for this period of Egyptian history, working back from this date to determine his date for the accession of Shishak. Therefore, even though Wente's date for Shishak differs by only one year from that of Kitchen and Hornung, it should be emphasized that the two dates were ascertained by entirely different means.

external synchronism by which one might date his reign, and the Egyptian chronological data themselves remain too fragmentary to permit chronological precision. Therefore, I am forced to remain skeptical: although the currently accepted date of c. 945 for Shishak's accession accords nicely with the date of c. 932 for the disruption of the Israelite monarchy as derived from the Phoenician chronological material (assuming antedating practice, Rehoboam's fifth year would then correspond with Shishak's 18th year), the lack of external control precludes my placing much weight upon this happy correspondence (indeed, the Egyptologists have tended to rely upon the biblical synchronism with Rehoboam to calculate their date for Shishak; to reverse the process would be a clear case of circular reasoning). In contrast to this uncertainty concerning Shishak, Baer's firm date for Takelot II, dependent only upon an astronomical calculation, seems to me to be considerably more reliable. A comparison between Albright's and Baer's chronology for the Twenty-second Dynasty may be found in Table IV.

At the very least, whether Baer's hypothesis of a full moon (without an eclipse) occurring on IV *šmw* 25 of the 15th year of Takelot II is accepted or rejected, Albright's suggestion to link that date with the lunar eclipse of 822 seems quite unlikely (not a single Egyptologist, so far as I am aware, has embraced it). Therefore, it is fair to say that his appeal to the Egyptian chronological evidence for the 22nd Dynasty to support his 922 date for the disruption of the Israelite Monarchy (over against 932 or any such date in this general time period) is invalid. All this is to say that at the present time one cannot confirm or deny *either* Hebrew date from the Egyptian evidence--the necessary chronological precision is simply not there.

TABLE IV
THE PHARAOHS OF THE TWENTY-SECOND DYNASTY:
TWO CHRONOLOGICAL RECONSTRUCTIONS

Albright[a]		Baer[b]	
Shoshenq I	935-914	Shoshenq I	945-924
Osorkon I	914-874	Osorkon I	924-909
Takelot I	874-860	Takelot I	909-
		Shoshenq II	-883
Osorkon II	860/59-	Osorkon II	883-855
(Shoshenq II)	---		
Takelot II[c]	837/36-	Takelot II[d]	860-835
Shoshenq III	822-770?	Shoshenq III	835-783
Pemi	770-765?	Pami	783-773
Shoshenq IV	765-725?	Shoshenq V[e]	773-735
		Osorkon IV[f]	735-712

[a]W. F. Albright, "New Light from Egypt on the Chronology and History of Israel and Judah," *BASOR* 130 (1953) 10. All dates are approximate.

[b]Klaus Baer, "The Libyan and Nubian Kings of Egypt: Notes on the Chronology of Dynasties XXII to XXVI," *JNES* 32 (1973) 11. Again, all dates are approximate.

[c]His year 15, fourth month of *šmw*, 25th day, understood as corresponding to the lunar eclipse dated to Feb. 24 (Julian), 822 B.C.E. (cf. my above discussion on pp. 63-64, and n. 16).

[d]His year 15, IV *šmw* 25, understood as corresponding to the full moon (with no eclipse) dated to March 10-11 (Julian), 845 B.C.E. (cf. my above discussion on pp. 65-66, and nn. 21-23).

[e]Shoshenq IV is generally assigned to the 23rd Dynasty; his dates (according to Baer) are c. 803-797.

[f]Osorkon III is also generally assigned to the 23rd Dynasty; his dates (according to Baer) are c. 783-778.

But, it will be recalled, Albright had supported his chronological reconstruction from two directions: from Takelot's supposed eclipse on up to Shishak, and from the accession of Ramesses II on down to Shishak. It is to this latter issue that I now turn. Albright himself had noted how he had relied heavily upon the chronological results of M. B. Rowton, and especially upon his suggested date of 1290 for the accession of Ramesses II.[27] But Rowton later changed his own mind concerning this date: in his later articles he suggested a revised date of 1304 for the accession of Ramesses II, and he carefully worked out the implications this date would have for the international diplomatic situation obtaining at that time.[28] Albright, of course, was well aware of all this: in some of his own later works he explicitly noted (and accepted) Rowton's change of mind;[29] but, to my knowledge, Albright never commented in print about the implications this change of date had for later Egyptian (or for monarchical Israelite) chronology. Notwithstanding this silence, it remains quite evident that the revised date of Rowton for the accession of Ramesses II, which was some 14 years higher than his original date, tended only to weaken Albright's contention that the Egyptian chronological evidence from the New Kingdom supported his low chronology for the Divided Monarchy of Israel.

More recently, however, the situation has become even more complicated. In an important article on the chronology of the New Kingdom published in 1976, Edward F. Wente and Charles C. Van Siclen III presented a strong case for dating the accession of Ramesses II to 1279 B.C.E., the *lowest* of the three astronomically possible

---

[27]Rowton, "Manetho's Date" (see above, n. 17). Parker, "Thutmose III and Ramesses II" (see above, n. 23), pp. 42-43, calculated that there are three astronomically possible dates for the accession of Ramesses II (1304, 1290, and 1279 B.C.E.); he agreed with Rowton in opting for 1290.

[28]See Rowton, "Comparative Chronology at the Time of Dynasty XIX," *JNES* 19 (1960) 15-22; and Rowton, "The Material from Western Asia and the Chronology of the Nineteenth Dynasty," *JNES* 25 (1966) 240-58.

[29]E.g., Albright, *Yahweh and the Gods of Canaan* (New York: Doubleday & Co., 1968), pp. 159-60; Albright, "Syria, the Philistines, and Phoenicia," *The Cambridge Ancient History*, 3rd ed., Vol. II, Part 2, History of the Middle East and the Aegean Region c. 1380-1000 B.C. (Cambridge: University Press, 1975), pp. 514-15.

dates.[30] Unlike Rowton, who tended to emphasize the Manethonian numbers and the international diplomatic correspondence in his own chronological reconstructions, Wente and Van Siclen based their own chronology primarily on the extant Egyptian epigraphic data themselves (which for the period of the New Kingdom are quite extensive).[31] After demonstrating that the Egyptian chronological data for the 18th Dynasty and the early part of the 19th Dynasty (up to the accession of Ramesses II) decisively support their low date for his accession, they proceeded to examine the Ramesside period itself. They concluded that the chronological data for this period also accord quite comfortably with their low date of 1279 for the accession of Ramesses II.[32]

At first glance, this low date for Ramesses II appears to provide striking confirmation for Albright's original contention that the Egyptian chronological evidence (at least from the period of the New Kingdom) strongly supports his low chronology for the Israelite monarchy. However, it should be emphasized that Wente and Van Siclen themselves dated Shishak's accession to c. 946 B.C.E., notwithstanding their low date for the accession of Ramesses II.[33] Thus, their date for Shishak is some 11 years higher than the one proposed by Albright; it accords well with a date such as 932 for the disruption of the Israelite monarchy, but not at all with Albright's date of 922.

To be sure, any detailed evaluation of the work of Wente and Van Siclen goes far beyond the scope of the present inquiry; nevertheless, this much should be said: an acceptance of their low date of 1279 B.C.E. for the accession of Ramesses II (which to the present

---

[30]Wente and Van Siclen, "A Chronology of the New Kingdom" (see above, n. 24), pp. 223-47; for the three possible dates for the accession of Ramesses II as fixed by astronomical calculation, see above, n. 27.

[31]Cf. the discussion in Wente and Van Siclen, "A Chronology of the New Kingdom," pp. 246-47, where they noted that for a span of some 140 years (from Year 32 of Ramesses II to Year 3 of Ramesses X) only a total of nine years lack some sort of documentation (and there is no definite instance of any two such years in succession).

[32]Ibid., p. 246.

[33]Ibid., p. 224; cf. n. 26 above. Wente and Van Siclen however did acknowledge that this date for Shishak could be raised or lowered, in view of the chronological uncertainties surrounding the reign of Takelot I and the possibilities of coregencies as yet undocumented.

writer seems entirely possible) by no means necessarily entails a lowering of the chronology for the later 22nd (Bubastite) Dynasty of Egypt, nor for that of the Divided Monarchy of Israel. Indeed, as I have just noted, Wente and Van Siclen themselves saw no reason to lower the date of the accession of Shishak. I therefore conclude that not only is there no incompatibility between a low date for the accession of Ramesses II and the traditional date for the accession of Shishak, but also that the burden of proof remains on those who would want to lower Shishak's date (whether on the basis of the Egyptian chronological evidence from the New Kingdom, or the evidence from a later period).

In summary, once again my conclusions are largely negative: the Egyptian chronological evidence is too imprecise to confirm or deny decisively any particular biblical chronology. The Egyptian evidence which can be firmly dated (e.g., the accession of Takelot II in 860, and probably the accession of Ramesses II in 1279) tends to support the 932 date for the disruption of the Israelite monarchy, but frankly in less than a compelling manner. Certainly, *contra* Albright, the Egyptian chronological evidence which is now extant may not be said to demonstrate the unique accuracy of his own particular chronology for the early part of the Divided Monarchy of Israel.

CHAPTER IV

THE CHRONOLOGICAL EVIDENCE FROM EGYPT:
B. DATING "TIRHAKAH KING OF ETHIOPIA"

As I have already noted above, the books of Kings contain only some three or four references to Egyptian pharaohs which are specific enough to be useful for chronological research. Undoubtedly the most problematic of these references--as well as the most notorious--is the brief notice found in 2 Kgs 19:9 which informs us that a certain "Tirhakah king of Ethiopia" (MT *Tirhāqāh melek kûš*)[1] was threatening to confront the invading armies of the Assyrian king Sennacherib on the coastal plains of Palestine. Now the actual identification of this "Tirhakah" is not in dispute: biblical scholars concur that the reference in question is to Taharqa, the third and most influential pharaoh of the 25th (Ethiopian or Nubian) Dynasty.[2] This identification, however, presents us with a major chronological difficulty: the Egyptian monumental evidence[3] firmly fixes the accession of Taharqa to c. 690 B.C.E., considerably later than the Palestinian invasion of Sennacherib in the summer of 701.[4] Therefore,

---

[1]LXX Θαρα(κα) βασιλέως Αἰθιόπων. Hebrew *kûš* was frequently used to designate the kingdom of Nubia, which was located on the Nile River south of Egypt (thus roughly equivalent in location to the modern Republic of the Sudan). For a useful discussion of the geography and history of the Nubian kingdom, see O. Wintermute, "Cush," *IDBS*, pp. 200-201.

[2]Manetho Ταρ(α)κος. For convenient summaries of the reign of Taharqa, see Gardiner, *Egypt of the Pharaohs*, pp. 344-47, and Kitchen, *Third Intermediate Period*, §§ 348-54. Concerning the Hebrew vocalization of *tirhāqāh*, see Kitchen, *ibid.*, § 421, n. 136.

[3]For a convenient discussion of this evidence, see Siegfried H. Horn, "Did Sennacherib Campaign Once or Twice Against Hezekiah?" *AUSS* 4 (1966) 3-11, and the references cited there. More recently, Egyptologists have raised the date of the commencement of the 26th Dynasty by a year (to 664); cf. Kitchen, *Third Intermediate Period*, § 119, and the references cited there.

[4]This date, like many derived from the Assyrian or Babylonian chronologies of the

we are confronted by a dilemma: either we must dismiss the Tirhakah reference in 2 Kgs 19:9 as a simple error or anachronism in the biblical tradition (Taharqa being the best known pharaoh of the relatively obscure 25th Dynasty), or we must reject the plain sense of the verse (and/or of its context) and reinterpret it in some manner. Scholars who have opted for some sort of reinterpretation have generally followed one of two approaches: either they have taken the phrase *melek kûš* as proleptic ("Tirhakah, the one who later became king of Ethiopia"); or, as part of a grand reinterpretation of the Sennacherib narrative, they have suggested that the Tirhakah reference corresponds with a hypothetical second invasion of Sennacherib (to be dated after 690, when Tirhakah was indisputably on the throne). Reputable scholars have championed each of these options for more than a century,[5] and it is fair to say that no consensus has yet been manifest (or is likely ever to be manifest, barring the future discovery of some sort of unambiguous evidence from Egypt or Assyria). Therefore, I dare not presume to settle this issue once and for all in the following discussion; all I hope to accomplish in the next several pages is to review the recent literature

---

first millennium B.C.E., is chronologically quite firm; cf. Hayim Tadmor, "The Chronology of the First Temple Period: A Presentation and Evaluation of the Sources," *The World History of the Jewish People, First Series: Ancient Times, The Age of the Monarchies: Political History*, vol. 4, pt. 1, Abraham Malamat, ed. (Jerusalem: Massada Press, 1979), pp. 53-55, and his references cited in n. 31.

[5]For a thorough review of the Assyrian and biblical evidence concerning the invasion(s) of Sennacherib, as well as a detailed analysis of the various solutions proposed by scholars to account for all these historical data, cf. the still very useful monograph of Leo L. Honor, *Sennacherib's Invasion of Palestine: A Critical Source Study* (New York: Columbia University Press, 1926); unhappily, however, he declined to present any historical conclusions of his own. This fault also besets another otherwise excellent examination of the biblical data, that of Brevard S. Childs, *Isaiah and the Assyrian Crisis* (London: SCM Press, 1967). I must confess that, as I reviewed these two works, I was in full sympathy with the statement made by John Bright concerning their utility:

> "Admittedly, any conclusions must be highly tentative. But the historian cannot be satisfied to draw none, but is obligated to indicate where the balance of probability in the matter seems to him to lie."

(Bright, "Excursus I: The Problem of Sennacherib's Campaigns in Palestine," *A History of Israel*, 3rd ed. [Philadelphia: Westminster Press, 1981], p. 298, n. 2; his entire excursus is a concise, useful introduction to the problem, including selected bibliography, much of it recent.)

on this controversial problem and to suggest where the balance of probability seems to lie.

At the outset, the following observation should be made: whatever interpretation of the Tirhakah reference one ultimately accepts will probably not seriously affect his or her reconstruction of the overall chronology of Judah for this period, for by the end of the eighth century B.C.E. the Assyro-Judahite synchronisms are sufficiently numerous as to enable us to date most of the kings of Judah to within a year or so.[6] Nevertheless, I do expect that the following review of the issues surrounding the Tirhakah reference in 2 Kgs 19:9 will prove worthwhile, not only to refine our understanding of the extent and nature of Sennacherib's military activity in Palestine, but also to sharpen our analysis of the biblical traditions themselves. It is to this latter issue which I now turn.

The Hebrew Bible actually contains three separate accounts of Sennacherib's military activity against Judah (2 Kgs 18:13-19:37; Isa 36:1-37:38; and 2 Chr 32:1-23). The passages in Kings and Isaiah closely parallel each other, and they probably represent two versions of one original narrative of Dtr provenance.[7] The Chronicles passage, on the other hand, basically represents a later abridgment of this same Dtr narrative, with some of the details suppressed (e.g., the notice about Tirhakah), and others emphasized or reinterpreted.[8] For the sake of economy, I will generally refer only to the Kings narrative in the following discussion, citing variations found in the Isaiah and Chronicles accounts only when appropriate to the overall argument.[9]

---

[6]Cf. the discussion of Tadmor, "Chronology of the First Temple Period," pp. 55-57; also his fuller discussion in "Chronology" [Hebrew], *Encyclopedia Miqra'it*, vol. 4 (Jerusalem: Bialik Institute, (1962), cols. 274-79.

[7]John Gray, *I & II Kings: A Commentary*, 2nd ed., The Old Testament Library (Philadelphia: Westminster Press, 1970), pp. 658-59; cf. the discussion in Childs, *Isaiah and the Assyrian Crisis*, pp. 137-40.

[8]Cf. the excellent discussion in Childs, *ibid.*, pp. 104-11.

[9]Good, albeit brief, textual notes comparing the versions of Kings and Isaiah may be found in Childs, *ibid.*, pp. 69-70, 76, 94. Honor, *Sennacherib's Invasion*, pp. 68-69, nn. 3-4, contains a fuller textual apparatus citing most of the differences between the Kings and Isaiah accounts; but probably the most complete and detailed comparative study of these two parallel versions remains that of Abraham Kuenen, *Historisch-Kritische*

At first glance, the Sennacherib account in 2 Kgs 18:13-19:37 appears to be a relatively smooth, continuous narrative, apparently recounted in chronological order. Thus we are told that Sennacherib invaded Judah in the fourteenth year of Hezekiah; he captured "all" of the fortified cities of Judah, compelling Hezekiah to sue for peace. The terms are severe: tribute so heavy that Hezekiah is forced to strip the inlaid gold from the doors of the temple of Yahweh. However, it appears that even this is not enough to satisfy the Assyrian king, for soon Sennacherib sends three important Assyrian officials (the Tartan, the Rabsaris, and the Rabshakeh) "with a great army" from Lachish (which apparently has not yet fallen) to Jerusalem to demand the surrender of the capital city. The Rabshakeh publicly delivers his scornful message in the hearing of the Jerusalemite citizenry assembled on the city walls; he speaks in the Judahite dialect to ensure their comprehension, even though the Judahite officials urge him to speak in Aramaic. Hezekiah despairs when he hears the report of the Rabshakeh's speech; he sends for Isaiah the prophet. Isaiah assures him that Sennacherib will not prevail, for Yahweh will cause him to hear a rumor and return to his own land where he will fall by the sword. Meanwhile, the Rabshakeh returns to the Assyrian king who has left Lachish and is now fighting against Libnah. When Sennacherib hears of the advance of Tirhakah king of Ethiopia, he sends messengers again to Hezekiah demanding surrender. This time Hezekiah takes the letter which they have brought, and he "spreads it out before Yahweh." Hezekiah prays for deliverance, and then Isaiah sends word that Yahweh has heard his prayer. Isaiah predicts that Sennacherib will not succeed in entering the city, indeed he will not even besiege it. We are then told that on that very night an angel of Yahweh slew 185,000 in the Assyrian camp; Sennacherib then departed for home and dwelt in Nineveh. The narrative ends with the notice that Sennacherib was assassinated by two of his own sons while he was worshipping in the temple of Nisroch his god.

Although a surface reading of the Sennacherib narrative such as the one summarized in the previous paragraph retains a certain amount of plausibility, biblical scholars have long pointed out a number of uneven features and unanswered questions which inevitably arise from the text. For example, why did Sennacherib threaten to attack

Einleitung in die Bücher des Alten Testaments (Leipzig, 1892), 2:74-79.

Jerusalem after being paid such a heavy tribute? Again, why did the Rabshakeh make two trips to Jerusalem only to deliver virtually the same message both times? And again, what really happened in the Assyrian camp that fateful night, and what relationship, if any, was there between that catastrophe and the advance of the military forces of Tirhakah? Finally, there is the general question of how the biblical account squares with the now accessible Assyrian and (to a lesser degree) Egyptian archival records. It is, to be sure, beyond the scope and purpose of the present investigation to rehearse even a fraction of the voluminous and varied scholarly literature on these two chapters of Kings; nevertheless, even a brief examination of one representative source-critical analysis of the Sennacherib narrative should sharpen our response to many of these questions.

In an important monograph entitled *Isaiah and the Assyrian Crisis*,[10] Brevard Childs analyzed the Sennacherib material as found in 2 Kgs 18-19 (and its parallels in Isaiah and Chronicles) in close detail. In line with most biblical scholars, he suggested dividing the narrative into two unequal parts: an "Account A" (2 Kgs 18:13-16) based upon some sort of annalistic or archival source,[11] and an "Account B" (2 Kgs 18:17-19:37), noticeably different in style, and making virtually no reference to the events recounted in Account A. Childs further delimited Account B into two parallel strands as follows: an Account B[1] (18:17-19:9a, 36-37) containing the first speech of the Rabshakeh, the first response of King Hezekiah and the prophet Isaiah, and the latter's confident prediction that Sennacherib would hear a rumor and return to his own land, where he would fall by the sword; and an Account B[2] (19:9b-35) containing another speech (and/or letter) of the Rabshakeh, another response of Hezekiah and of Isaiah, and a prediction by the prophet that Yahweh himself would defend his city

---

[10]Childs, *Isaiah and the Assyrian Crisis*, Studies in Biblical Theology, Second Series, No. 3 (London: SCM Press, 1967), pp. 69-111, 137-40.

[11]*Ibid.*, pp. 69-73. As is often pointed out, vv 14-16 of 2 Kings 18 are lacking in the parallel passage in Isaiah. Commentators generally suggest that the Isaianic text was purposely abbreviated (presumably to avoid mention of events which place Hezekiah in an unfavorable light), but I concur with Childs (pp. 69-70, and especially n. 1), in his preference for a text-critical solution. He suggested that a simple case of haplography (homeoarkton due to the repetition of the verbs *wayyišlah* in vv 14, 17) led to the omission in the Isaiah text.

Jerusalem. Thus, Account B^1 concludes with Sennacherib's abrupt departure home to Nineveh after receiving word that Tirhakah was on the march against him, and with his eventual assassination there by his own sons; but Account B^2 ends with Yahweh's sudden destruction of 185,000 Assyrian soldiers.[12] Childs characterized B^1 as a unified Dtr narrative largely based upon ancient tradition with a genuinely historical setting;[13] in contrast, B^2 is based upon a legendary source, heavily reflects Dtr theology (e.g., the role of Hezekiah as pious king), and contains a lengthy interpolation (vv 22-32).[14] Childs concluded his analysis as follows:

> The final question regarding the relation of the two accounts, B^1 and B^2, has, in large measure, already been answered indirectly. There is a common body of oral tradition shared by both accounts which appears in the similar structure of the stories and in the sections of parallel material. The many non-tendentious variations would rule out a literary relationship. However, the process through which the common material developed up to its final stage varied in the two sources. The work of the Dtr. redactor is evident in both accounts, but to a lesser degree in B^1. There is also some evidence for a mutual influencing of the two sources. It is possible for this blurring of lines to have been effected by the Dtr. redactor when he combined the sources or at an even later date.[15]

This brief overview of Childs' source-critical examination neither conveys adequately the thoroughness of his analysis nor the attractiveness of many of his conclusions. Nevertheless, it does illustrate how one competent scholar has delineated several heterogeneous sources in the narrative, two of which are basically parallel with each other. Furthermore, it notes how, especially in the case of Account B^2, he has drawn attention to the tendentious nature of much of the material, lending weight to the following caveat which concluded his overall discussion:

---

[12]*Ibid.*, pp. 73-76.

[13]*Ibid.*, pp. 76-93.

[14]*Ibid.*, pp. 94-103.

[15]*Ibid.*, p. 103.

The effort [in Account B[2]] to picture Hezekiah as the type of the faithful king has emerged as a dominant concern. The understanding that there is a radical alteration of traditional material which serves a new function of the author should provide a warning against a simple-minded historical reading of the text.[16]

We will do well to keep this caveat in mind as we now turn to an overview of some of the various historical reconstructions of Sennacherib's Palestinian campaign(s) proposed by biblical scholars. Once again, the literature on this topic is simply immense, making any attempt at an adequate survey out of the question.[17] Happily, for our purposes we can separate the great majority of these scholarly reconstructions into two general categories: those who suggest (in one form or other) that all the biblical accounts essentially refer to the one and only clearly attested Palestinian campaign of Sennacherib which took place in 701 B.C.E. (this category would probably still include the majority of scholars),[18] and those who posit a second Palestinian campaign of Sennacherib to account for the biblical data which do not accord easily with the 701 campaign. Although a second such campaign is not attested in the Assyrian records, it is nevertheless hypothetically possible inasmuch as no dated historical records for the last seven years of Sennacherib's reign (689-681) have as of yet come to light.[19] This two-campaign hypothesis was first suggested over a

---

[16]*Ibid.* Recently, Ehud Ben Zwi ("Who Wrote the Speech of Rabshakeh and When?" *JBL* 109 [1990] 79-92) has concluded that the entire Rabshakeh speech is inauthentic, largely derived from later Isaianic and Dtr traditions.

[17]For an extensive bibliography up to 1926, see Honor, *Sennacherib's Invasion*, pp. 117-22; for more recent literature, see H. H. Rowley, "Hezekiah's Reform and Rebellion," *BJRL* 44 (1962) 395-431 (the entire article is reprinted as chapter 4 of Rowley's *Men of God: Studies in Old Testament History and Prophecy* [London: Thomas Nelson, 1963], pp. 98-132), especially the notes on pp. 405-407 (= Men of God, pp. 107-109). For literature after 1962, John Bright's third edition of his *History of Israel* (see above, n. 5) probably represents the best single bibliographic source.

[18]Cf. the statement of Bright, *History of Israel*, 3rd ed., p. 298; curiously enough, the comments of D. J. Wiseman in *Documents from Old Testament Times*, D. Winton Thomas, ed. (London: Thomas Nelson and Sons, 1958), pp. 64-65, imply just the opposite.

[19]Horn, "Sennacherib against Hezekiah" (see above, n. 3), pp. 12-13.

century ago,[20] and, although it has never commanded the allegiance of a majority of biblical scholars, it has increasingly gained in favor among a significant number of competent scholars, including W. F. Albright and several of his students.[21]   Some of the reasons for suggesting the existence of a second Palestinian campaign are the following: 1) the biblical reference to Tirhakah may be retained as accurate inasmuch as he is clearly on the throne during the latter part of Sennacherib's reign; 2) the tensions and apparent contradictions between the biblical accounts A and B (as delineated above) may be more easily accounted for (i.e., Account A clearly refers to the 701 campaign, but Account B could be linked with the hypothetical second campaign); 3) the otherwise curious ambivalence in the utterances of Isaiah the prophet concerning the invading Assyrians (i.e., in some places he counselled surrender, in others defiance) could be more easily resolved; and 4) the significance of the closing remarks of the Sennacherib narrative citing the assassination of the Assyrian king in Nineveh by two of his sons would be heightened (since the twenty year gap between the 701 invasion and the assassination in 681 would be significantly reduced).   For these and other reasons (e.g., the issues of Egyptian chronology concerning the career of Tirhakah, to be discussed below in some detail), not a few biblical scholars have embraced the two-campaign hypothesis in one form or another.   It will be my task, therefore, to consider, at least in brief, the relative strength of these two positions, and to indicate which position seems more adequately to account for all the extant biblical, Assyrian, and Egyptian historical data.

Some time ago, H. H. Rowley[22] presented a strong defense of the one-campaign hypothesis, addressing many of the arguments advanced by scholars preferring the two-campaign hypothesis, and suggesting an attractive solution to the related problem of the chronol-

---

[20]W. F. Albright, "New Light from Egypt on the Chronology and History of Israel and Judah," *BASOR* 130 (1953) 8; but cf. Horn, "Sennacherib against Hezekiah," pp. 22-23, n. 59.

[21]Cf. Bright, *History of Israel*, 3rd ed., p. 298, and n. 4.

[22]Rowley, "Hezekiah's Reform and Rebellion" (see above, n. 17, for full bibliographic details, including reference to the reprint of the article in Rowley's *Men of God*), pp. 395-431. Page references in the next several notes will be to the original *BJRL* article, with the equivalent page(s) in the reprinted version indicated in parentheses and with the siglum "*MG*."

ogy of the accession of Hezekiah. In the course of his discussion, he referred to each of the four issues which I have just enumerated as follows: 1) Concerning Tirhakah: contemporary Egyptian records indeed do demonstrate the impossibility that he was already pharaoh in 701, and in fact seem to indicate that he was only about nine years old at that time (but cf. my discussion below); yet it remains far more plausible to recognize an anachronism in the biblical text for what it is, than to invent a second Assyrian invasion otherwise unattested in the ancient records.[23] 2) Concerning the tensions between the biblical accounts A and B: a judicious examination of the Assyrian annals (noting both what they claim and what they do not claim), coupled with a careful reading of the biblical texts themselves, can lead quite successfully to an entirely plausible historical reconstruction without resorting to the invention of a second campaign.[24] 3) Concerning the oracles of Isaiah: indeed it is the case that he had opposed the original revolt of Hezekiah, and predicted disaster, and had even declared that Assyria was the rod of Yahweh's anger;[25] nevertheless, once the rest of Judah had been devastated by the Assyrians and Jerusalem herself severely threatened, he suddenly seemed to be full of confidence, predicting that Jerusalem would be miraculously spared, and that Assyria herself would be humbled for her blasphemy.[26] This does seem quixotic on the part of the prophet (or at least, a remarkable change of mind in a brief period of time), but, as Rowley went on to argue:

> The apparently quixotic change of attitude on the part of the prophet arose from a single and consistent point of view. Hezekiah had been in the wrong in violating his oath to his Assyrian overlord, but now it was Sennacherib who was in the wrong in seeking to impose new terms that were not provided for in the instrument of surrender. Moreover, he was blaspheming against Yahweh and boasting of an invincible power that Yahweh Himself could not challenge. Resistance was now doubly justified, and since there were no human

---

[23]*Ibid.*, pp. 424-25 (= *MG*, p. 126).

[24]*Ibid.*, pp. 415-25 (= *MG*, pp. 116-26).

[25]*Ibid.*, p. 422 (= *MG*, pp. 123-24); cf., e.g., Isa 10:5-7; 18:1-6; 22:1-14; 30:1-5.

[26]*Ibid.*, p. 422 (= *MG*, p. 124); cf., e.g., Isa 10:8-19; 31:1-3, 8-9.

resources on which confidence could rest, Isaiah was sure that Yahweh would manifest His power and no human friends or allies would be able to share with Him the glory of the deliverance.[27]

Finally, 4) concerning the period of time between the return home of Sennacherib and his eventual assassination: to be sure, dating the hypothetical second invasion after 690 would definitely reduce the interval of time between its presumably disastrous outcome and Sennacherib's eventual assassination in 681; but, inasmuch as Hezekiah was by any scholar's reckoning dead by 686,[28] at least a five year interval would remain between the two events. Therefore, any advantage gained by the two-campaign hypothesis does not seem to be that pronounced. As Rowley himself pointed out:

> Once the disaster that overtook the Assyrian armies is removed from immediate connection with the assassination of the king, there is no reason to be troubled by few or many years. The Biblical author was not concerned to write the history of Assyria, and it sufficed for him to record that the king who had proudly challenged Israel's God had come to a bad end.[29]

Furthermore, it should be noted that if Hezekiah's death is dated earlier than 686 (and not a few scholars suggest that such is the case),[30] the years of overlap for a second invasion of Sennacherib dated after 690

---

[27]*Ibid.*, pp. 422-23 (= *MG*, p. 124).

[28]Albright originally proposed 686 for the end of Hezekiah's reign (see his comments in "The History of Palestine and Syria," *JQR* 24 [1934] 371, which I have quoted at some length below on p. 85); he later raised his date by one year (cf. "The Chronology of the Divided Monarchy of Israel." *BASOR* 100 [1945] 22, and especially n. 28, where he explained the reasons for his change). John Bright (*History of Israel*, 3rd ed., p. 288), E. R. Thiele ("The Chronology of the Kings of Judah and Israel," *JNES* 3 [1944] 179), and S. H. Horn ("Did Sennacherib Campaign Once or Twice Against Hezekiah?" *AUSS* 4 [1966] 23, n. 60) all concurred with the year 687/86 for Hezekiah's death. Many other scholars, however, prefer an earlier date; cf. Rowley, "Hezekiah's Reform and Rebellion," pp. 410-13 (= *MG*, pp. 112-15), and bibliography cited there.

[29]Rowley, "Hezekiah's Reform and Rebellion," p. 408 (= *MG*, pp. 110-11).

[30]See above, n. 28.

(the year of the accession of Tirhakah) coming against Hezekiah would be correspondingly diminished, if not altogether eliminated.

It is at this point of his discussion that Rowley presented his own solution to the thorny problem of dating the accession of Hezekiah. I have just pointed out that biblical scholars suggest dating the death of Hezekiah on or before 686 B.C.E.; such a date, however, is in fact largely dependent upon the corresponding date for his accession, some 29 years earlier. It will be recalled that I have already discussed this latter issue in some detail back in the first chapter (see above, p. 3), and only the essential points need be repeated here. If Hezekiah's 14th year is to be linked with Sennacherib's Palestinian invasion of 701 (as the synchronism in 2 Kgs 18:13 seems to indicate), then either the repeated Dtr synchronisms in 18:1-10 are in error (so, e.g., Albright, Thiele),[31] or some sort of coregency must be posited (so S. H. Horn).[32] Rather than dismissing the repeated synchronisms at the beginning of 2 Kgs 18 as inaccurate, Rowley instead queried the accuracy of the synchronism in 18:13, and suggested that the relatively minor emendation of "fourteen" (*'arba' 'eśrēh*) to "twenty-four" (*'arba' wĕ-'eśrîm*) would alleviate many of the difficulties.[33] However, if Rowley's emendation be accepted, then Hezekiah's death would have to be dated to c. 697, which would eliminate completely any possibility of dating a campaign of Sennacherib against Hezekiah after the accession of Tirhakah some seven years later. In other words, any scholar who wishes to espouse some form of the two-campaign theory which includes Tirhakah as pharaoh (presumably one of the most basic motivations for such a theory in the first place) *must* presume a late date for the accession of Hezekiah, and therefore must deny the validity

---

[31]Albright, "Chronology," *BASOR* 100 (1945) 22, n. 28; Thiele, "Chronology," *JNES* 3 (1944) 174-77.

[32]Horn, "The Chronology of King Hezekiah's Reign," *AUSS* 2 (1964) 49-51.

[33]Rowley, "Hezekiah's Reform and Rebellion," pp. 410-13 (= *MG*, pp. 112-15); some time earlier, Yohanan Aharoni ("The Chronology of the Kings of Israel and Judah" [Hebrew], *Tarbiz* 21 [1950] 97) also had suggested that the number "14" (in 2 Kgs 18:13) probably resulted from the corruption of an original "24." In contrast, A. K. Jenkins ("Hezekiah's Fourteenth Year: A New Interpretation of 2 Kings xviii 13-xix 37," *VT* 26 [1976] 284-98) argued for retaining the number "14" as authentic, but originally referring to Sargon's Palestinian campaign of 714-712, and only later reinterpreted by Dtr to refer to Sennacherib.

of the synchronisms at the beginning of 2 Kgs 18.[34] In essence, he or she must deny the whole import of the chapter as it now stands: for it maintains in no uncertain terms that Hezekiah was king of Judah during and after those fateful days when the Northern Kingdom came to an end. Indeed, as Rowley himself hinted, in attempting to eliminate one anachronism (the reference to Tirhakah as king of Ethiopia when Sennacherib campaigned in Palestine), the scholar is liable to create another (denying that Hezekiah was king of Judah when Samaria fell).[35]

It will be recalled that W. F. Albright indicated his own clear preference for the two-campaign hypothesis on a number of occasions.[36] It is to a brief examination of the reasons for this preference of his that I now turn. I have already noted that, on the strength of the synchronism found in 2 Kgs 18:13, Albright dated Hezekiah's accession

---

[34]Strictly speaking, of course, one could deny both the accuracy of the synchronism in 18:13 as well as the length of reign in 18:2, but retain the synchronisms in 18:1, 9, 10 as accurate, and then be free to propose some sort of two-campaign theory with Tirhakah as pharaoh; but I know of no scholar willing to do this. An easier approach is that of Horn (see above, n. 32), who proposed a 13 year coregency between Hezekiah and his father Ahaz (thus preserving, at least in some form, all the various synchronisms and regnal totals in 2 Kings 18); the problem with this kind of approach, however, is that it forces one to posit an extraordinary number of coregencies (even more than Thiele was willing to propose), many of which overlap a large part of the reign of the elder king, and for most of which there is really no evidence in the biblical text apart from the disparities in the numbers themselves (see Horn, "Hezekiah's Reign," chart opposite p. 40, for a clear illustration of the results of his approach).

[35]Rowley, "Hezekiah's Reform and Rebellion," pp. 410-13 (= MG, pp. 112-15); in n. 2 of p. 411 (= MG, p. 113, n. 2), Rowley quoted with approval the apt comment of J. Skinner, The Book of the Prophet Isaiah: Chapters I-XXXIX, The Cambridge Bible (Cambridge, 1896), p. lxxvi, "It would argue an almost incredible degree of carelessness in a historian to assign so important an event as the fall of Samaria to the wrong reign." Essentially the same point was made by Yohanan Aharoni, "Chronology" (see above, n. 33), pp. 96-97.

[36]E.g., "The History of Palestine and Syria," JQR 24 (1934) 370-71; cf. his comments in "The Biblical Period," Louis Finkelstein, ed., The Jews: Their History, Culture, and Religion (New York: Harper & Brothers, 1949), 1:42-44, and nn. 101-102. Refinements in his argumentation (based largely upon the Egyptian chronological data) may be found in his "New Light from Egypt on the Chronology and History of Israel and Judah," BASOR 130 (1953) 8-11, and his "Further Light on Synchronisms Between Egypt and Asia in the Period 935-685 B.C." BASOR 141 (1956) 25-26.

to c. 715 B.C.E.[37]   Although such a low date accords nicely with a two-campaign hypothesis (especially inasmuch as it permits an overlap of several years between Hezekiah and Tirhakah), the one need not entail the other. Nevertheless, Albright embraced both positions, and in one place suggested that this overlap between the reigns of the two kings provided "almost decisive" confirmation for his chronology.[38] This was not his only reason, however, for preferring the two-campaign theory, as the following quotation from an early article should make clear:

> The reviewer [Albright] still believes in the two campaign theory of Sennacherib's invasion of Judah. . . . The position of the reviewer is based mainly upon the fact that Taharko's accession is to be dated 689 B.C.E., while Hezekiah's reign extended from 714 to 686 (the reviewer's chronology). It is hardly possible to harmonize the main account in Kings and Isaiah, in which Sennacherib is reported to have besieged Lachish first, then Libnah, while the Rabshakeh was sent on a mission to Jerusalem [= Account B, as delineated above], with the succinct statement, II Kings 18.13-16 [= Account A], which agrees perfectly with Sennacherib's own description of the campaign in 701. Nor can we discard the main account so easily as is done by most of those who reject the two campaign theory. The route of Sennacherib's advance, from Lachish northward to Libnah, is out of harmony with the direction of Sennacherib's march as described in his own inscriptions.[39]

Albright's emphasis on the historical accuracy of Account B reappeared in a later *BASOR* article:

---

[37]Albright, "Chronology," *BASOR* 100 (1945) 22, and n. 28; cf. my discussion in Chapter I, p. 3. Interestingly enough, as I have already discussed at some length in Chapter I, pp. 4-7, Albright usually placed more confidence in the accuracy of the Judahite synchronisms than in the regnal totals; however, it is evident that he did not do so here (i.e. he retained Hezekiah's regnal total of 29 years as "very well attested in our sources" [Albright, *ibid.*, n. 28], while rejecting the Judahite synchronisms of 2 Kgs 18:9-10 inasmuch as they conflict with 18:13).

[38]Albright, "Chronology," p. 22, n. 28.

[39]Albright, "History of Palestine and Syria," *JQR* 24 (1934) 370-71. As I have already pointed out in another context (see above, n. 28), Albright later raised his chronology for Hezekiah and Tirhakah by one year.

The present text [Account B] is altogether too precise and correct in its historical background (cf. II Kings 19:12-13 = Isa. 37:12-13, which mentions nine distinct historical events of the ninth-eighth century, nearly all of which can be validated from the Assyrian records!) to admit of such distortion. That the Deuteronomic compiler telescoped two parallel campaigns is now certain, but there is no evidence that he distorted the material which had come down to him.[40]

Probably the most decisive argument for the two-campaign theory remained for Albright the question of the dating of Tirhakah, and all the more so after the publication of the Kawa inscriptions by M. F. Laming Macadam in 1949.[41] It is to an evaluation of this evidence from Egypt that I now turn.

As a result of the Oxford Excavations in Nubia, undertaken in the 1930s at Kawa in the Northern Province of what is now the Republic of the Sudan, several important stelae of Tirhakah have come to light.[42] The expedition's epigrapher, M. F. L. Macadam, eventually published them in 1949; his careful notes included a suggested reconstruction of the previously murky chronology of the pharaohs of the 25th (Ethiopian or Nubian) Dynasty. I will mainly be concerned with the inscriptions which Macadam designated as Stelae IV and V, for these two inscriptions enable us to ascertain within a reasonable degree of certainty a number of details concerning Tirhakah's background and early career as pharaoh. For example, we learn the following data from

---

[40]Albright, "New Light," *BASOR* 130 (1953) 9; in his 1956 *BASOR* article (see above, n. 36), he raised the number to ten such places. Cf. also the comments of John Bright (*History of Israel*, 3rd ed., pp. 300-301, and especially nn. 11-12), where he argues strongly for the historical accuracy of both Accounts A and B.

[41]M. F. Laming Macadam, *The Temples of Kawa: I. The Inscriptions* (London: Oxford University Press, 1949), text and plates in two separate volumes.

[42]Macadam, *Kawa I*, pp. 4-44, and plates 5-14; Stela III is dated to Tirhakah's years 2-8, Stelae IV and V to his year 6, Stela VI to years 8-10, and Stela VII to year 10. The inscriptions either list various gifts made to the temple of Amon-Rē' at Gematen (= Kawa) (Stelae III, VI), or describe its restoration under Tirhakah (Stelae IV, VII), or recount the auspicious events in Tirhakah's sixth year which helped motivate such repairs (Stela V).

Stela IV:[43]

1. Tirhakah, a brother of the ruling pharaoh Shebitku, spent his youth in Nubia; at the request of Shebitku "who loved him more than all his brothers," he came north to Thebes.[44]
2. On his trip to Thebes, he was accompanied by an army.
3. On his way, he passed by the temple of Amon-Rē' in Gematen (= Kawa); he was saddened to see it in serious disrepair.
4. After he had become pharaoh, he set out to repair the temple; he sent a large contingent of craftsmen to Gematen to reconstruct the temple in grand style.
5. At that time, Tirhakah was in Memphis.
6. The work was initiated in his sixth year, the date of the inscription.

In addition, according to Macadam's suggested translation of ll. 12-13, we may infer that Tirhakah had seen the ruined temple "in the first year of his reign"; i.e. he had been crowned as king (or according to Macadam's chronological reconstruction, coregent) the same year he had left Nubia.[45] As will be discussed below, quite a number of Egyptologists have disagreed, however, with this interpretation.

Stela V, also dated to the sixth year of Tirhakah, provides us with the following information:[46]

1. Certain "wonders" took place in the sixth year of the king's reign, including heavy rains in Nubia and an unusually high flooding of the Nile.
2. Tirhakah had been praying to Amon-Rē' for just such an inundation (to prevent the outbreak of famine); after his prayer was answered, he multiplied his devotion "to all the gods."

---

[43]Macadam, *Kawa I*, pp. 14-21, and plates 7-8; cf. also the discussion in Horn, "Sennacherib against Hezekiah" (see above, n. 28), pp. 7-8.

[44]Macadam, *Kawa I*, p. 15, and especially n. 19 on p. 17.

[45]*Ibid.*, p. 15; cf. his lengthy discussion in n. 30 on pp. 18-20.

[46]*Ibid.*, pp. 22-32, and plates 9-10. The stela actually is a duplicate text of several previously known inscriptions: the first part is paralleled by two nearly complete texts; the concluding portion, however, is paralleled only by a single fragmentary text, which was, in fact, greatly misunderstood until the discovery of Kawa V.

3. In the present inscription, Tirhakah seems to express his gratitude to Amon-Rē' in particular for "four goodly wonders," all of which are also said to have occurred in his sixth year. These four wonders probably are the following:[47]

    A. He (Amon-Rē') gave good cultivation throughout the land.

    B. He slew the rats and snakes within it.

    C. He kept away the locusts.

    D. He prevented the south winds from reaping it.

4. The result was an "incalculable" harvest from both Upper and Lower Egypt.

5. Tirhakah was crowned in Memphis after the death of his brother Shebitku.

6. Tirhakah was twenty years old when he originally had been summoned away from Nubia by Shebitku; since that time he had not seen his mother Abar until her recent visit to Lower Egypt "after an interval of years." Presumably this reunion took place in Tirhakah's sixth year as well.

Even the above summary should demonstrate that the major concern of Stela V is to recount the various "wonders" which took place in the sixth year of Tirhakah, as well as to express gratitude to Amon-Rē' for these indications of his blessing. At one point (l. 10 of the inscription; cf. above, my item no. 3), a particular number of wonders ("four goodly wonders") is specified; however, it is by no means obvious from the inscription itself which of the wonders are to be included under this

---

[47]See Jean Leclant and Jean Yoyotte, "Notes d'histoire et de civilisation éthiopiennes," *BIFAO* 51 (1952) 22-24, where they pointed out that the four parallel clauses of ll. 11-12 (*rdi.n.f . . . sm'.n.f . . . ḥsf.n.f . . . n rdi.n.f . . .*, "he gave . . . he slew . . . he repelled . . . he did not permit . . .") are likely to be the "four goodly wonders" of l. 10, and that the deity Amon-Rē' is probably the subject of each clause. Less plausible is Macadam's original rendering of ll. 11-12:

> "It [the inundation] caused the cultivation to be good throughout for my sake; it slew the rats and snakes that were in the midst of it; it kept away from it the devouring of the locusts. It prevented the south winds from reaping it . . ." (*Kawa I*, p. 27).

As Leclant and Yoyotte argued, the inundation could hardly have been credited with keeping away the locusts and the south winds, whereas Amon-Rē' (who is named in l. 10 as bringing forth the four goodly wonders) certainly could have been. Concurring with this is the translation of Jozef M. A. Janssen (*Biblica* 34 [1953] 28); cf. also the discussion in Kitchen, *Third Intermediate Period*, § 136.

rubric. Macadam, as part of his overall chronological reconstruction of the pharaohs of the 25th Dynasty, proposed to delineate these four wonders as follows:[48]

1. The great inundation of the Nile (ll. 5-8)
2. The rainstorm in Nubia (ll. 9-10)
3. Tirhakah's coronation (ll. 13-16)
4. The visit of the Queen Mother (ll. 16-22).

This delineation, however, calls for a word of explanation. Macadam ingeniously proposed that a careful reading of Kawa Stelae IV and V indicates that Tirhakah was not crowned as sole king until the sixth year of his reign; i.e. that he served as coregent under his brother Shebitku for his first five years (until the latter's death). This would help explain both the delay in the rebuilding of the temple of Amon-Rē' at Gematen (which did not start until Tirhakah's sixth year), as well as the delay in the reunion of the Queen Mother with her son (which apparently also occurred in Tirhakah's eventful sixth year).

I have already noted briefly that Macadam's suggested translation of Stela IV, ll. 12-13 supports his coregency hypothesis.[49] At this point in the discussion, however, a closer look at these two lines is appropriate. The following is Macadam's translation: "When the Double Diadem was established upon his head [i.e. when he, Tirhakah, became sole king after the death of Shebitku] . . . , he called to mind this temple [the temple at Gematen], which he had seen as a youth in the first year of his reign [i.e. on his journey north to be crowned as Shebitku's coregent, some six years previously]." Hence, although Tirhakah counted his regnal years from the inauguration of this coregency (the same year he had noticed the disrepair of the Gematen temple), he did not (indeed, as coregent probably could not) commence rebuilding the temple until his sixth year (= the first year of his sole

---

[48]Macadam, *Kawa I*, n. 30, pp. 18-19; cf. the discussion in Horn, "Sennacherib against Hezekiah," *AUSS* 4 (1966) 8-9.

[49]See above, p. 87. Macadam (*Kawa I*, n. 30, p. 19) cited Nile-level Text No. 33 at Karnak as evidence for a three year coregency between Shabako and Shebitku, thus setting a precedent for Shebitku and Tirhakah. More recently, Anthony Spalinger ("The Year 712 B.C. and its Implications for Egyptian History," *JARCE* 10 [1973] 98) proposed a two year coregency between Shabako and Shebitku based on the same evidence; but, it should be noted that Spalinger nonetheless concurred with Leclant and Yoyotte in rejecting Macadam's proposal for a six year coregency between Shebitku and Tirhakah.

reign, according to Macadam's reconstruction). Furthermore, inasmuch as ll. 16-17 of Stela V mention that Tirhakah had been 20 years old when he had left Nubia, he must have been only about 26 years old when he became sole king in c. 690;[50] hence not more than nine years old in 701, the year of Sennacherib's invasion of Palestine. Thus, if Macadam's reconstruction of the Egyptian chronological data for the 25th Dynasty be sound, one must reject completely any possibility of Tirhakah's participation in any significant way in the events of that year. It will, of course, be immediately apparent that Macadam's chronological reconstruction strengthened the position of those biblical scholars (such as W. F. Albright) who preferred the two-campaign hypothesis: for one may still retain the biblical notice concerning Tirhakah's arrival in Palestine as accurate, but, now out of necessity, date it to after 690 B.C.E., during the putative second invasion of Sennacherib. As Albright himself concluded:

> The new Egyptian evidence which we have marshalled in this paper [i.e. the chronology of Tirhakah's early life, as reconstructed by Macadam], demonstrates the substantial--perhaps exact--correctness of our chronology of the tenth-ninth century; it also proves the accuracy of our reconstruction of the chronology and history of Hezekiah's reign.[51]

However, few, if any, Egyptologists have embraced these conclusions of Macadam. As I have already noted, Leclant and Yoyotte

---

[50]Thus, Macadam's suggested reconstruction of the chronology for the early years of Tirhakah is as follows:

Birth of Tirhakah	709
Association of Tirhakah with Shebitku	689
Death of Shebitku, Tirhakah sole ruler, visit of Abar, exceptionally high Nile, and building of temple at Gematen	684
Official opening of temple at Gematen	680

These dates are from Macadam, *Kawa I*, n. 30, p. 19, and are based upon the date of 663 for the commencement of the 26th Dynasty. However, Egyptologists have more recently raised this last date by a year; cf. above, p. 73, n. 3.

[51]Albright, "New Light," *BASOR* 130 (1953) 9; cf. the comments of Horn, "Sennacherib against Hezekiah," p. 11.

in an important discussion of Macadam's proposals[52] suggested a quite different delineation of the "four goodly wonders" of Kawa Stela V, l. 10 (cf. my above discussion, pp. 87-88, and especially n. 47). But this alternative view immediately endangers an important premise of Macadam's chronology: *viz.*, that the accession of Tirhakah as sole king took place in his eventful sixth year; indeed, that it comprised one of the "four goodly wonders" which occurred that year. Leclant and Yoyotte, on the other hand, proposed an alternative interpretation of the reference to Tirhakah's coronation as king in Stela V: they argued that indeed it is true that the reference in l. 15 to the enthronement of Tirhakah as king "after the Hawk had soared to heaven" indicates that it took place after the death of Shebitku, but this coronation ought to be dated, not to the sixth year of Tirhakah, but back to his original enthronement in his first year; and it is included in its present context only as an introduction to the account of the visit of the Queen Mother (which indeed did probably occur in Tirhakah's sixth year).[53]   In support of their alternative interpretation, they pointed out the following: when the reference in l. 15 is compared with Kawa IV, ll. 11-13, it becomes clear that Tirhakah had not yet officially ascended the throne (*ḫ' m nsw*), he had not yet been acknowledged as King of Upper and Lower Egypt (*nsw-bit*), the "double Diadem" had not yet been established upon his head (*smn nbty tp.f*), and he had not received his Horus name (*ḫpr rn.f m Hr k[.] ḫ'w*) until this coronation ceremony took place after the death of Shebitku.[54] However, elsewhere in a number of dated inscriptions, Tirhakah is unmistakably pictured as full king before his sixth year: e.g., in a stela commemorating his repairs of the enclosure wall of the temple at Medinet Habu dated to his third year;[55] in private papyri dated to his third and fifth years;[56] and

---

[52]Leclant and Yoyotte, "Notes d'histoire," *BIFAO* 51 (1952) 1-39, and especially pp. 15-29.

[53]*Ibid.*, pp. 23-24.

[54]*Ibid.*, p. 24. Macadam agreed that both V 15 and IV 11-13 referred to the official coronation of Tirhakah (see *Kawa I*, nn. 28, 30, 31, on pp. 18-20), but he dated this event, of course, to Tirhakah's sixth year.

[55]Leclant and Yoyotte, "Notes d'histoire," p. 24, and n. 1. For a brief description and a drawing of the stela, see Howard Carter, "Report of Work Done in Upper Egypt (1902-1903)," *ASAE* 4 (1903) 171-80, and the "Note additionnelle" by G. Maspero on

indeed in Kawa Stela III, which records his numerous donations made to the temple of Amon-Rē' at Gematen in his years 2-5 (as well as his years 6-8).[57] These data, therefore, raise serious doubts as to the likelihood of Macadam's suggested six year coregency between She-bitku and Tirhakah.

---

p. 180. Tirhakah is pictured on the stela as presenting an offering to the god Amon-Rē' who is seated upon a throne with the goddess Mut standing behind him. A translation of the text of the stela may be found in Uvo Hölscher, *The Excavations of Medinet Habu, Vol. 2: The Temples of the Eighteenth Dynasty*, The University of Chicago Oriental Institute Publications, Vol. 41 (Chicago: University of Chicago Press, 1939), p. 34; at the time of this publication the stela was in the Cairo Museum (No. 36140). Cf. also the note of H. Gauthier, "Les Steles de l'an III de Taharqa de Medinet-Habou," *ASAE* 18 (1919) 90, which indicated that a virtually identical copy of the Medinet Habu stela was to be found in London.

[56]Year 3--Louvre Papyrus 3228 A, the sale of a slave: see F. Ll. Griffith, *Catalogue of the Demotic Papyri in the John Rylands Library*, Vol. 3 (Manchester, 1909), pp. 15, 57-58 for notes and translation; cf. also Eugène Revillout, *Notice des papyrus démotiques archaïques* (Paris, 1896), pp. 230-46. Year 5--Cairo Papyrus 30884, a financial account (fragmentary): see Wilhelm Spiegelberg, *Die Demotischen Papyrus II*, Catalogue général des antiquités égyptiennes du Musée du Caire, Vol. 39, Text (Strassburg, 1908), p. 194, and *ibid.*, Vol. 40, Tafeln (Strassburg, 1906), Tafel 67. For other papyri probably to be dated in Tirhakah's fourth or fifth year, see references in Leclant and Yoyotte, "Notes d'histoire," p. 25, n. 3, and G. Schmidt, "Das Jahr des Regierungsantritts König Taharqas," *Kush* 6 (1958) p. 127, nn. 34-35.

[57]Macadam, *Kawa I*, pp. 4-14, and plates 5-6. Both Leclant and Yoyotte ("Notes d'histoire," p. 24, n. 1) as well as Schmidt ("Taharqas," p. 127, and n. 36) cited a Nile-level text (no. 34) as also dated in Tirhakah's year 5, but this is erroneous: for both G. Legrain's original publication of the Karnak Nile-level texts (*ZÄS* 34 [1896] 115, no. 34) as well as von Beckerath's more recent recollation (*JARCE* 5 [1966] 53, no. 34; cf. also pp. 47-48, and n. 36) read quite clearly year 6, ⟨glyph⟩. Inasmuch as this Nile-level text (along with no. 35, dated also to Tirhakah's year 6) record the highest inundation level of any recorded on the quay, it surely corresponds with the famous inundation of year 6 which is commemorated in Kawa Stela V 5-8; cf. von Beckerath's Figure 1 on p. 44 of his article, also Macadam's comments in *Kawa I*, p. 29, n. 25.

Finally, for the sake of completeness, one additional inscription should be cited. A demotic stela which records the death of an Apis bull attests either year 2 or year 5 of Tirhakah: the name of the pharaoh is certain, but the exact reading of the year number is not; cf. the discussion of J. Vercoutter, "The Napatan Kings and Apis Worship," *Kush* 8 (1960) 67-69, and plate 21b. For a convenient listing of all the extant dated inscriptions of Tirhakah, arranged in chronological sequence, see Anthony Spalinger, "The Foreign Policy of Egypt Preceding the Assyrian Conquest," *CdÉ* 53 (1978) 44-47.

Furthermore, Leclant and Yoyotte also pointed out that one can in fact interpret quite easily the crucial ll. 12-13 of Kawa Stela IV to agree with the evidence just cited (even though these were the very lines Macadam had cited as strong evidence for his six year coregency hypothesis).[58] This last point requires further discussion. It will be recalled (cf. above, p. 89) that Macadam had translated Kawa IV, ll. 12-13 as follows:

> When the Double Diadem was established upon his head and his name became Horus Lofty of Diadems, he called to mind this temple, which he had beheld as a youth in the first year of his reign.[59]

It will be readily apparent how this translation permits Macadam's proposal of a six year coregency between "the first year of his reign" when Tirhakah as a youth had beheld the Gematen temple in disrepair, and his later coronation as full king (after the death of Shebitku, dated by Macadam to Tirhakah's sixth year) "when the Double Diadem was established," and when "he called to mind this temple." However, as Leclant and Yoyotte pointed out, one can interpret these lines in another way, as simply indicating that already in the first year of his reign Tirhakah called to mind the neglected state of the temple (which he had originally beheld as a youth).[60] Support for this alternative interpretation may be found in Kawa Stela III which indicates that already in Tirhakah's second year he is demonstrating his concern for the Gematen temple by his generous offerings (which are then listed in the

---

[58]Leclant and Yoyotte, "Notes d'histoire," pp. 20-21.

[59]Macadam, *Kawa I*, p. 15.

[60]Leclant and Yoyotte, "Notes d'histoire," p. 20. For a vigorous defense of their alternative interpretation relying upon recent advances in syntactical analysis of Egyptian, see Anson F. Rainey, "Taharqa and Syntax," *Tel Aviv* 3 (1976) 38-41; his comments on p. 40 are worth quoting here:
"The whole point is that Taharqa turned his attention to this temple during the first year of his reign. It cannot possibly be taken to mean that he was a youth when he began to reign! Therefore, Macadam's rendering (1949:18-20 n. 30), which he uses to prove his proposed chronology, is conclusively refuted by the syntax of the passage. The view of Leclant and Yoyotte (1952:20-21) is thoroughly vindicated."

stela).[61] Indeed, according to Leclant and Yoyotte, ll. 12-13 of Stela IV should be understood as comprising the final part of a "preamble" to the royal proclamation (ll. 13-20) announcing Tirhakah's intent to rebuild the temple. This preamble recounts his previous concern for the care of the temple of "his father" Amon-Rē', such concern which now leads (in his sixth year) to his decision to rebuild the structure completely.

To conclude: according to Leclant and Yoyotte, neither the Kawa stelae themselves nor the other dated monumental and papyrological evidence give us any reason to posit a six year coregency between Shebitku and Tirhakah. On the contrary, Tirhakah is clearly depicted as full king as early as his second year of reign, and we must therefore date Shebitku's death to before that time.[62] The following is a chronological reconstruction of Tirhakah's activities as described in Kawa Stelae III-VII (based upon the interpretations of Leclant and Yoyotte):[63]

Year 1 (= c. 690 B.C.E.): After the death of Shebitku, the coronation of Tirhakah takes place in Memphis (IV 12-13, V 15); at this time he recalls the temple of Amon-Rē' at Gemathen which is lying in disrepair (IV 12-13). Some (unspecified) time earlier, when Tirhakah was only a youth of some twenty years of age, he had been summoned north from Nubia to Thebes by his brother Shebitku; it was during that trip that he had first visited the temple at Gemathen and noticed its deteriorated condition (IV 7-12, V 13-17).[64]

---

[61]The year-number "2" is lacking for col. 1 of Stela III, but as Macadam (*Kawa I*, p. 9, n. 1) pointed out, the year numbers are present on the stems of all the other Υ-scepters running beside the columns, and they increase by one for each successive year (thus indicating years 3-8 inclusive); therefore, the restoration of "2" in the broken portion of col. 1 is quite certain.

[62]This was also clearly recognized by Schmidt, "Taharqas" (above, n. 56), pp. 127-28, who argued that any possible coregency between the two brothers could not have been for much more than a year in length, and more likely was only for a few months. Kitchen, *Third Intermediate Period*, §§ 132-34, argued against the possibility of any overlap at all.

[63]Leclant and Yoyotte, "Notes d'histoire," pp. 20-21.

[64]It is this last historical datum which administers, in my opinion, the *coup de grâce* to the suggestions of Schmidt ("Taharqas," pp. 127-29, and especially n. 43) and Horn ("Sennacherib against Hezekiah," pp. 9-11, and especially n. 34) that Tirhakah was only

Years 2-5: Tirhakah makes generous donations to the temple (III 1-9).

Year 6 (c. 685): A year of unusually heavy rains, an exceptionally high Nile, and the "four goodly wonders" of Amon-Rē' (V 5-13)--this probably is also the year of the visit of the Queen Mother Abar (V 16-22), who had not seen her son since his original departure from Nubia "after an interval [*ḥnty*] of years." Finally, this year is also the year Tirhakah announces his decision to rebuild the Gematen temple, for which preparation he amasses an army as well as a large contingent of craftsmen (IV 13-27). Not surprisingly, the list in Stela III of the donations to the Gematen temple for this year is considerably shorter than for any of the other years 2-10 (cf. III 10).

Years 7-10: Both generous donations (III 11-22, VI 1-14) and lavish efforts at reconstruction (VI 14-21, VII 1-5) continue throughout these years.[65]

Year 10 (c. 681): A solemn consecration of the newly reconstructed temple takes place on New Year's Day of the civil calendar (VII 1).[66]

---

20 years of age in 690 B.C.E., the year of his coronation. As I have just discussed at some length, Kawa IV 11-12 is best understood as indicating that, already in the first year of his reign, Tirhakah *remembered* (*sḫ'.n.f*) the disrepair of the temple at Gematen. We are, on the one hand, given no indication that this was the year of his original journey north from Nubia (when he had first visited the Gematen temple); but, on the other hand, we are explicitly told that he was but a youth when he had first beheld that dilapidated structure (cf. the apt comments of Rainey, as quoted above in n. 60). Admittedly, the time interval between Tirhakah's original trip from Nubia and the first year of his reign is nowhere explicitly stated, but it would seem to have been at least several years in length, and very possibly a decade or more (cf. the "interval [*ḥnty*] of years" between that original journey from Nubia and the later visit of the queen mother when Tirhakah was on the throne [V 16-18]). Finally, as will be discussed below, if the death of Tirhakah's father Piye (Piankhy) is indeed to be dated on or before 713, as is probably the case, then Tirhakah would have been (at the bare minimum) at least 22 years of age in 690, and in all probability considerably older.

[65]Leclant and Yoyotte ("Notes d'histoire," p. 21) provided a useful analysis of the complementary nature of these three texts, pointing out how they all attest (explicitly or implicitly) the progress of the efforts at reconstruction.

[66]It is by no means certain that the pharaohs of the 25th Dynasty reckoned their regnal years to accord with the New Year's Day (I *'ḫt* 1) of the civil calendar; although such was the case for the 12th and the 26th Dynasties, it was demonstrably not the case for the 18th Dynasty (in which regnal years were reckoned from the exact date of each

For our immediate purposes, the result of this rather extended discussion of the Egyptian materials may be summarized as follows: Tirhakah's accession can be confidently dated to c. 690 B.C.E., well after Sennacherib's Palestinian campaign of 701; but, *contra* Albright and others, there is no evidence that he was only twenty years of age at the time of his coronation. Furthermore, Macadam's suggestion of a six year coregency between Shebitku and Tirhakah is, in the light of the critique of Leclant and Yoyotte, at best quite unlikely. On the contrary, Shebitku's death may be dated, with a reasonable degree of certitude, to c. 690, the year of Tirhakah's accession to the throne.[67]

Now, the question inevitably arises as to whether one can date the accession of Shebitku with any degree of precision, for if this date can be determined, one can then ascertain more exactly the possible age of Tirhakah at his own accession in c. 690. A survey of recent discussions on this issue indicates that, due to the paucity of firmly datable materials, chronological certainty concerning the accession of Shebitku still eludes us.[68] Nevertheless, some progress has been made: several

---

king's accession, regardless of the corresponding date on the civil calendar). For an extended discussion of these variant methods of dating regnal years, see Alan H. Gardiner, "Regnal Years and Civil Calendar in Pharaonic Egypt," *JEA* 31 (1945) 11-28. Schmidt ("Taharqas," p. 128) argued that the pharaohs of the 25th Dynasty (known for their love of ancient tradition) probably followed the former method (i.e. they reckoned their regnal years in accordance with the civil calendar). Cf. also the comments of Donald B. Redford, "Sais and the Kushite Invasions of the Eighth Century B.C." *JARCE* 22 (1985) 5-6.

[67]This would still leave room for Schmidt's brief coregency of a few months between the two brothers (see above, n. 62); but I suspect that positing even such a short coregency is not necessary (cf. my comments in n. 64 above which call into question Schmidt's suggestion that Tirhakah had not left Nubia until 690; also cf. Kitchen, *Third Intermediate Period*, § 132). In a recent monograph entitled *Ancient Egyptian Coregencies* (The Oriental Institute of Chicago: Studies in Ancient Oriental Civilization, No. 40 [Chicago: The Oriental Institute, 1977]), William H. Murnane came to basically the same conclusion (see pp. 190-93 of his study).

[68]Cf. the comments of Klaus Baer ("The Libyan and Nubian Kings of Egypt: Notes on the Chronology of Dynasties XXII to XXVI," *JNES* 32 [1973] 250, who noted that, inasmuch as the highest attested regnal date for Shebitku is only year 3, the conventional tendency among Egyptologists to give him most of the years not otherwise accounted for before the accession of Tirhakah is "a mere guess." Baer dated Shebitku's reign to 698-690, but cautioned that it may well have been shorter. Alan Gardiner (*Egypt of the Pharaohs* [Oxford: Clarendon Press, 1961], p. 450) suggested the date of 695 for the

recent studies of the historical issues attending the earlier pharaohs of the 25th Dynasty have led to an increasing measure of chronological precision concerning these Kushite kings. It is to a brief overview of some of these proposals that I now turn.

Anthony Spalinger, in an important article entitled "The Year 712 B.C. and its Implications for Egyptian History,"[69] argued convincingly for dating Shabako's conquest of Lower Egypt to that year. Following the revised chronology of the military campaigns of Sargon II by Hayim Tadmor,[70] he pointed out that, according to the Assyrian annals, in the year 713 (or, less likely, in early 712) a certain usurper Yamani of Ashdod contacted a *Pir'u* of Egypt to request assistance in his rebellion against Assyria.[71] Although the pharaoh is not named, and although it is probable that both Bocchoris of Sais as well as Osorkon (IV) Akheperre of Bubastis[72] were still on the throne in that year, Spalinger suggested that Yamani's pleas were probably directed

---

accession of Shebitku. However, as Baer pointed out, most Egyptologists have preferred an earlier date for his accession: e.g., Leclant and Yoyotte ("Notes d'histoire," p. 27) suggested the year 701 (*"au plus tôt"*); the same year was proposed by Spalinger ("Year 712," pp. 98-101) with a two year coregency with Shabako (701-699); finally, Kitchen in 1973 (*Third Intermediate Period*, §§ 126-27) expressed his preference for 702 for Shebitku's accession, and he rejected a coregency with Shabako (*ibid.*, § 137). Nevertheless, it should be noted that in 1982 Kitchen modified his position slightly, now allowing for the two year coregency with Shabako (to be dated 702-700; see Kitchen, "Further Thoughts of Egyptian Chronology in the Third Intermediate Period," *RdÉ* 34 [1982-83] 59-69, and especially 64-69, §§ 15-17, 20; but cf. his later comments in §§ 468-69, 527 of the 2nd ed. of his *Third Intermediate Period* [copyrighted, 1986]).

[69]Spalinger, "Year 712," *JARCE* 10 (1973) 95-101.

[70]Tadmor, "The Campaigns of Sargon II of Assur: A Chronological-Historical Study," *JCS* 12 (1958) 22-40, 77-100; cf. Tadmor, "Philistia Under Assyrian Rule," *BA* 29 (1966) 86-102.

[71]Spalinger, "Year 712," p. 97; cf. *ANET*, pp. 285-87. The usurper Yamani was not a Greek, as some suppose (e.g., Oppenheim in *ANET*); cf. the comments of Spalinger in "Year 712," p. 97, n. 14, and the references cited there.

[72]The reference to *Šilḫanni* king of *Muṣri* in a prism fragment of Sargon II datable to 716 B.C.E. is probably a reference to Osorkon IV, the last king of the 23rd Dynasty, as first recognized by F. W. von Bissing, and eventually endorsed by Albright (see his discussion in "Further Light on Synchronisms between Egypt and Asia in the Period 935-685 B.C." *BASOR* 141 [1956] 23-24); cf. also the restorations suggested by Tadmor ("Campaigns of Sargon II," pp. 77-78).

to Bocchoris inasmuch as Bubastis (unlike Sais) was following a distinctly conciliatory policy toward Assyria at the time.[73] At any rate, in the year 712 Yamani was forced to flee to Egypt (having received no Egyptian help, as far as we are aware); he eventually found himself (according to the Display Inscription) at the "border of Egypt which is (at) the border (or: territory) of Ethiopia," *ana itê Miṣri ša pât Meluḫḫa*.[74] Spalinger then concluded his analysis of the Assyrian data as follows:

> Yamani did not meet the Pir'u of Egypt whom he had contacted less than a year earlier. He simply went south, into Upper Egypt, and finally met the King of Kush. This monarch must have been Shabako (see part II of our study), and he seems to have been in no mood to incur the wrath of the Assyrian King. Yamani was sent back to Nineveh--extradited; not the normal Egyptian custom if we regard the affairs of Hadad the Edomite (I Kings 11.17ff.) and Jeroboam (I Kings 11.40) as typical, as well as the refugees of Judah who fled

---

[73]Spalinger, "Year 712," pp. 96-97. Concerning Bubastis: in the prism fragment mentioned in the previous note, we are told that *Šilḫanni* (Osorkon IV) sent a gift of "twelve large horses" to the Assyrian king; such action on the part of the Bubastite ruler would demonstrate some sort of friendly relationship between Bubastis and Assyria. The evidence concerning Sais is more indirect: it consists of an oracle (transmitted in Manetho, fragments 64 and 65, as well as in a Demotic papyrus of the first century B.C.E.) in which a lamb is said to have foretold the destruction of Egypt after the sixth year of Bocchoris (which turned out to be, not coincidentally, the year of his death). It predicted that the Assyrians would invade Egypt and that the local gods of Egypt would be removed to Nineveh. Spalinger then pointed out:

> "As the prophecy is revealed, it appears clear that Dynasty 24 is regarded as the last legitimate house of Egypt and that the ensuing foreign domination includes the Kushites as well as [the] Assyrians. For our purposes here, it is sufficient to note that Sais, according to the prophecy, is no friend to the Assyrians" (p. 96, n. 10).

In connection with this discussion, Spalinger also cited the reference in 2 Kgs 17:4 concerning the appeal of Hoshea of Israel to "So" king of Egypt, presumably for help against Assyria; he followed Goedicke ("The End of 'So, King of Egypt,'" *BASOR* 171 [1963] 64-66) in understanding "So" as originally a reference to the Delta city of Sais. (An extended discussion of this hypothesis, which I find quite attractive, will be found in the second Excursus following this chapter.) Spalinger saw this as further proof that Sais was following an active policy of opposition to Assyria.

[74]Spalinger, "Year 712," p. 97; the translation is his. Cf. his n. 17, where he pointed out his reasons for rejecting Oppenheim's translation (*ANET*, p. 286), "and he fled into the territory of Musru--which belongs (now) to Ethiopia."

to Egypt after the destruction of the Temple in 587 B.C., but then, Shabako was not Egyptian. His attitude was certainly not reflective of the Saite monarch's. Note that neither Sais nor Bubastis appear in the Assyrian annals for 712 B.C.; nor do we read anymore of a Pir'u of Egypt. The King of Kush makes his appearance and the situation changes dramatically.[75]

Spalinger's conclusions in Part II of his study can be summarized more briefly. Arguing from the firm date of 690 B.C.E. for Tirhakah's accession, he suggested taking seriously the Manethonian regnal total (as transmitted in Eusebius) of 12 years for Shebitku,[76] and he then posited a two year coregency with Shabako dating from 701 to 699.[77] Inasmuch as the highest attested regnal year for Shabako is 15, his accession could then be dated to c. 713, and, as it appears that his conquest of the Delta had already been completed by his second regnal year (according to the evidence from a stela from Horbeit in the Eastern Delta cited by Leclant and Yoyotte),[78] it is not surprising that that year would correspond with the year 712 B.C.E. as derived from the independent chronological evidence of the Assyrian annals. In other words, it is now possible to conclude (apart from the troublesome unknowns of Egyptian chronology) that Year 2 of Shabako, the first year of his domination of both Upper and Lower Egypt, almost certainly

---

[75]Spalinger, "Year 712," p. 97.

[76]Manetho, frag. 67. Africanus attests 14 years for Shebitku (frag. 66). As a general rule, the Manethonian regnal totals for the kings of the 25th Dynasty are demonstrably too low; cf. the helpful discussion in Kitchen, *Third Intermediate Period*, § 421.

[77]Spalinger, "Year 712," p. 98, and n. 25; cf. my comments above, n. 49. It should be pointed out that, *contra* Spalinger (p. 98), Shabako was Shebitku's uncle, not his brother. Concerning the question of the various relationships within the Nubian royal family, see Dows Dunham and M. F. Laming Macadam, "Names and Relationships of the Royal Family of Napata," *JEA* 35 (1949) 139-49; but note that the otherwise useful genealogical chart on p. 149 of the article also mistakenly depicts Shabako as a brother of Shebitku (contrast the correct notation found on p. 147, no. 68). The error in the chart may well have been the source of Spalinger's confusion. Genealogical charts correctly depicting the relationship between these two pharaohs may be found in Macadam, *Kawa I*, p. 131, and Kitchen, *Third Intermediate Period*, p. 478.

[78]Spalinger, "Year 712," p. 99, and n. 27. Kitchen, *Third Intermediate Period*, § 340, adduced further evidence for dating his reconquest of Egypt by the second year of his reign.

corresponds with 712 B.C.E. Less certain, to be sure, are the dating of Shebitku's accession to 701 and the death of Shabako to 699 inasmuch as they depend on data from Manetho; nevertheless, even these latter two dates are unlikely to be more than a few years in error.[79]

The conclusions of Spalinger were cited with approval by both Klaus Baer[80] and K. A. Kitchen.[81] I have already noted Baer's cautions concerning the dating of the early Kushite pharaohs;[82] it is now appropriate to cite the important discussions of Kitchen in some detail. In his massive study of this period of Egyptian history published at about the same time as Spalinger's article,[83] Kitchen reconstructed the events of 716-712 B.C.E. in a manner analogous to that of Spalinger: *viz.*, the ruler of "Egypt *and Nubia*" in 712 could not have been either Osorkon IV nor Bakenranef (= Bocchoris of Manetho), neither of whom ruled any further south than Memphis; rather he must have been a pharaoh of the 25th (Nubian) Dynasty.[84] But Osorkon IV (= Shilḫanni of the Sargon inscription) was unquestionably the pharaoh who had dealt with the Assyrians in 716, only four years previously.

---

[79]Spalinger, "Year 712," pp. 99-100.

[80]Baer, "Libyan and Nubian Kings," *JNES* 32 (1973) § 5, p. 7; Baer was familiar with an earlier version of Spalinger's work.

[81]Kitchen, "Further Thoughts," *RdÉ* 34 (1982-83) § 17, p. 66. Also cf. the recent comments of Donald B. Redford, "Sais and the Kushite Invasions" (see above, n. 66), pp. 6-7.

[82]See above, n. 68.

[83]Kitchen, *Third Intermediate Period*, copyright date given on p. iv as 1973; however, according to the reviewer's note accompanying E. P. Uphill's review of Kitchen's book (*JEA* 61 [1975] 277), the date should have read 1972. At any rate, Spalinger was able to examine Kitchen's work soon after the completion of his own paper; see the postscript which follows his "Year 712" article (p. 100), where he noted his general agreement with Kitchen concerning the events of 712 B.C.E. A second edition of Kitchen's *Third Intermediate Period*, unchanged except for a lengthy supplement incorporating a number of additions and corrections keyed to the original text, was published in 1986.

[84]Kitchen, *Third Intermediate Period*, § 115; as he noted, the pharaoh in question could only have been Piye (Piankhy) or Shabako, and inasmuch as Piye ruled only briefly in the Delta, it is far more likely that Shabako was the ruler who returned the hapless Yamani to the Assyrians; cf. also Kitchen's comments in § 341, and n. 778.

Therefore, Shabako's conquest of Lower Egypt, which must have already taken place on or before his second regnal year (as attested by a wall-inscription at Memphis commemorating the burial of an Apis-bull),[85] is to be dated to within the four year span of 716-712. Again, inasmuch as Shabako's highest known regnal figure is 15, his reign must have extended at least to 702/698 B.C.E.[86]

It is at this point that Kitchen proposed an intriguing reconstruction of the events of 701 B.C.E. from the Egyptian point of view. He noted that Sennacherib's annals cited the presence of hostile Egyptian and Nubian forces in Palestine in that year, which was a marked departure from the neutral policies of the Egyptian pharaohs of the recent past. It is virtually certain that these forces were sent either by Shabako or by his successor Shebitku (or possibly by both, if a coregency between the two be posited). But, as Kitchen went on to argue:

New policies, in a basic situation virtually unchanged, are commonly the mark of new men. Therefore, the drastic change of policy in Egypt at this time may well imply the death of Shabako (who had been neutral) and the accession of a new king, Shebitku, who favoured direct intervention in Palestine. On *this* basis, Shebitku's accession would fall not later than early in 701 B.C., possibly in the latter part of 702 B.C., if one allows for prior parleys between the

---

[85]*Ibid.*, § 114, and especially n. 247.

[86]*Ibid.*, § 125. Indeed, he argued that Shabako's death must have taken place within these dates. However, his reasoning for this last assertion seems imprecise: although he was certainly correct in concluding that the evidence from the British Museum Statue No. 24429 (which attests Shabako's year 15) compels us to extend his reign to 702/698, it is not clear why his reign cannot conceivably be extended even further (e.g., for as much as five or more years). Admittedly, there currently exists no documentation for any such additional years, but that is precisely the problem (as I shall discuss below) which also exists with Shabako's successor Shebitku (to whom Kitchen allotted 12 regnal years, although his highest attested regnal year is only year 3). In other words, I fail to see how Kitchen (who is generally both very meticulous with his documentation as well as lucid in his reasoning) felt he could conclude his § 125 with such a close dating of Shabako's death (*viz.*, within the years 702-699). (It should be noted that my query also affects his statement in § 126 [p. 154] asserting that Shebitku must have reigned "*not less than 8 years*" [emphasis his]; as far as the extant data indicate, he need only have reigned for 3 years.)

new king and the emissaries of the anti-Assyrian Palestinians who were seeking his help.[87]

Citing the evidence from Kawa Stelae IV and V which indicated that Tirhakah was a youth of 20 when summoned north from Nubia with an army, Kitchen then proposed the following sequence of events:

1. Ekron and other petty states of Palestine reject Assyrian rule and prepare against attack.
2. In Egypt, Shabako dies and Shebitku is crowned pharaoh.
3. Ekron and her allies appeal for help from the new young pharaoh.
4. Shebitku decides on an active role in Palestinian affairs (a marked change of policy from that of his immediate predecessor); he prepares his own military forces.
5. It is at this time that Shebitku summons his brothers (including Tirhakah, "a youth of twenty years" according to Kawa V 17) from Nubia; they journey north along with an army and meet Shebitku in Thebes, and together proceed to Lower Egypt.
6. Egyptian and Nubian forces join those of the rebel Palestinian states; in 701 B.C.E., Sennacherib claims to defeat them at Eltekeh.[88] As will be readily apparent, a reconstruction such as this permits the inclusion of prince Tirhakah on the field of battle at Eltekeh, in line with 2 Kgs 19:9 and Isa 37:9 (where his designation as *melek Kûš* would have to be seen as proleptic).[89] In support of this proposal, Kitchen argued that a 20 or 21 year old Tirhakah may well have acted as the titular head of the expedition (as the representative of his brother the reigning pharaoh), thus "nominally in command but supplied

---

[87]*Ibid.*, § 126, p. 155; emphasis his. In a later article (see my discussion above, n. 68), he did allow for a two year coregency between Shabako and Shebitku.

[88]*Ibid.*, § 127; events 2-6 would then be dated to the years 702-701. Essentially the same reconstruction (albeit presented in more picturesque language) may be found in Kitchen's "Late-Egyptian Chronology and the Hebrew Monarchy: Critical Studies in Old Testament Mythology, I," *JANES* 5 (1973) [The Gaster Festschrift], pp. 225-31.

[89]Kitchen, *Third Intermediate Period*, § 129 (also cf. his 2nd ed., § 467).

with generals to do the real tactical planning."[90] Furthermore, it was not unusual for royal princes to accompany Egyptian armies on Syro-Palestinian campaigns.[91]

Such a reconstruction of the events of 701 B.C.E. does seem attractive, and several scholars have embraced it with enthusiasm.[92] Certainly, it makes sense out of what seems to be an odd biblical anachronism, especially inasmuch as it is part of a narrative which, as Albright repeatedly emphasized, is otherwise filled with accurate historical details. Secondly, it accords well with an emerging consensus (at least among Egyptologists) concerning the chronology of the early Kushite pharaohs, and it presents a useful synchronism by which to date more accurately the accession of Shebitku. Thirdly, it eliminates once and for all any need to posit a second Palestinian campaign of Sennacherib in order to account for the biblical texts. Nevertheless, despite these attractive features, I hesitate to endorse this reconstruction. My caveats, which are spelled out in some detail below, cluster around the following three areas of concern: 1) the uncertainties which still attend the dating of the accession of Shebitku; 2) the question of the extent of Tirhakah's military activity in Palestine after 690 B.C.E. (when he was unquestionably *melek Kûš*); and 3) the nagging question of the nature and purposes of the biblical narratives themselves. Any reconstruction which attempts to link the biblical references to Tirhakah

---

[90]Kitchen, *Third Intermediate Period*, § 127, p. 158. Frank J. Yurco ("Sennacherib's Third Campaign and the Coregency of Shabaka and Shebitku," *Serapis* 6 [1980] 223 and n. 21) suggested that Tirhakah may well have been a military commander (cf. Kawa Stela V 13, which Yurco translated, "Indeed, it was that I might be with him that I came from Nubia in the midst of the king's brothers whom his majesty had marshalled [*ts.n*] therefrom"). Yurco pointed out that Egyptian princes commonly received military training at quite a young age.

[91]Kitchen, *Third Intermediate Period*, § 127, and especially n. 308.

[92]Most notably, Rainey, "Taharqa and Syntax," *Tel Aviv* 3 (1976) 38-41; but also cf. Yurco, "Sennacherib's Third Campaign," pp. 221-40, where his reconstruction of the events of 701 accorded quite closely with that of Kitchen (two minor exceptions: he denied Tirhakah's presence at the battle of Eltekeh, preferring to see him leading a relief unit to rescue Hezekiah in Jerusalem; secondly, he dated Shebitku's accession to 701, and gave him a three year coregency with Shabako in line with the Manethonian data). Finally, Murnane, *Ancient Egyptian Coregencies* (see above, n. 67), pp. 189-90, although not expressly following Kitchen's reconstruction, nonetheless basically concurred with it.

with the events of 701 must, of necessity, reckon with these three issues.

1. Concerning the question of the dating of Shebitku's accession: as I have already noted, and as Kitchen himself conceded, the highest regnal figure extant for Shebitku is only year 3 (from the Nile-level Text No. 33 at Karnak).[93] However, as his reign must have extended at least to 690, the date of the accession of Tirhakah, one must be prepared to grant him at least 11 regnal years (Kitchen opted for 12) in order to date his accession on or before 701.[94] I submit that the complete absence of any documentation for nearly a decade of rule should be disquieting, despite Kitchen's protestations to the contrary.[95] Admittedly, this is an argument from silence, but in the light of the relatively full documentation for most of Shabako's regnal years,[96] and the very full documentation for the early years of Tirhakah,[97] I think the absence of such documentation for Shebitku cannot be dismissed as

---

[93]Kitchen, *Third Intermediate Period*, § 126; for the publications of the Nile-level texts, see above, n. 57. Although it is true that Shebitku did leave his architectural mark on Egypt (see Kitchen, *ibid.*, § 347, and references cited there), this fact in no way necessitates a reign for him of a decade or more (*contra* Kitchen, *ibid.*, § 126, p. 156). Furthermore, it should be pointed out that Kitchen's discussion of the Apis-bull evidence (in *ibid.*, § 126, pp. 156-57) proves absolutely nothing as to the length of *Shebitku's* reign: although it demonstrates quite convincingly that some 16 years may well have separated Shabako's 14th year from Tirhakah's 4th year, an interval which indeed corroborates well with the other evidence already adduced for the dating of the accession of *Shabako*, the Apis evidence does not in any way clarify the issue of the dating of the accession of *Shebitku*.

[94]Kitchen preferred the year 702; cf. my above discussion, n. 68.

[95]Kitchen, *Third Intermediate Period*, § 126; see my comments in n. 93.

[96]A cursory examination of Kitchen's useful overview of Shabako's reign (as found in *ibid.*, §§ 340-44) indicates that dated inscriptions are extant for the following regnal years of Shabako: year 2 (*bis*), year 3, year 4 (?), year 6, year 12, year 14 (?), and the aforementioned year 15; plus Nile-level Text No. 32, whose regnal year is now lost. In the 2nd ed. of his *Third Intermediate Period* (§ 527), Kitchen also cites a legal document dated to Shabako's 10th year.

[97]See, conveniently, Spalinger's listing in "Foreign Policy," *CdÉ* 53 (1978) 44-47, where he cited dated inscriptions for every regnal year of Tirhakah between years 2-10, plus the years 13, 14, 16, 19, 20, 24, and 26. For more detailed bibliography concerning the inscriptions attesting Tirhakah's regnal years 2-5, see nn. 55-57 above.

insignificant. Furthermore, if Spalinger's suggested equation of Shabako's year 2 with the date of 712 be accepted, as I think it should,[98] then Shabako's death cannot be dated before the year 699 (Spalinger's date), and may well have occurred several years later.[99] Thus, at the bare minimum, one must posit a 2 year coregency between Shabako and Shebitku to permit the latter's accession by the year 701.[100] As is becoming evident, on the one hand the chronological fit for Shabako's reign is extremely tight, whereas on the other hand Shebitku's length of reign seems embarrassingly broad. Therefore, I prefer the approach of Klaus Baer[101] who aptly characterized the general tendency among Egyptologists to give most (or, in Kitchen's case, all) of the undocumented years to Shebitku as "a mere guess." It will be recalled that he preferred dating Shebitku's accession to 698, and implied that it may well have been even later. To conclude: until more epigraphic data come to light concerning the latter years of Shabako and/or Shebitku, it must be conceded that we cannot preclude altogether the possibility that Shebitku came to the throne on or before the fateful year 701 B.C.E., but the extant data certainly cast considerable doubt upon the likelihood of such a high date for his accession.[102]

---

[98]Again it should be recalled that his suggested synchronism evades completely the unknowns of Egyptian chronology, being dependent rather on the Assyrian chronology (which for this period is accurate to within a year); cf. Baer (above, n. 80), and, to a lesser degree, Kitchen himself (in his 1982 article; see above, n. 81). In addition, Yurco ("Sennacherib's Third Campaign" [cf. above, nn. 90, 92], p. 221), whose suggested reconstruction of the events of 701 generally accorded with that of Kitchen, also acknowledged the attractiveness of Spalinger's synchronism; indeed it compelled Yurco to extend his own dating of Shabako's death to 699/98, thus necessitating (in his opinion) a three year coregency with Shebitku (*ibid.*, pp. 228-29).

[99]Cf. above, n. 86.

[100]So, even Kitchen in his 1982 article (see above, n. 68), except that he continued to date Shebitku's accession to the year 702. As I have just noted (above, n. 98), Yurco preferred a three year coregency between the two kings, to be dated 701-698.

[101]Baer, "Libyan and Nubian Kings," *JNES* 32 (1973) § 35e, p. 25; cf. above, n. 68.

[102]Yurco, "Sennacherib's Third Campaign," pp. 237-40, contains further evidence pointing to a significant role for Shabako after the year 701. For example, the two seal impressions with Shabako's cartouche which were discovered in the ruins of Sennacherib's palace at Nineveh (for references, see Yurco, *ibid.*, pp. 237-38, and nn. 132-35), although commonly connected with the events of 712 in relation to the affair of Yamani,

2. Concerning Tirhakah's military activity in Palestine after 690: again it will be necessary to draw upon the relevant work of Anthony Spalinger. In his 1978 article entitled "The Foreign Policy of Egypt Preceding the Assyrian Conquest,"[103] Spalinger examined in some detail the evidence concerning Tirhakah's diplomatic and military activity in Palestine during the early part of his reign. For our purposes only his conclusions need be summarized. Although the relevant inscriptional data are somewhat ambiguous, they do tend to suggest that (at least between Tirhakah's accession in 690 and the victorious Palestinian campaign of Esarhaddon in 679) Tirhakah probably was able to exert considerable control over much of Palestine. In other words, the later Greek traditions of "Tirhakah the Conqueror" are probably more accurate than the usual impression of a relatively impotent pharaoh (at least in foreign affairs) characteristic of recent scholarship.[104] It may well be, as Spalinger suggested, that by the year 679 Tirhakah's decade of dominance in the Levant was coming to an end,[105] but what remains significant for us is the realization that at least from 690 until (and beyond) the death of Sennacherib in 681, the power to be reckoned with (from the Judahite point of view) was

---

may well have dated to the reign of Sennacherib (accession year, c. 704), inasmuch as Nineveh was the capital of Sennacherib, but not that of Sargon II. If this be the case, then the seal impressions probably have to be dated after the events of 701 (presuming that they come from diplomatic documents, as is likely), for prior to that date, Hezekiah and other Palestinian states were in full revolt against Assyria, and enjoying the support of Egypt. Inasmuch as the events of 701 may best be considered to have resulted in a stalemate (at least from the Egyptian point of view), Shabako may well have sought a treaty of peace with Sennacherib, especially one which permitted the Egyptians access to the trade which passed through the coastal cities of Philistia. Sennacherib, perennially preoccupied with the problem of Assyria's other frontiers (not least, Babylon), was probably only too willing to agree. At any rate, the fact that Esarhaddon later had to resort to severe military measures to curtail such Egyptian trade with Philistia indicates that his policy was, in all probability, considerably more restrictive than that of his father Sennacherib (on this last point Yurco was following a proposal found in Spalinger, "Foreign Policy" [see next note], pp. 41-43).

[103]Spalinger, "Foreign Policy," *CdÉ* 53 (1978) 22-47.

[104]*Ibid.*, p. 22; on the Greek traditions, cf. Godifroy Goossens ("Taharqa le conquérant," *CdÉ* 22 [1947] 239-44), who, however, largely discounted their historicity.

[105]Spalinger, "Foreign Policy," pp. 42-43.

Egyptian, not Assyrian, i.e. Pharaoh Tirhakah from Kush, not Sennacherib from Nineveh.[106] Consequently, I would urge that the problematic biblical reference to Tirhakah *melek Kûš* probably reflects the Palestinian political reality of the 680s (when the narrative in question may well have been first formulated)[107] more than it does some par-

---

[106]Yurco ("Sennacherib's Third Campaign," pp. 238-40, and especially nn. 142, 145-46) preferred describing the situation in Palestine between Egypt and Assyria after 701 as a neutral standoff between the two major powers. More specifically, he suggested that Spalinger's emphasis on Tirhakah's military activity in Palestine required qualification: for Hezekiah, after all, did pay up his tribute, and Manasseh, who smoothly succeeded his father Hezekiah as king, was manifestly pro-Assyrian. Although, admittedly, one ought not to over-emphasize Tirhakah's domination of the Levant *vis-à-vis* the Assyrians (especially in the light of the paucity and the ambiguity of the available evidence); nevertheless I would point out the following: first, Hezekiah's tribute, though indeed heavy, represents a considerably less severe punishment (especially for one of the leaders of the revolt) than, e.g., the deportation of the king of Ashkelon or the death (and subsequent exposure) of the leaders of Ekron. This relatively humane treatment of Hezekiah does not, of course, represent any magnanimity on the part of the Assyrian king; rather it indicates obliquely the less than successful outcome of his campaign in Palestine. Along with a number of other scholars, I suspect that Sennacherib's annals conclude with a description of Hezekiah's tribute, not so much for reasons of chronology, but rather as an attempt to divert attention from his inability to capture either Hezekiah or the city of Jerusalem. Secondly, although Manasseh's pro-Assyrian policies are indeed well known, it must be emphasized that they need not characterize the entirety of his long reign, for we simply do not know about the early years of his reign. If the Dtr synchronisms dating Hezekiah's accession to before the fall of Samaria are accepted as accurate (as, e.g., argued by Hayim Tadmor; cf. below, nn. 124, 127), then Manasseh's accession may well have dated to around 697, the year of the death of his father. It is entirely possible that Manasseh may have been able to enjoy nearly two decades of quasi-independent rule, largely free of Assyrian (and Egyptian) pressure; although certainly by the time of Esarhaddon's extensive military activity against Egypt in the 670s, any such freedom came to an end. At any rate, although dogmatism is of course to be avoided, I see no reason to deny a strong role for Tirhakah in Palestine at least throughout the decade of the 680s.

[107]I.e. in a form somewhat analogous to that of the present text, with the assassination of Sennacherib providing the climax of the story. Undoubtedly, earlier versions of the story were told and retold throughout the first two decades of the seventh century, as the Judahites relished recounting their amazing (albeit very costly) deliverance from what must have seemed to be certain destruction at the hands of the Assyrian king. However, as will be discussed below, the present form of the narrative undoubtedly postdates Sennacherib's assassination by several decades or more; as Childs pointed out, Account B[1] appears to be a unified narrative of Dtr provenance, and Account B[2] contains exilic touches reminiscent of Deutero-Isaiah.

ticular petty detail about an Egyptian response to a campaign of Sennacherib back in 701. Although this last point will need to be developed
further in the next section, it is appropriate here to emphasize the brute
fact that the military reputation of Tirhakah *as Pharaoh* must have been
all too well known to the biblical narrator(s) of 2 Kgs 18-19.

      3. Concerning the nature and purposes of the biblical narra-
tives themselves: I have already discussed to some extent the careful
source-critical work of Brevard Childs.[108] As will be recalled, Childs
suggested the following delineation of the Sennacherib material found
in 2 Kgs 18-19: an Account A (2 Kgs 18:13-16), essentially annalistic
in origin; an Account B[1] (18:17-19:9a, 36-37), representing a unified
narrative of Dtr provenance and largely based upon generally accurate
tradition; and an Account B[2] (19:9b-35), more heterogeneous, based
upon a legendary source, and heavily reflecting Dtr theology. Finally,
the caveat of Childs concerning the use of the historical data of these
narratives (especially those recounted in Account B[2]) should also be
recalled: recognition of the tendentious nature of much of the material
militates strongly against any simple-minded historical reading of the
text.[109] But this caveat may well be extended to the material found
in Account B[1] (such as the reference to Tirhakah); as Childs pointed
out:

> The Dtr. redactor of II Kings 19 not only stood within a circle of
> tradition, but he made creative use of them to illustrate his own
> theology of history. Once again the author fused older and newer
> elements into a whole. The B[1] account of the Assyrian threat is
> brought to a close by the prophecy of retreat and ultimate destruction
> of the enemy. The fact that the death of Sennacherib occurred some
> twenty years after his return is lost in his scheme. The impression of
> the author's being at a considerable distance from the historical events
> of Sennacherib's death in 681 is not removed even bythose who place
> much historical weight on the mention of Tirhakah.[110]

He then concluded his discussion of Account B[1] as follows:

---

[108]See above, pp. 77-79.

[109]Childs, *Isaiah and the Assyrian Crisis* (see above, n. 10), pp. 69-103.

[110]*Ibid.*, p. 93.

To summarize: The analysis of the B[1] account has pointed out the highly complex nature of the traditions which make up the account. On the one hand, the study has shown a large layer of the material which reflects ancient tradition with a genuinely historical setting. On the other hand, we have seen also that newer elements have entered into the account and have been formed into a unified story which bears the stamp of the Dtr. author.[111]

I have chosen to quote Childs' conclusions at some length in order to lend plausibility to two general proposals of my own, both of which attempt to specify what can and what cannot be deduced from the biblical narratives themselves:

A. As has already been mentioned, I strongly suspect that the Tirhakah reference in 2 Kgs 19:9 (as well as its parallel in Isaiah) represents a reflection on the part of the Judahite tradition of Tirhakah's general domination of the Palestinian coastline in the decade of the 680s over against a Sennacherib who was either too weak, or (as is more likely) too preoccupied to reassert Assyrian claims of suzerainty. Of course, this was the same infamous Sennacherib who had nearly triumphed over King Hezekiah, and nearly captured the Judahite capital city of Jerusalem, some 20 years previously, but (and this is where both Accounts B[1] and B[2] become hazy) something clearly happened: whether it be a devastating plague (so B[2]),[112] or the advance of the Egyptians (so B[1]),[113] or conceivably some combination of the two--at

---

[111]*Ibid.*

[112]Cf. 2 Kgs 19:35; the total of 185,000 slain Assyrians, an impossibly high figure, may have originally been 5180 (cf. Horn, "Sennacherib against Hezekiah" [see above, n. 3], pp. 27-28). As is often pointed out in this context, Herodotus (II, 141) also recounted a story about the sudden devastation of Sennacherib's army: one night as the Assyrians were encamped near the Egyptian frontier, a multitude of field mice swarmed over the camp, devouring their quivers, bows, and the handles of their shields, thus forcing them to flee the next day unarmed, with many casualties. Although this story in Herodotus diverges in many details from the biblical tradition (e.g., the location of the battle, the identity of Sennacherib's opponents, the cause of the Assyrian debacle), the interesting correlation between the mice (known as notorious bearers of plague, cf. 1 Sam 6:3-5) and the biblical account of a sudden devastation from Yahweh (again, a plague?) may indeed be more than coincidental.

[113]Again, linking 2 Kgs 19:9a with vv 36-37. It is probably not accidental that the message in Account B[2] which parallels the Rabshakeh's speech in B[1] omits all mention

any rate, Yahweh intervened, with the result that both Hezekiah and Jerusalem were spared. And, as far as the Dtr redactor was concerned, Sennacherib's untimely death at the hands of his own sons could be considered as much a part of Yahweh's timely intervention as any particular advance (or general domination) of an Egyptian army under a Kushite king a decade or so earlier. In short: what is clear is that we cannot read Account B[1] as straight history; rather we must read it as an account (almost apologetic in nature) of the vindication of Yahweh over against the taunts of the Assyrian Rabshakeh, whose speech, after all, has been quoted at length in the earlier part of the narrative.[114] In essence, the Rabshakeh had scornfully challenged the leaders of Judah concerning two topics: where is Yahweh, whose high places have been removed by Hezekiah?[115] and secondly, where is Egypt, that "bruised staff of a reed," upon whom the Judahites have trusted?[116] The conclusion of Account B[1] implicitly gives the answer to *both* of these questions: just as it was in the temple of his god Nisroch where Sennacherib had been scandalously murdered (implicitly by Yahweh?), likewise it was the rumor of the advance of the *Egyptians* which had originally led to Sennacherib's retreat back to Nineveh. It was of little concern to the Dtr narrator that Tirhakah's domination of Palestine at the expense of Sennacherib probably had not taken place until a decade or so after the 701 invasion, no more than it concerned him that Sennacherib's death took place some two decades after the portentous events of the year 701. Consequently, I submit that it is as foolhardy

---

of Egypt, for the narrator of B[2] wants to give all the credit for the deliverance of Jerusalem directly to Yahweh.

[114] 2 Kgs 18:19-25 as well as vv 28-35. It is in the earlier speech that the Rabshakeh twice mentions the futility of trusting in Egypt (vv 21, 24).

[115] 2 Kgs 18:22; as Childs (*Isaiah and the Assyrian Crisis*, p. 82) pointed out, the strange combination found in the Rabshakeh's argument of an intimate awareness of Hezekiah's cultic reform along with a blatantly pagan point of view indicates the presence of genuine historical tradition.

[116] 2 Kgs 18:21; on the worthlessness of Egypt as an ally, cf. Isa 30:2-5, 7. The Rabshakeh's further argument concerning the futility of trusting in Egyptian horses and chariotry (2 Kgs 18:24) is also paralleled in Isa 31:1-3. On the high value generally placed upon horses from Egypt, see Albright, "Further Light," *BASOR* 141 (1956) 24-25, and the references cited there.

(not to mention foreign to the intent of the text itself) to base the dating of the accession of some particular Egyptian pharaoh (such as Shebitku) upon this text as it would be to posit some sort of second invasion of Sennacherib from the same text. Tirhakah--it is just barely conceivable--may have indeed been the one who had led an Egyptian advance into Palestine in the summer or fall of the year 701 B.C.E.: the historical data adduced above have not totally forestalled this possibility (although they have, in my opinion, made it exceedingly remote). But to read the biblical text here as dispassionate history rather than as a parenetic presentation of Yahweh's activity does a disservice both to the Bible itself as well as to the various scholarly efforts at historical reconstruction by those who are more sensitive to such issues.[117]

B. Finally, it will be appropriate before drawing this discussion of the Sennacherib narratives to a close to direct some attention to the larger issue of the overall context in which these narratives are found. It is, therefore, to a brief examination of this issue (as well as to some ideas of my own which are prompted by such a discussion) that I now turn.

I have already noted the important conclusion of H. H. Rowley[118] that proponents of the two-campaign hypothesis must, of chronological necessity, deny the validity of the Dtr synchronisms at the beginning of 2 Kgs 18 which firmly link the beginning of Hezekiah's reign to the fall of Samaria. Once again, the adherents of such a view end up implicating the Dtr editor(s) of a more fundamental anachronism than any such attending the brief reference to Tirhakah *melek Kûš*. Whether the synchronisms found at the beginning of 2 Kgs 18 are as accurate (to the exact year) as Rowley might have thought is not my

---

[117]E.g., Kitchen's caustic dismissal (*Third Intermediate Period*, § 128, n. 311) of the approach of Childs as well as his later sharp condemnation ("Further Thoughts," *RdÉ* 34 [1982-83] 65, nn. 30, 33) of Spalinger's work illustrate well my point: for Kitchen's own tendency to read the biblical texts basically as a collection of historical facts blinds him not only to their disparate literary character (an understanding of which is crucial for correctly appropriating the "facts" contained therein), but also to a sympathetic appreciation of the work of other scholars not so insensitive to literary matters (cf. also the polemical tone found in his supplement to the 2nd ed. of his *Third Intermediate Period*, §§ 467-68). For a recent, far more sensitive reading of the text in its final form, see Danna Nolan Fewell, "Sennacherib's Defeat: Words at War in 2 Kings 18.13-19.37," *JSOT* 34 (1986) 79-90.

[118]See above, pp. 83-84, and especially n. 35.

concern for the moment; rather, my desire is to focus upon the larger context of these chapters (thus, in essence, to pursue Rowley's mode of inquiry even further) in order to ascertain what pertinent implications may be gained from a closer look at the Dtr editing of these materials. P. R. Ackroyd, in a useful study entitled "An Interpretation of the Babylonian Exile: A Study of 2 Kings 20, Isaiah 38-39,"[119] has, in my opinion, advanced this discussion significantly; the following observations represent my appropriation of some conclusions of his which are particularly relevant to the present inquiry:

(1) The study of Childs (much of which has already been summarized above), though at many points valuable, nonetheless suffers some disadvantage in failing to include an analysis of the two narratives found in 2 Kgs 20 (viz., Hezekiah's illness, and the visit of the Babylonian ambassadors), texts closely linked chronologically (at least in the opinion of the redactor) to the previously recounted narratives concerning Sennacherib's invasion and withdrawal.[120]

(2) This chronological link, though admittedly fraught with vexing problems, should be examined more closely. At least this much is clear: in the opinion of the Dtr narrator, Hezekiah's illness lay some 15 years before the end of his reign (20:6). Less clear is the Dtr dating of the arrival of the Babylonian envoys (20:12-19), although v 12 seems to imply a close chronological link between the two incidents.[121]

(3) Although in the Dtr narrative sequences the invasion of Sennacherib precedes the accounts of Hezekiah's illness and the arrival of the Babylonian ambassadors, in actual historical sequence the reverse is far more likely to have been the case: the sending of Merodach-baladan's envoys probably coincided with the anti-

---

[119]Ackroyd, "Babylonian Exile," *SJT* 27 (1974) 329-52.

[120]*Ibid.*, pp. 329-31. The historical résumé of the reign of Hezekiah which is preserved virtually entire in both 2 Kgs 18-20 and Isa 36-39 is also presupposed in the abbreviated version found in 2 Chr 32:1-31 (cf. especially v 31 which gives the Chronicler's interpretation of the visit of the Babylonian envoys, an interpretation which only makes sense if the reader is already familiar with the Dtr account).

[121]*Ibid.*, pp. 330-31.

Assyrian activity of Hezekiah which prompted Sennacherib's invasion in the first place.[122]

(4) Ackroyd's major thesis in the article, although somewhat tangential to the present inquiry, is nevertheless worthy of note: he argued quite persuasively that the narrative concerning the Babylonian ambassadors is intended by the Dtr narrator to foreshadow the Babylonian exile, both prophetically and legally.[123]

For our purposes, Ackroyd's contributions are several. First, he has clarified the overall direction of the Dtr narratives of 2 Kgs 18-20: despite appearances to the contrary (the parade example being the fall of Samaria), not Assyrian exile but Babylonian exile is to be the final fate of Judah. The (non-chronological) arrangement of the various

---

[122]*Ibid.*, pp. 331-32, where he cited the pertinent study of J. A. Brinkman, "Sennacherib's Babylonian Problem: An Interpretation," *JCS* 25 (1973) 89-95, and especially p. 91 and n. 10. See below, n. 128, for further details.

[123]Ackroyd, "Babylonian Exile," pp. 332-43. As is evident in the text, Isaiah *prophetically* declares the inevitability of the Babylonian exile in response to Hezekiah's boast that he showed the emissaries everything in his palace; however, Ackroyd also suggested the intriguing possibility that (at least in the eyes of the Dtr narrator) the very act of viewing all this royal property on the part of the Babylonians may have indicated a *legal* transfer of the property to them as well. He followed a proposal first made by David Daube to the effect that a number of biblical texts seem to presuppose the following legal custom: in the case of the sale of something unable to be physically handed over to the new owner (e.g., a house or land), a formal viewing of the property would be scheduled, at which time the exchange is deemed to have taken place. Daube noted that such a viewing must be accompanied by the intention of the owner to hand over the property in question. Ackroyd then went on to suggest that in the Hezekiah narrative as found in 2 Kgs 20:

"The king shows the ambassadors from Babylon everything in palace and kingdom; the prophetic judgment explicates this by saying that everything in effect now belongs to Babylon. It is true that there is absent from this the feature of 'owner's intention to sell' noted by Daube, but here we may legitimately trace the further interpretation of the analogy. It is in fact God who had decreed the handing over of the land--it is his, after all--and Hezekiah has become his unwitting agent in bringing about the loss of the land. By letting these ambassadors see everything, Hezekiah has handed over the possession of everything in Judah to the enemy and has anticipated the exile. Though the disaster itself belongs to the future--the time is coming--the essential legal take-over has already ensured that exile will take place" (p. 341).

Hezekiah narratives contributes strikingly to this impression (miraculous success against the armies of Assyria, triumph over a life-threatening illness, but shortsighted pride in the presence of the Babylonian representatives). Secondly, inasmuch as the chronological links which are found in these chapters should be seen as interpretative rather than strictly factual, this phenomenon increases our suspicion that the numbers themselves (especially the "14th year" in 18:13, although possibly also the "15 years" of 20:6) may be secondary as well.[124] Finally, Ackroyd has demonstrated convincingly the subtle artistry of the Dtr narrator(s), lending plausibility to future efforts at recovering programmatic, even schematic structures which elsewhere may underlie the present Dtr text. One such possibility will be presented in the next chapter.

For these and other reasons (some of which will be spelled out in the next chapter), I have for some time suspected that the synchronism in 2 Kgs 18:13, the one which has so influenced the chronologies of both Thiele and Albright,[125] is editorial in origin, hence valueless. Unhappily, the present state of knowledge concerning the historical situation obtaining at the end of the eighth century in the Levant still forbids dogmatism on this point, but at least this much can be said: it is precarious to cite 2 Kgs 18:13 as a firm external synchronism by which the accession of Hezekiah may be dated. *Contra*

---

[124]It should be noted that this specific point was not made by Ackroyd; however, a number of other scholars have not hesitated to query the accuracy of the synchronism found in 18:13. As I have already pointed out (see above, n. 33), both Rowley and Aharoni independently suggested that the number 14 was probably a corruption of an original 24. Tadmor, who also doubted the accuracy of the synchronism in 18:13, followed a different approach: he suggested that the chronological heading in 18:13 had originally introduced the stories about Hezekiah's illness and the subsequent visit of the Babylonian ambassadors (20:1-19; cf. especially v 6 where the promised 15 additional years would have yielded the expected regnal total for Hezekiah of 29 years as recorded in 18:2). Later, it was placed in its present position by the Dtr redactor, who thus connected all the prophetic stories about Isaiah and Hezekiah to the fateful year of Sennacherib's campaign and the miraculous deliverance of Jerusalem. Hence, although the number 14 may well have been accurate in its original position, it did not remain such in its present location (for further details concerning this thesis, which I consider quite attractive, see below, n. 127).

[125]E. R. Thiele, "The Chronology of the Kings of Judah and Israel," *JNES* 3 (1944) 164; W. F. Albright, "The Chronology of the Divided Monarchy of Israel," *BASOR* 100 (1945) 22, n. 28.

both Albright and Thiele, neither the biblical text itself (when properly understood) nor the evidence from Egypt and Mesopotamia unequivocally support this synchronism; on the contrary, unnecessary violence both to the biblical narratives themselves as well as to the Dtr redaction of these narratives inevitably results.[126] Definitely preferable, it seems to me, is the approach of Hayim Tadmor, who upholds the essential accuracy of the Dtr synchronisms in 2 Kgs 18:1-10 and thus concurs with the Dtr redactor(s) in dating Hezekiah's accession to before the destruction of Samaria.[127]   At any rate, before multiplying Assyrian

---

[126]E.g., severely reducing the overlap between the reign of Merodach-baladan (who was king of Babylon in 722-710, and again briefly in 703; cf. discussion in n. 128, below) and Hezekiah (whose accession would then have to be dated to c. 715), with the result that, if the "15 additional years" of 20:6 be taken at all seriously, then any contact between the two kings would have to be dated very near to the end of the century; secondly, casting considerable doubt not only upon the Dtr synchronisms in the first part of ch. 18, but also upon what seems to me to be the intentional editorial juxtaposition of Hoshea's disastrous end brought about by the pagan Assyrians over against Hezekiah's miraculous triumph *vis-à-vis* the same Assyrians. (Admittedly, one might argue that the very desire to sharpen such a contrast might have motivated an editorial decision to advance Hezekiah's accession to before the fall of Samaria, but I seriously doubt that any editor as ostensibly conscientious as the Dtr editors would have taken such liberties with what must have been a well-remembered tradition.)

[127]For a concise summation of Tadmor's approach, see "The Chronology of the First Temple Period: A Presentation and Evaluation of the Sources," *The World History of the Jewish People, First Series: Ancient Times, The Age of the Monarchies: Political History*, vol. 4, pt. 1, p. 58, and nn. 36-38; a fuller presentation may be found in his "Chronology" article in the *Encyclopedia Miqra'it* [Hebrew], vol. 4 (Jerusalem: Bialik Institute, 1962), cols. 278-79. Tadmor's arguments may be summed up as follows: According to the chronological datum found in Isa 14:28-29, in the year Ahaz died (presumably the same year Hezekiah first became king), we are told that the "rod which smote Philistia" was no more. Although more specific identification is lacking in the text itself, the reference is probably to the death of the infamous Tiglath-pileser III, the only Assyrian king from this time who was worthy of such an epithet. Since according to the Babylonian Chronicle the death of Tiglath-pileser took place in late 727 or early 726, it therefore seems likely that the death of Ahaz should also be dated to around this time. Furthermore, such a date accords well with the synchronism found in 2 Kgs 18:10, which equates the sixth year of Hezekiah with the fall of Samaria in 722/21; assuming antedating practice, his accession would then be dated to 727/26. All this, of course, is in striking contradiction to the synchronism in 18:13, which equates Hezekiah's 14th year with 701. However, as I have already briefly pointed out above in n. 124, Tadmor suggested that this aberrant chronological datum may have originally prefaced only the stories found in ch. 20. If this be the case, then we can date the visit of the Babylonian embassy to around 714, the time of Ashdod's rebellion under Yamani against Sargon II (which eventually led to the

invasions or creating youthful campaigns for Tirhakah, we must read the biblical texts for what they are (and are not), and conform our historical speculations to the data as they presently exist.

In drawing this discussion to a close, it will be appropriate first to present some reasonably firm conclusions concerning the chronology of Assyria and Egypt concurrent with the time of Hezekiah, and then offer a necessarily more tentative reconstruction of the events, both military and diplomatic, which took place in the Ancient Near East around the end of the eighth century B.C.E., especially as they impinged upon the fortunes of Judah. First, concerning chronology: the Assyrian dates are generally quite reliable for this period, usually accurate to within a single year. After the death of Shalmaneser V in late 722, Sargon II came to the throne; his reign may fairly be characterized as some 17 years of nearly continuous warfare.[128] Indeed, in 705 Sargon

---

usurper's extradition in 712 by the Kushite pharaoh Shabako; see above, pp. 97-99). Such a visit, when Merodach-baladan was indeed king of Babylon, fits in well at this time, inasmuch as his envoys may have attempted to encourage Hezekiah's participation in the revolt against Assyria. Presumably, Hezekiah instead heeded the advice of the prophet Isaiah (see, e.g., Isaiah's dire warning in Isa 20:1-6), and thus avoided the fierce reprisals of Sargon's generals. At any rate, when the stories in 2 Kgs 20 were coupled to the accounts of Jerusalem's later deliverance from Sennacherib (these last stories, which apparently lacked a chronological heading, being placed first on account of their greater importance), the redactor prefaced the whole collection of stories about Hezekiah and Isaiah with the attribution originally intended only for the stories in ch. 20, thus in essence dating all the events to the same year (cf. 20:6b, where it seems the invasion of Sennacherib is in view). Although these suggestions of Tadmor are somewhat speculative, I would submit (especially in the light of Ackroyd's observations concerning the Dtr sequencing of the Hezekiah narratives in 2 Kgs 18-20) that they point the way toward the eventual solution of what must be one of the most frustrating chronological puzzles in the entire Hebrew Bible. As I will point out in the next chapter, the 14/15 patterning in the Dtr discussions of both Amaziah and Hezekiah may possibly be schematic (note that these two kings are also said to have been 25 years old when they began to reign, and that they reigned 29 years), yet even if such a pattern be somewhat artificial, it need not have departed too far from the genuine historical situation.

[128]See, e.g., William W. Hallo and William Kelly Simpson, *The Ancient Near East: A History* (New York: Harcourt Brace Jovanovich, 1971), pp. 137-41. On the activities of Merodach-baladan (Marduk-apla-iddina II), who was king of Babylon during most of the reign of Sargon II (as well as briefly during the reign of Sennacherib), cf. Brinkman, "Sennacherib's Babylonian Problem" (see above, n. 122), pp. 90-91, and especially Brinkman's lengthy study in the Oppenheim festschrift ("Merodach-Baladan II," *Studies Presented to A. Leo Oppenheim, June 7, 1964* [Chicago: The Oriental Institute, 1964],

pp. 6-53); the comments which follow are heavily dependent upon this last article of Brinkman's.

The following is a brief résumé of the activities of Merodach-baladan during the last third of the eighth century B.C.E.: Already in the waning years of the reign of Tiglath-pileser III (late 730s), Merodach-baladan is depicted in the Assyrian historiographical sources as a prominent chieftain from the Yakin tribe of southern Babylonia. But it was not until the death of Shalmaneser V in 722 that this tribal chief was able to consolidate his rule over the whole of Babylonia. By Nisan 722, only some three months after the death of the Assyrian monarch, Merodach-baladan assumed kingship in the city of Babylon; he was not ousted from that position until 710. Two years after his accession to the throne, he was involved (at least indirectly) in a major reverse for the Assyrians at the battle of Der (for details, see below, n. 139). Although the outcome of the battle remains ambiguous, the Assyrians refrained from interfering with Babylonia for the next ten years. As might be expected, throughout this time Babylonia flourished: temples were repaired, royal land grants made, business transacted as usual. Little is known about the foreign relations of Merodach-baladan during this decade; however, he reappears in the Assyrian annals in 710-709 when Sargon marched against Babylonia and Elam. After major reversals, Merodach-baladan fled the city of Babylon; Sargon officially became sovereign of Babylonia at the New Year Festival in 709. Meanwhile, the dethroned Chaldean chieftain collected his forces in the south at his old tribal capital of Dur-yakin. The Assyrians succeeded in capturing and destroying the city, but the wounded Merodach-baladan apparently eluded their capture. Sargon ruled Babylonia until his death in Iran in 705; however, soon after his son Sennacherib ascended to the throne, he too was challenged by Babylonian opposition. Once again Merodach-baladan reappears as king of Babylonia, deposing the shadowy usurper Marduk-zakir-shumi (either in the year 704 or in 703, the precise chronology for this period being unclear; for bibliography, see below, n. 130). Indeed, Sennacherib directed his self-styled "first campaign" against this familiar nemesis of Assyria. According to his annals, Sennacherib defeated the Babylonian and Elamite forces at Kish, and then proceeded to Babylon where he installed one Bel-ibni, a Babylonian who had been educated at the Assyrian court, as king (he was later deposed in 700, when Sennacherib installed his own crown prince, Asshur-nadin-shumi, on the Babylonian throne). Merodach-baladan meanwhile had fled Kish in the face of the overwhelming Assyrian advance, retreating to his familiar refuge in the southern swamps, and thus once again successfully eluding capture. Rebellion continued throughout this region, necessitating further Assyrian military activity. Indeed, Sennacherib's campaign of 700 was directed primarily against Bit-yakin, the homeland of Merodach-baladad. Yet again, the Chaldean chieftain eluded Assyrian efforts at capture, although this is the last we hear about him (he is said to have fled to Elam with his national gods and the bones of his ancestors, but abandoning members of his own family, if Sennacherib is to be believed).

The question of Merodach-baladan's contacts with Hezekiah of Judah remains to be discussed. Brinkman, heavily influenced by Thiele's chronology, suggested dating the Babylonian mission to shortly before Sennacherib's Palestinian campaign in 701, fitting in well with the theory that the outbreak of rebellion in Babylonia and in Palestine in 703-702 were related. It is likely that the ambassadors were sent to cement an alliance with

finally met his own death on the field of battle, leaving the throne for his son Sennacherib.[129] He, in turn, was soon confronted by rebellion in both the east and the west.[130] By the turn of the century he had succeeded in reasserting some semblance of order throughout most of the Assyrian empire, although sporadic flareups continued to tax his patience.[131] At any rate, his own death was also untimely; by 681 his son Esarhaddon was on the throne.[132]

Hezekiah--the bestowal of gifts by the Babylonians accords well with Merodach-baladan's known monetary benefactions to Elam to insure their military support on a number of occasions, and Hezekiah's display of his own treasures substantiates the theory that the ambassadors came to assess his strength. However, I would submit that one need not preclude an earlier date for such a mission: e.g., Tadmor's suggestion (see the previous note) that the embassy be dated to around 714, again a time of Palestinian revolt (also cf. the comments of Gray, *I & II Kings*, 2nd ed., pp. 668-69, 700-703; and Bright, *History of Israel*, 3rd ed., pp. 284-85, and especially n. 44).

[129]Brinkman, "Merodach-Baladan II," p. 22; cf. Hayim Tadmor, "The Campaigns of Sargon II of Assur: A Chronological-Historical Study," *JCS* 12 (1958) 97, and nn. 312-15. On the chronological problem of dating the first regnal year of Sennacherib, see the next note.

[130]Bright, *History of Israel*, 3rd ed., pp. 284-85; cf. Tadmor, "Philistia Under Assyrian Rule," *BA* 29 (1966) 95-96. As has been briefly noted above, there remains a measure of chronological uncertainty concerning the exact dating of Sennacherib's accession as well as his first campaign against Babylonia: the various Assyrian and Babylonian sources (which seem to be in some contradiction) lend support to the years 705, 704, or even 703 for dating his first regnal year. For a penetrating analysis of the evidence, see Brinkman, "Merodach-Baladan II," pp. 22-24, and the sources cited there; Brinkman opted for dating Sennacherib's first official regnal year to 704, and the campaign against Merodach-baladan to 703. More recently, however, Louis D. Levine ("Sennacherib's Southern Front: 704-689 B.C." *JCS* 34 [1982] 29-35) argued plausibly for dating both events to the year 704.

[131]Cf. the comments of Hallo ("From Qarqar to Carchemish: Assyria and Israel in the Light of New Discoveries," *BA* 23 [1960] 57-60; an updated version of which is in *BAR* 2, pp. 182-85; cf. also Hallo and Simpson, *History* [above, n. 128], pp. 141-42) who characterized the accession of Sennacherib as inaugurating a new phase of the Assyrian domination of western Asia: a *Pax Assyriaca* replacing the militarism which exemplified the reign of Sargon II. However, throughout most of Sennacherib's reign, the "Babylonian problem" continued to haunt him; cf. Levine, "Sennacherib's Southern Front," pp. 28-29.

[132]Concerning the Assyrian evidence for the identity of Sennacherib's assassin (one Arda-Mulišši, the second eldest son of the king; cf. the biblical Adrammelech of 2 Kgs

The chronological data for Egypt are, as we have already seen, less straightforward: Tirhakah had become pharaoh by the year 690, age at accession uncertain. Prior to Tirhakah's accession, his elder brother Shebitku had been on the throne for at least three years (presumably more). Tirhakah's accession took place after Shebitku's death, any coregency between the two lasting a year or less. Some 23 years previous to all this, Tirhakah's uncle, Shabako, had come to the throne after the death of his brother Piye (Piankhy); this date (713) is quite firm.[133] Shabako reigned at least until 699 inasmuch as his year 15 is attested. A coregency between Shabako and Shebitku is possible, although undocumented. This much we do know: Shebitku could not have reigned as sole king until 699 *at the earliest*, and in all probability not until several years later.[134] Thus, *contra* Kitchen, it is extremely unlikely that Shebitku could have summoned Tirhakah from Nubia prior to the Sennacherib invasion of 701 inasmuch as he (Shebitku) could only have been (at best) a junior coregent at that time.

The above conclusions, I submit, are reasonably solid, and not likely to be overturned by future discoveries. The following historical reconstruction is far more tentative (due to the paucity and ambiguity of the sources, dogmatism, of necessity, being avoided); nevertheless, as John Bright pointed out,[135] any would be biblical historian (or chronographer) would be remiss in neglecting to present (at least in a summary fashion) the historical reconstruction which in his or her opinion best accommodates all the data. The following comments represent, therefore, my own brief contribution to this end.

It was probably not long after the death of Sargon in 705 when Hezekiah helped to instigate revolt in the Levant: he formally withheld tribute from Assyria (2 Kgs 18:7), and prepared both his capital city and

---

19:37), see the recent article of Simo Parpola ("The Murderer of Sennacherib," *Death in Mesopotamia*, Mesopotamia: Copenhagen Studies in Assyriology, Vol. 8, Bendt Alster, ed. [Copenhagen: Akademisk Forlag, 1980], pp. 171-82). I am indebted to Professor Moran for this reference.

[133]See above, pp. 97-100.

[134]See above, pp. 104-105.

[135]Cf. above, n. 5, p. 74.

his military forces for war (2 Chr 32:3-5; cf. 2 Kgs 20:20).[136] Mean-while, soon after Sennacherib's own accession to the Assyrian throne, Merodach-baladan once again seized the Babylonian throne; Assyrian efforts to dislodge him and to pacify the region (the goals of the first two campaigns of Sennacherib) lasted until 702.[137] During this time, revolt continued to spread throughout Syria-Palestine: possibly in-cluding Edom, Moab, and Ammon, certainly involving much of Phoe-nicia, and most notably, heavily involving both the state of Judah and the Philistine cities of Ashkelon and Ekron (where, possibly due to Judahite pressure [cf. 2 Kgs 18:8], the citizenry deposed Padi, their pro-Assyrian king, and handed him over in chains to Hezekiah). It seems probable that pharaoh Shabako promised Egyptian military support to the rebels as well; in any case, Hezekiah (over the strong objections of Isaiah the prophet) apparently relied upon the backing of Egypt as he continued to play a central role as one of the leaders of the revolt.[138]

By the spring of 701 Sennacherib was ready to march to the west. Quickly subduing Phoenicia, he moved down the coast to Philis-tia and punished Ekron especially severely for her insurrection. It is probably around this time that the battle of Eltekeh took place; according to Sennacherib's annals, he overcame both forces from Egypt and from Nubia (it remains unclear, however, whether this battle corre-

---

[136]Presumably, the cutting of the famous Siloam tunnel would also date from around this time (cf. 2 Chr 32:30); such a diversion of Jerusalem's water source would not only have insured an uninterrupted supply to the besieged inhabitants of the city, but also have effectively deprived the invading army of convenient access to that all-important commodity (thus contributing to the distinct possibility of the outbreak of plague; cf. below, n. 146). If, as is likely, the arrival of Sennacherib's forces would have occurred in mid or late summer, such a lack of water would have been especially grievous to the Assyrians; the nearest available perennial spring (Bir 'Ayyub, some 250 meters south of the city) would probably have been blocked up as well.

[137]Levine ("Sennacherib's Southern Front," pp. 35-40), noting that Sennacherib in his annals nowhere claims to have returned to Assyria at the end of his first campaign nor started out from Assyria at the beginning of his second campaign, suggested that in actuality the second campaign represented a continuation of the first (a proposal whose plausibility is further enhanced by a close look at the geography of the region).

[138]Once again, this may have occasioned the visit of Merodach-baladan's envoys; but cf. my above comments in nn. 127-28.

sponds with the Tirhakah reference in 2 Kgs 19:9).[139] At any rate,

<hr />

[139]Yohanan Aharoni (*The Land of the Bible: A Historical Geography*, revised ed., trans. and ed. by A. F. Rainey [Philadelphia: Westminster, 1979], p. 388) drew attention to the summary nature of the Assyrian annals, ordered as they are often on topical rather than chronological grounds; he preferred equating the Eltekeh battle with the biblical notice of Tirhakah's advance, asserting that the biblical chronological sequence (i.e. placing the confrontation with Egypt after the fall of Lachish) is more accurate. However, Tadmor ("Philistia Under Assyrian Rule," *BA* 29 [1966] 96-97) preferred following the Assyrian sequencing more closely; he suggested that the battle of Eltekeh took place during (and thus interrupting) the siege of Ekron. His subsequent remarks are worth quoting in full:

> "Though Sennacherib's annals describe the defeat of the Ethiopians, it is quite apparent that the 'victory' was rather exaggerated; no cogent details of the defeat are given (except the statement about prisoners taken 'in the midst of the battle'), no numbers are mentioned, no booty is listed. Instead, the royal scribe introduces the booty taken from Eltekeh and Timna, two small fortresses of the Ekronites. Finally, the Egyptians were not pursued, as would have been natural had they been totally defeated" (p. 97).

Tadmor's incisive comments about the very limited nature of the Assyrian "victory" at Eltekeh could actually be used to support an identification of this battle with the Egyptian military activity mentioned in 2 Kgs 19:9; but, even given the paucity and ambiguity of the available evidence, such an identification seems to me quite doubtful (cf. also the suggestions of Yurco, as cited below in n. 145).

Not so incidental to all this is the comparison (as first made by Hallo) to similar ambiguities in the extant epigraphic evidence concerning the battle of Der (for the general history, see above, n. 128). In this case, we have access to primary sources representing three different viewpoints concerning the battle (not surprisingly, each source claiming victory). (Hallo's comments may be found in his article "From Qarqar to Carchemish," *BA* 23 [1960] 53, 59; cf. *BAR* 2, pp. 178, 184; also Hallo and Simpson, *History* [above, n. 128], pp. 139, 142.) Citing with approval the suggestions of C. J. Gadd ("Inscribed Barrel Cylinder of Marduk-Apla-Iddina II," *Iraq* 15 [1953] 128) that the then recently discovered barrel cylinder of Merodach-baladan attests yet a third differing account of the battle of Der in 720 (the first two accounts consisting of various inscriptions of Sargon claiming Assyrian victory, and the Babylonian Chronicle claiming victory for Umbanigash, the Elamite king, while contemptuously dismissing Merodach-baladan as arriving too late for the action), Hallo then concluded: "we are thus warned against an uncritical reading of our primary sources even where they rely on eye witnesses" (Hallo and Simpson, *History*, p. 139). (Concerning the question of how to reconcile these three disparate versions of the battle, see Brinkman, "Merodach-Baladan II," pp. 13-15, and especially n. 53; he suggested that Sargon had been attacked by the Elamites, had suffered considerable reverses, but had probably retained possession of the area; the Babylonians nevertheless subsequently enjoyed a ten year respite from Assyrian meddling; and as for Merodach-baladan, his claim of victory may well have been only a "figurative statement" inasmuch as no allusion to his participation in a specific battle is made, and if the Elamites had been fighting under hire to him as they later did in 703, the outcome of the

Sennacherib was then able to turn his full attention toward Judah; according to his annals he reduced some 46 Judahite cities and shut Hezekiah up in Jerusalem "like a bird in a cage."[140]   The fall of Lachish, although not specifically mentioned in the annals, must have been especially gratifying to the Assyrian king, for he later had it portrayed in striking detail on the palace reliefs in Nineveh.[141]

At some point (very possibly after the fall of Lachish and the [initial?] defeat of the Egyptians at Eltekeh), Hezekiah sued for peace. The terms were severe.[142]   Padi was eventually restored to his throne, and portions of western Judah were annexed to Ashdod, Ekron, and Gaza.   Unhappily, both the Assyrian annals as well as the biblical

---

battle could have been technically ascribed to him [even if he had not been physically present].)

All this is background information for Hallo's subsequent comment (*History*, p. 142; cf. *BA*, p. 59, *BAR* 2, pp. 183-84) concerning Sennacherib's Palestinian campaign: "Sennaherib's [*sic*] campaign against Hezekiah in 701 is well known. We have an unusually complete account of this event told from both sides--if indeed it was a single event. In part because of the very different interpretations put on it by the Biblical and the Assyrian sources, some have argued that there were actually two contests between Sennaherib and Hezekiah and that the Assyrians won the first but lost the second. This theory is plausible, for it would not be out of character for the Deuteronomist to dismiss the defeat of a good king in three verses, nor for Sennaherib to pass over his defeat in total silence. By the same reasoning, however, we would have to suppose that there had been two or even three battles of Der."

[140]Cf. the two recent discussions of Nadav Na'aman ("Sennacherib's 'Letter to God' on His Campaign to Judah," *BASOR* 214 [1974] 25-39; and "Sennacherib's Campaign to Judah and the Date of the *LMLK* Stamps," *VT* 29 [1979] 61-86) concerning a cuneiform text probably to be connected with this campaign of Sennacherib to Judah in 701 (for a brief description of this text, see below, Excursus I, part 1).

[141]See *ANEP*, plates 371-74.

[142]According to both the Assyrian annals as well as the Bible, Hezekiah was forced to give up some 30 talents of gold as well as much silver (but here different figures are given, 800 talents according to the annals, but only 300 according to the Bible). Concerning this apparent disparity between these two sources, see the comments and bibliography in Rowley, "Hezekiah's Reform and Rebellion" (see above, n. 17), p. 415, and n. 3 (= *Men of God*, p. 117, and n. 2); as he noted, a number of scholars have maintained that these two figures actually correspond with each other inasmuch as the Assyrian silver talent was not the same as the Hebrew talent (while the gold talent was the same in both cases).

narratives are unclear as to the final outcome of the campaign. Sennacherib did not claim that he captured Jerusalem; rather he ends his annalistic entry with a description in loving detail of Hezekiah's tribute![143] As for the biblical narratives, as we have already seen, they too become hazy. One thing, however, remains clear: Jerusalem, although probably besieged,[144] was not captured. I suspect that some sort of renewed Egyptian military activity may well have had something to do with this remarkable deliverance, although our sources are essentially mute.[145] Indeed, a sudden outbreak of plague (quite possible in the hot Palestinian summer, especially in a location lacking a regular water supply),[146] perhaps coupled with the threat (or actuality) of

---

[143]Presumably delivered after Sennacherib's withdrawal and return to Nineveh; but cf. the comments of Siegfried Herrmann (*A History of Israel in Old Testament Times*, revised and enlarged ed., trans. John Bowden [Philadelphia: Fortress, 1981], pp. 258-59), who suggested the possibility that Hezekiah may have sent his tribute and ostentatiously reasserted his allegiance to the Assyrian king before the latter's departure. In any case, although it seems evident that the concluding focus in Sennacherib's annals upon Hezekiah's tribute was partly meant to obscure the fact that Jerusalem was not conquered and Hezekiah (probably the ringleader of the original revolt) not apprehended, this point should not be overstressed--for as A. Leo Oppenheim (*IBD*, 4:271) pointed out:

"Seen from the Assyrian military point of view, the purpose of the entire campaign, the third of Sennacherib, was to enforce the delivery of tribute and to make a show of military power toward Egypt. . . . It has to be stressed that, however suddenly Sennacherib left for home, he cannot have suffered any patent losses through pestilence or the like, because the entire region would have rebelled immediately, and we know nothing about unrest in that part of the Assyrian Empire."

[144]At least according to Sennacherib's annals; contrast, however, the impression given by the biblical Account B[2] which seems to insist that Jerusalem was totally spared the threat of siege (e.g., 2 Kgs 19:32).

[145]Certainly this seems to be the contention of Account B[1] (cf. my above discussion, pp. 109-11); Yurco ("Sennacherib's Third Campaign" [see above, n. 90], pp. 224-36), noting that the battle of Eltekeh probably represented only a confrontation with a specialized forward unit of the Egyptian army (i.e. the highly mobile elite chariotry, cavalry, and archers originally stationed in the delta), argued plausibly that the subsequent advance of the main Egyptian army (possibly coupled with an outbreak of plague) may well have convinced Sennacherib to quit the field early, even though Jerusalem had not yet fallen.

[146]Cf. above, n. 136. For a strong defense of the hypothesis that an outbreak of plague caused Sennacherib's early withdrawal from Jerusalem, see Wolfram von Soden,

renewed Egyptian pressure may well have forced Sennacherib to break off the siege. At any rate, in the year 700 we find him campaigning elsewhere, once again against the ever resilient Merodach-baladan.

A decade later (690 B.C.E.), Tirhakah was on the Egyptian throne, and, in all probability, the youthful Manasseh was on the Judahite throne. For the balance of the reign of Sennacherib, the Assyrian king seemingly had no reason to confront either of these two monarchs; and, as has been discussed above, it may well have been the Nubian pharaoh rather than the Assyrian king who exercised *de facto* dominion over the Palestinian coastlands in the 680s.[147] Whether Sennacherib remained somewhat chastened by the outcome of his third military campaign, we may never know, but this much is clear: whatever happened in Judah in the fall of the year 701 continued to have serious repercussions (at least among the Judahites) throughout most of the next century. As the traditions about the apparent inviolability of Zion assumed the character of sacred dogma, they would color strongly many of the religious attitudes among those who considered themselves to be true worshippers of Yahweh (and thus eventually contributing greatly to the frustration of the late seventh century prophet Jeremiah who was forced to speak against such "pious" rhetoric).[148] And, indeed, at least in one sense, Jerusalem did remain inviolate--at least beyond the close of the seventh century--which is, after all, more than can be said about Sennacherib's grand capital of Assyria herself, the city of Nineveh.

"Sanherib vor Jerusalem 701 v. Chr." *Antike und Universalgeschichte: Festschrift Hans Erich Stier* (Münster, 1972), pp. 43-51, and especially pp. 49-51.

[147]Cf. above, pp. 106-108.

[148]Perhaps the parade example being his "temple sermon" (Jer 7:1-15).

EXCURSUS I

A CRITIQUE OF SHEA'S RECENT DEFENSE OF THE TWO CAMPAIGN THEORY

While in the process of completing the previous chapter, I came across the recent article by William A. Shea entitled "Sennacherib's Second Palestinian Campaign" (*JBL* 104 [1985] 401-18). Citing various kinds of recent uncovered (or recently reinterpreted) evidence from Mesopotamia, Palestine, and Egypt, Shea attempted to demonstrate how these disparate data indicate the strong probability of a second Palestinian campaign of Sennacherib to be dated some time after his conquest and destruction of Babylon in 689. Although in my opinion his conclusions remain less than convincing (the available data are still too sparse to permit dogmatism), Shea has nonetheless succeeded in opening up several new lines of investigation concerning this vexing issue. More specifically, he has pointed to some five quite diverse areas of inquiry, each of which represent topics heretofore absent in previous discussions (including my own) of the subject. Therefore, my comments which follow will, of necessity, include a brief introduction to each of these five topics as well as a critique of Shea's analysis and conclusions (when appropriate). My order of presentation will follow that of Shea's.

1. Nadav Na'aman's recent discovery (*BASOR* 214 [1974] 25-39; cf. also *VT* 29 [1979] 61-86) of a join between two cuneiform fragments in the British Museum, and his attribution of the resultant text to Sennacherib (previously, one fragment had usually been associated with Tiglath-pileser III, and the other with Sargon II) shed new light upon the Palestinian military activity of that king. In particular, the text describes his campaign against the city of Azekah as well as a certain royal city in Philistia (whose name is now lost, but probably to be identified with Gath). In l. 5 of the inscription, Azekah is described as being "between my [bo]rder and the land of Judah," a situation which must be dated to after Sargon's campaign of 712 when he annexed portions of Philistia. Inasmuch as Sargon did not participate personally in that campaign (whereas the present text indicates the presence of the

Assyrian king in the field of battle), Na'aman seems justified in connecting the events described in this text to those of Sennacherib in 701. Shea readily concurred with Na'aman's suggested identification for the Assyrian king, but he then noted the problematic spelling of *Anšar* in the text for the king's patron deity (in contrast to the spelling *Aššur* found elsewhere in Sennacherib's historical texts). Na'aman himself had called attention to this peculiar spelling (indeed, this was the very feature which had originally led Hayim Tadmor in 1958 to deny that the fragment could be attributed to Sennacherib), but he concluded that a recognition of the literary genre of the text (*viz.*, a "letter to God," which was meant to be read before Asshur in his main temple in the city of that name [however, cf. *VT* 29, p. 63, n. 4]) sufficiently accounts for the odd spelling (other documents from the time of Sennacherib originating from the city of Asshur attest the same spelling). Shea noted, however, that these other texts from Asshur date to after the year 689, the year of Sennacherib's conquest of the city of Babylon; hence Na'aman's text should also be dated to after that year as well (thus attesting a second Palestinian invasion of Sennacherib!).

Such a conclusion, however, although certainly not impossible, remains in my opinion far from compelling. First of all, the extant text is unlikely to have been the original (it was found in Asshurbanapal's library in Nineveh, thus representing, in all probability, a later copy of the original text which presumably remained in the city of Asshur). Inasmuch as the spelling *Anšar* was extensively used in the historical inscriptions of both Esarhaddon and Asshurbanapal, a scribe recopying this inscription may well have substituted the more common form. Secondly, the inscription itself, not being a typical historical or annalistic text, need not necessarily have conformed to their orthographic practice (cf. the Assyrian recension of Enuma Elish, with its systematic replacement of "Marduk" by "Anshar," also dated to the reign of Sennacherib).

2. Hayim Tawil recently suggested (*JNES* 41 [1982] 195-206) that the reference to the rivers of *Māṣôr* in 2 Kgs 19:24 (= Isa 37:25) should be connected with Sennacherib's Nineveh irrigation project (completed by the year 694) which tapped the waters of Mount Musri northeast of the city, rather than, as is commonly supposed, a reference to "the rivers of Egypt." Shea cited Tawil's study with approval and pointed out that it supported dating Isaiah's oracle (as well as the occasion which prompted it) to some time after 694, thus implicitly

supporting a second Palestinian invasion of Sennacherib to be dated to after that time. Indeed, Tawil himself acknowledged the possibility of such an interpretation, but remained noncommittal. Tawil's approach seems to me to be the more prudent one: for it will be recalled that this section of Kings (part of Childs' Account B[2]) appears to be a later interpolation, remarkably close both in language and in thought to that of Deutero-Isaiah, hence valueless in ascertaining the date (or dates) of Sennacherib's military activity in Palestine (cf. Childs, *Isaiah and the Assyrian Crisis*, p. 103).

3. Recently, Bezalel Porten (*BA* 44 [1981] 36-52), upon examination of the Adon Papyrus in the Cairo Museum, discovered a line of demotic Egyptian on the verso of the papyrus; several Demoticists agreed (with varying degrees of enthusiasm) that a reference to the king of the city of Ekron is probably to be found there. Although the reference in l. 4 to the king of Babylon coming to Aphek has led most scholars (including Porten himself) to date this letter to the time of Nebuchadnezzar, Shea cited a short note by Charles Krahmalkov (in *BA* 44 [1981] 197-98) which suggested dating the papyrus to the time of Sennacherib (indeed, Krahmalkov suggested that that very name should be reconstructed in the last part of the last line of the text, where the legible letters read *sn*[   ]). As for the "king of Babylon," he identified him with Merodach-baladan, whose diplomatic activity in Palestine is well known. Thus Adon is to be identified as the rebel king of Ekron (who is unnamed in the Assyrian annals), the one whom Sennacherib deposed after his seemingly unsuccessful appeal to the Egyptian pharaoh for help. Krahmalkov found some confirmation for such an early dating in his proposal that the name *šndwr* in l. 9 of the papyrus is a reference to the rebel king Sanduarri, ruler of Kundu and Sizu, who allied himself with the Sidonians against Assyria, and who was eventually executed by Esarhaddon in 676.

Shea's own suggestion is predictable: if *šndwr* of the papyrus is indeed to be identified with Sanduarri, then an early seventh century date is preferable to the late eighth century date urged by Krahmalkov. As a corollary to this, however, Shea is virtually compelled to identify the "king of Babylon" as Sennacherib himself (who after all did subdue that city and assume its throne). Nonetheless, an odd title for a Philistine prince to use for the Assyrian king, it seems to me to be. In light of the fragmentary state of the papyrus and the highly speculative nature of Krahmalkov's proposals, I would urge caution in attempting to establish a second invasion of Sennacherib from such ambiguous material.

4. Julian Reade, in his provocative but idiosyncratic article entitled "Mesopotamian Guidelines for Biblical Chronology" (*Syro-Mesopotamian Studies* 4 [1981] 1-9) (my favorite sentence in the article: "Now the field of Biblical chronology is notoriously littered with scholars who have lost their heads" [p. 3]), pointed out that the Lachish chariot depicted on the Nineveh palace reliefs as booty taken from the local governor's palace is virtually identical with the Assyrian chariots of that time; Reade concluded that, inasmuch as the Assyrian artists would probably have indicated any distinctive features of the enemy's chariot had there been any, it appears that the Lachishites were indeed using efficient, up-to-date models, and that "military technology usually travels fast" (p. 5). Shea quoted Reade's argument at length in an attempt to strengthen his own hypothesis of a later, second invasion of Sennacherib (the Judahites thus having had time to prepare some imitative models after having seen the Assyrian chariots in action in 701). Again, this is possible, but highly speculative; I doubt that such a close chronological dating of military technology (i.e. to within a decade or so) is even at all feasible.

5. Finally, the important discussion of Anthony Spalinger (*CdÉ* 53 [1978] 22-47), of which I have already made mention (see above, pp. 106-108), comes under review. Citing Pascal Vernus' recent publication (*BIFAO* 75 [1975] 1-66 + Plate V) of a Karnak text of Tirhakah (which was found inscribed on the back of the annals of Thutmose III, a feature which enabled Vernus to reconstitute the original sequence of columns), Spalinger attempted to clarify our knowledge of Tirhakah's foreign policy toward western Asia in the light of several incidental details contained in the inscription. The text, although broken in many places, still remains clear enough: it is a poetic invocation to Amon-Rē', Tirhakah's patron deity (cf. the Kawa Inscriptions as discussed above, pp. 86-96), and it seems to be concerned with some disaster (apparently a military reversal in Syria-Palestine [cf. col. 16], although the details are [probably intentionally] most obscure). At any rate, Tirhakah never blames his god (nor himself); rather he seems to blame the event itself (cf. cols. 5-6). He then asks for guidance from Amon-Rē' for future action; in particular, confirmation for him to march again into battle (cols. 19-20). Both Vernus and Spalinger date the composition of this inscription to a time

around the year 675, some time before Tirhakah's defeat of Esarhaddon's army in 674/73. In particular, Spalinger, in connection with
his proposal that Tirhakah was able to exert considerable control over
much of Palestine throughout the 680s, suggested dating the Vernus text
to after this decade, when Esarhaddon had begun to reassert Assyrian
authority over Syria-Palestine. Already in 679, Esarhaddon, campaigning right to the border of Egypt, was laying claim to those lands;
in 677 he began his conquest of Tyre which was completed within a
year, by which time Philistia was supporting him as well. Hence, by
676, all Egyptian claims to control over the Levant had come to an end,
and inasmuch as the Vernus text seems to reflect dissention in the
Egyptian royal court over this situation (cf. col. 18), a date around 675
(predating Tirhakah's counter-offensive against Esarhaddon in 674/73)
seems justified.

      Shea, relying heavily upon his own suggested dating of the
Na'aman text (see my no. 1, above) for "proof" of a Palestine military
campaign by Sennacherib after 689, and noting that there is no clear
reference to Assyrian clashes with Egyptian forces during Esarhaddon's
Palestinian campaigns of 679 and 677 (of course, there is no such
reference in the Na'aman text either), concluded that the Vernus text
must reflect the results of this heretofore hypothetical second Palestinian
campaign of Sennacherib (cf. the biblical notice in 2 Kgs 19:9, where,
however, Tirhakah seems, if anything, to have triumphed). I find all
this speculative in the extreme: especially in the light of Spalinger's
overall contention that Egypt, and not Assyria, exercised effective
control over the Levant during the latter years of Sennacherib's reign.
Almost certainly, the Egyptian debacle in Palestine which seems to be
presupposed in the Vernus inscription must have occurred on or after
the year 679 B.C.E.

      The foregoing critique of Shea's work is not meant overly to
diminish his positive contributions to the ongoing debate concerning
Sennacherib's Palestinian military activity, however. For example, on
pp. 415-16 of his article, he has correctly pointed out that (as I have
argued above on p. 119) the Egyptian chronological evidence precludes
altogether dating any Palestinian campaign for Tirhakah in 701.
Secondly, Shea has succeeded in drawing upon a number of important
areas of inquiry, several of which will require further examination
in future discussions of this topic. Indeed, closer analysis of both the
Na'aman and the Vernus texts should prove to shed valuable light upon

the historical situation obtaining in the Ancient Near East in the late eighth and the early seventh centuries B.C.E.

EXCURSUS II

THE IDENTITY OF "SO, KING OF EGYPT"

The reference to "So, king of Egypt" (*sô' melek-miṣrayim*) in 2 Kgs 17:4 has perplexed scholars for years, and not a few proposals have been advanced to identify or otherwise explain this cryptic notice. It is not my purpose here to rehearse the literature on the subject,[1] but rather merely to examine a few of the most recent proposals and to indicate where I think the most likely solution seems to lie.

It will be immediately apparent that a successful identification of "So" would serve as a helpful external synchronism both for the chronology of the end of the Northern Kingdom of Israel as well as for the corresponding murky period of Egyptian history. Certain possibilities can now be eliminated once and for all: past attempts to identify "So" as one of the pharaohs of the 25th (Nubian) Dynasty[2] are now to be relegated to the realm of the impossible inasmuch as it seems extremely unlikely that any extended Nubian control of the Delta predated 712 B.C.E.[3] Rather, the pharaonic possibilities must now be limited to the 22nd Dynasty (Osorkon IV Akheperre, ruling from Tanis

---

[1]Extensive bibliography may be found in Hans Goedicke, "The End of 'So, King of Egypt,'" *BASOR* 171 (1963) 64-65; for more recent proposals, see Donald B. Redford, "A Note on II Kings, 17, 4," *The SSEA Journal* 11 (1981) 75.

[2]Such efforts indeed date back to the (proto-) Lucianic recension of the LXX, which reads rather curiously: Ἀδραμέλεχ τὸν Αἰθίοπα τὸν κατοικοῦντα ἐν Αἰγύπτου.

[3]See my above discussion, pp. 97-100. Likewise, the suggested identification of "So" with a certain "*Sib'e, turtan* of Egypt" mentioned in the annals of Sargon II, at one time quite widely held (cf. *ANET*, p. 285), more recently has been shown to be untenable; see Goedicke, "The End of 'So,'" pp. 64-65, and especially R. Borger, "Das Ende des Ägyptischen Feldherrn Sib'e = ﬡﬢ ﬡ," *JNES* 19 (1960) 49-53, where he demonstrated that the name *Sib'e* should rather have been read as *Re'e*.

in the eastern Delta) and the 24th Dynasty (Tefnakht, ruling from Sais in the western Delta).[4]

Recently, K. A. Kitchen[5] suggested that "So" represents an abbreviated form of the name (O)so(rkon)[6] of the 22nd Dynasty. Arguing that his territorial domain in the east Delta and his capital of Tanis (the biblical Zoan)[7] would be the most likely destination for Israelite envoys seeking military assistance for their revolt against Assyria, Kitchen concluded that the apparent lack of success resulting from the diplomatic effort only typified the actual lack of resources on the part of this "shadow monarch."

Some time ago, however, Hans Goedicke[8] presented what seems to me to be a more satisfying solution to this crux. Suggesting that Tefnakht was the most powerful pharaoh in the Delta during the decade of the 720s, he noted that his capital of Sais in the western Delta would probably have been regarded as the political center of Egypt by Hoshea and his envoys. Thus the Hebrew $Sô'$ should be understood as a reference to the capital city of Sais, and not as a reference to any particular pharaoh. As Albright in his postscript to Goedicke's article pointed out, the Hebrew text of 2 Kgs 17:4 may well have originally

---

[4]The shadowy Iuput II of the 23rd Dynasty probably reigned in Leontopolis around this time as well (see Kitchen, *Third Intermediate Period*, § 323; cf. Klaus Baer, "Libyan and Nubian Kings," *JNES* 32 [1973] § 30a, p. 22), but inasmuch as he probably enjoyed only locally effective rule in and around his dynastic capital, he would have been an extremely unlikely candidate for Hoshea's diplomacy.

[5]Kitchen, *Third Intermediate Period*, §§ 333-34 (in his 2nd ed., see also §§ 463-64, 526).

[6]I.e. Osorkon IV Akheperre Setepenamun, dated by Kitchen (*ibid.*, § 147; cf. p. 467) to c. 730-715, and by Baer ("Libyan and Nubian Kings," § 12) to c. 735-712. Kitchen (*ibid.*, § 334, n. 751) cited a number of similar abbreviations for pharaohs (e.g., "Sesse" for Ramesses II, "Shosh" for Shoshenq) as well as names of private citizens from the New Kingdom onwards.

[7]Both the Hebrew "Zoan" ($sô'an$), and the Greek Τάνις represent the Egyptian $\underline{D}'n.t$ (surviving in Coptic as $Ǧa'ne$); see T. O. Lambdin, "Zoan," *IDB*, 4:961.

[8]*BASOR* 171 (1963) 64-66; see above, n. 1. In a postscript entitled "The Elimination of King 'So,'" W. F. Albright enthusiastically endorsed Goedicke's proposal, declaring it "among the most important clarifications of biblical history in recent years" (p. 66).

read *'el Sô' <'el> melek Miṣrayim*, "to Sais, to the king of Egypt," with the loss of the second *'el* through haplography.[9]

A number of other scholars have embraced this solution as well.[10] Indeed, as Anthony Spalinger has argued from other evidence,[11] the pharaohs of Sais never considered themselves friends of Assyria, in stark contrast to the Bubastite pharaoh Shilḫanni (= Osorkon IV)[12] who later sent gifts to Assyria.[13] Thus, it seems to me definitely more probable that Hoshea would seek help from Tefnakht, the ruler in the western Delta at that time.[14]

In a recent article, Donald B. Redford further confirmed the basic identification of "So" with Sais (although in somewhat of an

---

[9]Albright, *ibid.*; he also noted that both the contemporary Arabic *Sā el-Hagar* as well as the Babylonian *Sa-a-a* indicate the presence of a long vowel in the Egyptian name. Analogy with the Phoenician shift of stressed *ā* [< *ấ*] > *ō* probably accounts for the Hebrew form (cf. Hebrew "Zoan" [*sô'an*] for Egyptian *Ḏ'n.t*, Greek *Tanis*, Coptic *Ǧa'ne*).

[10]E.g., Hayim Tadmor ("Philistia Under Assyrian Rule," *BA* 29 [1966] 91, n. 19), Siegfried Herrmann (*A History of Israel in Old Testament Times*, revised and enlarged ed., trans. John Bowden [Philadelphia: Fortress, 1981], p. 250), and Anthony Spalinger ("The Year 712 B.C. and its Implications for Egyptian History," *JARCE* 10 [1973] 96, and n. 11).

[11]Spalinger, *ibid.*, pp. 96-97; cf. my above discussion, pp. 97-100, and especially n. 73.

[12]On this identification, see above, n. 72, p. 97.

[13]As Spalinger pointed out (*ibid.*, pp. 86-97), this good will policy toward Assyria may have been the result of the ill-fated *turtan* affair in 720 (cf. above, n. 3, for references); thus it need not necessarily have reflected Osorkon's policy prior to that date (such an about-face would, of course, have to be presupposed for Kitchen's equation of "So" with Osorkon to remain viable).

[14]Extant Egyptian evidence seems to indicate that Tefnakht (father of Bocchoris) never took the title of pharaoh, preferring to be known as "Chief of the West" or "Great Chief of the West and Administrator of the Domains of Lower Egypt"; see Spalinger, "Year 712," p. 96, n. 8, and the references cited there (this may also explain why no extant fragments of Manetho appears to mention his name--the *Stephinates* of the 26th Dynasty probably corresponds with Tefnakht II, the son of Bocchoris [cf. Kitchen, *Third Intermediate Period*, §§ 116-18]).

oblique manner).[15]   Looking to Manetho and his "inflated" list for the 26th (Saite) Dynasty, Redford pointed to the entry *Nechepso*,[16] which as John Ray had already noted,[17] is most probably a reduplication of the name Necho followed by an epithet *-pso*. Redford then went on to explain this last term as reflecting the Egyptian *p,' s,'w(w)*, "the Saite," the Greek name thus originally designating "Necho the Saite." Citing an analogous Aramaic transliteration of an Egyptian name (פסא), and noting its similarity with the biblical סוא, Redford concluded that this form may well lurk behind the biblical "So" as well.[18]

     Finally, a word about chronology is in order. Scholars are in general agreement that Hoshea's overtures to "So" probably date to several years after the death of Tiglathpileser III and the succession of his son Shalmaneser V in 727.[19] Following Tadmor's Judahite chronology,[20] the death of Ahaz would seem to have occurred around this time as well. I would suggest that it is not without significance that according to the Chronicler (2 Chr 29:3; 30:1-4, 13) this was around the time of Hezekiah's cleansing of the Jerusalem temple as well as his triumphant Passover. Whether the Chronicler is here reflecting an independent, accurate chronological tradition is not certain, I admit, but such a Yahwistic revival (with its clear political overtones) would certainly

---

[15]Redford, "Note on II Kings" (see above, n. 1), pp. 75-76. In his more recent article entitled "Sais and the Kushite Invasion of the Eighth Century B.C." (*JARCE* 22 [1985] 5-15), he is more forthright in this identification (see p. 15, and especially n. 69).

[16]Manetho, frag. 68-69.

[17]J. D. Ray, "Pharaoh Nechepso," *JEA* 60 (1974) 255-56.

[18]Although Redford refrained from advancing a specific translation for the Hebrew term, he apparently wishes to equate it with the Egyptian form *(p,') s,'w(w)*, "the Saite," a nisbe appellative designating the pharaoh as such rather than a place name denoting his capital city. This is certainly possible, although I still prefer Goedicke's approach as doing less violence to the Hebrew text. Duane L. Christensen's recent article ("The Identity of 'King So' in Egypt [2 Kings xvii 4]," *VT* 39 [1989] 140-53), while rejecting Goedicke's specific identification of biblical "So" with Sais, nonetheless refutes Kitchen's Osorkon proposal at length, and argues on historical grounds that the pharaoh in question must have been Tefnakht, the Saite ruler.

[19]E.g., Goedicke ("End of 'So,'" p. 64) suggests the year 724, which seems to me to be about right.

[20]For details, see above, pp. 114-16, nn. 124, 127.

fit well at this time of Assyrian weakness. It would indeed be an irony of history if Hoshea of Israel were seeking military support from the land of Egypt at the very same time that Hezekiah of Judah was proclaiming renewed allegiance to the God who had long ago attained victory for Israel over against that same land.

CHAPTER V

THE JUDAHITE KING LIST HYPOTHESIS

Most of the discussion found in the preceding chapters may be characterized as evaluative, and largely dependent upon the results and controversies of recent scholarship. This is, of course, important: for any effort toward erecting a viable biblical chronology for the period of the divided monarchy must be based upon such a sober analysis in order to ascertain which conclusions appear to be largely beyond controversy (e.g., among Egyptologists and Assyriologists) and which conclusions are not. Thus, the dating of the founding of Carthage, or of the initial domination of the 25th Egyptian Dynasty in the Delta seem to be reasonably well established, with serious implications for biblical chronology. Conversely, the date for the accession of Shishak appears not to be established with reasonable certainty at the present time, again with important consequences for the biblical chronographer. Such an approach, while important, nevertheless becomes rather tedious: lengthy analysis and discussion often producing few tangible results.

Whatever the weaknesses of the present chapter, tedium and caution are not likely to be included among them. What I propose to do in the next several pages is to present a hypothesis, one which to my knowledge has not been heretofore suggested, and one which will attempt (at least to a limited extent) to account for the Judahite regnal data as presently found in both the books of Kings and of Chronicles. As is well known, the subject of biblical chronology has evoked numerous grand hypotheses (perhaps the best recent example--both in its austere methodology and surprising success in accounting for nearly all of the biblical chronological data, as well in its resultant violence to the Dtr editing of those data--is the work of E. R. Thiele),[1] and I remain in full sympathy with those who are not anxious to labor through yet another one. Nevertheless, it is hoped that the following discussion will prove worthwhile, not so much in sharpening the dating of the Judahite monarchs (several years of research has convinced me

---

[1]See above, pp. 12-27, for an extended evaluation of this theory.

that only external synchronisms have any real hope of accomplishing that task), but rather in clarifying our understanding of some of the chronistic sources underlying the books of Kings (and Chronicles) as well as the editorial process which led to their present form.

The relevant article by Shoshana R. Bin-Nun should be mentioned at this point.[2] She has made the important observation that the accession formulae for the kings of the divided monarchy reflect two different sources (both of which predate the Dtr editing of Kings), and that these two sources are best characterized as "king lists" (cf. the Tyrian King List as discussed above in Chapter II). Thus, the regnal totals for the Judahite kings (as found in both the books of Kings and Chronicles) reflect an original Judahite king list, and for the Israelite kings, an originally separate Israelite king list. Inasmuch as Bin-Nun's conclusions have recently been sharply challenged,[3] it seems appropriate to analyze them in closer detail.

In general, the "accession formulae" which introduce each Israelite and Judahite king will include his name, (usually) his patronymic, and his length of reign.[4] However, even a superficial analysis of the various accession formulae will disclose significant differences between the formulae for the Israelite kings and the formulae for their Judahite counterparts: the Judahite formulae usually include both the age at accession of the monarch as well as the name of the Queen Mother; the Israelite formulae, on the other hand, never contain either of these last two items. All this, of course, has long been recognized, and need not necessarily indicate the existence of two different king lists underlying the present formulae, only differing sources or interests on the part of the Dtr editor. However, Bin-Nun has pointed out another more subtle variation between the two sets of formulae: the Israelite formulae consistently place the length of reign at the end of

---

[2]Bin-Nun, "Formulas from Royal Records of Israel and of Judah," *VT* 18 (1968) 414-32.

[3]See the otherwise fine work by Richard D. Nelson, *The Double Redaction of the Deuteronomistic History*, Journal for the Study of the Old Testament Supplement Series, No. 18 (Sheffield: JSOT Press, 1981), pp. 30-31.

[4]The synchronisms which usually introduce the accession formulae are almost certainly secondary; cf. Bin-Nun, "Formulas from Royal Records," pp. 419, 424-27.

each formula, while the Judahite formulae never do.[5] Thus, the Israelite formulae may fairly be typified as:

> bišnat X (šānāh) lĕ-C melek yĕhûdāh mālak A (ben-B)
> 'al-yiśrā'ēl (bĕtirṣāh/bĕšōmrôn)[6] Y šānāh[7]

Less common is the two part formula:

> wĕ-A ben-B mālak 'al-yiśrā'ēl
> bišnat X (šānāh) lĕ-C melek yĕhûdāh
> wayyimlōk ('al-yiśrā'ēl) Y šānāh[8]

The Judahite formulae differ strikingly from the above Israelite patterns, and not only by the inclusion of additional details:

> bišnat X (šānāh) lĕ-C (ben-D) (melek yiśrā'ēl)
> mālak A (ben-B) (melek yĕhûdāh)
> ben Z šānāh hāyāh bĕmolkô wĕ-Y šānāh mālak bîrûšālaim
> wĕ-šēm 'immô E (bat-F) (mîn-G)[9]

As Bin-Nun argued, it is unlikely that the Judahite syntactical sequence was motivated secondarily by the presence of the age at accession in the regnal formulae, since even in the cases of Abijam and Asa where the ages at accession are lacking, the characteristic sequence is still to be found.[10] Rather it is far more likely that the Israelite formulae derived from one king list (most likely originally of Israelite origin); the

---

[5]*Ibid.*, pp. 418-20.

[6]Four times the capital city appears after the regnal total (1 Kgs 16:15, 23; 2 Kgs 10:36; 15:17).

[7]A total of thirteen examples: 1 Kgs 15:33; 16:8, 15, 23; 2 Kgs 10:36; 13:1, 10; 14:23; 15:8, 17, 23, 27; 17:1.

[8]A total of five examples: 1 Kgs 15:25; 16:29; 22:52; 2 Kgs 3:1; and 2 Kgs 15:13 (where *bĕšōmrôn* follows the regnal total).

[9]1 Kgs 15:1-2, 9-10; 2 Kgs 8:16-17, 25-26; 14:1-2; 15:1-2, 32-33; 16:1-2; 18:1-2; cf. 1 Kgs 14:21, 22:41-42; 2 Kgs 12:1-2 (especially 𝔊[L]).

[10]See 1 Kgs 15:1-2, 9-10.

Judahite formulae from another. The synchronisms with their stereo-typical phrasing, on the other hand, are most likely the result of later Dtr editing. At any rate, it is clear that the Dtr editors took great pains not only to include regnal data for every Israelite and Judahite king, but also to intersperse their discussions of each of these kings in strictly chronological order (whether they correctly ascertained this order is another matter, of course). As Bin-Nun pointed out:

> A summary of the information contained in the Book of Kings gives but a vague picture of the history of Israel and of Judah from the division of the kingdom until their destruction. Many important political events are not even mentioned. On the other hand, the unbroken lines of the kings of both states form a surprising contrast with the author's fragmentary reports. Not a single king is left out, neither usurpers nor even Atalia, although, not being regarded a legitimate ruler, she has no formulas.[11]

But the question then arises as to how the synchronisms were first calculated and the Dtr "leap-frog" ordering of the monarchs formulated. I suspect that around the time of Hezekiah when the Northern Kingdom had just fallen, the Deuteronomistic school (newly trans-planted in the south?) was already concerned about formulating a theological history of the two kingdoms,[12] thus motivating them to calculate the synchronisms in order to construct the chronological skeleton for their work. As Bin-Nun pointed out, it would be extremely unlikely that such synchronisms were present in the original king lists or royal chronicles inasmuch as these latter sources would not likely head their entries with the name of foreign kings.[13]

---

[11]Bin-Nun, "Formulas from Royal Records," p. 423.

[12]Cf. the Dtr *Grundschrift* (Dtr G) hypothesis as suggested by E. W. Nicholson (*Deuteronomy and Tradition* [Philadelphia: Fortress Press, 1967], pp. 113-18), and re-cently elaborated upon by Steven L. McKenzie (*The Chronicler's Use of the Deuterono-mistic History*, Harvard Semitic Monographs, No. 33 [Atlanta: Scholars Press, 1985], p. 175, and especially n. 29 on p. 180). For a recent, positive assessment of Hezekiah's role in the compilation of the works of the four eighth century prophets (Amos, Hosea, [proto-]Isaiah, and Micah), see D. N. Freedman, "Headings in the Books of the Eighth-Century Prophets," *AUSS* 25 (1987) 9-26, especially pp. 24-25.

[13]Bin-Nun, "Formulas from Royal Records," p. 425, n. 1.

Recently, Steven L. McKenzie has argued convincingly that the Chronicler was familiar only with the Josianic edition of Dtr (Dtr 1):

> In this survey of the material from the death of Josiah to the exile we have found that in every passage Chr [1] relies on sources other than K[ings] for his account. This phenomenon stands in striking contrast to the situation for the material surveyed earlier. There it is clear that DH [i.e. the Deuteronomistic History] is C[hronicles'] main source for every king. Even for the reign of Hezekiah where Chr uses other sources extensively, it is still obvious that he knows K and has abbreviated some of its accounts. In the earlier material I suggested that where Chr uses DH he generally follows it closely. . . . It is, therefore, very striking to find no truly parallel passages beginning with Josiah's death. This evidence, then, provides the answer to the question of the extent of Chr's use of DH, which has been born in mind throughout this survey. Chr uses DH up to the account of Josiah's death, but not thereafter.
>
> Why would Chr cease to use DH from the time of Josiah's death on? This change obviously cannot be attributed to his bias nor to textual corruption or text type. It must, therefore, have to do with a change in Chr's sources, specifically his Deuteronomistic source. I have already expressed agreement with the theory that the Dtr 1 edition of DH was a program for the Josianic reform and that DH was subsequently extended by an exilic editor. The fact that Chr's use of K ceases with the death of Josiah fits well with this theory of two editions of DH. I suggest, therefore, that Chr uses the work of Dtr 1 as a source but not the work of Dtr 2.[14]

However, if this is the case, then there immediately arises the question of the source of the Chr accession formulae for Jehoahaz, Jehoiakim, Jehoiachin, and Zedekiah.[15] Except that the names of the queen mothers are lacking, the formulae correspond quite closely with their Dtr counterparts in Kings.[16] Closer analysis suggests the likely solu-

---

[14]McKenzie, *Chronicler's Use* (see above, n. 12), p. 187. For the different redactional levels of Dtr and Chr, see above, Chapter I, nn. 1, 17.

[15]2 Chr 36:2, 5, 9, 11.

[16]2 Kgs 23:31 = 2 Chr 36:2; 2 Kgs 23:36 = 2 Chr 36:5; 2 Kgs 24:8 = 2 Chr 36:9, except that Jehoiachin is said in Kings to have been 18 years old upon accession and reigned 3 months, whereas in Chronicles he was but 8 years old upon accession and

tion to the problem: as McKenzie notes, the absence of the names of
the queen mothers in Chronicles actually began with Manasseh (the
name of Ahaz's mother is lacking in both Kings and Chronicles); this
observation as well as analogous changes in the formulation of the
death-burial notices point to a subtle but definite change in Chr's
sources datable to the time of Hezekiah (again indirect evidence for Dtr
G?).[17] At any rate, the evidence from Chronicles seems to indicate the
existence of some sort of Judahite king list known to Chr 1 which was
similar to, but independent of, the source underlying Dtr 2.

The idea of such king list(s) underlying the present regnal data
of Dtr and Chr is not that controversial;[18] what remains problematic,
however, is the question of how closely such a king list (e.g., of the
Judahite monarchs) dating to the time of Dtr 2 corresponded to the
sources which were known to Dtr 1 or Dtr G. Certainly, a number of
the synchronisms fail to line up in any obvious way with the regnal
totals as we now have them. Why this is so remains unclear; however,
at least the possibility of variant regnal totals drawn from a later king
list replacing some of the regnal data from earlier sources (meanwhile
leaving at least some of the synchronisms unchanged) should be entertained. I will have reason to return to this question below.

The hypothesis of some sort of king list as the source of the
regnal data in the books of Chronicles helps to explain another interesting phenomenon which, so far as I am aware, has not been accounted
for in any other way. Twice in Chronicles, the Judahite regnal formulae
are repeated as a sort of inclusio bracketing the discussion of a king:
first in the case of Jehoram (2 Chr 21:5, 20), and secondly in the case

---

reigned 3 months and 10 days--apparently a case of a misplaced "10"; finally, 2 Kgs
24:18 = 2 Chr 36:11.

[17]McKenzie here is relying upon an unpublished Ph.D. thesis by H. R. Macy entitled
"Sources of the Books of Chronicles" (Harvard University, 1975), pp. 115-65; as Macy
argued (p. 119), neither scribal error nor any alleged theological bias can adequately
account for the omission of all the names of the queen mothers (a total of seven): scribal
error tends to be less extensive and more random, and such a sudden shift in Chr's
theology (motivation unknown) after the Hezekiah section is extremely unlikely.

[18]Cf., e.g., the comments of Julian Reade, "Mesopotamian Guidelines for Biblical
Chronology," *Syro-Mesopotamian Studies* 4/1 (May, 1981) 5, and n. 11; I cannot accept
his suggestion, however, that the names Pekah and Pekahiah originally represented the
same individual.

of Jotham (2 Chr 27:1, 8). The reason for these repetitions is not obvious; they are lacking in the Dtr parallels, and there seems to be no reason for the Chronicler to highlight these two (rather nondescript) monarchs. A third analogous phenomenon seems easier to explain: Josiah (the "hero" of Dtr 1) has a dual notice in both Kings and Chronicles concerning his all-important 18th year (see 2 Kgs 22:3; 23:23; 2 Chr 34:8; 35:19); they bracket the discussion of his famous Passover which is dated to that year. Here, at least, a theologically portentous event is signalled by this literary device; something which, however, seems not to be the case in the first two examples. Nonetheless, I would suggest that the following "king list" of the Judahite monarchs might suggest a solution for all three of these odd repetitions:

	(David)
	(Solomon)
1.	Rehoboam
2.	Abijah
3.	Asa
4.	Jehoshaphat
*5.	Jehoram (double regnal formula)
6.	Ahaziah
	(Athaliah)
7.	Joash
8.	Amaziah
9.	Uzziah
*10.	Jotham (double regnal formula)
11.	Ahaz
12.	Hezekiah
13.	Manasseh
14.	Amon
*15.	Josiah (double reference to 18th year)
16.	Jehoahaz
17.	Jehoiakim
18.	Jehoiachin
19.	Zedekiah

Is the Chronicler signalling some sort of pattern--every fifth king war-ranting some sort of cipher to mark his reign?[19]   At least, such a hypothesis prompted me some time ago to examine more closely the Dtr regnal data for the Judahite monarchs--with interesting results. An exilic "king list" of the Davidic dynasty drawn from the data as they are preserved in the MT (the versions are in virtually total agreement)[20] would look like this:

---

[19]F. M. Cross ("A Reconstruction of the Judean Restoration," *JBL* 94 [1975] 12-14) has presented a strong case for the likelihood that Chr 1 supported a program of resto-ration of the Davidic kingdom under Zerubbabel. If this were the case, then Chr 1 would have surely reckoned Zerubbabel (grandson of the exiled king Jehoiachin, cf. 1 Chr 3:17-19) as "king" no. 20 on the king list (whence the rationale for the peculiar flagging of every fifth king by a double date formula on the part of Chr?).

[20]As Albright pointed out some time ago; cf. above, Chapter I, p. 20, n. 64.

HYPOTHETICAL DTR JUDAHITE KING LIST

Antedated Regnal Year Subtotals	Judahite King--Age at Accession; Length of Reign	Dtr Reference
39	David--30 yrs old; reigned 40 yrs	2 Sam 5:4
39	Solomon--no age given; reigned 40 yrs	1 Kgs 11:42
16	Rehoboam--41 yrs old; reigned 17 yrs	1 Kgs 14:21
2	Abijam--no age given; reigned 3 yrs	1 Kgs 15:2
40	Asa--no age given; reigned 41 yrs	1 Kgs 15:10
24	Jehoshaphat--35 yrs old; reigned 25 yrs	1 Kgs 22:42
7	Jehoram--32 yrs old; reigned 8 yrs	2 Kgs 8:17
0	Ahaziah--22 yrs old; reigned 1 yr	2 Kgs 8:26
(6)	(Athaliah--"reigned" 7 yrs)	(2 Kgs 11:1-4)
39	Joash--7 yrs old; reigned 40 yrs	2 Kgs 12:1-2
28	Amaziah--25 yrs old; reigned 29 yrs ("lived 15 yrs after. . .")*	2 Kgs 14:2; (2 Kgs 14:17)
51	Azariah--16 yrs old; reigned 52 yrs	2 Kgs 15:2
15	Jotham--25 yrs old; reigned 16 yrs	2 Kgs 15:33
15	Ahaz--20 yrs old; reigned 16 yrs	2 Kgs 16:2
28	Hezekiah--25 yrs old; reigned 29 yrs ("add 15 yrs to your life")*	2 Kgs 18:2; (2 Kgs 20:6)
54	Manasseh--12 yrs old; reigned 55 yrs	2 Kgs 21:1
1	Amon--22 yrs old; reigned 2 yrs	2 Kgs 21:19
30	Josiah--8 yrs old; reigned 31 yrs	2 Kgs 22:1
0	Jehoahaz--23 yrs old; reigned 3 mos	2 Kgs 23:31
10	Jehoiakim--25 yrs old; reigned 11 yrs	2 Kgs 23:36
(36)	Jehoiachin--18 yrs old; reigned 3 mos	2 Kgs 24:8
--	Zedekiah--21 yrs old; reigned 11 yrs	2 Kgs 24:18
480 total yrs in 37th yr of exile of Jehoiachin, 2 Kgs 25:27		

* Note the curiously palistrophic correspondences between Amaziah and Hezekiah--not only in age at accession and length of reign, but also in the parallel reference to "15 yrs" as a significant chronological datum in the career of each king (for further discussion, see below, n. 27).

As the reader will no doubt recall, the book of Kings ends on a rather quiet note: in the 37th year of the exiled king Jehoiachin, the Judahite monarch was freed from prison by the Babylonian king Evil-merodach (= Amel-marduk); every day, we are then told, he dined at the king's table. Now, it is undoubtedly not coincidental that according to the Judahite regnal totals as extant in Kings, exactly 480 years separated this event from the original coronation of King David over Judah. (Once again, the actual historical situation need not concern us at this point, although it would seem that only some 449 years actually separated these two events.)[21] As other biblical chronological evidence indicates,[22] Jehoiachin was considered to be the legitimate Davidic king by many of the Judahite population even after his exile and Zedekiah's accession to the throne. Therefore, it would not have been unusual to continue reckoning by the "regnal years" of Jehoiachin, as seems to be the case in 2 Kgs 25:27. At any rate, reckoning by the process of antedating (the time-honored system for chronological calculation),[23] one obtains the exact total of 480 years between that time so long ago when David was recognized as king by his Judahite compatriots in Hebron (2 Sam 5:1-5) and the most recent (for Dtr 2) positive turn of events in Babylon. It will be readily recalled that another 480 year period of time has been mentioned already in Kings: the time interval between the exodus from Egypt and the founding of

---

[21]Assuming the essential accuracy of David's 40 year reign, and then reckoning backwards from the date of 971 for Solomon's accession as calculated from the Tyrian King List (cf. above, Chapter II, especially pp. 53-55).

[22]Cf. Bright, *History of Israel*, 3rd ed., pp. 328-29, and nn. 53-54 (concerning an earlier date for the Eliakim seal, see also F. M. Cross, Jr., "The Seal of Miqnêyaw, Servant of Yahweh," *Ancient Seals and the Bible*, Occasional Papers on the Near East, Vol. 2/1, Leonard Gorelick and Elizabeth Williams-Forte, eds. [Malibu: Undena Publications, 1983], p. 58, and n. 26).

[23]On the use of the antedating system in the regnal calculations, cf. Albright, "Chronology," p. 22, n. 29. I concur with Albright and others in suggesting that Judah switched to the Assyrian postdating system around the time of Manasseh (see the Appendix below). Nonetheless, the antedating system remained the more natural method of reckoning, and may well have been used even in Mesopotamia (cf. Albright, "The Original Account of the Fall of Samaria in II Kings," *BASOR* 174 [1964] 66-67, and the references cited there; however, I cannot accept his proposal that the Hezekiah synchronisms in 2 Kgs 18:9-10 originally referred to the Assyrian king Shalmaneser V).

Solomon's temple (1 Kgs 6:1).[24] (Again the actual historical interval, although almost certainly considerably less than this round number, need not concern us here.) Is it not likely that such a significant number would have impressed itself upon the Deuteronomistic school, to the end that Jehoiachin's release from prison in 561[25] in his 37th year (and according to the Dtr regnal totals, in the 480th year of the Davidic monarchy) may well have provided the occasion for the updated exilic redaction of the Dtr history (Dtr 2)?[26] At least this much is clear: the biblical numbers for the Judahite regnal totals as extant in the MT and the ancient versions undoubtedly correspond very closely with those which were available to Dtr 2. The question of whether this exilic version of the Judahite King List differed greatly from that known by Dtr G or Dtr 1 may never be answered, but the extant synchronisms seem to indicate at least some changes took place. At any rate, the Judahite regnal totals as extant tend to correspond (with a few exceptions) quite well with the actual historical situation (cf. my proposed chronological reconstruction in the Appendix). Although a few of the ages at accession appear to be corrupt,[27] most of them seem reasonably

---

[24]For a valiant attempt to account for these 480 years, see Martin Noth, *The Deuteronomistic History*, Journal for the Study of the Old Testament Supplement Series, Vol. 15 (Sheffield: JSOT Press, 1981), pp. 18-25. Concerning the possibility of other similar "chronological idealizations," see the comments of Frederick H. Cryer, "To the One of Fictive Music: OT Chronology and History," *Scandinavian Journal of the Old Testament* (2/1987) 1-27, especially pp. 25-27; cf. also James Barr, "Why the World Was Created in 4004 B.C.: Archbishop Ussher and Biblical Chronology," *BJRL* 67 (1985) 575-608, especially pp. 603-606.

[25]For this date, see Hayim Tadmor, "Chronology of the Last Kings of Judah," *JNES* 15 (1956) 230.

[26]Gerhard Larsson ("The Documentary Hypothesis and the Chronological Structure of the Old Testament," *ZAW* 97 [1985] 316-33) has recently argued that the present chronological framework as found in Dtr (as well as in P, Chronicles, Jeremiah, and Ezekiel) is of "comparatively late origin": 3rd century B.C.E., or even later.

[27]Most notably, the 25 years for Hezekiah, making him a father at age 42 and Ahaz a father at age 11 (even earlier if his regnal total is reduced, as I shall urge in the Appendix). Emending "25" to "15" would make Ahaz a father at age 15 (my chronology), and Hezekiah a father at age 32. (Jehoiakim's age at accession seems a bit high as well.) As I have already pointed out briefly (see above, n. 127, p. 116, also the chart on p. 145), the 25/29 age at accession/regnal total pattern for both Amaziah and Hezekiah (with both also having been said to have lived an additional 15 years after an important

accurate as well. The synchronisms, on the other hand, often do not reflect historical reality (cf., e.g., the string of synchronisms in 2 Kgs 15 which are dependent upon the impossibly high regnal total of 52 for Azariah); they appear to be the result of secondary and even tertiary calculations based upon traditions of varying levels of accuracy.[28]

---

event in their reigns) seem somewhat schematic and suspiciously secondary. As the positions of the two kings on the following chart indicate, this curious correspondence is probably not accidental:

Rehoboam
Abijam
Asa
Jehoshaphat
*Jehoram
Ahaziah
Joash
⤢Amaziah
   Azariah
   *Jotham
   Ahaz
⤡Hezekiah
Manasseh
Amon
*Josiah
Jehoahaz
Jehoiakim   * denotes double regnal/date
Jehoiachin   formulae in Chronicles
Zedekiah

It will be recalled that I have already had reason to query the accuracy of the reference in 2 Kgs 18:13 to Hezekiah's 14th year as the year of Sennacherib's Palestinian invasion (see above, pp. 114-16); I suspect (but cannot prove) that this number too may well be the result of this later Dtr schematization. Alternatively, a dislocation in the regnal data analogous to that attested in the two variants of Jehoiachin's regnal data in Kings and Chronicles (see above, n. 16) might have occurred; quite possibly the original entry in the Judahite king list read somewhat as follows: "Hezekiah was 14 years old when he became king and he reigned 29 years in Jerusalem; in his 25th year Sennacherib king of Assyria came up. . . ." (and then a substitution, whether accidental or deliberate, of the "25" for the age at accession and the "14" for the synchronism with Sennacherib having taken place). However, considering the uncanny correspondences of the regnal data between Amaziah and Hezekiah, I suspect that some version of the former alternative is the more likely.

[28]For a recent, helpful attempt to delineate the origins of a number of the errors and

Although exceptions may be found (cf. my comments in the Appendix), on the whole they are best ignored (thus following the lead of the Chronicler[s], who almost invariably deleted all synchronistic references to the kings of Israel).[29]   Untangling the various redaction levels of Kings will undoubtedly continue to elicit much scholarly effort; although several recent studies have clarified significantly our understanding of Dtr G, Dtr 1, and Dtr 2, much work remains yet to be done. It is hoped, however, that the observations advanced in this chapter will, at least to some extant, lead to a deeper understanding of the complex Dtr tradition lying behind the present books of Samuel and Kings, as well as a deeper appreciation of that anonymous final redactor we call Dtr 2, who saw in what was probably only a fleeting gesture of generosity by an obscure Babylonian monarch in his accession year reason enough to update and edit the Israelite and Judahite history which has long since eclipsed in fame and influence any other such historiographic work from ancient times.

---

misunderstandings underlying these synchronisms, see Antti Laato, "New Viewpoints on the Chronology of the Kings of Judah and Israel," *ZAW* 98 (1986) 210-21.

[29]The book of Chronicles, although virtually free of the synchronisms which introduce nearly every accession formula in Kings (see, however, 2 Chr 13:1), contains a number of additional synchronisms not in Kings. As Albright ("Chronology," pp. 18-20, and especially nn. 10, 14) pointed out, there are a number of synchronisms for the reign of Asa which are independent of Kings (e.g., 2 Chr 15:10, 19; 16:1, 12, 13); two of these (15:19 and 16:1) are in clear contradiction with the regnal totals of both Kings and Chronicles, leading Albright to embrace them as original. The origin of these synchronisms is indeed obscure; Thiele (*Mysterious Numbers*, 1st ed., pp. 58-59) may well be correct in suggesting that these latter synchronisms originally did not refer to the reign of Asa but rather to the years since the disruption of the United Monarchy. At any rate, one must be careful about relying too heavily upon these synchronisms from Chronicles, for they will make shambles out of what otherwise proves to be a reasonably straightforward chronological reconstruction for the early kings of the divided monarchies of Israel and Judah, based on the regnal totals (see the Appendix for details).

APPENDIX

A CHRONOLOGY FOR THE UNITED AND DIVIDED MONARCHY OF ISRAEL

The following Table represents a *tentative* chronological reconstruction for the period of the Davidic dynasty from the late eleventh to early sixth centuries B.C.E.; as will be evident in the notes, it draws heavily upon the work of Albright and Tadmor, and somewhat upon Thiele as well. It should be noted that the dates which seem reasonably secure (mostly those fixed by external synchronisms) are indicated by a double-underscoring (e.g., 968); all other dates are approximate. Although I hesitate to claim much improvement over Albright's five-year margin of error, I suspect that (especially due to the evidence from the Tyrian King List) the margin of error for the early kings has been successfully diminished to about that point. Dating the accession of Hezekiah, of course, remains problematic,[1] and this has profound

---

[1]While in the process of compiling this section, I came across the recent article of Nadav Na'aman entitled "Historical and Chronological Notes on the Kingdoms of Israel and Judah in the Eighth Century B.C." (*VT* 36 [1986] 71-92); although disagreeing with a number of his proposed dates, I was gratified to find myself in close agreement with his early date for the accession of Hezekiah. Na'aman, along with many other biblical chronographers (not least, Albright), placed much emphasis on the Dtr synchronisms (which he suggested were probably derived from a source independent of those for the regnal years; see p. 90 of his article). After several years of juggling with the figures, I have come to a different conclusion: I suspect that the synchronisms (at least those connected with the regnal accession formulae) represent secondary calculations of Dtr provenance based upon originally separate Judahite and Israelite king lists (cf. my discussion above in Chapter V). However, other synchronisms which were imbedded in narrative material may well have been more primitive (e.g., 2 Kgs 14:17; 15:30; 18:10; and possibly 18:13, although this remains, as we have seen, problematic).

Inasmuch as the regnal totals may be, quite apart from the synchronisms, relatively easily aligned with the extra-biblical dates (with only a few alterations necessary), while chaos ensues if one attempts to accommodate the synchronisms (e.g., the 10 years of Menahem between the 39th and the 50th years of Azariah [2 Kgs 15:17, 23], especially if one attempts to antedate); I remain skeptical of any value of these synchronisms to "correct" the regnal totals. As noted in the discussion in the previous chapter, I concur with those who would posit coregencies among the Judahite monarchs in order to explain

implications for several of the monarchs of the mid to late eighth century. Unless otherwise noted, the dates represent spring New Years for Judah (i.e. starting in Nisan), and fall New Years for Israel (probably corresponding not to the seventh, but to the eighth month of the Judahite calendar).[2]

(some) of their high regnal totals; however, I do not consider seemingly aberrant synchronisms sufficient reason to posit a coregency without further biblical or extra-biblical evidence (I fear Na'aman has fallen too quickly into this trap). At any rate, I doubt that the Dtr editors were themselves aware of any such coregencies (even of the rather well attested one between Azariah and Jotham; contrast 2 Kgs 15:5 with the synchronisms found in 15:32 and 16:1).

[2]The question of whether the Judahite and/or the Israelite New Year began in the spring or the fall remains unsettled; I am following Tadmor ("First Temple Period" [see above, p. 2, n. 4], pp. 50-51; cf. the references cited in his nn. 21-22), who suggested that the Judahite kings reckoned their reigns using a spring New Year whereas the Israelite kings used a fall New Year. In addition, as S. Talmon ("Divergences in Calendar-Reckoning in Ephraim and Judah," *VT* 8 [1958] 48-74; reprinted in his *King, Cult and Calendar in Ancient Israel: Collected Studies* [Jerusalem: Magnes, 1986], pp. 113-39) has pointed out, it appears that the calendars of the two kingdoms may have differed by a month with the Israelite calendar lagging behind its Judahite counterpart by that amount (cf. the analogous variation in the agricultural year between the two regions as well as Jeroboam's apparent delay of the feast of Tabernacles [1 Kgs 12:32-33] and Hezekiah's delay of Passover, probably for the sake of the recently displaced Northerners [2 Chr 30:2]). For a different interpretation of these one month delays, see J. B. Segal, "Intercalation and the Hebrew Calendar," *VT* 7 (1957) 250-307, and especially pp. 256-59.

CHRONOLOGICAL TABLE FOR THE UNITED AND DIVIDED MONARCHY OF ISRAEL[a]

United Monarchy		
David	40[b]	1010-971[c]
Solomon	40	971-932[d]
Founding of the First Temple		968[e]

Divided Monarchy					
Judah			Israel		
Rehoboam	17	932-916	Jeroboam I	22	932-911
Abijam	3	916-914	Nadab	2	911-910
Asa	41	914-874	Baasha	24	910-887
			Elah	2	887-886
			Zimri	7 days[e]	886
			(interregnum)		886-884[f]
Jehoshaphat	25	874-850	Omri	12	884-873[g]
			Ahab	22	873-852
Jehoram	8	850-843	Ahaziah	2	852-851
Ahaziah	[1] 2[h]	843-842	Joram	[12] 10	851-842[i]
Athaliah	7	842-836	Jehu	28	842-815[j]
Jehoash	40	836-797	Joahaz	17	815-799
Amaziah	29	797-769	Joash	16	799-784[k]
Azariah	[52] 42[l]	783-742[m]	Jeroboam II	41	784-744
Jotham	16	751-736[n]	Zechariah	6 mos	744-743
			Shallum	1 mo	743
			Menahem	[10] 8[o]	743-737
			Pekahiah	2	737-736

Divided Monarchy						
Judah			Israel			
Ahaz	[16] 10	736-727[p]	Pekah		[20] 5[o]	736-732[q]
Hezekiah	29	727-698[r]	Hoshea		9	732-724
Fall of Samaria in 722/21[s]						
Manasseh	55	697-642[t]				
Amon	2	641-640[u]				
Josiah	31	639-609				
Jehoahaz	3 mos	609				
Jehoiakim	11	608-598				
Jehoiachin	3 mos	597				
Zedekiah	11	596-586[v]				
Fall of Jerusalem in 587/86[v]						

[a]Biblical regnal totals which differ from those adopted here appear in brackets (e.g., for Azariah [52]); antedating practice is assumed until the reign of Manasseh (cf. Albright, "Chronology" [see above, p. 4, n. 8], p. 22, n. 29).

[b]Although the suspicion tends to linger that both the 40 year reigns of David and Solomon are only round numbers, chronological data found in 1 Kgs 2:11 (cf. 2 Sam 5:4-5), which indicate that David reigned for 7 years (or 7 years and 6 months) in Hebron and then 33 years in Jerusalem, seem to support the accuracy of at least the first figure of forty regnal years. If Solomon reigned as coregent for a few of David's last years as king, as the narrative sequence in 1 Kgs 1-2 seems to imply, then the Davidic dates would naturally have to be adjusted downward.

[c]On the accuracy of these dates, firmly fixed as they are by the Tyrian King List, see above, Chapter II.

[d]Admittedly, this date depends upon the 40 year regnal total for Solomon, but inasmuch as the following Judahite regnal figures (down to the death of Ahaziah in 842) accord almost exactly with this date, its accuracy seems reasonably well assured.

[e]So MT and $\mathfrak{G}^L$; $\mathfrak{G}^B$ reads "seven years." The subsequent chronological reconstruction of the Omrides remains difficult, with the Greek texts attesting a different chronology from that of the MT. As has been noted above in Chapter I (see above,

pp. 23-25), J. D. Shenkel proposed that the "Old Greek" chronology preceded that of the MT (the "Hebrew" chronology); however, this thesis was sharply challenged by D. W. Gooding (see above, p. 24, n. 58) on a number of points (cf. also the recent study by Alberto Green, "Regnal Formulas in the Hebrew and Greek Texts of the Books of Kings," *JNES* 42 [1983] 167-80). While I suspect that Gooding was too optimistic about the chronology of the MT (he essentially followed Thiele's approach), he did raise several important queries about the Greek evidence. Both Gooding and Shenkel agree that the "seven years" of $\mathbb{G}^B$ for Zimri is secondary; Gooding is probably right to discount as well the odd synchronism of both $\mathbb{G}^B$ and $\mathbb{G}^L$ in 3 Reigns 16:6 (Elah's accession = 20th year of Asa) as a secondary harmonization. However, these admittedly secondary developments do not vitiate the importance of the (at least for the Hebrew chronology) strangely aberrant synchronism in 17:23, the one which introduces Shenkel's Old Greek chronology for the Omride kings (see pp. 38-42 of his book). In other words, while the chronology of $\mathbb{G}^B$ as reflected in 3 Reigns 16:6-15 (cf. Gooding's review, pp. 124-25; Shenkel, *Chronology and Recensional Development*, pp. 32-36) probably represents a secondary, backward adjustment to align the reigns of Elah and Zimri to the Old Greek chronology for the Omrides (3 Reigns 16:23, 28a, 29 [contrast 16:29 MT]; 22:41), I still think Shenkel's major thesis is correct: the Old Greek chronology (for the Omride kings) predates the Hebrew, and is probably original. Thus, I am not surprised that the Old Greek chronology accords almost exactly with my own suggested chronological reconstruction of the Omride kings, whereas the Hebrew chronology remains self-contradictory (e.g., contrast 1 Kgs 16:23 with vv 18 and 29; cf. the comments of Albright, "Chronology," n. 15, pp. 20-21).

   [f]Presumably the period of time in which Omri and Tibni contended for power; cf. 1 Kgs 16:21-22. Inasmuch as Ahab was still alive in 853 (cf. Albright, "Chronology," p. 21, n. 17), assuming correct regnal totals for both Omri and Ahab, the latter must have ascended to the throne by 873 (possibly 874) and the former by 884 (or, less likely, by 885).

   [g]I am assuming that the anomalous synchronism found in 1 Kgs 16:23 is original. Again, it should be noted that my chronological reconstruction for this period accords almost exactly with that of the Old Greek (see above, note e), although the two were derived by entirely different means.

   [h]As Tadmor ("First Temple Period" [see above, p. 2, n. 4], p. 52), has pointed out, normally one would have expected either two regnal years (if Ahaziah had reigned beyond the New Year, reckoning by the antedating system), or the exact number of months (if he had reigned for less than a year; cf. Zechariah and Shallum); probably the best assumption to make here is that the original source listed one year plus several months, and that this was later reduced to just one year.

   [i]See next note. As both Tadmor ("First Temple Period," p. 59) and Albright ("Chronology," p. 21, n. 17) have pointed out, the 12 year regnal total for Joram of Israel

is too large (it may have resulted from contamination with the 12s, 24s, and 22 + 2s representative of the rest of the early regnal totals of the Israelite kings (cf. Tadmor, "First Temple Period," p. 52). For a recent defense of the provocative theory that Jehoram of Judah and Joram of Israel were the same person (the difference in orthography being consistent with the respective regional dialects), see John Strange, "Joram, King of Israel and Judah," *VT* 25 (1975) 191-201.

[j]Jehu paid tribute to Assyria in the 18th year of Shalmaneser III, i.e. after Nisan of the year 841 B.C.E. Presumably his rebellion took place the previous winter while Joram was recovering from his wounds in the Omride winter residency at Jezreel (see Tadmor, "First Temple Period," p. 59; cf. Albright, "Chronology," p. 21, n. 17).

[k]It was probably in the year 796 that Joash paid tribute to Adad-nirari III; see A. R. Millard and H. Tadmor, "Adad-nirari III in Syria: Another Stele Fragment and the Dates of His Campaigns," *Iraq* 35 (1973) 57-64; also H. Tadmor, "The Historical Inscriptions of Adad-nirari III," *Iraq* 35 (1973) 141-50.

[l]The extant regnal total for Azariah (Uzziah), even including the years of probable coregencies (see next note), is still too large; cf. Albright, "Chronology," p. 21, nn. 21-22. In the light of Albright's suggestion (following a proposal first made by Thiele) that a careful analysis of the records of Tiglath-pileser III indicates Azariah's participation in the events of the year 743, only to seemingly disappear the next year (see Albright, *ibid.*, p. 18, n. 8), I cannot accept Tadmor's suggestion to retain his biblical regnal total of 52 (Tadmor proposed dating him to 785-733, including a 16+ year coregency with Amaziah [785-769] and a 16 year coregency with Jotham [758-743], and thus outliving his son Jotham by some 10 years; note that Tadmor's rationale for these dates rests largely upon the synchronisms with the Israelite kings--synchronisms which, in my opinion, are almost certainly secondary calculations made by the Dtr editors).

[m]For the date of 742 for the death of Azariah, see the previous note. I have presupposed a 15 year coregency between Azariah and his father Amaziah, in basic agreement with Tadmor, Aharoni, and now Na'aman (see my above discussion in Chapter I, pp. 9-11, and especially nn. 20, 24; for Na'aman's article, see above, n. 1 on p. 151). The seemingly aberrant synchronism of 2 Kgs 15:1, although apparently 12 years out of line (cf. my above discussion in Chapter I, p. 19), still may be used as a check of the dating of the accession of Jeroboam II, some 15 years before that of Azariah's sole reign in 769. For the clearly attested coregency between Azariah and his son Jotham, see Albright, "Chronology," p. 21, and n. 23. Further confirmation of the essential accuracy of my proposed chronology for this period may be found in the odd synchronism found in 2 Kgs 15:30, which links Jotham's 20th year with the first of Hoshea (almost certainly to be dated to 732; see below, notes p and q).

[n]Concerning the external evidence for these dates, see the previous and the following notes. Presumably Jotham lived to 732, some four years after Ahaz's accession as king (or coregent?).

[o]On the secondary nature of these numbers, see Albright, "Chronology," pp. 21-22, nn. 24, 26. In the year 738, Menahem paid tribute to Pul (= Tiglath-pileser III); cf. Tadmor, "First Temple Period," p. 54 (event no. 4), also the recent references cited in his n. 30 on p. 319.

[p]The regnal figure one adopts for Ahaz will closely depend upon the date one adopts for the accession of Hezekiah. Albright and Thiele (who both dated Hezekiah's accession to 715) were forced to increase this regnal total to 20 (concerning Thiele's vacillations on this topic, see my above discussion, pp. 21-23); Tadmor (who preferred the date of 727 for Hezekiah's accession) retained the biblical total of 16 for Ahaz by pushing Jotham's reign back to 758-743 (see above, note l). The synchronisms are of no help here inasmuch as they are clearly secondary (depending upon the improbable 20 year regnal total for Pekah). Since Hoshea's reign is able to be closely dated (see next note), and since according to 2 Kgs 15:30 Jotham's 20th year is to be equated with Hoshea's accession year (732), I prefer reducing Ahaz's regnal total from 16 (reminiscent of Jotham?) to 10. Alternatively, one could posit a coregency between Ahaz and Hezekiah, as Na'aman does, but this approach seems more problematic, especially in the light of the chronological datum found in Isa 14:28-29 which apparently links the death of Ahaz to the same year as the death of Tiglath-pileser III (727/26). (For further discussion concerning this last reference, see above, p. 115, n. 127.)

[q]The date of 732 for the death of Pekah and the accession of Hoshea is virtually certain (cf. Albright, "Chronology," p. 22, n. 26; Tadmor, "First Temple Period," p. 54). At least two conclusions follow from this datum: 1) the biblical regnal total of 20 years for Pekah is impossibly too large (Menahem was still king in 738, whereas Hoshea must have ascended the throne by 731 at the latest); and 2) the Dtr synchronisms based upon Pekah's regnal total (e.g., 2 Kgs 15:32; 16:1) are secondary, hence valueless. Probably a third conclusion should be listed here as well: Tadmor ("Chronology" [Hebrew], *Encyclopedia Miqra'it*, vol. 4, cols. 287-88) has pointed out that the synchronisms of 2 Kgs 18:1, 9-10 are probably also secondary calculations, predicated upon the assumption that the fall of Samaria (correctly dated to the 6th year of Hezekiah in v 10) must have taken place in Hoshea's 9th year (when in reality, his reign probably ended some two years earlier [see the next note]; cf. Albright's suggested dates of 732-724 for Hoshea, but 722/21 for the fall of Samaria). I have for some time suspected that the Dtr editors, when they were calculating their synchronisms from the king lists, probably worked backwards from the original synchronism of the fall of Samaria in Hezekiah's sixth year, but got into trouble almost immediately with Hoshea's dates, and fell hopelessly into error with the alleged 20 year reign of Pekah (recently Na'aman [see above, note 1, p. 151] also discussed the likelihood of such a "backwards counting" theory for Pekah, citing analogous procedures in both Egyptian and Mesopotamian sources).

Therefore, only the seemingly aberrant synchronisms (e.g., 2 Kgs 14:17; 15:1 [?], 30) can be used with any confidence to reconstruct the actual chronological situation.

ʳThe question of the dating of Hezekiah's accession, of course, remains in dispute. My own reasons for following Tadmor's early date have already been spelled out (see above, pp. 114-16, and especially nn. 124, 127). Perhaps a relatively subtle piece of corroborating evidence may be found in 2 Chr 29:3; 30:1-2, where Hezekiah's famous Passover (apparently dated to his first [or accession] year) is said to have taken place in the second month. S. Talmon ("Calendar-Reckoning" [see above, n. 2, p. 152], pp. 58-62) may well be right in suggesting that this one month delay was prompted by the difference between the calendars of the two kingdoms. However, I would submit that there would have been a real need for such a calendrical concession only if the Northern Kingdom (and its calendar) were still in existence; i.e. only if Hezekiah's Passover had taken place before the fall of Samaria. Thus, even the incidental detail of the timing of Hezekiah's Passover tends to support an early date for his accession.

ˢConcerning this date, cf. Albright, "Chronology," p. 22, n. 27. Tadmor ("The Campaigns of Sargon II of Assur: A Chronological-Historical Study," *JCS* 12 [1958] 37-39) argued strongly for dating the fall of Samaria to the late summer or early autumn of 722, following a two year siege of the city (at the beginning of which Hoshea had already been deported to Assyria).

ᵗAs Albright ("Chronology," p. 22, n. 29) has noted, the Assyrian system of postdating has replaced the earlier antedating system by this time. Note, however, that, *contra* Albright, there is no need to emend Manasseh's regnal total.

ᵘConcerning these dates for Manasseh's successors, most of which are quite firm, see Tadmor, "Chronology of the Last Kings of Judah," *JNES* 15 (1956) 226-30. Note that under the postdating system Amon's accession year would have been 642, but his first regnal year 641, etc.

ᵛThe fall of Jerusalem is traditionally dated to 587 B.C.E., but see Tadmor, "First Temple Period," pp. 55-56, and nn. 32-33, where he followed 2 Kgs 25:8 in synchronizing the 11th and last year of Zedekiah with the 19th year of Nebuchadnezzer (= 1 Nisan 586); also cf. Tadmor, "Chronology of the Last Kings of Judah," p. 230 (however, cf. his n. 26 on that page).

BIBLIOGRAPHY

Ackroyd, P. R. "An Interpretation of the Babylonian Exile: A Study of 2 Kings 20, Isaiah 38-39." *SJT* 27 (1974) 329-52.

Aharoni, Yohanan. "The Chronology of the Kings of Israel and Judah" [Hebrew]. *Tarbiz* 21 (1950) 92-100.

_____. *The Land of the Bible: A Historical Geography.* Revised ed. Trans. and ed. by A. F. Rainey. Philadelphia: Westminster Press, 1979.

Albright, W. F. "Alternative Chronology." *Interpretation* 6 (1952) 101-103.

_____. *Archaeology and the Religion of Israel.* Baltimore: Johns Hopkins Press, 1942.

_____. "The Biblical Period." *The Jews: Their History, Culture, and Religion.* Louis Finkelstein, ed. New York: Harper & Brothers, 1949, 1:3-69.

_____. "The Chronology of the Divided Monarchy of Israel." *BASOR* 100 (1945) 16-22.

_____. "Egypt and the Early History of the Negeb." *JPOS* 4 (1924) 131-61.

_____. "Further Light on Synchronisms between Egypt and Asia in the Period 935-685 B.C." *BASOR* 141 (1956) 23-27.

_____. "The History of Palestine and Syria." *JQR* 24 (1934) 363-76.

_____. "The Nebuchadnezzar and Neriglissar Chronicles." *BASOR* 143 (1956) 28-33.

_____. "The New Assyro-Tyrian Synchronism and the Chronology of Tyre." *Annuaire de l'Institut de Philologie et Histoire Orientales et Slaves* 13 (1953) [Mélanges Isadore Lévy (Bruxelles, 1955)] 1-9.

_____. "New Light from Egypt on the Chronology and History of Israel and Judah." *BASOR* 130 (1953) 4-11.

_____. "The Original Account of the Fall of Samaria." *BASOR* 174 (1964) 66-67.

_____. "Syria, the Philistines, and Phoenicia." *The Cambridge Ancient History.* 3rd ed. Vol. II, Part 2. History of the Middle East and the Aegean Region c. 1380-1000 B.C. Cambridge: University Press, 1975. Pp. 507-36.

_____. *Yahweh and the Gods of Canaan.* New York: Doubleday & Co., 1968.

Andersen, K. T. "Die Chronologie der Könige von Israel und Juda." *Studia Theologica* 23 (1969) 69-114.

_____. "Noch einmal: Die Chronologie der Könige von Israel und Juda." *Scandinavian Journal of the Old Testament* (1/1989) 1-45.

Astour, Michael C. "841 B.C.: The First Assyrian Invasion of Israel." *JAOS* 91 (1971) 383-89.

Baer, Klaus. "The Libyan and Nubian Kings of Egypt: Notes on the Chronology of Dynasties XXII to XXVI." *JNES* 32 (1973) 4-25.

Barnes, Timothy D. *Constantine and Eusebius.* Cambridge: Harvard University Press, 1981.

Barr, James. "Why the World Was Created in 4004 B.C.: Archbishop Ussher and Biblical Chronology." *BJRL* 67 (1985) 575-608.

Barta, Winfried. "Die Mondfinsternis Im 15. Regierungsjahr Takelots II. und die Chronologie der 22. bis 25. Dynastie." *RdÉ* 32 (1980) 3-17.

Beckerath, Jürgen von. "The Nile Level Records at Karnak and Their Importance for the History of the Libyan Period (Dynasties XXII and XXIII)." *JARCE* 5 (1966) 43-55.

Begrich, Joachim. *Die Chronologie der Könige von Israel und Juda.* Tübingen, 1929.

Bin-Nun, Shoshana R. "Formulas from Royal Records of Israel and of Judah." *VT* 18 (1968) 414-32.

Borger, R. "Das Ende des Ägyptischen Feldherrn Sib'e = ‫סוא‬." *JNES* 19 (1960) 49-53.

Bright, John. *A History of Israel.* 3rd ed. Philadelphia: Westminster Press, 1981.

Brinkman, J. A. "Merodach-Baladan II." *Studies Presented to A. Leo Oppenheim, June 7, 1964.* Chicago: The Oriental Institute, 1964. Pp. 6-53.

_____. "Sennacherib's Babylonian Problem: An Interpretation." *JCS* 25 (1973) 89-95.

Caminos, Ricardo A. *The Chronicle of Prince Osorkon.* Analecta Orientalia, Vol. 37. Rome: Pontifical Biblical Institute, 1958.

_____. "Gebel Es-Silsilis No. 100." *JEA* 38 (1952) 46-61 + Plates X-XIII.

Carter, Howard. "Report of Work Done in Upper Egypt (1902-1903)." *ASAE* 4 (1903) 171-80. With a "Note additionnelle" by G. Maspero on p. 180.

Childs, Brevard S. *Isaiah and the Assyrian Crisis.* Studies in Biblical Theology. Second Series, No. 3. London: SCM Press, 1967.

Christensen, Duane L. "The Identity of 'King So' in Egypt (2 Kings xvii 4)." *VT* 39 (1989) 140-53.

Cramer, J. A., ed. *Anecdota Graeca e Codd. Manuscriptis Bibliothecae Regiae Parisiensis.* Vol. 2. Oxford, 1839.

Cross, F. M., Jr. *Canaanite Myth and Hebrew Epic.* Cambridge: Harvard University Press, 1973.

_____. "An Interpretation of the Nora Stone." *BASOR* 208 (1972) 13-19.

_____. "A Reconstruction of the Judean Restoration." *JBL* 94 (1975) 4-18.

_____. "The Seal of Miqnêyaw, Servant of Yahweh." *Ancient Seals and the Bible.* Occasional Papers on the Near East, Vol. 2/1. Leonard Gorelick and Elizabeth Williams-Forte, eds. Malibu: Undena Publications, 1983. Pp. 55-63 + Plates IX-XI.

Cryer, Frederick H. "To the One of Fictive Music: OT Chronology and History." *Scandinavian Journal of the Old Testament* (2/1987) 1-27.

Dever, W. G. *et al.* "Further Excavations at Gezer, 1967-1971." *BA* 34 (1971) 94-132.

De Vries, S. J. "Chronology of the OT." *IDB*. 1:580-99.

_____. "Chronology, OT." *IDBS*. Pp. 161-66.

Dunham, Dows, and Macadam, M. F. Laming. "Names and Relationships of the Royal Family of Napata." *JEA* 35 (1949) 139-49 + Plates XV and XVI.

Fewell, Danna Nolan. "Sennacherib's Defeat: Words at War in 2 Kings 18.13-19.37." *JSOT* 34 (1986) 79-90.

Freedman, David Noel. "Headings in the Books of the Eighth-Century Prophets." *AUSS* 25 (1987) 9-26.

Gadd, C. J. "Inscribed Barrel Cylinder of Marduk-Apla-Iddina II." *Iraq* 15 (1953) 123-34.

Gardiner, Alan. *Egyptian Grammar.* 3rd revised ed. London: Oxford University Press, 1957.

_____. *Egypt of the Pharaohs: An Introduction.* Oxford: Clarendon Press, 1961.

_____. "Regnal Years and Civil Calendar in Pharaonic Egypt." *JEA* 31 (1945) 11-28.

Gauthier, H. "Les Steles de l'an II de Taharqa de Medinet-Habou." *ASAE* 18 (1919) 90.

Goedicke, Hans. "The End of 'So, King of Egypt.'" *BASOR* 171 (1963) 64-66.

Gooding, D. W. Review of *Chronology and Recensional Development in the Greek Text of Kings* by J. D. Shenkel. *JTS* 21 (1970) 118-31.

Goossens, Godifroy. "Taharqa le conquérant." *CdÉ* 22 (1947) 239-44.

Grant, Robert M. *Theophilus of Antioch: Ad Autolycum.* Oxford, 1970.

Gray, John. *I & II Kings: A Commentary*. The Old Testament Library. London: SCM Press, 1964. 2nd ed. Philadelphia: Westminster Press, 1970.

Green, Alberto R. "Regal Formulas in the Hebrew and Greek Texts of the Books of Kings." *JNES* 42 (1983) 167-80.

Griffith, F. Ll. *Catalogue of the Demotic Papyri in the John Rylands Library*. Vol. 3. Manchester, 1909.

Hallo, William W. "From Qarqar to Carchemish: Assyria and Israel in the Light of New Discoveries." *BA* 23 (1960) 34-61.

_____, and Simpson, William Kelly. *The Ancient Near East: A History*. New York: Harcourt Brace Jovanovich, 1971.

Herrmann, Siegfried. *A History of Israel in Old Testament Times*. Revised and enlarged ed. Trans. John Bowden. Philadelphia: Fortress Press, 1981.

Hölscher, Uvo. *The Excavations of Medinet Habu, Vol. 2: The Temples of the Eighteenth Dynasty*. The University of Chicago Oriental Institute Publications, Vol. 41. Chicago: University of Chicago Press, 1939.

Honor, Leo L. *Sennacherib's Invasion of Palestine: A Critical Source Study*. Contributions to Oriental History and Philology, No. 12. New York: Columbia University Press, 1926.

Horn, Siegfried H. "The Chronology of King Hezekiah's Reign." *AUSS* 2 (1964) 40-52.

_____. "Did Sennacherib Campaign Once or Twice Against Hezekiah?" *AUSS* 4 (1966) 1-28.

Hornung, Erik. *Untersuchungen zur Chronologie und Geschichte des Neuen Reiches*. Ägptologische Abhandlungen, Band 11. Wiesbaden: Otto Harrassowitz, 1964.

Janssen, Jozef M. A. "Que sait-on actuellement du Pharaon Taharqa?" *Biblica* 34 (1953) 23-43.

Jenkins, A. K. "Hezekiah's Fourteenth Year: A New Interpretation of 2 Kings xviii 13-xix 37." *VT* 26 (1976) 284-98.

Josephus, Flavius. *Contra Apionem*. The Loeb Classical Library. Vol. 1. Trans. by H. St. J. Thackeray. Cambridge: Harvard University Press, 1946.

Katzenstein, H. Jacob. *The History of Tyre*. Jerusalem: Goldberg's Press, 1973.

Kitchen, K. A. "Further Thoughts on Egyptian Chronology in the Third Intermediate Period." *RdÉ* 34 (1982-83) 59-69.

_____. "Late Egyptian Chronology and the Hebrew Monarchy: Critical Studies in Old Testament Mythology, I." *JANES* 5 (1973) [The Gaster Festschrift], pp. 225-33.

_____. "On the Princedoms of Late-Libyan Egypt." *CdÉ* 52 (1977) 40-48.

_____. *The Third Intermediate Period in Egypt (1100-650 B.C.* Warminster: Aris & Phillips, 1973; 2nd ed. with supplement, *idem*, 1986.

Krahmalkov, Charles R. "The Historical Setting of the Adon Letter." *BA* 44 (1981) 197-98.

Kuenen, Abraham. *Historisch-Kritische Einleitung in die Bücher des Alten Testaments*. 3 vols. Leipzig, 1892.

Kugler, F. X. *Von Moses bis Paulus*. Münster, 1922.

Laato, Annti. "New Viewpoints on the Chronology of the Kings of Judah and Israel." *ZAW* 98 (1986) 210-21.

Lambdin, T. O. "Zoan." *IDB*. 4:961.

Larsson, Gerhard. "The Documentary Hypothesis and the Chronological Structure of the Old Testament." *ZAW* 97 (1985) 316-33.

Leclant, Jean, and Yoyotte, Jean. "Notes d'histoire et de civilisation éthiopiennes." *BIFAO* 51 (1952) 1-39.

Legrain, G. "Textes gravés sur le quai de Karnak." *ZÄS* 34 (1896) 111-21.

Levine, Louis D. "Sennacherib's Southern Front: 704-689 B.C." *JCS* 34 (1982) 28-58.

Lipiński, E. "Ba'li-Ma'zer II and the Chronology of Tyre." *Rivista degli studi orientali* 45 (1970) 59-65.

Liver, J. "The Chronology of Tyre at the Beginning of the First Millennium B.C." *IEJ* 3 (1953) 119-20.

Macadam, M. F. Laming. *The Temples of Kawa: I. The Inscriptions.* Texts and plates in two separate volumes. London: Oxford University Press, 1949.

Macy, H. R. "Sources of the Books of Chronicles." Unpublished Ph.D. Thesis. Harvard University, 1975.

McCarter, P. Kyle. "'Yaw, Son of 'Omri': A Philological Note on Israelite Chronology." *BASOR* 216 (1974) 5-7.

McKenzie, Steven L. *The Chronicler's Use of the Deuteronomistic History.* Harvard Semitic Monographs, No. 33. Atlanta: Scholars Press, 1985.

Millard, A. R., and Tadmor, Hayim. "Adad-nirari III in Syria: Another Stele Fragment and the Dates of His Campaigns." *Iraq* 35 (1973) 57-64.

Miller, J. Maxwell. "Another Look at the Chronology of the Early Divided Monarchy." *JBL* 86 (1967) 276-88.

Moscati, Sabatino, ed. *An Introduction to the Comparative Grammar of the Semitic Languages: Phonology and Morphology.* Porta Linguarum Orientalium. Wiesbaden: Otto Harrassowitz, 1969.

Mosshammer, Alden A. *The Chronicle of Eusebius and Greek Chronographic Tradition.* Lewisburg: Bucknell University Press, 1979.

Mowinckel, Sigmund. "Die Chronologie der israelitischen und jüdischen Könige." *Acta Orientalia* 10 (1932) 161-277.

Murnane, William H. *Ancient Egyptian Coregencies.* The Oriental Institute of Chicago: Studies in Ancient Oriental Civilization, No. 40. Chicago: The Oriental Institute, 1977.

Na'aman, Nadav. "Historical and Chronological Notes on the Kingdoms of Israel and Judah in the Eighth Century B.C." *VT* 36 (1986) 71-92.

_____. "Sennacherib's Campaign to Judah and the Date of the *LMLK* Stamps." *VT* 29 (1979) 61-86.

_____. "Sennacherib's 'Letter to God' on His Campaign to Judah." *BASOR* 214 (1974) 25-39.

Nelson, Richard D. *The Double Redaction of the Deuteronomistic History.* Journal for the Study of the Old Testament Supplement Series, No. 18. Sheffield: JSOT Press, 1981.

Nicholson, E. W. *Deuteronomy and Tradition.* Philadelphia: Fortress Press, 1967.

Niese, Benedictus, ed. *Flavii Iosephi Opera.* Berlin, 1889.

Noth, Martin. *The Deuteronomistic History.* Journal for the Study of the Old Testament Supplement Series. David J. A. Clines, Philip R. Davies, and David M. Gunn, eds. Sheffield: JSOT Press, 1981.

Oppenheim, A. Leo. "Sennacherib." *IDB.* 4:270-72.

Otto, J. C. T., ed. *Theophili Episcopi Antiocheni Ad Autolycum Libri Tres* [= Corpus Apologetarum Christianorum Saeculi Secundi, Vol. 8]. Jena, 1861.

Parker, Richard A. *The Calendars of Ancient Egypt.* The Oriental Institute of the University of Chicago: Studies in Ancient Oriental Civilization, No. 26. Chicago: University of Chicago Press, 1950.

_____. "The Length of Reign of Taharqa." *Kush* 8 (1960) 267-69.

_____. "The Lunar Dates of Thutmose III and Ramesses II." *JNES* 16 (1957) 39-43.

_____. "The Names of the Sixteenth Day of the Lunar Month." *JNES* 12 (1950) 50.

Parpola, Simo. "The Murderer of Sennacherib." *Death in Mesopotamia.* Mesopotamia: Copenhagen Studies in Assyriology, Vol. 8. Papers read at the XXVIe Rencontre assyriologique internationale. Bendt Alster, ed. Copenhagen: Akademisk Forlag, 1980. Pp. 171-82.

Peñuela, J. M. "La Inscripción Asiria IM 55644 y la Cronología de los reyes de Tiro" [in two parts]. *Sefarad* 13 (1953) 217-37 and 14 (1954) 1-39.

Picard, G. C., and Picard, C. *The Life and Death of Carthage.* Trans. Dominique Collon. London: Thomas Nelson, 1968.

Porten, Bezalel. "The Identity of King Adon." *BA* 44 (1981) 36-52.

Rainey, Anson F. "Taharqa and Syntax." *Tel Aviv* 3 (1976) 38-41.

Ray, J. D. "Pharaoh Nechepso." *JEA* 60 (1974) 255-56.

Reade, Julian. "Mesopotamian Guidelines for Biblical Chronology." *Syro-Mesopotamian Studies* 4/1 (1981) 1-9.

Redford, Donald B. "A Note on II Kings, 17, 4." *The SSEA Journal* 11 (1981) 75-76.

_____. "Sais and the Kushite Invasions of the Eighth Century B.C." *JARCE* 22 (1985) 5-15.

_____. "Studies in Relations Between Palestine and Egypt during the First Millenium B.C.: II. The Twenty-second Dynasty." *JAOS* 93 (1973) 3-17.

Reliefs and Inscriptions at Karnak. Vol. III. *The Bubastite Portal.* University of Chicago Oriental Institute Publications, No. 84. Chicago: University of Chicago Press, 1954.

Renouf, P. Le Page. "The Eclipse in Egyptian Texts." *PSBA* 7 (1885) 163-70.

Revillout, Eugène. *Notice des papyrus démotiques archaïques.* Paris, 1896.

Rowley, H. H. "Hezekiah's Reform and Rebellion." *BJRL* 44 (1962) 395-431.

_____. *Men of God: Studies in Old Testament History and Prophecy.* London: Thomas Nelson, 1963.

Rowton, M. B. "Comparative Chronology at the Time of Dynasty XIX." *JNES* 19 (1960) 15-22.

_____. "The Date of the Founding of Solomon's Temple." *BASOR* 119 (1950) 20-22.

_____. "Manetho's Date for Ramesses II." *JEA* 34 (1948) 57-74.

_____. "The Material from Western Asia and the Chronology of the Nineteenth Dynasty." *JNES* 25 (1966) 240-58.

Safar, Fuad. "A Further Text of Shalmaneser III from Assur." *Sumer* 7 (1951) 3-21 + Plates I-III.

Schedl, Claus. "Textkritische Bemerkungen zu den Synchronismen der Könige von Israel und Juda." *VT* 12 (1962) 88-119.

Schmidt, G. "Das Jahr des Regierungsantritts König Taharqas: Ein Beitrag zur Chronologie der 25. Dynastie." *Kush* 6 (1958) 121-30.

Schoene, A., ed. *Eusebi Chronicorum Libri Duo*. Vol. 1. Berlin, 1875.

Segal, J. B. "Intercalation and the Hebrew Calendar." *VT* 7 (1957) 250-307.

Shea, William A. "Sennacherib's Second Palestinian Campaign." *JBL* 104 (1985) 401-18.

Shenkel, James Donald. *Chronology and Recensional Development in the Greek Text of Kings*. Harvard Semitic Monographs, Vol. 1. Cambridge: Harvard University Press, 1968.

Skinner, J. *The Book of the Prophet Isaiah: Chapters I-XXXIX*. The Cambridge Bible. Cambridge, 1896.

Soden, Wolfram von. "Sanherib vor Jerusalem 701 v. Chr." *Antike und Universalgeschichte: Festschrift Hans Erich Stier*. Münster: Verlag Aschendorff, 1972. Pp. 43-51.

_____. *Grundriss der Akkadischen Grammatik*. Rome: Pontifical Biblical Institute, 1952.

Spalinger, Anthony. "The Foreign Policy of Egypt Preceding the Assyrian Conquest." *CdÉ* 53 (1978) 22-47.

_____. "The Year 712 B.C. and its Implications for Egyptian History." *JARCE* 10 (1973) 95-101.

Spiegelberg, Wilhelm. *Die Demotischen Papyrus II.* Catalogue général des antiquités égyptiennes du Musée du Caire. Vol. 39: Text. Strassburg, 1908. Vol. 40: Tafeln. Strassburg, 1906.

Strange, John. "Joram, King of Israel and Judah." *VT* 25 (1975) 191-201.

Syncellus, Georgius. *Chronographia.* Vol. 1. Guilielme Dindorfi, ed. [= *Corpus Scriptorum Byzantinae*, Vol. 12]. Bonnae, 1829.

Tadmor, Hayim. "Amaziah" [Hebrew]. *Encyclopedia Miqra'it.* Vol. 1. Jerusalem: Bialik Institute, 1950. Cols. 438-39.

_____. "The Campaigns of Sargon II of Assur: A Chronological-Historical Study." *JCS* 12 (1958) 22-40, 77-100.

_____. "Chronology" [Hebrew]. *Encyclopedia Miqra'it.* Vol. 4. Jerusalem: Bialik Institute, 1962. Cols. 245-310.

_____. "The Chronology of the First Temple Period: A Presentation and Evaluation of the Sources." *The World History of the Jewish People, First Series: Ancient Times, The Age of the Monarchies: Political History.* Vol. 4, Part 1. Abraham Malamat, ed. Jerusalem: Massada Press, 1979. Pp. 44-60; 318-20.

_____. "Chronology of the Last Kings of Judah." *JNES* 15 (1956) 226-30.

_____. "The Historical Inscriptions of Adad-nirari III." *Iraq* 35 (1973) 141-50.

_____. "Philistia Under Assyrian Rule." *BA* 29 (1966) 86-102.

Talmon, S. "Divergences in Calendar-Reckoning in Ephraim and Judah." *VT* 8 (1958) 48-74.

Tawil, Hayim. "The Historicity of 2 Kings 19:24 (= Isaiah 37:25): The Problem of *Ye'ōrê Māṣôr*." *JNES* 41 (1982) 195-206.

Thiele, Edwin R. "An Additional Chronological Note on 'Yaw, Son of 'Omri.'" *BASOR* 222 (1976) 19-23.

_____. "The Chronology of the Kings of Judah and Israel." *JNES* 3 (1944) 137-86.

_____. "A Comparison of the Chronological Data of Israel and Judah." *VT* 4 (1954) 185-95.

_____. "Coregencies and Overlapping Reigns among the Hebrew Kings." *JBL* 93 (1974) 174-200.

_____. *The Mysterious Numbers of the Hebrew Kings*. 1st ed., Chicago: University of Chicago Press, 1951. 2nd revised ed., Grand Rapids: Eerdmans, 1965. 3rd re-revised ed., Grand Rapids: Zondervan, 1983.

_____. "New Evidence on the Chronology of the Last Kings of Judah." *BASOR* 143 (1956) 22-27.

Thomas, D. Winton, ed. *Documents from Old Testament Times*. London: Thomas Nelson and Sons, 1958.

Uphill, E. P. Review of K. A. Kitchen's *Third Intermediate Period*. *JEA* 61 (1975) 277-83.

Vercoutter, J. "The Napatan Kings and Apis Worship: Serapeum Burials of the Napatan Period." *Kush* 8 (1960) 62-76 + Plates 21 and 22.

Vernus, Pascal. "Inscriptions de la troisième période intermédiaire (I): Les inscriptions de la cour péristyle nord du VIe pylône dans le temple de Karnak." *BIFAO* 75 (1975) 1-66 + Plate V.

Waddell, W. G. *Manetho*. The Loeb Classical Library. Cambridge: Harvard University Press, 1940.

Weippert, Manfred. "Jau(a) Mār Ḥumrî--Joram oder Jehu von Israel?" *VT* 28 (1978) 113-18.

Wente, Edward F. Review of K. A. Kitchen's *Third Intermediate Period*. *JNES* 35 (1976) 275-78.

_____, and Van Siclen, Charles C. III. "A Chronology of the New Kingdom." *Studies in Honor of George R. Hughes*. The Oriental Institute of the University of Chicago: Studies in Ancient Oriental Civilization, No. 39. Chicago: The Oriental Institute, 1976. Pp. 217-61.

Wifall, Walter R. "The Chronology of the Divided Monarchy of Israel." *ZAW* 80 (1968) 319-37.

Wintermute, O. "Kush." *IDBS*. Pp. 200-201.

Yurco, Frank J. "Sennacherib's Third Campaign and the Coregency of Shabaka and Shebitku." *Serapis* 6 (1980) 221-40.

Zwi, Ehud Ben. "Who Wrote the Speech of Rabshakeh and When?" *JBL* 109 (1990) 79-92.

REFERENCE INDEX

Biblical References

(A) Hebrew Bible

Extra-Biblical References

(A) Akkadian Texts/Sources

ADAD-NIRARI III

AUTHOR INDEX

Hölscher, U.	92n55
Honor, L. L.	74n5, 75n9, 79n17
Horn, S. H.	73n3, 79n19, 80n20, 82n28, 83, 84n34, 87n43, 89n48, 90n51, 94n64, 109n112
Hornung, E.	66n26
Hughes, G. R.	59n6, 60n7
Janssen, J. M. A.	88n47
Jenkins, A. K.	83n33
Katzenstein, H. J.	33n10, 34n11, 44nm, 51nn25-26
Kitchen, K. A.	59nn5-6, 60nn7-8, 61n10, 63n14, 64n20, 66nn25-26, 73nn2-3, 88n47, 94n62, 96n67, 97n68, 99nn76-78, 100-103, 104, 105, 111n117, 119, 132, 133nn13-14
Krahmalkov, C. R.	127
Kuenen, A.	75n9
Kugler, F. X.	51n25
Laato, A.	148n28
Lambdin, T. O.	132n7
Larsson, G.	147n26
Leclant, J.	88n47, 89n49, 90-96, 97n68, 99
Legrain, G.	92n57
Levine, L. D.	118nn130-131, 120n137
Lipiński, E.	34, 35n16, 42nk, 46-47, 47n23, 49nc, 52-53, 54nn36-37
Liver, J.	51
Macadam, M. F. L.	86-94, 96, 99n77
Macalister, A.	62n12
Macy, H. R.	142n17

- not as good
  as expected
- but useful

Beginnings of the Cold War

- emphasis on _Poland_ issue
- little or no discussion
  of _internal_ Polish questions
  or relative merits of
  London vs. Lublin
  govts.
- ditto for social forces in
  other E. Europe nations

- nice, quick review
  had by reading ch. 7

- a _very_ useful
  book for teaching

Beginnings of
the Cold War

Martin F. Herz

McGraw-Hill Book Company
New York • St. Louis • San Francisco • Toronto • London • Sydney

Contents

A Few Basic Texts

Passages from Allied declarations and agreements whose breach by the Soviet Union is discussed in this narrative.

ATLANTIC CHARTER, AUGUST 14, 1941

. . . First, their countries seek no aggrandizement, territorial or other;

Second, they desire to see no territorial changes that do not accord with the freely expressed wishes of the people concerned;

Third, they respect the right of all peoples to choose the form of government under which they will live; and they wish to see sovereign rights and self-government restored to those who have been forcibly deprived of them. . . .

Proclaimed by President Roosevelt and Prime Minister Churchill, subscribed to (with a reservation*) by the

* The Russian reservation was as follows:

"Considering that the practical application of these principles will necessarily adapt itself to the circumstances, needs, and historic

A Few Basic Texts

Soviet government on September 24, 1941; reaffirmed in the United Nations Declaration of January 1, 1942; reaffirmed in the Yalta Protocol of February 11, 1945

MOSCOW DECLARATION, NOVEMBER 1, 1943

... jointly declare:

6. That after the termination of hostilities they will not employ their military forces within the territories of other states except for the purposes envisaged in this declaration and after joint consultation.

> *Signed by Foreign Minister Molotov, Foreign Secretary Eden, Secretary of State Hull, and Chinese Ambassador Foo*

---

peculiarities of particular countries, the Soviet Government can state that a consistent application of these principles will secure the most energetic support on the part of the government and peoples of the Soviet Union." Statement by I. M. Maisky, Soviet ambassador to Great Britain, in accepting the principles of the Atlantic Charter on behalf of his government. *Report of Proceedings, Inter-Allied Meeting held in London at St. James Palace on September 24, 1941* (London: H. M. Stationery Office, 1941), Cmd. 6315. (This statement does not appear in the U.S. official documentation series published by the Department of State.) Cf. also Churchill's comment documented in note 11, chap. 2, below.

According to the Hull *Memoirs*, Maisky "indicated that his Government felt it should have been consulted beforehand regarding the Atlantic Charter." *The Memoirs of Cordell Hull* (New York: Macmillan, 1948), II, 1165. Proclamation of the Atlantic Charter took place two months after the German attack on Russia and one month after conclusion of the mutual assistance agreement between Great Britain and the Soviet Union.

As for Great Britain, Churchill declared that the Atlantic Charter would not apply to the British Empire. Speech to the House of Commons on September 9, 1941, *H. C. Debates, 5th series*, vol. 374, coll. 68-69.

A Few Basic Texts

... The establishment of order in Europe and the rebuilding of national economic life must be achieved by processes which will enable the liberated peoples to destroy the last vestiges of Nazism and Fascism and to create democratic institutions of their own choice. This is a principle of the Atlantic Charter—the right of all peoples to choose the form of government under which they will live—the restoration of sovereign rights and self-government to those peoples who have been forcibly deprived of them by the aggressor nations.

To foster the conditions in which the liberated peoples may exercise these rights, the three governments will jointly assist the people in any European liberated state or former Axis satellite state in Europe where in their judgment conditions require (a) to establish conditions of internal peace; (b) to carry out emergency measures for the relief of distressed peoples; (c) to form interim governmental authorities broadly representative of all democratic elements in the population and pledged to the earliest possible establishment through free elections of governments responsive to the will of the people; and (d) to facilitate where necessary the holding of such elections. . . .

When, in the opinion of the three governments, conditions in any European liberated state or any former Axis satellite state in Europe make such action necessary, they will immediately consult together on the measures necessary to discharge the joint responsibilities set forth in this declaration. . . .

> *Signed at Yalta by Prime Minister Churchill, President Roosevelt, and Premier Stalin.*

DECLARATION ON POLAND, FEBRUARY 11, 1945

We came to the Crimea Conference resolved to settle our differences about Poland. . . . We reaffirm our common desire to see established a strong, free, independent and democratic Poland. As a result of our discussions, we have agreed on the conditions in which a new Polish Provisional Government of National Unity may be formed in such a manner as to command recognition by the three major powers. . . .

A new situation has been created in Poland as a result of her complete liberation by the Red Army. This calls for the establishment of a Polish Provisional Government which can be more broadly based than was possible before the recent liberation of western Poland. The Provisional Government which is now functioning in Poland should therefore be reorganized on a broader democratic basis with the inclusion of democratic leaders from Poland itself and from Poles abroad. This new Government should then be called the Polish Provisional Government of National Unity.

. . . This Polish Provisional Government of National Unity shall be pledged to the holding of free and unfettered elections as soon as possible on the basis of universal suffrage and secret ballot. In these elections all democratic and anti-Nazi parties shall have the right to take part and to put forward candidates. . . .

> *Signed at Yalta by Prime Minister Churchill, President Roosevelt, and Marshal Stalin*

note this phrase. re: Korea + pro-Japs

BEGINNINGS OF THE COLD WAR

1

Introduction and Perspective

I call this little book an analytical compilation. It is a modest effort with a limited purpose. It does not try to lay bare the ideological roots of the Cold War, which other authors have done very well, or to survey its entire development. The purpose of this study is, simply, to summarize and highlight a few chapters of recent world history which encompass the major *beginnings* of the Cold War.

When did the Cold War begin? Its origins go back, no doubt, to Marx and Lenin. Experts may differ as to when, after the last war, the term "Cold War" became applicable to our relations with Soviet Russia. But surely the period covered here—essentially, the early months of 1945—helps to understand how it came about that we and the Russians weren't able to exist together more peacefully after World War II.

This summary represents something I had wanted to do for many years. Human memory being limited, it is perhaps not surprising that so many of us in the Foreign Service who lived through that period have forgotten just how our present conflict with Soviet Russia came to pass. Of course, we all know most of the important elements, but we have forgotten the sequence of events, and even some important facts have sunk below the level of ready recall.

We need to remember.

Also, it occurred to me that if the memories of those of us who lived through that period are no longer fresh, how much more difficult it must be for our younger colleagues in the Foreign Service, who were still in school at that time and who probably didn't follow the events even in the newspapers, to put the basic facts into perspective. They may not have found it possible to consult the many official documents and biographies and other works of scholarship on the subject.

For the existing source material is overwhelming. Virtually everything of significance has long since been published. The trouble is that the subject matter is complicated, and it takes a great deal of time to sift through even the most important material. If the Department of State had not assigned me to the Senior Seminar in Foreign Policy, thus giving me time for reading, study and reflection, I should not have been able to undertake this task.

And this is a suitable point at which to state that although in surveying the available historical material I received help from many quarters, including some friends in the Department of State, any views expressed in this book are those of the author and do not necessarily represent the views of the United States government. As will be seen, however, the author expresses few views of his own in this book. Essentially, we are surveying historical facts—but of course the highlighting of those facts and the significance attributed to them are always matters of individual judgment.

One of the things that strikes one most forcefully as one starts out on such a retrospective enterprise is that our memories are selective and that, especially, we tend to forget our *expectations.* *yes* This is a strange psychological phenomenon. When an important event comes to pass, our recollection of the actual event is likely to overlay, to supersede, to crowd out the memory of our original expectations about that event.

Let me cite some examples which have a bearing on this study:

We all know that Japan capitulated about three months after the end of the war in Europe, but how many of us remember our earlier expectations about the duration of the Pacific war? We read today with amazement that at the Yalta Conference the Combined (U. S.-British) Chiefs of Staff recommended that "the planning date for the end of the war against Japan should be set at eighteen months after the defeat of Germany."[1] Today, of course, we have the benefit of hindsight. We know that the atomic bomb became available, and we know that even without the atomic bomb Japan would probably have been forced to give up, alone through bombing and the attrition on her shipping, perhaps not very long after we had captured Okinawa and Iwo Jima in the spring of 1945. That, however, was emphatically not the view of our most qualified military men in the early months of that year.

In the judgment of our most qualified military leaders, the entry of Russia into the war against Japan was highly desirable. We note, in particular, that our Joint Staff planners considered it militarily important that Russia "conduct an all-out offensive

5

against Manchuria to contain Japanese forces and resources in North China and Manchuria that might otherwise be employed in the defense of Japan."[2] Ten years later, one of our most illustrious military leaders publicly denied that he had favored Russia's entry into the war against Japan.[3] He was a victim of the phenomenon that I describe. His earlier anticipations were obviously overlaid, superseded, crowded out by his knowledge that, as it turned out, we did not need Russian help. The Department of Defense, after some historical research, brought out documentary evidence that the illustrious military leader had himself clearly advocated Russia's entry into the war even as a specific preparation for the launching of our own invasion of the Japanese home islands.[4] So fallible is human memory, especially when it comes to expectations.

Or take our expectations about the postwar period. How many of us remember our enormous preoccupation, as the war drew to its end, with the problems of "reconversion" and unemployment when, as it seemed, our vastly increased industrial potential would be no longer fully needed? Those who, like myself, had been unemployed before the war remember this poignantly, but even then we are in retrospect astounded by the statistics about U.S. unemployment immediately prior to our entry into the war: it had been 10.4 million in 1938, 9.4 million in 1939, and still 8.1 million in 1940 when the impact of the European war began to be felt. (By comparison, unemployment during the height of the depression had been 12.8 million,[5] in 1933.) We had been in what was termed an economic "recession" before World War II and there was widespread fear that the aftermath would involve another such prolonged period of under-use of our economy.

Is it surprising, then, to recall—even if it requires quite an effort—that the rush of our army to demobilize, the whole sen-

6

timent in favor of the speediest possible return of our soldiers, was not unrelated to the quest for jobs? We all wanted to get home quickly because those who would return last were expected to have the hardest times ahead of them. Today we know that no postwar recession developed and that, in fact, we soon moved into a period of further economic expansion. But most of our economic experts, and certainly the general public in the United States, had no such expectations in early 1945.

Nor, one may assume, did the Russians—steeped in the teachings of Marx and Lenin—have any expectation that the United States would be able to use its productive plant to capacity after the war. They were, as a matter of fact, reinforced in their expectations by the fact that the United States seemed interested in long-term credit arrangements for postwar trade with Russia. Thus Donald Nelson, chairman of the War Production Board, talked with Stalin and Mikoyan as early as October 1943 about the expected great American postwar "surplus" that would be available on advantageous terms to our Russian partners;[6] and in July 1944 Eric Johnston, president of the U.S. Chamber of Commerce, discussed the possibility of large-scale American postwar credits with the same Russian leaders.[7] How this expectation was disappointed will be part of our narrative.

The most important expectation, of course, related to the political shape of the postwar world. Here again, our knowledge of what actually happened may dim our recollection of the great hopes most of us held for a future of peace, order, and democratic development throughout the length and breadth of the world. For this purpose, the complete defeat and "re-education" of the Axis aggressors was our first requirement. The second requirement, it seemed, was a new world organization in which disputes would henceforth be settled on their merits. It seemed inconceivable that the world would break up into separate

7

camps or spheres of influence, and the full weight of American diplomacy was directed to the avoidance of a political line of demarcation across Europe.

We were, or so it seemed, summoned once more by history to take a leading role in the establishment of a world organization to keep the peace, in partnership with our wartime allies. However, we were not ready for a world parliament in which constraints might be applied against us. "The veto power," Cordell Hull told a group of Congressional leaders in 1944, "is in the document [of proposals for the future United Nations organization] primarily on account of the United States. It is a necessary safeguard in dealing with a new and untried world arrangement. . . . We cannot move any faster than an alert public opinion in perfecting a permanent peace organization, but we should not be deterred for an instant from pursuing the sole course that is open, the alternative being international chaos such as we have had heretofore."[8]

While great hopes were placed in the future world organization (which had no name as yet, for the words "United Nations" originally applied only to the wartime alliance), there were doubts whether Russia would cooperate with it wholeheartedly. Accordingly, there was rejoicing when the Yalta Conference seemed to have brought agreement on the voting arrangements for the new organization; and there was dismay when Russia announced in March 1945 that it would not send Foreign Minister Molotov to the San Francisco Conference, where the new organization was to be formally created. How many of our hopes rode on the future world organization is apparent from rereading the newspapers of those days. Indeed, our disappointments over the abuse of the veto in the United Nations were a measure of our erstwhile expectation that, somehow, that organization would abate all frictions and rivalries between the great powers.

Yes, we were comrades-in-arms with Russia and we looked forward to a long period of peace and ever increasing cooperation and understanding. There were difficulties and troubles that came to the fore increasingly as the year 1945 wore on. They will be described and summarized. But there were also many things the general public did not know. We did not know, for instance, that Stalin in March 1945 had accused Churchill and Roosevelt in highly offensive terms of negotiating with Germany behind his back. We did not know of the acrimonious correspondence between these leaders about fulfillment of the Yalta Agreement on Poland. Throughout the war, information damaging to the alliance was purposely withheld from the American public, and some was withheld even after the defeat of Germany.

An American officer, for instance, who returned from a prisoner-of-war camp in Germany and presented evidence to our War Department that the Russians had been guilty of massacring thousands of Polish officers at Katyn (as had been claimed by Nazi propaganda during the war) received a letter ordering him "neither to mention nor discuss this matter with anyone in or out of the service without specific approval in writing from the War Department." Many years later, in 1952, the general who had issued that order was summoned before a committee of our House of Representatives and gave an explanation which thoroughly reflects our attitudes and expectations in early 1945.

Said Major General Clayton Bissell with soldierly directness: "I was very concerned all of this particular time with events that were even more critical to America's war with Japan, and this [disclosure] wasn't going to help win the Japanese war one bit, except in a different way. And that was the reason I was so careful about this thing. . . . Our number one objective, other than defeating Japan at that time, was to get the UNO going. We didn't know whether we could get Russia to come in."[9]

Beginnings of the Cold War

The Katyn massacre, as we shall see, played a fateful role in the political history of the war and of the postwar settlements.

How well I personally recall the attitude reflected in General Bissell's statement! I was among the first American officers to enter Vienna in the summer of 1945, after the Russians had been in occupation there for four months, raping and pillaging on an enormous scale. Hardly had we arrived when we were inundated with stories about the misdeeds of the Russian soldiery. We turned those stories aside with remarks that the Russians were our allies; that they had suffered terribly in the war; that we intended to fight jointly with them to bring about the defeat of Japan; and that we hoped to cooperate with them, however difficult it might be, to assure the peace of the world. This was a widespread attitude, for an enormous amount of good will for Russia had accumulated in the United States during the war.[10] How this good will was quickly dissipated in the space of very few months is the subject of this narrative.

There can be no better way to start our consideration of the evidence than to examine one of the most fascinating diplomatic documents of the period, the record of the conversations between Harry L. Hopkins and Josef Stalin in which they reviewed the reasons—some apparent, some real—why relations between the wartime allies were so rapidly deteriorating. The time of the first conversation was May 26, 1945, three weeks after the defeat of Germany. The place was Stalin's office in the Kremlin. Present were, on the Russian side, Marshal Stalin, Foreign Minister Vyacheslav Molotov, and Mr. Pavlov, an interpreter; and on the American side, Mr. Hopkins, Ambassador W. Averell Harriman, and Mr. Charles E. Bohlen. There were six conversations between these men in the space of ten days, reviewing some of the root causes of the Cold War.

10

Introduction and Perspective

Hopkins had only a few more months to live. He had risen from a hospital bed to be present at the funeral service for President Roosevelt, whom he had served in many capacities including that of Secretary of Commerce and, more important, as personal assistant, agent, and confidant. For almost four years he had lived in the White House. He had been present at the Tehran and Yalta Conferences, though at the latter he had been too ill to attend all the meetings. He had been bedridden in his home when President Truman asked him to undertake this mission to Moscow. The new President felt that Hopkins was best able to interpret the American position to Stalin because he had been so closely associated with President Roosevelt and because of the role he had played in starting the program of American aid that had meant so much to Russia during the war.

The careful reader will note in the next following narrative chapter the differing meanings attached by Hopkins and Stalin to the phrases "friendly government" and "strong and democratic Poland"; the use of the words "vital interest" by Stalin to describe the Russian desire for what he called a "strong and friendly Poland"; and the growing bluntness of Hopkins in describing Poland as the test case of American-Russian postwar relations. Although the United States had many other grievances against the Soviet Union stemming from unilateral actions in eastern Europe—some of which will be brought out in later sections of this study—the Hopkins conversations revolved very largely around the Polish question.

Russia lost about 15,000,000 dead in World War II, or 9 per cent of its population. The United States lost about 400,000 dead, or 0.3 per cent of its population. But the country that lost the greatest proportion, 14 per cent of its population, was Poland. Out of a prewar population of 35,000,000, it lost approximately 5,000,000 dead.[11] This becomes understandable when we think about the unique position of Poland as the only country that was attacked by *both* Germany and the Soviet Union during the same war and that experienced the full fury of both totalitarian occupations and of mass exterminations, plus a civil war between two rival undergrounds. It is useful to keep this background in mind as one reads the following narrative.

At the time that we are discussing here, the term "satellite" was not yet used to describe states subservient to and controlled by the Soviet Union. (The term was then used to describe Rumania, Bulgaria and Hungary, which were, or had been, in the sphere of influence of Nazi Germany.) It is well to recall, at the same time, that the Western hemisphere was regarded not only by us but also by our allies as an absolute preserve of the United States. The idea that Cuba, for instance, or any other neighbor of the United States might adopt a system or an allegiance hostile to the United States would at that time have seemed utterly fantastic. As far as Europe was concerned, the United States would not hear of spheres of influence and, as we shall see, throughout the period reviewed in this study we felt that Russian security could be adequately protected by freely elected governments in the countries on Russia's borders. But it soon turned out that such governments would—for good reason—have been bitterly hostile to the Soviet Union; and, as we shall see at the end of Chapter 5, that damaging fact was even admitted by Stalin at the Potsdam Conference.

Poland was the most important case in point, as is clearly brought out in the Stalin-Hopkins conversations summarized in the next chapter.

NOTES

1. Report of the Combined Chiefs of Staff to President Roosevelt and Prime Minister Churchill, 9 February 1945, in *Foreign Relations of the United States—The Conferences of Malta and Yalta* (Washington: Government Printing Office, 1955, hereafter cited as *Yalta Papers*), p. 830.

2. Report by the Joint Staff Planners, 18 January 1945, Conclusions, para. 6 b. (1) (a) (ii). Ibid., p. 392.

The Joint Chiefs of Staff, in a memorandum to the President dated January 23, 1945, stated that "Russia's entry at as early a date as possible consistent with her ability to engage in offensive operations is necessary to provide maximum assistance to our Pacific operations." Ibid., p. 396.

3. General Douglas MacArthur declared on March 23, 1955 that his views had not been sought for the Yalta Conference, but that if they had he "would most emphatically have recommended against bringing the Soviet into the Pacific war at that late date." *New York Times*, March 24, 1955.

4. U. S. Department of Defense, *The Entry of the Soviet Union into the War Against Japan: Military Plans, 1941-1945*—press release of October 19, 1955, in *New York Times* of October 20, 1955. Report by Brig. Gen. George A. Lincoln of his conversation with Gen. MacArthur on February 25, 1945: "Concerning over-all plan, General MacArthur considers it essential that maximum number of Jap divisions be engaged and pinned down on Asiatic mainland before United States forces strike Japan proper." Also memorandum by Col. Paul L. Freeman, Jr. on conversation with Gen. MacArthur on February 13, 1945: "He [Gen. MacArthur] was in thorough agreement that the only means of defeating Japan was by the invasion of the industrial heart of Japan. He stressed the potency of the Japanese Army and stated that when we entered Japan we must be prepared to reckon with the Japanese Army in far greater strength than is now there. He was apprehensive as to the possibility of the movement of the bulk of the Manchurian Army and other Japanese forces from China to the defense of the homeland. He emphatically stated that

we must not invade Japan proper unless the Russian Army is previously committed to action in Manchuria. . . ."

Cf. also *The Forrestal Diaries* (New York: Viking, 1951), p. 31, entry for Wednesday, February 28, 1945: "On the . . . question of the war against Japan afterward, he [MacArthur] expressed the view that the help of the Chinese would be negligible. He felt that we should secure the commitment of the Russians to active and vigorous prosecution of a campaign against the Japanese in Manchukuo of such proportions as to pin down a very large part of the Japanese Army; that once this campaign was engaged, we should then launch an attack on the home islands, giving, as he expressed it, the *coup de main* from the rear while substantial portions of the military power of Japan were engaged on the mainland of Asia. . . . He said he felt that our strength should be reserved for use in the Japanese mainland, on the plain of Tokyo, and that this could not be done without the assurance that the Japanese would be heavily engaged by the Russians in Manchuria. He expressed doubt that the use of anything less than sixty divisions by Russia would be sufficient. . . ."

5. U.S. Department of Commerce, *Historical Statistics of the United States* (Washington: Government Printing Office, 1957), p. 73.

6. Herbert Feis, *Churchill, Roosevelt, Stalin—The War They Waged and the Peace They Sought* (Princeton, N.J.: Princeton University Press, 1957), p. 641.

7. *New York Times,* July 14, 1944.

8. *The Memoirs of Cordell Hull* (New York: Macmillan, 1948), II, 1662. Mr. Hull added, however, that it was his expectation that "none of the permanent members of the Council would exercise its right of veto capriciously or arbitrarily" and that any of the great powers would "call this [veto] power forth only on a matter of the gravest concern to itself, never on secondary matters and never in a way to prevent thorough discussion of any issue" (II, 1663).

9. *Hearings Before the Select Committee to Conduct an Investigation of the Facts, Evidence and Circumstances of the Katyn Forest Massacre,* 82nd Congress, House, Second Session, February/March 1952 (hereafter cited as *Katyn Forest Massacre*), p. 1877.

10. Secretary of State James F. Byrnes, for instance, reconstructed this state of mind as follows in 1947: "It is a trite but true statement that 'hindsight is better than foresight'. But, if one can recall the

attitude of the people of the United States toward the Soviets in the days immediately following the German surrender, he will agree that, as a result of our sufferings and sacrifices in a common cause, the Soviet Union then had in the United States a deposit of good will, as great, if not greater, than that of any other country. It is little short of a tragedy that Russia should have withdrawn that deposit with the recklessness and the lack of appreciation shown during the last two and a half years. Our assumption that we could co-operate, and our patience in trying to co-operate, justify the firmness we now must show." *Speaking Frankly* (New York: Harper, 1947), p. 71.

11. Encyclopaedia Britannica, Inc., *10 Eventful Years* (Chicago, 1947). Population figures for Russia from the 1939 census; for the United States, from the 1940 census; and for Poland, estimated as of 1939. Casualty figures for Russia have never been published and are unofficial estimates. The U.S. casualty figure is based on official sources. Polish casualties are estimated and include some 3,000,000 Jews murdered in Nazi concentration camps.

According to some Polish sources, Poland lost not 5 but 6 million human lives during the war. Cf. Stanislaw Mikolajczyk, *The Rape of Poland—Pattern of Soviet Aggression* (New York: McGraw-Hill, 1948), p. 123.

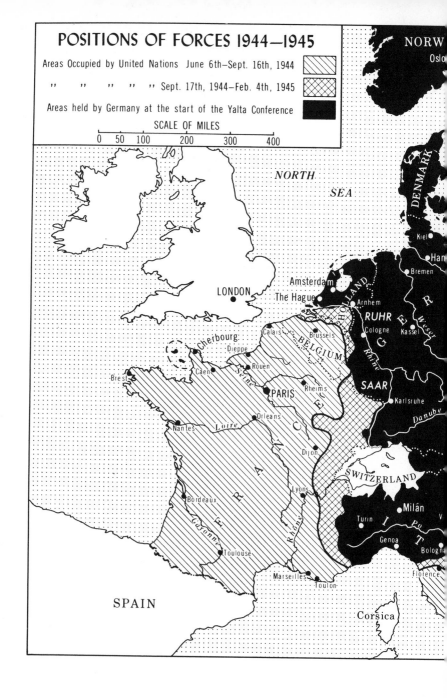

POSITIONS OF FORCES 1944—1945

Areas Occupied by United Nations June 6th—Sept. 16th, 1944

  "   "   "   "   " Sept. 17th, 1944—Feb. 4th, 1945

Areas held by Germany at the start of the Yalta Conference

SCALE OF MILES

0   50   100   200   300   400

NORW

Oslo

NORTH
SEA

DENMARK

Kiel

Han

Bremen

Amsterdam

The Hague

Arnhem

HOLLAND

RUHR

Cologne   Kassel

G E R

Wesel

Calais

Brussels

BELGIUM

Rhine

SAAR

Karlsruhe

Danube

LONDON

Cherbourg

Dieppe

Caen

Rouen

Seine

PARIS

Rheims

Orleans

E

C

Dijon

SWITZERLAND

Brest

Nantes

Loire

Lyons

Rhône

Milán

Turin

I

Po

V

Bordeaux

R   A

Genoa

T

Bologna

Garonne

Toulouse

Marseilles

Toulon

Florence

SPAIN

Corsica

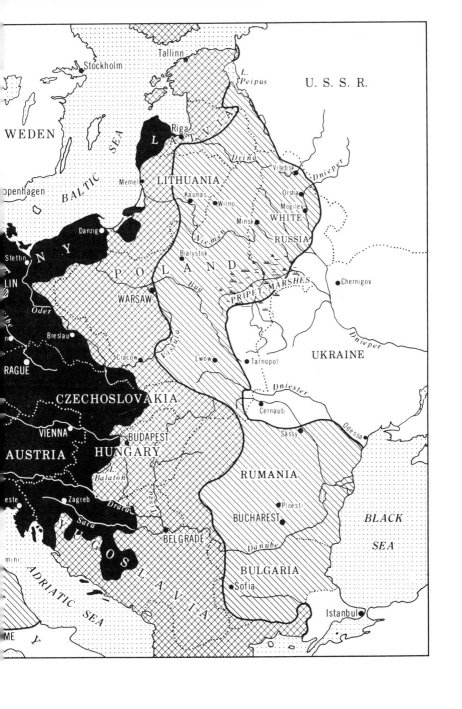

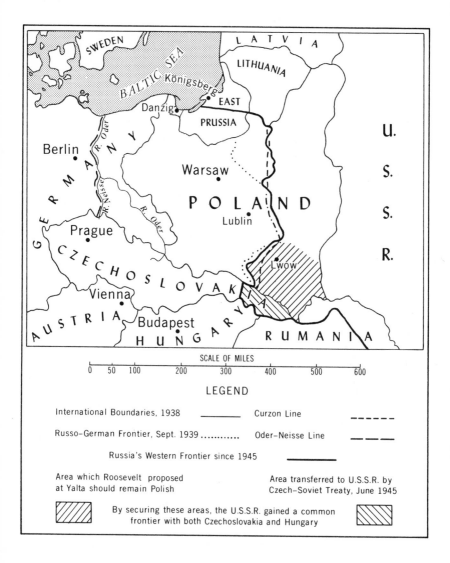

SCALE OF MILES

```
0    50   100        200        300        400        500        600
```

LEGEND

International Boundaries, 1938 ——————— Curzon Line — — — — —

Russo–German Frontier, Sept. 1939 ············ Oder–Neisse Line — — — —

Russia's Western Frontier since 1945 ———————

Area which Roosevelt proposed   Area transferred to U.S.S.R. by
at Yalta should remain Polish   Czech–Soviet Treaty, June 1945

By securing these areas, the U.S.S.R. gained a common
frontier with both Czechoslovakia and Hungary

2

Stalin-Hopkins Conversations

EXTRACT FROM THE BOHLEN MINUTES[1]

Mr. Hopkins began the conversation by reporting on the circumstances of the death of President Roosevelt six weeks before. He said that on his trip home from Yalta the President had frequently reviewed with him the results of the Crimea Conference and that he had come away from the Conference with renewed confidence that the United States and the Soviet Union could work together in peace as they had in war. President Roosevelt on the trip home had frequently spoken of the respect and admiration he had for Marshal Stalin and he had looked forward to their next meeting which the President hoped would be in Berlin.

Marshal Stalin remarked that he recalled the toast at the Crimea Conference to their next meeting in Berlin.

Mr. Hopkins said that he recalled his first meeting with the Marshal in July 1941, during the troubled and anxious days of the German offensive. He said he remembered vividly the

19

frankness with which Marshal Stalin had told him of the Soviet position and of the unalterable determination of the Soviet Union to wage war against Germany until final victory was assured. He had returned to the United States and conveyed to President Roosevelt his own conviction that the Soviet Union would hold fast and President Roosevelt had thereupon initiated the program of assistance to the Soviet Union. At that time, most people believed that a German victory was inevitable but President Roosevelt, in spite of all such opinions, had decided otherwise and through his leadership he had put through a program of aid to Russia.

Marshal Stalin observed that at that time there had been many doubts of the ability of the Soviet Union to keep going. . . .

Mr. Hopkins then said that a few days ago President Truman had sent for him and had asked him to come to Moscow to have a talk with Marshal Stalin. There were a number of things that he and Mr. Harriman hoped to discuss with Marshal Stalin and Mr. Molotov while he was in Moscow, but before going into those specific questions he wished to tell the Marshal of the real reason why the President had asked him to come, and that was the question of the fundamental relationship between the U. S. and the Soviet Union.

Two months ago, Mr. Hopkins said, there had been overwhelming sympathy among the American people for the Soviet Union and complete support for President Roosevelt's policies which the Marshal knew so well. . . . The American people at that time hoped and confidently believed that the two countries could work together in peace as well as they had in war. Mr. Hopkins said there had always been a small minority, the Hearsts and the McCormicks, who had been against the policy of cooperation with the Soviet Union. These men had also been bitter political enemies of President Roosevelt but had never had any backing from the American people as was shown by the fact that against their bitter opposition President Roosevelt had been four times elected President. He said he did not intend to discuss this small minority but to discuss the general state of American opinion and particularly the present attitude of the millions of Americans who had supported President Roosevelt's policy in regard to the Soviet Union and who believed that despite the different political and economic ideologies of the two countries, the U. S. and the Soviet Union could work together after the war in order to bring about a secure peace for humanity.

Mr. Hopkins said he wished to assure the Marshal with all the earnestness at his command that this body of American public opinion who had been the constant support of the Roosevelt policies were seriously disturbed about our relations with Russia. In fact, in the last six weeks the deterioration of public opinion had been so serious as to affect adversely the relations between our two countries. He said he wished to emphasize that this change had occurred in the very people who had supported to the hilt Roosevelt's policy of cooperation with the Soviet Union. . . . It was obvious to them that if present trends continued unchecked the entire structure of world cooperation and relations with the Soviet Union which President Roosevelt and the Marshal had labored so hard to build would be destroyed.

Prior to his departure, Mr. Hopkins continued, President Truman had expressed to him his great anxiety at the present situation and also his desire to continue President Roosevelt's policy of working with the Soviet Union and his intention to carry out in fact as well as in spirit all the arrangements, both formal and informal, which President Roosevelt and Marshal Stalin had worked out together. Mr. Hopkins added that as

21

the Marshal knew he had not been well and he would not be in Moscow unless he had felt the situation was serious. He also said he would not have come had he not believed that the present trend could be halted and a common basis found to go forward in the future.

Mr. Hopkins said that it was not simple or easy to put a finger on the precise reasons for this deterioration but he must emphasize that without the support of public opinion and particularly of the supporters of President Roosevelt it would be very difficult for President Truman to carry forward President Roosevelt's policy. He said that, as the Marshal was aware, the cardinal basis of President Roosevelt's policy which the American people had fully supported had been the concept that the interests of the U. S. were world-wide and not confined to North and South America and the Pacific Ocean and it was this concept that had led to the many conferences concerning the peace of the world which President Roosevelt had had with Marshal Stalin. President Roosevelt had believed that the Soviet Union had likewise world-wide interests and that the two countries could work out together any political or economic considerations at issue between them.

After the Yalta Conference, Mr. Hopkins continued, it looked as though we were well on the way to reaching a basic understanding on all questions of foreign affairs of interest to our respective countries. . . . He said in a country like ours public opinion is affected by specific incidents and in this case the deterioration in public opinion in regard to our relations with the Soviet Union had been centered in our inability to carry into effect the Yalta Agreement on Poland. There were also a train of events, each unimportant in themselves, which had grown up around the Polish question and which contributed to the deterioration in public opinion. President Truman felt, and so did the

American public, although they were not familiar with all the details, a sense of bewilderment at our inability to solve the Polish question.

Marshal Stalin replied that the reason for the failure on the Polish question was that the Soviet Union desired to have a friendly Poland, but that Great Britain wanted to revive the system of *cordon sanitaire** on the Soviet borders.

Mr. Hopkins replied that neither the Government nor the people of the U. S. had any such intention. . . . He stated that the U. S. would desire a Poland friendly to the Soviet Union and in fact desired to see friendly countries all along the Soviet borders.

Marshal Stalin replied if that be so we could easily come to terms in regard to Poland.

Mr. Hopkins said that during his visit there were a number of specific questions that he and Mr. Harriman hoped to discuss with Marshal Stalin and Mr. Molotov but that the general statement he had just made concerning public opinion in the U. S. was the principal reason for his coming and the principal cause of anxiety at the present time. He said he had wished to state frankly and as forcibly as he knew how to Marshal Stalin the importance that he, personally, attached to the present trend of events and that he felt that the situation would get rapidly worse unless we could clear up the Polish matter. He had therefore been glad to hear the Marshal say that he thought the question could be settled.

[Hopkins then detailed the matters he hoped to discuss during his stay in Moscow, reemphasizing the importance of the Polish question, and Stalin said that he had also several disturbing questions on his mind in regard to the United States. It

---

* The post-World-War-I system of anti-Communist buffer states on Russia's borders in Europe.

was agreed to pursue these matters at a later meeting. These were subsequently discussed the evening of May 27, as follows, still according to the Bohlen minutes:]

Marshal Stalin said he would not attempt to use Soviet public opinion as a screen but would speak of the feeling that had been created in Soviet governmental circles as a result of recent moves on the part of the U. S. Government. He said these circles felt a certain alarm in regard to the attitude of the U. S. Government. It was their impression that the American attitude towards the Soviet Union had perceptibly cooled once it became obvious that Germany was defeated, and that it was as though the Americans were saying that the Russians were no longer needed. He said he would give the following examples:

(1) The case of Argentina and its invitation to the San Francisco Conference. At Yalta, it had been agreed that only those states which had declared war on Germany before the first of March would be invited, but at San Francisco this decision had been overturned. He said it was not understood in the Soviet Union why Argentina could not have been asked to wait three months or so before joining the world organization. He added that the action of the Conference and the attitude of the U. S. had raised the question of the value of agreements between the three major powers if their decisions could be overturned by the votes of such countries as Honduras and Porto Rico [sic].

(2) The question of the Reparations Commission. At Yalta, it had been agreed that the three powers would sit on this Commission in Moscow and subsequently the U. S. had insisted that France should be represented on the same basis as the Soviet Union. This he felt was an insult to the Soviet Union in view of the fact that France had concluded a separate peace with Germany and had opened the frontier to the Germans. . . . To at-

24

tempt to place France on the same footing as the Soviet Union looked like an attempt to humiliate the Russians.

(3) The attitude of the U. S. Government towards the Polish question. He said that at Yalta it had been agreed that the existing government was to be reconstructed and that anyone with common sense could see that this meant that the present government was to form the basis of the new. He said no other understanding of the Yalta Agreement was possible. Despite the fact that they were simple people the Russians should not be regarded as fools, which was a mistake the West frequently made, nor were they blind and could quite well see what was going on before their eyes. It was true that the Russians were patient in the interests of a common cause but their patience had its limits.

(4) The manner in which Lend-Lease had been curtailed. If the U. S. was unable to supply the Soviet Union further under Lend-Lease that was one thing but that the manner in which it had been done had been unfortunate and even brutal. For example, certain ships had been unloaded and while it was true that this order had been cancelled the whole manner in which it had been done had caused concern to the Soviet Government. If the refusal to continue Lend-Lease was designed as pressure on the Russians in order to soften them up then it was a fundamental mistake. Marshal Stalin said he must tell Mr. Hopkins frankly that if the Russians were approached frankly on a friendly basis much could be done but that reprisals in any form would bring about the exact opposite effect.

(5) The disposition of the German Navy and merchant fleet which surrendered to the Allies. Stalin said that as we knew certain units of the German Army who had been fighting against the Russians had been anxious to surrender to the Western allies but not to the Russians, but under the surrender terms

German troops were supposed to surrender to the army against which they had fought. He said, for example, General Eisenhower as an honest man had correctly turned over to the Soviet Command in Czechoslovakia some 135,000 German troops who had tried to surrender to the American Army. This was an example of fair and honest behavior. However, as regards the German fleet which had caused so much damage to Leningrad and other Soviet ports not one vessel had been turned over to the Soviet Union. . . . He said that the Soviet Government had certain information leading it to believe that both the U. S. and England intended to reject the Soviet request and he must say that if this turned out to be true it would be very unpleasant. The Marshal concluded by saying that he had completed the range of his account.

Mr. Hopkins said he first of all wished to express appreciation of the frankness with which Marshal Stalin had exposed his worries. [He then proceeded to explain the U. S. position on the German naval vessels, which was that we did not intend to keep any of them, and then went into a lengthy explanation of the status of Lend-Lease during and after the European war, concluding that the incident to which Marshal Stalin referred did not have any fundamental policy significance.]

Marshal Stalin said he wished to make it clear that he fully understood the right of the U. S. to curtail Lend-Lease shipments to the Soviet Union under present conditions . . . but what he had in mind was the manner and form in which it was done. He felt that what was after all an agreement between the two Governments had been ended in a scornful and abrupt manner. . . . He added that the Soviet Government had intended to make a suitable expression of gratitude to the U. S. for the Lend-Lease assistance during the war but the way in which this program had been halted now made that impossible.

Mr. Hopkins replied that what disturbed him most about the Marshal's statement was the revelation that he believed that the U. S. would use Lend-Lease as a means of showing our displeasure with the Soviet Union. He wished to assure the Marshal that however unfortunate the impression this question had caused in the mind of the Soviet Government, he must believe that there was no attempt or desire on the part of the U. S. to use it as a pressure weapon. He said the U. S. is a strong power and does not go in for those methods. Furthermore, we have no conflict of immediate interests with the Soviet Union and would have no reason to adopt such practices.

[Hopkins then turned to the question of the Reparations Commission. He pointed out, *inter alia*, that in any event the three powers would in the first instance begin their discussions in Moscow without France. Marshal Stalin replied that Poland, which had suffered even more than France, should certainly be represented if France was to be, and that Yugoslavia also deserved a place. The discussion then turned to the Argentine question. Ambassador Harriman explained that the U. S. had obtained Latin American support for the admission of the Ukraine and White Russia as separate members of the new world organization, as had been agreed at Yalta. However, the Latin American countries had immediately tried to connect this question with that of the admission of the Argentine. Mr. Stettinius had made it plain that he would not make any such connection and in the end the Latin American countries did vote solidly in support of the Yalta decision regarding Ukraine and White Russia. Mr. Harriman said that if Mr. Molotov had not then introduced the question of an invitation to the Warsaw Government, we might have been successful in persuading the Latin American countries to postpone the question of Argentina. Marshal Stalin finally said that in any event what had been done could not be put right and the Argentine question now belonged to the past.]

Mr. Hopkins then said with the Marshal's permission he would like to review the position of the U. S. in regard to Poland. He said first of all he wished to assure the Marshal that he had no thought or indeed any right to attempt to settle the Polish problem during his visit here in Moscow, nor was he intending to hide behind American public opinion in presenting the position of the U. S.

Marshal Stalin said he was afraid that his remark concerning Soviet public opinion had cut Mr. Hopkins to the quick and that he had not meant to imply that Mr. Hopkins was hiding behind the screen of American public opinion. In fact, he knew Mr. Hopkins to be an honest and frank man.

Mr. Hopkins said that he wished to state this position as clearly and as forcibly as he knew how. He said the question of Poland *per se* was not so important as the fact that it had become a symbol of our ability to work out problems with the Soviet Union. He said that we had no special interests in Poland and no special desire to see any particular kind of government, that we would accept any government in Poland which was desired by the Polish people and was at the same time friendly to the Soviet Government. He said that the people and Government of the U. S. felt that this was a problem which should be worked out jointly between the U. S., the Soviet Union and Great Britain and that we felt that the Polish people should be given the right to free elections to choose their own government and their own system and that Poland should genuinely be independent.

The Government and people of the U. S., Mr. Hopkins continued, were disturbed because the preliminary steps towards the reestablishment of Poland appeared to have been taken unilaterally by the Soviet Union together with the present Warsaw Government and that in fact the U. S. was completely excluded. He said he hoped that Stalin would believe him when he said that this feeling was a fact. . . . He hoped that the Marshal would put his mind to the task of thinking up what diplomatic methods could be used to settle this question, keeping in mind the feeling of the American people. . . . Poland had become a symbol in the sense that it bore a direct relation to the willingness of the U. S. to participate in international affairs on a world-wide basis and that our people must believe that they are joining their power with that of the Soviet Union and Great Britain in the promotion of international peace and the well-being of humanity.

Mr. Hopkins concluded by saying that he felt the overwhelming majority of the people of the U. S. felt that the relations between the U.S. and the USSR could be worked out in a spirit of cooperation despite the differences in ideology and that with all these factors in its favor he wished to appeal to the Marshal to help find a way to the solution of the Polish problem.

Marshal Stalin replied that he wished Mr. Hopkins would take into consideration the following factors: He said it may seem strange, although it appeared to be recognized in U. S. circles and Churchill in his speeches also recognized it, that the Soviet Government should wish for a friendly Poland. In the course of twenty-five years the Germans had twice invaded Russia via Poland. Neither the British nor American people had experienced such German invasions which were a horrible thing to endure and the results of which were not easily forgotten. He said these German invasions were not warfare but were like the incursions of the Huns. He said that Germany had been able to do this because Poland had been regarded as a part of the *cordon sanitaire* around the Soviet Union and that previous European policy had been that Polish Governments must be hostile to Russia. In these circumstances either Poland had been too weak to oppose Germany or had let the Germans come through. Thus Poland had served as a corridor for the German attacks on Russia.

Stalin said Poland's weakness and hostility had been a great source of weakness to the Soviet Union and had permitted the Germans to do what they wished in the East and also in the West since the two were mixed together. It was therefore in Russia's vital interest that Poland should be both strong and friendly. He said there was no intention on the part of the Soviet Union to interfere in Poland's internal affairs, that Poland would live under the parliamentary system, which is like Czechoslovakia, Belgium and Holland, that any talk of an intention to Sovietize Poland was stupid. He said even the Polish leaders, some of whom were communists, were against the Soviet system since the Polish people did not desire collective farms or other aspects of the Soviet system. In this the Polish leaders were right since the Soviet system was not exportable— it must develop from within on the basis of a set of conditions which were not present in Poland. He said that all the Soviet Union wanted was that Poland should not be in a position to open the gates to Germany and in order to prevent this Poland must be strong and democratic.

Stalin then said that before he came to his suggestion as to the practical solution of the question he would like to comment on Mr. Hopkins' remarks concerning future U. S. interests in the world. He said that whether the U. S. wished it or not it was a world power and would have to accept world-wide interests.

Not only this war but the previous war had shown that without U. S. intervention Germany could not have been defeated and that all the events and developments of the last thirty years had confirmed this. In fact the U. S. had more reason to be a world power than any other state. For this reason he fully recognized the right of the U. S. as a world power to participate in the Polish question and that the Soviet interest in Poland did not in any way exclude those of England and the U. S. Mr. Hopkins had spoken of unilateral action in Poland and U. S. public opinion concerning it. It was true that Russia had taken such unilateral action but they had been compelled to.

Stalin recalled that the Soviet Government had recognized the Warsaw Government and concluded a treaty with it at a time when their allies did not recognize this government. These were admittedly unilateral acts which would have been much better left undone but the fact was they had not met with any understanding on the part of their allies. The need for these actions had arisen out of the presence of Soviet troops in Poland and it would have been impossible to have waited until such time as the allies had come to an agreement on Poland. The logic of the war against Germany had demanded that the Soviet rear be assured and the Lublin Committee had been of great assistance to the Red Army at all times and it was for this reason that these actions had been taken by the Soviet Government. He said it was contrary to the Soviet policy to set up a Soviet administration on foreign soil since this would look like occupation and be resented by the local inhabitants.

It was for this reason, Stalin continued, that some Polish administration had to be established in Poland and this could be done only with those who had helped the Red Army. He said he wished to emphasize that these steps had not been taken with any desire to eliminate or exclude Russia's allies. He must point out, however, the Soviet action in Poland had been more successful than British action in Greece and at no time had they been compelled to undertake the measures which the British had taken in Greece. Stalin then turned to his suggestion for the solution of the Polish problem.

Marshal Stalin said that he felt that we should examine the composition of the future Government of National Unity. He said there were eighteen or twenty ministries in the present Polish Government and that four or five of these portfolios could be given representatives of other Polish groups taken from the list submitted by Great Britain and the U. S. (Molotov whispered to Stalin who then said he meant four and not five posts in the government.) He said he thought the Warsaw Poles would not accept more than four ministers from other democratic groups. [The discussion then turned to personalities, and Hopkins said he would require some time to consider the Marshal's suggestion.]

[The third conversation dealt with the Far East and need not be detailed here since it involved no disagreements. This was the conversation in which, according to the Bohlen notes, Stalin declared that "the Soviet people would not be a factor in any way hindering Chinese unity but on the contrary would help the Chinese to achieve it. In regard to the Generalissimo the Marshal said he knew little of any Chinese leader but that he felt that Chiang Kai-Shek was the best of the lot and would be the one to undertake the unification of China. He said he saw no other possible leader and that for example he did not believe that the Chinese communist leaders were as good or would be able to bring about the unification of China. . . . In Manchuria as in any part of China where Soviet troops went the Chinese administration would be set up under Chiang. . . ." The future occupation regime for Germany was also discussed. During the fourth conversation, on May 30, the question of Poland came up again:]

Mr. Hopkins said he would like to continue the discussion on Poland. He said first of all he would like to make a general observation. Historically speaking the people of Russia and, since the revolution, the people of the Soviet Union, had distrusted successive Polish Governments and to some extent the Polish people. Likewise, for many years the Polish people had feared Russia and, since the revolution, the Soviet Union. He said that at their first meeting he had indicated to Marshal Stalin as clearly as he could that the U. S. was not only not interested in the establishment of a *cordon sanitaire* around Russia but on the contrary was aggressively opposed to it; that the U. S. had no economic interests of substantial importance in Poland and that we believed that the U. S., the Soviet Union and England in working to help create a new Polish state that would be friendly to Russia could have an immense moral and political effect in the task of bringing about genuine Polish-Soviet friendship. He said that the Soviet Union alone working directly with Poland would find this a more difficult task and in those circumstances Poland might remain a troublesome and even threatening area for Russia. However, if the three nations genuinely got together and were associated with the creation of a new Polish state, we believed that would have a most helpful effect in the establishment of a friendly and independent Poland which would be genuinely friendly to the Soviet Union.

Marshal Stalin said he agreed. There was no intention on the part of the Soviet Government to exclude her allies England and America from participation in the solution of this problem.

Mr. Hopkins inquired if the Marshal believed it would be a fact that the U. S. and British participation would be helpful.

Marshal Stalin said that undoubtedly the solution would carry more weight if it was tripartite.

Mr. Hopkins said he would like to accent once again the reasons for our concern in regard to Poland, and indeed, in regard to other countries which were geographically far from our borders. He said there were certain fundamental rights which, when infringed upon or denied caused concern in the U. S. These were cardinal elements which must be present if a parliamentary system is to be established and maintained. He said for example:

(1) There must be the right of freedom of speech so that people could say what they wanted to, the right of assembly, the right of movement and the right to worship at any church that they desired;

(2) All political parties, except the fascist party and fascist elements, who represented or could represent democratic governments should be permitted the free use, without distinction, of the press, radio, meetings and other facilities of political expression;

(3) All citizens should have the right of public trial, defense by counsel of their own choosing, and the right of habeas corpus.

He concluded that if we could find a meeting of minds in regard to these general principles which would be the basis for future free elections, then he was sure we could find ways and means to agree on procedures to carry them into effect. He then asked the Marshal if he would care to comment in a general sense or more specifically in regard to the general observations he had made concerning the fundamentals of a new Polish state.

Marshal Stalin replied that these principles of democracy are well known and would find no objection on the part of the Soviet Government. He was sure that the Polish Government, which in its declarations had outlined just such principles, would not only not oppose them but would welcome them. He said, however, that in regard to the specific freedoms mentioned by Mr. Hopkins, they could only be applied in full in peace time, and even then with certain limitations. He said, for example, the fascist party, whose intention it was to overthrow democratic governments, could not be permitted to enjoy to the full extent these freedoms. He said secondly there were the limitations imposed by war. All states when they were threatened by war or their frontiers were not secure had found it necessary to introduce certain restrictions. This had been done in England, France, the Soviet Union and elsewhere and perhaps to a lesser extent in the U. S. which was protected by wide oceans. It was for these reasons that only in time of peace could consideration be given to the full application of these freedoms. For example, he said that in time of war no state will allow the free unrestricted use of radio transmitters which could be used to convey information to the enemy. With reference to freedom of speech, certain restrictions had to be imposed for military security. . . . He said, to sum up: (1) during time of war these political freedoms could not be enjoyed to the full extent, and (2) nor could they apply without reservations to fascist parties trying to overthrow the government. . . .

Mr. Hopkins said he thoroughly understood the Marshal's opinions. He added that when he had left the Crimea Conference President Roosevelt had thought the Polish matter was virtually settled. Mr. Hopkins said he and all the other American representatives thought the same and felt that in very short time Mr. Molotov, Mr. Harriman and Sir Archibald Clark Kerr* would be able to carry out the Crimea Decision. . . . He must confess that he had been bewildered and disturbed that

* The then British ambassador to the Soviet Union.

35

one thing after another had seemed to occur to prevent the carrying out of the decision which all had thought was clear and sure. . . . Mr. Hopkins said that he must say that rightly or wrongly there was a strong feeling among the American people that the Soviet Union wished to dominate Poland. . . .

[Twice again, during the Hopkins visit, was the question of Poland discussed. The record of the fifth conversation, which concerned the Poles who were to be called to Moscow to "consult" on the formation of the Provisional Government of National Unity, has not yet been published. Hopkins also attempted to persuade Stalin to release fourteen Polish underground leaders who had been arrested by Soviet troops and charged with subversive activities against the Soviet forces. In an after-dinner conversation on June 1, Hopkins according to a memorandum of record[2] "reminded Stalin again of the many minority groups in America who were not sympathetic to the Soviet Union" and told him very forcefully that he must "believe me when I told him that our whole relationship was threatened by the impasse of Poland." Stalin was adamant against release of the arrested Polish leaders, inveighed against alleged British connivance with the Polish Government in Exile in London, and observed that "we must take into consideration Russian opinion as well as American opinion; that it was the Russian forces that had liberated Poland and if they had not gained the victory in Poland, with such a great loss of Russian life, nobody would be talking about a new Poland. . . ."]

NOTES

1. The language of this chapter is taken from the Bohlen notes, first published in Robert E. Sherwood's *Roosevelt and Hopkins* (New York: Harper, 1948) and later officially in Volume I of *Foreign Relations of the United States—Conference of Berlin (Potsdam)* (Washington: Government Printing Office, 1960; hereafter cited as *Potsdam Papers*), pp. 24 ff. Some condensations have been made, so as to focus on the principal issues. Sentences within brackets are condensations, and dots indicate deletions of nonessential detail. In a few cases the grammar of the original, probably hastily written, minutes has been improved.

2. Ibid., p. 57.

3

Poland: Roots of Conflict

Under a secret protocol to the Molotov-Ribbentrop pact of August 23, 1939 Poland was in effect divided between Russia and Germany. "In the event of a territorial and political rearrangement of the areas belonging to the Polish state," the protocol said, "the spheres of influence of Germany and the USSR shall be bounded approximately by the line of the rivers Narew, Vistula, and San."[1] This line of demarcation, subsequently modified by a secret supplementary protocol dated September 28, corresponded in the center to the so-called Curzon Line, which had been proposed in 1919 by the Allied Supreme Council as representing the approximate ethnic boundary between Poles on the one hand and Ukrainians and White Russians on the other. In its northern and southern portions, the demarcation line between Russia and Germany ran to the west of the Curzon Line, i.e., it gave Russia more territory.

As the Polish army was crushed by the German Wehrmacht and its remnants retreated to the east, the Germans encouraged the Russians to attack the Poles from the rear.[2] The German government desired that Russia should occupy its entire sphere of influence in Poland to preclude the continued existence of a Polish rump state in that area.[3] After Poland had thus been divided between them, Germany and Russia concluded a Boundary and Friendship Treaty with a secret supplementary protocol which declared: "Both parties will tolerate in their territories no Polish agitation which affects the territories of the other party. They will suppress in their territories all beginnings of such agitation and inform each other concerning suitable measures for this purpose."[4] Russia annexed its portion of Poland, incorporating it into the Ukrainian and White Russian Soviet Republics. Poland had ceased to exist.

Poland had suffered this fate before, only to rise again. Once a great empire that included most of the Ukraine and White Russia as well as German and Baltic populations, it had been "partitioned" between Russia and Prussia in 1772 and again in 1793. But the Poles rose under Kosciuszko and regained most of their lost territory, only to be decisively defeated in 1795, when the country was divided up between Russia, Prussia, and Austria. However, the Poles never stopped fighting for the re-establishment of their nation. For a while their hopes were pinned on Napoleon, and a Polish army accompanied him against Russia. After Napoleon's defeat, the Congress of Vienna permitted a small "Congress Poland" to exist, but it was placed under the Czar and by 1820 it had become a Russian province. Still the Poles continued to fight for their freedom until a century later, in 1919, a new Polish state once more emerged on the international scene.

The problem of Poland between World War I and World War II was thus how to maintain independence in the face of two covetous neighbors, and the aim of Polish diplomacy was to obtain effective Western guarantees that would deter both Germany and Russia. The peculiar Polish security interests (which were shared by other states bordering on Russia) were the reason why no collective security agreement could be reached between Russia and the West in the face of the Nazi threat in 1939. As Churchill has written: "The obstacle to such an agreement was the terror of these same border countries of receiving Soviet help in the shape of Soviet Armies marching through their territories to defend them from the Germans and incidentally incorporate them in the Soviet-Communist system of which they were the most vehement opponents. Poland, Rumania, Finland and the three Baltic states did not know whether it was German aggression or Russian rescue that they dreaded more. It was this hideous choice that paralyzed British and French policy."[5]

If Poland had ceased to exist after September 1939, there were nevertheless Poles who kept up the fight in accordance with age-old tradition. Thousands of Polish soldiers who had escaped the Nazi-Soviet pincers made their way to the West, as did some distinguished Polish statesmen. On September 30 a Polish government-in-exile was established in France and promptly recognized by France, Great Britain, and, shortly later, the United States. Some 84,000 Polish troops were under arms in France at the time of the debacle there in 1940, and many of them were evacuated to England, as was the Polish government-in-exile. That government came to be known as the London Polish government (as distinguished from the later Lublin government), and it maintained especially close relations with the British government. This was understandable, for it had been Britain's guarantee to Poland which had resulted in its declaration of war against Germany in 1939 when Hitler had sent his Wehrmacht into Poland.

Poland: Roots of Conflict

When Hitler later launched his attack against Russia in 1941, and after Great Britain had concluded a mutual assistance agreement with the Soviet Union, the London Polish government sought ways and means of establishing relations with the Soviet Union—but it did so as an aggrieved party and in a proud spirit of national assertiveness. As Prime Minister Mikolajczyk has written: "Unlike Britain and the U. S. . . . we had certain conditions to present to the Russians in exchange for our pledge of support. The conditions we offered were generous. We ruled out reparations and indemnities, though entitled to both. We promised to forgive, if not forget. To our astonishment, when we sat down with Russian Ambassador Ivan Maisky in London to draw up a new pact, we learned that Russia was not willing to accept our modest claims."[6] The Polish claims were the re-establishment of Poland in its pre-1939 boundaries. This Russia, even at the time when it was most sorely beset by the German invaders, was unwilling to guarantee.

The Soviet position in the Polish-Soviet negotiations in 1941 was completely inflexible: they regarded their annexation of eastern Poland as final; they claimed that it corresponded to ethnographic realities; they referred to the fact that the British government had in 1920 sponsored a frontier line (the Curzon Line) which was almost the same; and they argued that the experience they were undergoing at the hands of the German army proved how essential these areas were to the defense of the Soviet Union. They were prepared to free Polish prisoners of war in Russia and to permit the formation of a Polish army on Russian soil by recruitment among the released prisoners and other Poles. They were prepared to establish diplomatic relations with the London Polish government, but in the end they were only willing to state publicly, in the agreement with that government, that they regard "the Soviet-German treaties of

1939 as to territorial changes in Poland as having lost their validity."

On the public record, this statement seemed to leave the matter of Poland's future eastern frontiers in doubt, but when Polish Prime Minister Sikorski after signing the Polish-Soviet agreement declared that Poland's pre-1939 frontiers should be restored, he received an immediate answer from *Izvestia* (August 3, 1941) to the effect that the Soviet Union had promised nothing in that regard. The British government also confined itself to a declaration that "His Majesty's Government do not recognize any territorial changes which have been effected in Poland since August 1939," and Foreign Minister Eden explained in answer to a question in the House of Commons that this did not involve any British guarantee of Poland's frontiers.[7] The U.S. position was that all territorial questions should be postponed until after the war.[8] This was, in fact, the position of some of the Polish leaders, who felt that a war-weakened Russia would in the end not be able to oppose Polish national aspirations.[9]

Meanwhile, as Polish-Russian relations were formally normalized, the Soviet authorities began to release Polish prisoners of war in Russia, but it turned out that the only Poles who were made available for service in a new Polish army on Russian soil were those who came from western Poland, plus ethnic Poles from eastern Poland (i.e., excluding Ukrainians, White Russians, and Jews from the latter area). Although Stalin agreed with General Sikorski, the Polish Prime Minister, that six or seven Polish divisions were to be formed in Russia, the Poles quickly noted that most of the officers who were known to have fallen into Russian captivity were not among the soldiers being released from prisoner-of-war camps. Since the new Polish divisions were to be equipped with American arms, and since the supply situation was terribly strained, the Polish divisions were very slow in being formed.

On every occasion of contact with Western leaders, Stalin pressed for recognition of eastern frontiers that would extend Russian territory after the war. When Foreign Minister Eden visited Moscow in December 1941, Stalin offered assurances of Russian support for a privileged British security position in western Europe in return for British recognition of the Soviet boundaries roughly as they had been before the German attack. When Molotov was in London in May 1942 to conclude a mutual assistance treaty with Great Britain, he pressed hard for British recognition of the Russian position and would have obtained it but for American objections.[10] (Churchill considered that such an extension of Russian frontiers to where they had been at the time of the Nazi attack would be compatible with the Atlantic Charter.[11]) In January 1943 the Soviet government informed the Polish government-in-exile that henceforth those refugees in Russia who had come from the former eastern provinces of Poland would be treated as Soviet citizens. The Polish government-in-exile, of course, protested this pronouncement as illegal and unacceptable.

Meanwhile, the position of the nascent new Polish army in Russia became more and more difficult. In October 1941 the London Polish government addressed a note to the Soviet ambassador expressing disquiet about the whereabouts of "several thousand Polish officers who have not returned to Poland and who have not been found in Soviet military camps." The Russian ambassador's reply, one month later, was to the effect that all Polish officers on the territory of the U. S. S. R. had been set free.[12] In November 1941, the Polish ambassador in Moscow obtained an audience with Stalin and raised, more specifically, the question of what had happened to approximately 15,000 Polish officers and noncoms who were known to have been in camps at Starobielsk, Kozielsk, and Ostashkov. The Polish underground had knowledge that those prisoners had been transferred from their camps in early 1940 to an unknown destination, but only between 350 and 400 had reported to the Polish army in Russia. Stalin replied that the Russian "amnesty" knew no exceptions, and he declined to discuss the matter further. In December 1941 General Sikorski flew to Moscow and put the same question to Stalin at a time when the Germans were pressing at the very gates of Moscow. Stalin insisted that the Polish officers had been liberated and suggested that they might be "somewhere in Manchuria."[13]

As the supply situation of the Polish army became more difficult, it was arranged that the Polish troops should be permitted to leave Russia through Iran to join the Allied forces in the Middle East. In the course of his discussions of the modalities of that withdrawal, the Polish commander-in-chief, General Anders, had an interview with Stalin in March 1942, when he again raised the question of the missing Polish officers. According to a record of this conversation, Anders said: "Many of our people are still in prisons and labor camps. Only recently released prisoners are reporting all the time. So far, not a single officer removed from Kozielsk, Starobielsk or Ostashkov has turned up. You certainly must have them. We have collected additional information about them. Where can they be?" Stalin replied: "I have already given all necessary orders that they are to be freed. They say they are even in Franz Joseph Land, but there is no one there. I don't know where they are. Why should we retain them? Perhaps they were in camps in territories which were taken over by the Germans and were dispersed."[14] The Poles immediately explained that this was impossible since they were in contact with the underground in Poland itself and would have heard if some of the missing officers had turned up there.

The London Polish government had, in fact, excellent information about the former inmates of the three prisoner-of-war camps as they not only represented the bulk of the Polish officer corps but included political leaders, lawyers, physicians, scientists, and clergymen—the cream of the Polish leadership elements. At Ostashkov there had been between 6,500 and 6,600 officers, many of them reservists who in private life had held important civil posts; at Starobielsk most of the 4,000 prisoners had been noncoms; while at Kozielsk there had been 4,500 personnel of various military ranks, including some of Poland's highest ranking officers, as well as some civilians. According to information available to the London Polish government, Lavrenty Beria, the head of the Soviet secret police, had declared to some Polish representatives as early as the spring of 1940 that in regard to the missing officers, "a great mistake had been made."[15] The London Polish government thus had every reason to suspect that the former occupants of the three prison camps, from whom all news had ceased since early 1940, had been the victims of foul play. But they did not know what kind of foul play it had been.

On April 13, 1943 the German radio announced that on the basis of information furnished by the local population, the German authorities had found in the forest of Katyn near Smolensk "the spot where in secret mass executions, the Bolsheviks murdered 10,000 Polish officers." German authorities, the broadcast said, had found a pit 28 meters long and 16 meters wide in which, twelve deep, lay the bodies of 3,000 Polish officers. In full uniform, and in some cases shackled, all had wounds from pistol bullets in the back of the neck. The Germans said that "search and discovery of other pits were continuing." In a cal-

45

culated expression of horror, they called for an on-the-spot investigation by the International Red Cross. Two days afterward, the Soviet news agency Tass rejected the German revelation as a dastardly provocation and for the first time gave an explanation of what was supposed to have happened to the missing prisoners: "The Polish prisoners in question," the Soviet story went, "were interned in the vicinity of Smolensk in special camps and were employed in road construction. It was impossible to evacuate them at the time of the approach of the German troops, and as a result they fell into their hands. If, therefore, they have been found murdered, it means they have been murdered by the Germans who for reasons of provocation claim now that the crime has been committed by the Soviet authorities."[16]

The London Polish government was placed in an exceedingly difficult position by the German propaganda campaign. Although nauseated by the German effort to derive propaganda advantage by embroiling Polish relations with the Soviet Union, it felt that it could not ignore the allegations. On April 16 the London Polish government thus issued a statement detailing the known facts about the missing prisoners and about its unsuccessful efforts to obtain an accounting from the Soviet government, and asked that "the facts alleged be verified by a competent international body, such as the International Red Cross." It announced that it had already approached that organization "with a view to their sending a delegation to the place where the massacre of the Polish prisoners of war is said to have taken place."[17] In the view of one eminent historian of Russia's relations with the West, "it is hard, in retrospect, to see how the Poles could have done less."[18]

The Soviet reaction to the Polish statement was exceedingly violent. Stalin informed Churchill and Roosevelt that he in-

46

tended to break (he used the word "interrupt") relations with the London Polish government for having "struck a treacherous blow at the Soviet Union to help Hitler tyranny" and he claimed that "the fact that the anti-Soviet campaign has been started simultaneously in the German and Polish press and follows identical lines is indubitable evidence of contact and collusion between Hitler—the allies' enemy—and the Sikorski Government in this hostile campaign." In vain did Churchill and Roosevelt urge Stalin to withhold action. They deplored the Polish government's action, but both pointed out that the London Poles were certainly not trying to help Hitler. Roosevelt cabled Stalin: "Incidentally, I have several million Poles in the U. S., a great many of whom are in the Army and Navy. I can assure you that all of them are bitter against the Hitlerites. However, the overall situation would not be helped by the knowledge of a complete diplomatic break between the Soviet and Polish Governments." Churchill also warned that "public announcement of a break would do the greatest possible harm in the U. S., where the Poles are numerous and influential." However, Stalin broke relations with the London Polish government even before these messages reached him, claiming that "Soviet public opinion was deeply outraged by such conduct, and hence the Soviet government could no longer defer action."[19]

The breakdown of relations between the Polish government in London and the Soviet government was a disaster for the Western allies. In Russia an organization called the "Union of Polish Patriots in the USSR" came to the fore with a declaration denouncing the London Polish government, and it was obvious that that pro-Communist group was being groomed to take over in Poland when Soviet forces reached Polish soil. To make matters worse, General Sikorski, who had been both prime minister and commander-in-chief of the Polish armed forces, was

47

killed in an airplane crash in July 1943. His successor, Stanislaw Mikolajczyk, was an able and moderate political leader who had to harness together a number of differing political tendencies plus the Polish military. It must be remembered that the Polish government in London sponsored not only some 150,000 Polish troops in the Mediterranean and the Middle East but also a Polish Air Force in England and, last but not least, an important underground network in Poland (called the Polish Home Army). The Poles in London were in close contact with the underground. Ominously, they began to receive reports of Polish pro-Communist partisans who were being parachuted into Poland by the Russians.

The United States generally left the lead to the British in the efforts to restore Polish-Russian relations. Roosevelt toyed with the idea of a compromise on the territorial issue involving modification of the Curzon Line that would give the city of Lwow to Poland and "a plebiscite . . . after the shell shock of war had subsided."[20] In general, however, the position of the United States remained that territorial issues should await the peace conference.[21] The British, on the other hand, felt that the sooner the territorial question was settled, the better were the chances that the Russians would acquiesce in a free Poland. A joint U. S.-British demarche in Moscow in September to patch up Soviet-Polish relations met with uncompromising Russian opposition. When Eden, before the Moscow Conference of October 1943, asked Mikolajczyk to empower him to discuss the frontier question with the Russians, the Polish premier flatly refused, reminding Eden of the principles expressed in the Atlantic Charter and warning that if the West bargained away Poland's eastern territories, "it would be only the beginning of Russian demands."[22]

The Polish position prior to the Moscow Conference was set

48

forth in detail to both Hull and Eden. It asked the American and British governments to guarantee Poland's independence, integrity, and security. Ambassador Ciechanowski told Hull that "anxious to maintain good Polish-Soviet relations in the future, my government would deem undesirable either temporary or partial occupation of Polish territories by the Soviet armies. However, if such occupation were unavoidable as a result of military operations against Germany, it should be dependent on a previous Polish-Soviet understanding, based on the reestablishment of diplomatic relations." The right of the Polish government to administer the country should be guaranteed, and "to safeguard such a guarantee, American-British troops . . . should enter and be stationed on the territory of Poland to protect the population against eventual Soviet reprisals and the creation of accomplished facts."[23] This position, of course, left no room whatever for compromise.

At the Moscow Conference, the Polish question was thus only briefly discussed. Litvinov denounced the London Polish government; declared that the Poles must learn to live as a small national state within their "correct" boundaries, and give up the idea that they were a great power; and asserted that when their interests collided with Russia's interests, they would have to give way. Molotov listened to Eden's plea that the Polish-Russian quarrel be ended, but indicated that he thought the question one for the Soviet government to settle; he affirmed that the Soviet government wanted to see an "independent" Poland; but its government would have to be "friendly" to the Soviet Union, and the group in London was decidedly not. Hull confined his intervention to generalities.[24] The entry made in the final Protocol of the Conference said merely about this item of the agenda that "an exchange of views took place."

On the other hand, the Conference spent a great deal of time

49

on the Four-Power Declaration, which set forth certain principles that would govern the policies of the signatories during the remainder of the war. Paragraph six of that Declaration, in the original American proposal, read: "That they will not employ their military forces within the territories of other states except for the purposes envisaged in this Declaration and after joint consultation *and agreement.*" Molotov objected to the words "and agreement" and made it clear that while Russia was willing to consult, it was not willing to submit to a veto over action.[25] Accordingly, the Declaration was issued without the words "and agreement" (see page viii). The Moscow Four-Power Declaration was subsequently hailed as the harbinger of a new era of international understanding because it recorded agreement on "the necessity of establishing . . . a general international organization, based on the principle of the sovereign equality of all peace-loving states," but it did not advance the solution of the questions of Russia's western boundaries and Russia's relations with its neighbor states in Europe.

Cordell Hull nevertheless said, when he reviewed the accomplishments of the Moscow Conference before Congress in November 1943: "As the provisions of the Four-Nation Declaration are carried into effect, there will no longer be need for spheres of influence, for alliances, for balance of power, or any other of the special arrangements through which, in the unhappy past, the nations strove to safeguard their security or to promote their interests." He reasoned that "in the atmosphere of mutual understanding and confidence which made possible [the movement toward an international organization] in Moscow, many of the problems which are difficult today will, as time goes on, undoubtedly become more possible of satisfactory solution through frank and friendly discussion."[26]

The London Polish government did not share this optimistic

interpretation of the meeting, and it concentrated all its efforts to assure that the Western allies would support its uncompromising position at the forthcoming meeting of heads of state at Tehran. The Polish ambassador to the United States handed Hull a memorandum which threatened that, if Soviet troops entered Polish territory without previous resumption of Polish-Soviet relations, the Polish government would "undertake political action against this violation of Polish sovereignty, while the Polish local administration and army in Poland would have to continue to work underground." In London, Mikolajczyk warned that "decisions taken without full consultation with the Polish government upon which the underground in Poland staked its hopes would undoubtedly lead to a serious crisis in that quarter, would create a crisis in Polish circles in England and the Middle East, and might have serious repercussions among Americans of Polish origin."[27] In other words, the London Polish government was threatening that in the event Russian troops entered Poland without its consent, the Polish underground would fight the Russians, and it threatened that if the United States made an agreement with Russia over the head of the Polish government, the latter would mobilize Polish opinion in the United States against the U. S. government.

At the Tehran Conference, Stalin raised the idea that Poland's Western frontier should include an enormous chunk of German territory up to the river Oder, and Churchill readily fell in with that suggestion. Churchill reports that he said to Stalin: "I have no power from Parliament nor, I believe, has the President, to define any frontier lines. But we might now, in Teheran, see if the three heads of governments, working in agreement, could form some sort of policy which we could recommend to the Poles and advise them to accept."[28] There ensued a prolonged discussion of the proposed future frontiers for the Polish state, in which Roosevelt sat by silently. In the end, although the exact modifications of the Curzon Line still were not precisely agreed, Churchill and Stalin agreed that the new Poland should go roughly from the Curzon Line to the Oder.

At a separate, private meeting with Stalin, Roosevelt explained the reason why he did not feel he could commit himself. He told the Soviet dictator that there were six or seven million Americans of Polish extraction who constituted an important voting bloc and whose opinions had to be taken seriously in determining American foreign policy.[29] He referred to the forthcoming electoral campaign in 1944 and, according to the Bohlen memo of that conversation, indicated that "personally he agreed with the views of Marshal Stalin as to the necessity of the restoration of a Polish state but would like to see the eastern border moved farther to the west and the western border moved even to the River Oder. He hoped, however, that the Marshal would understand that for political reasons outlined above, he could not participate in any decision here in Tehran or even next winter on this subject and that he could not publicly take part in any such arrangement at the present time." Roosevelt also appears to have spoken about the desirability of the city of Lwow going to Poland, although the record of this aspect of the confidential conversation is unclear.[30] (In another private talk at Tehran, when the prospective world peace organization was discussed, the President remarked that American naval and air forces could be used to help police the world, but any land armies needed to quell aggression would have to be provided by Russia and Britain.[31])

It was thus left to Churchill to attempt to get the London Polish government to accept a territorial settlement along the lines discussed at Tehran. The matter had become especially urgent because the Red Army was about to reach the old boundary of Poland. But the Poles were adamant: on January 4, 1944, the day when the Red Army crossed the line, Mikolajczyk in a broadcast reaffirmed the order given to the Polish underground to cooperate with the Soviet commanders "if relations [with the London Polish government] should be resumed"; demanded "respect for the rights and interests of the Polish Republic"; invoked the Atlantic Charter and the Four Freedoms; and announced that a delegate of the government had been empowered to act in its name in Poland "to carry out all the functions of the government concerning home administration."[32] The Russian reply, in equally uncompromising terms, denounced the "emigrant" Polish government as incapable of conducting friendly relations with the Soviet Union or of leading an active fight against the Germans in Poland; declared that it wished to see a strong and independent Poland with which it could be friendly; insisted that the eastern boundary, while it need not follow the 1939 line, must correspond to the ethnic situation; and only offered the Poles compensation in the West, "through incorporation with Poland of ancient Polish lands previously wrested by Germany." Pointedly, the Russian statement referred to the "Union of Polish Patriots in the USSR" and announced that a Polish Army Corps under its auspices was operating hand in hand with the Red Army in the battle for liberation.

Churchill was tough with Milolajczyk when he saw him on January 20. "The British Government takes the view that Poland must be strong, independent, and free," he began, and then quickly added, "from the Curzon Line to the Oder." In the premier's own words:

> . . . when I raised the first of my objections about this obvious unilateral partition of Poland, Churchill reminded me a bit tartly that the Anglo-Polish alliance pact, signed just before the outbreak of the war, had obliged Britain to de-

fend Poland and Poland's independence against the Germans but had not mentioned the eastern frontiers of Poland. "You must understand this, Mr. Mikolajczyk, Great Britain and the U.S. will not go to war to defend the eastern frontiers of Poland. If an agreement is reached now about those frontiers, this agreement could be guaranteed by Great Britain as well as the Soviet Union. It is not possible under the American Constitution for President Roosevelt to guarantee the frontiers of any foreign country. Therefore, I urge you to agree to the Curzon Line as the eastern frontier of Poland, in principle at least. . . . If you do not act quickly, I cannot be responsible for anything that might take place."[33]

The Polish government felt that it had to obtain the views of the underground before replying to the British initiative. Meanwhile, it tried to mobilize the support of the United States but obtained only an evasive reply. However, Ambassador Harriman in Moscow tried to exercise a moderating influence, and he reported that he felt an agreement was still possible if the Polish government would drop its most outspokenly anti-Soviet members and if it at least tacitly accepted the Soviet position on boundaries.[34] But the Polish underground was, if anything, more proudly unyielding than its government. It was willing to accept the German territory offered in the west, but refused to cede what was asked in the east and even objected to the acquisition of German territory (East Prussia) by Russia. It was willing, on the other hand, to accept a temporary line of demarcation but one substantially to the east of what Russia proposed. And it affirmed that changes in the Polish government and high command could not be made "in obedience to the demands of a foreign power." The Polish troops in the Mediterranean theatre took an equally unyielding position.[35] Mikolajczyk's reply to Churchill was therefore wholly negative.

While the American government continued to maintain silence in the matter, Churchill on February 22, 1944 made a
statement in the House of Commons in which he recalled that
the British government had never guaranteed any particular
boundary of Poland and had, in fact, not approved the Polish
occupation of certain territories to the east of the Curzon Line in
1920 (when the Polish army under Pilsudski had beaten the Red
Army). He went on to say: "I have an intense sympathy with the
Poles, that heroic race whose national spirit centuries of misfor-
tune cannot quench, but I also have sympathy with the Russian
standpoint. Twice in our lifetime Russia has been violently as-
saulted by Germany. . . . Russia has the right to reassurance
against future attacks from the West, and we are going all the
way with her to see that she gets it, not only by the might of her
arms but by the approval and assent of the United Nations."

The London Polish government immediately protested this
speech. Mikolajczyk repeatedly attempted to obtain a hearing
from Roosevelt, but the President sent him a letter stating that
he wanted to see him very much "but a visit at this time may
bring misunderstanding in public opinion."[36] When the Polish
premier finally succeeded in seeing Roosevelt in June, it was
on condition that he would make no public statement. The
meeting was amiable. The President ventilated the possibility
of a compromise on the boundary question and urged the Polish
premier to visit Stalin. Mikolajczyk agreed to see Stalin. But a
message from Roosevelt to the Soviet dictator, suggesting such
a meeting, met with a negative response since Mikolajczyk
made it clear to the Soviet ambassador in London that he refused to reorganize his government or to make any territorial
concessions.

The Western invasion of Europe was now imminent, while

55

in the east the Russian offensive had come to a halt. Meanwhile, the Polish question was further complicated by the fact that the Russians seemed about to set up a rival Polish government. However, the American government did not feel that it could afford to press the Russians too strongly. The landings in Normandy, as Cordell Hull has written, "had to be coordinated with Russian military movements in the East so that the Germans could not draw off too large a portion of their forces to meet us in the West. We could not afford to become partisan in the Polish question to the extent of alienating Russia at that crucial moment."[37] The Russians, as it turned out, kept the word they had given at Tehran by launching a major offensive with 130 divisions after the Western Allies had landed in France. While that offensive heartened the Allied military leaders, its momentum was such that it carried the Red Army for the first time into territory that the Russians themselves had recognized as Polish, thereby creating a new crisis in Polish-Russian relations.

Now it was Churchill's turn to ask Stalin to receive Mikolajczyk. Stalin replied that, since Russia did not wish to set up a Russian administration in Poland, and since "we have not found in Poland other forces capable of establishing a Polish administration," he was getting in touch with the Polish Committee of National Liberation which had been established at Lublin and which "intended" to set up such an administration. However, he would not refuse to see Mikolajczyk.[38] With great difficulty, the British government managed to persuade the Polish premier to go, but while he was on his way the Russian government signed an agreement with the Lublin group, entrusting it with the administration of the Polish liberated territory. When Mikolajczyk arrived in Moscow, preceded by messages from Churchill and Roosevelt urging reconciliation, he was coldly received. Molotov asked him why he had come. Stalin repeated the well-known Russian position on frontiers but suggested that if Mikolajczyk's group reached an accord with the Committee of National Liberation, some small changes to the benefit of the Poles might be made in the Curzon Line. While Russia had not yet recognized the Lublin group as a Polish government, Stalin was suggesting that the London Polish government could be recognized by Russia only if it accepted some if not all the members of the Lublin group, i.e., if it formed a coalition with them.

Mikolajczyk saw Stalin on August 3, 1944. On August 1 the Polish Home Army in Warsaw had risen against the Germans in expectation of freeing it before the Red Army reached the city. The anti-Communist Poles in Warsaw were of course not in touch with the Russian command, but they had decided that the time had come to strike because the city's suburbs on the eastern bank of the Vistula were already under Russian artillery fire and the Polish radio station in Moscow had called on the people of Warsaw to rise against the Germans.[39] The Polish underground in Warsaw was soon opposed by five picked German divisions and it was clear that the fate of the uprising depended on the speed of the Russian advance into the city. The Russian troops, however, arraigned themselves on the eastern bank of the Vistula to the north and south of Warsaw and marked time. The embattled Poles in Warsaw had food and ammunition only for about a week's fighting, and soon they pleaded in messages to London for supplies and for relief. Mikolajczyk in Moscow and Churchill in telegrams from London besought Stalin to help, but Stalin replied evasively, expressing doubt that a major uprising had taken place but promising some assistance. Molotov claimed that the Germans were counterattacking the Russian troops.

In the absence of any Russian assistance to the uprising in

Warsaw, the R. A. F. started dropping supplies from planes based in Italy, but its losses during these long trips were prohibitive and the flights had to be stopped. Mikolajczyk appealed to the U. S. Air Force, which had run a shuttle service between bases in Britain and Russia, to drop supplies to the Warsaw fighters. But when the United States asked for permission for its planes to land behind the Russian lines, Vyshinsky replied: "The Soviet Government cannot of course object to English or American aircraft dropping arms in the region of Warsaw, since this is an American and British affair. But they decidedly object to American or British aircraft, after dropping arms in the region of Warsaw, landing on Soviet territory, since the Soviet government do not wish to associate themselves either directly or indirectly with the adventure in Warsaw." In a message to Churchill, Stalin declared that he had become "convinced that the Warsaw action represents a reckless and terrible adventure which is costing the population large sacrifices. . . . In the situation which has arisen the Soviet command has come to the conclusion that it must dissociate itself from the Warsaw adventure, as it cannot take either direct or indirect responsibility for the Warsaw action."[40]

For sixty-three days the Poles in Warsaw kept up the fight against towering odds while Churchill and Roosevelt appealed to Stalin to come to their assistance. Meanwhile, Mikolajczyk, who had returned to London, was desperately trying to work out a political compromise which might save the lives of the remaining embattled freedom fighters. He told Churchill that he was prepared to offer the Lublin Committee fourteen seats, but his offer met with no response from Moscow. Churchill proposed to Roosevelt that American planes be sent over Warsaw with instructions to land behind the Russian lines even without Russian consent, but Roosevelt felt this would only create a major crisis with the Russians. Churchill seems to have agreed, for he later wrote that he "should have liked to say, 'we are sending our aeroplanes to land in your territory, after delivering supplies to Warsaw. If you do not treat them properly, all convoys will be stopped from this moment by us.' But the reader of these pages in after-years must realise that everyone always has to keep in mind the fortunes of millions of men fighting in a world-wide struggle, and that terrible and even humbling submissions must at times be made to the general aim."[41]

After the battle had gone on for six weeks, the Russians changed their tactics and began to give some artillery and air support to the Polish Home Army in Warsaw. Also some Polish troops under Russian command were ferried across the Vistula and tried to join up with the fighting within the city, but they suffered great losses and the survivors had to be brought back. Russian landing fields were made available and one large flight of American bombers was thus able to drop supplies, on September 18, but it was too late. On October 2, after a last broadcast in which they called down God's judgment on those responsible for their betrayal, the Polish forces in Warsaw ceased resistance. Of the 40,000 men and women of the underground army, about 15,000 had been killed. The German army lost 10,000 dead in the battle, and 9,000 wounded. The proportions, as Churchill suggests, attest to the bitter, hand-to-hand character of the fighting. When the Russians entered the city three months later, they found little but shattered streets and the unburied dead.

As one historian summed up the situation:

> The crisis in Polish affairs which had thus developed in the first part of August deserves a place in the history of the Second World War like that which Thucydides gave to the Athenian attack on Melos. The affair had all the elements

59

of tragedy, not only for Poland but for the world at large. Stalin's cold-blooded decision to destroy the Polish Home Army, to deprive the London Government of all effective power in Polish affairs, and to disregard the feelings of the population of Poland herself meant sacrificing much of the sympathy of the British and American public in favour of what he believed to be the security of his western frontier. Polish nationalism and folly had helped to bring the disaster to its climax; Russian brutality and ruthlessness, Roosevelt's failure to make his opinion about the Curzon Line clear to the Poles, and the bloodthirst of German revenge all united to make this passage of Polish history into unmitigated tragedy.[42]

The rest of the story between the fall of Warsaw and the Yalta Conference is quickly told. Churchill was in Moscow in October 1944 to discuss a whole range of difficulties that had accumulated in eastern Europe. At that conference, Roosevelt was unable to participate because of the election campaign. Churchill brought with him a proposal drawn up by Mikolajczyk which called for the formation of a Polish government in which the Communists would have one-fifth of the posts. On the territorial question, the proposal was ambiguous. Churchill urged Stalin to discuss the matter with the Polish premier, and when Stalin agreed he summoned Mikolajczyk urgently to Moscow. The discussion got nowhere as Mikolajczyk still refused to accept the Curzon Line. At one point Molotov intervened in the argument to remark that at Tehran all the Big Three had agreed on the Curzon Line as the proper frontier for the new Poland. (Ambassador Harriman subsequently rectified this impression by pointing out that Roosevelt had not participated in the discussions at Tehran on Poland's western frontier.) Again and again, Churchill attempted to bring the Polish and Russian points of view closer together, but each time he was rebuffed by one side or by both.[43] In the end, Stalin told Mikolajczyk to talk with the Lublin Committee. These pro-Communist Poles now claimed 75 per cent of the posts in any Polish government. In a final talk, Stalin made it clear that if Mikolajczyk were to form a government acceptable to Russia, the Lublin Poles must have a majority.[44]

In their extremity, the Poles in London again turned to the United States. It was now October, less than a month before the 1944 elections, and Roosevelt was fearful that a row over Poland could alienate the important Polish vote, especially in the Middle West. Particularly embarrassing was Mikolajczyk's reference to Molotov's claim that the American President had agreed to the Curzon Line a year before at the Tehran Conference. The President thus temporized while he tried to mend his fences with the Polish-American Congress, which was becoming restive.[45] Not until after he had been re-elected, on November 17, did he reply to Mikolajczyk in a letter delivered by Ambassador Harriman. The letter was as evasive as the U. S. reply to a similar plea in January: it declared that the U. S. government stood "unequivocally for a strong, free and independent Polish state with the untrammeled right of the Polish people to order their internal existence as they see fit"; but on the critical frontier question it offered no specific support, stating merely that if mutual agreement on the subject were reached between the Polish, Soviet, and British governments, the United States "would offer no objection." While the United States could not give any guarantee of specific frontiers, Roosevelt concluded, the prospective world organization would assure the inviolability of agreed frontiers.[46]

Within the London Polish government, there were some who felt that some concessions on the territorial issue were inevitable, but they were in a minority. There was extensive discussion whether some modification of the Curzon Line, notably through inclusion of the city of Lwow, might be negotiated with American help. Ambassador Harriman indicated to Mikolajczyk that he was prepared to talk along such lines with Stalin. But the parties represented in the government-in-exile, with the exception of Mikolajczyk's own Peasant Party, were all opposed to the suggestion. The Polish premier thus resigned his office on November 24. The succeeding government under Tomasz Arciszewski was even more unyielding than the previous one. It was clear that the Russians would now soon proclaim the Lublin group to be the legal government of Poland. President Roosevelt sent a message to Stalin asking him to stay his hand, but the message, dated December 20, was not strongly worded.[47] At the time when it was sent, the German Rundstedt offensive had just broken the American lines in the Ardennes and on December 18 Nazi panzer units had forged to within eight miles of the headquarters of the First U. S. Army.[48]

In a long debate on the Polish question in the House of Commons, Churchill was unsparing in his criticism of the London Poles. He explained that Mikolajczyk had resigned because he was "confronted with the obstinate and inflexible resistance of his London colleagues, whose veto was like the former *Liberum Veto*, which played so great a part in the ruin of Poland." Since Mikolajczyk's resignation, the Polish government had, he said, "been almost entirely reconstituted in a form which in some respects I certainly am not able to applaud." He predicted that because of the failure of the Polish government, troubles would arise between the Russians and the Polish underground as the Red Army advanced through Poland. Churchill defended the British government's support for the Soviet claim to the Curzon Line, including the claim that the territory of Lwow should be assigned to the Soviet Union. The Prime Minister also expressed his regret that various factors in the domestic situation in the United States had made it impossible for the position of that government to be stated with precision.[49]

On December 31, 1944 the Lublin Committee constituted itself as the Provisional National Government of the Polish Republic. On January 5, 1945 the Soviet government—overriding a final appeal by President Roosevelt—recogized the Provisional Government. On January 17 Stalin announced that the Red Army, together with the First Polish Army, had liberated Warsaw, and on the following day, members of the Provisional Government entered the city to establish themselves upon the rubble and ashes to which it had been reduced during the tragic uprising of August and September. Meanwhile, the U. S. and British governments continued to recognize the London Polish government. This was the situation when the Big Three met in Yalta in early February 1945.

NOTES

1. Department of State, *Documents on German Foreign Policy, 1918-1945*, Series D, Volume VII, pp. 246/247 (Document 229).

2. ". . . Please discuss this at once with Molotov and see if the Soviet Union does not consider it desirable for Russian forces to move at the proper time against Polish forces in the Russian sphere of interest and, for their part, occupy this territory." Telegram from Reich Foreign Minister to the German Ambassador in the Soviet Union, September 3, 1939. Ibid., pp. 540/541 (Document 567).

3. ". . . From the communication made to you by Molotov on September 14, we assume that the Soviet Government will take a hand militarily, and that it intends to begin its operations now. We wel-

come this. The Soviet Government thus relieves us of the necessity of annihilating the remainder of the Polish Army by pursuing it as far as the Russian boundary. Also the question is disposed of in case a Russian intervention did not take place, or whether in the area lying to the east of the German zone of influence a political vacuum might not occur. Since we on our part have no intention of undertaking any political or administrative activities in these areas, apart from what is made necessary by military operations, without such an intervention on the part of the Soviet Government there might be the possibility of the construction of new states there." Telegram from Reich Foreign Minister Ribbentrop to the German Ambassador in the Soviet Union, September 15, 1939. Stalin agreed wholeheartedly that anything that in the future might create friction between Germany and the Soviet Union must be avoided. From this point of view, he told the German Ambassador, "he considered it wrong to leave an independent Polish rump state." Department of State, *Documents on German Foreign Policy, 1918-1945*, Series D, Volume VIII, pp. 68-69 (Document 70) and p. 130 (Document 131).

4. Ibid., p. 166 (Document 160). A piquant footnote to this macabre chapter of history is found in the explanation that the Russians originally proposed to give for their invasion and annexation of eastern Poland. According to a telegram from the German ambassador in Moscow dated September 16, 1939, Molotov proposed that the Soviet Union issue a communiqué which would explain that since the Polish state had collapsed, all agreements concluded with Poland were void; that third powers might try to profit from the chaos which had arisen; and that the Soviet Union therefore considered itself obligated to intervene "to protect its Ukrainian and White Russian brothers and make it possible for these unfortunate people to work in peace." Molotov added rather ingenuously that, while the proposed statement was "jarring to German sensibilities . . . the Soviet Government unfortunately saw no possibility of any other motivation, since the Soviet Union had thus far not concerned itself about the plight of its minorities in Poland and had to justify abroad, in some way or other, its present intervention." As the Germans would not agree, a joint communiqué was later issued which did not mention Ukrainians or White Russians in eastern Poland. Ibid., pp. 44, 76, 96 (Documents 46, 78, 94).

5. Winston Churchill, *The Second World War* (Boston: Houghton Mifflin, 1948-1953). I: *The Gathering Storm* (1948). II: *Their Finest Hour* (1949). III: *The Grand Alliance* (1950). IV: *The Hinge of Fate* (1950). V: *Closing the Ring* (1951). VI: *Triumph and Tragedy* (1953). From *The Gathering Storm*, p. 362.

6. Stanislaw Mikolajczyk, *The Rape of Poland—Pattern of Soviet Aggression* (New York: McGraw-Hill, 1948), p. 16.

7. Royal Institute of International Affairs, *America, Britain, and Russia—Their Cooperation and Conflict, 1941-1946*, by William Hardy McNeill (London: Oxford University Press, 1953), p. 47.

8. *The Memoirs of Cordell Hull* (New York: Macmillan, 1948), II, 1166.

9. Prime Minister Sikorski is himself reported to have expressed the view that "the question of the Polish borders will be settled by the correlation of forces after the war." David J. Dallin, *Soviet Russia's Foreign Policy, 1939-1942* (New Haven: Yale University Press, 1942), p. 399.

10. The strongly negative U.S. reaction was described by Cordell Hull as follows: "We indicated that, if the treaty in its proposed form were signed, we might not be able to remain silent since silence might give tacit consent. On the contrary we might have to issue a separate statement clearly stating that we did not subscribe to its principles and clauses. This would be a sharp break within the United Nations, on this point at least, but there was no other course we could logically pursue." Hull *Memoirs*, II, 1172.

11. Prior to Molotov's visit, Churchill told Roosevelt on April 23, 1942: "The increasing gravity of the war has led me to feel that the principles of the Atlantic Charter ought not to be construed so as to deny Russia the frontiers she occupied when Germany attacked her. This was the basis on which Russia acceded to the Charter. . . . I hope therefore that you will be able to give us a free hand to sign the treaty which Stalin desires as soon as possible. Everything portends an immense renewal of the German invasion of Russia in the spring, and there is very little we can do to help the only country that is heavily engaged with the German armies. . . ." Churchill, *The Hinge of Fate*, p. 327.

12. Mikolajczyk, pp. 20-21.

13. Ibid., p. 22. Some historians regard this conversation, which

took place when Russia's military fortunes were at their lowest ebb, as having represented the best opportunity for a compromise between Russian and Polish territorial aspirations. Stalin raised the boundary issue with Sikorski not in terms of the Curzon Line but in terms of "a little" change. Mikolajczyk (p. 23) reports that Stalin referred to "very slight frontier alterations." According to W. W. Kulski in *Foreign Affairs,* July 1947 ("The Lost Opportunity for Russian-Polish Friendship"), Stalin added that he would not in any case claim the town of Lwow, which was ethnically Polish. In the opinion of Herbert Feis, "it may be that at this time the Polish government missed its best chance to win some measure of compromise from the Soviet government. Russian powers of resistance were being most exhaustively tried. Friendship and support in war probably meant more to the Soviet rulers just then than ever again." Herbert Feis, *Churchill, Roosevelt, Stalin—The War They Waged and the Peace They Sought* (Princeton, N.J.: Princeton University Press, 1957), pp. 33-34.

14. Record of Anders-Stalin conversation of March 18, 1942, *Katyn Forest Massacre* (see chap. 1, note 9), p. 961.

15. Ibid., p. 554; Mikolajczyk, p. 36.

16. This has been the Russian side of the story ever since. After the Red Army reoccupied the Smolensk area, the Soviet government appointed a "Special Commission for Ascertaining the Circumstances of the Shooting of Polish Officer Prisoners by the German Fascist Invaders in the Katyn Forest." The complete record is included in *Katyn Forest Massacre.* Thus the Russians produced a camp commander named Vetoshnikov who testified that "communications with Smolensk were cut. Then I myself with several staff members went to Smolensk to clarify the situation. . . . I applied to the chief of traffic of the Smolensk section of the Western Railway, Ivanov, asking him to provide the camp with railway cars for the evacuation of the Polish prisoners. But Ivanov answered that I could not count on receiving cars. I also tried to get in touch with Moscow to obtain permission to set out on foot, but I failed." An engineer Ivanov was also produced, who testified that "the administration of the Polish war prisoner camp applied to my office for cars for evacuation of the Poles, but we had none to spare. Besides, we could not send cars to the Gustino line

where the majority of the Polish war prisoners were, since that line was already under fire. . . . Thus the Polish war prisoners remained in the Smolensk region. *Katyn Forest Massacre*, p. 229.

Extensive analysis and rebuttal of the Russian "investigation," not only by the London Polish government but later in testimony before the House Committee, removes what little plausibility the Russian contentions may have had for some contemporary observers. It was not customary for the Russians to employ officer prisoners as road-building labor. It was the invariable rule, on the other hand, for prisoners to be evacuated well in advance of the arrival of German troops. The failure of the Russians to account for the disappearance of the prisoners prior to the German announcement has never been explained, even by their own propaganda. The Russian contention that mail dated up to the summer of 1941 was found on the bodies remains unsupported by any witness from inside Poland who might have testified to contact with the prisoners after the spring of 1940. On the other hand, there is much evidence that the Polish prisoners were taken from their camps in groups of 200 to 300—except for a contingent of 400 whom the Russians hoped to convert to Communism and who thus survived.

American officer war prisoners, who were forced by the Nazis to observe the corpses at Katyn, also noted—as did other witnesses—that the Polish dead were clad in winter uniforms in an excellent state of repair, showing practically no wear. This was especially noteworthy with regard to their boots. The American prisoners stated that from their own personal experience as prisoners of war in a German camp they knew that clothing could not have remained in that condition if it had been worn for a year in a prisoner camp. The body of mutually reinforcing evidence supporting the Polish case on the Katyn massacre has become so impressive that it seems surprising, from today's vantage point, that contemporary U.S. and British official opinion generally credited the Russian case. It must be remembered, of course, that at that time Russia was bearing the heaviest burden of the war. For additional information on the Katyn massacre, cf. J. K. Zawodny, *Death in the Forest* (Notre Dame, Ind.: University of Notre Dame Press, 1962).

17. Mikolajczyk, p. 31.

18. George F. Kennan, *Russia and the West Under Lenin and Stalin* (Boston: Little, Brown, 1960), p. 360. Churchill appears to have thought the Polish declaration a mistake. When Sikorski placed the evidence of the Soviet murder of the officers before him, Churchill says he replied: "If they are dead nothing you can do will bring them back." (Churchill, *The Hinge of Fate*, p. 759.) According to Feis it is unclear whether Sikorski himself "was fully advised that the statement was to be issued,and, if he was, whether he favored or resisted it. . . . What is certainly clear is that the military elements in his government, and the leaders of the Polish Army, felt that Polish honor and human justice made it imperative to break silence on this question and to hold the Soviet Government up for judgment. Whoever within the Polish group had sponsored the statement, some of them soon began to regret it." Feis, p. 193n.

19. *Correspondence Between the Chairman of the Council of Ministers of the U.S.S.R. and the Presidents of the U.S.A. and the Prime Ministers of Great Britain During the Great Patriotic War of 1941-1945* (Moscow: Foreign Language Publishing House, 1957), I, 120-22 and II, 60-62. (This source will be referred to later as *Stalin Correspondence*.)

20. Hull *Memoirs*, II, 1266.

21. "We wanted to see normal diplomatic relations restored between Russia and Poland; and we wanted the Soviet Government to agree to broad principles of international cooperation after the war, centered around the creation of an organization to maintain the peace. But we did not intend to insist on a wartime settlement of specific questions such as the determination of the future boundary between Poland and Russia. Raising this question, at the insistence of the Polish Government or of anyone else, would have reopened the whole question of numerous boundaries of interest to Russia—a Pandora's box of infinite trouble—which we had successfully postponed for the time being by the strong stand we had emphatically taken when the British-Soviet agreement of May 26, 1942, was under negotiation." Hull *Memoirs*, II, 1273.

22. Mikolajcyzk, p. 45.

23. Jan Ciechanowski, *Defeat in Victory* (Garden City, N.Y.: Doubleday, 1947), pp. 215-16; Hull *Memoirs*, II, 1271-72.

68

24. Hull *Memoirs,* II, 1305.

25. Feis, pp. 208-209. Equally significant, though not in connection with Poland, was the difference between the originally proposed language of paragraph 2 and that which was finally accepted: "That those of them at war with the common enemy will act together in all matters relating to the surrender and disarmament of that enemy, *and to any occupation of enemy territory and territory of other states held by that enemy.*" The clause appearing in italics was deleted because of Molotov's objections.

26. Hull *Memoirs,* II, 1314-15.

27. Ibid., II, 1316. The full text of the eloquent parallel note to the British government is contained in Mikolajczyk, note 11, pp. 267 ff. The quoted passage about resistance to the Soviets was modified by the additional sentence: "In that case the Polish Government foresee the use of measures of self-defense wherever such measures are rendered indispensable by Soviet methods of terror and extermination of Polish citizens. . . ." The note went on to say: "The Polish Government have, moreover, reasons to fear that in present conditions the life and property of Polish citizens may be exposed to danger after the entry of Soviet troops into Poland and the imposing on the country of Soviet administration. In that case desperate reaction of the Polish community may be expected, following the violation of the principle adopted in Quebec, assuring to the United Nations their liberty and their own administration. . . . Polish airmen, sailors, and soldiers in carrying out the fight against the common enemy must be assured that their families will be restored to them and that they can expect to return to a free and independent homeland."

28. Churchill, *Closing the Ring,* p. 362.

29. Robert E. Sherwood, *Roosevelt and Hopkins* (New York: Harper, 1948), p. 796. Stalin's reply was to suggest that some propaganda work should be undertaken to bend their minds to accord with state policy. McNeill (p. 364) comments: "Stalin probably did not take Roosevelt's remarks seriously. It is likely that he regarded the President's appeal to Polish-American opinion as a curiously devious trick to justify a policy of opposition to the Soviet Union."

30. *Foreign Relations of the United States—Conferences of Cairo and Tehran* (Washington: Government Printing Office, 1961; here-

after cited as *Tehran Papers*), p. 594. Feis (p. 285) comments: "in telling Stalin that he found no fault with the general ideas of shifting Polish frontiers to the west, Roosevelt, according to his own later interpretation, did not mean to bestow his approval on any particular frontier line—specifically the Curzon Line. But Stalin and Molotov both understood him to be doing so." Cf. also Stalin's version of what Roosevelt said, as reported by Churchill in 1944 (*Tehran Papers*, p. 885) and Roosevelt's own recollection at Yalta (*Yalta Papers*, [see chap. 1, note 1], p. 667).

31. Sherwood, p. 786. McNeill (p. 357) comments on this episode: "What effect did Roosevelt's casual statement that American ground troops would not be available for police duty abroad have on Stalin's calculations? Stalin was a man who greatly respected military force. If America were in truth getting ready to withdraw militarily from Europe and Asia after the end of the war, obviously the only rival to his political influence would be Great Britain. . . . If Stalin thought in terms such as these, it is probable that Roosevelt's statement encouraged him to raise his sights higher and made the Russians more unbending than before in claiming territorial and other concessions for themselves in Eastern Europe."

32. Mikolajczyk, note 13, pp. 270 ff.

33. Ibid., pp. 51-52. "I cannot make such an announcement, Mr. Prime Minister," Mikolajczyk reports himself as having answered. "Poland cannot emerge from this war diminished. You are asking for an intolerable concession. . . . Let me tell you that this will be a test case. It will compromise an Allied nation grossly and unjustly, and it will not bring peace to Europe. Don't you see, Mr. Prime Minister, that the Soviet Union's aim is not only to take the eastern half of our country but to take all of Poland—all of Europe? We have tried so diligently to keep the unity of the Allies, to cooperate. But do you realize that since the Red Army entered Poland it has been disarming and arresting the very members of the Polish underground who helped the Russians capture each point?" To which, the Polish premier reports, Churchill replied with a shrug. "That's more of a reason why you should now quickly agree to the Curzon Line."

It deserves to be noted that Mikolajczyk put the Polish case usually in terms of the diminution of territory he was asked to accept, rather than in terms of population. This was probably because, according to the Polish 1931 census, the last one before the war, the population to the east of the Curzon Line was predominantly Ukrainian and Byelorussian. Of a total population of 10.6 million living in that area, 5.7 million had given Russian languages as their mother tongues. Some 0.9 million had indicated Yiddish, and most of these had presumably been killed by the Germans by the end of the war. Competent analysts believe that the figures of Ukrainians may have been understated in the census, since Poland had launched a policy of forced pacification against the Ukrainian nationalists in 1930. Cf. U. S. Department of Commerce, Bureau of the Census, *The Population of Poland* (Washington: Government Printing Office, 1954), pp. 74-79 and p. 149.

To say that the population to the east of the Curzon Line was predominantly Ukrainian and Byelorussian does not, of course, mean that that population desired to belong to the U. S. S. R., notwithstanding the "plebiscite" held in that area by the Russians in 1939. According to the census figures, the area in any event also contained a sizable minority of some 3.9 million Poles. Churchill in his conversations with Mikolajczyk always stated that Poles to the east of the Curzon Line would have the right to be repatriated to Poland proper. Cf. Mikolajczyk, p. 51.

34. "Hull asked the Ambassador to impress both the Soviet and Polish Governments with the wisdom of not doing anything that might affect full military cooperation, spoil the possibilities of international cooperation after the war, or affect adversely the President's prospects for election. But judgment as well as expediency influenced the American treatment of the situation. Roosevelt thought, and Harriman's and Winant's reports gave ground for the belief, that the Soviet Government was not without cause in its refusal to deal with the Polish Government until it ejected certain of its members. Some of its inner group were, in truth, making no secret of their hatred and complete mistrust of the Soviet Union. They were saying that the only real hope for Poland lay in war between the West and the Soviet Union." Feis, p. 296.

35. Ibid., p. 297. General Anders, who was in command of the Second Polish Corps, which was in the center of the hardest fighting

in Italy, sent a message on February 25, 1944 saying that "all soldiers of the Polish Army in the east will refuse to consider the possibility of abandoning any scrap of Polish territory to the Bolsheviks."

36. Mikolajczyk, p. 56; Ciechanowski, pp. 308 and 317.

37. Hull *Memoirs*, II, 1441-42.

38. *Stalin Correspondence*, I, 241-42.

39. "The Polish Army now entering Polish territory, trained in the USSR, is now joined to the People's Army to form the corps of the Polish armed forces, the armed arm of our nation in its struggle for independence. Its ranks will be joined tomorrow by the sons of Warsaw. . . . It is . . . a hundred times more necessary than ever to remember that in the flood of Hitlerite destruction all is lost that is not saved by active effort and that by direct active struggle in the streets of Warsaw, in its houses, factories, and stores we not only hasten the moment of final liberation but also save the nation's property and the lives of our brethren. Poles, the time of liberation is at hand! Poles, to arms! There is not a moment to lose!" Radio Kosciuszko, Moscow, in Polish, 8:15 p.m., July 29, 1944.

40. Churchill, *Triumph and Tragedy*, pp. 133-34.

41. Ibid., p. 141. Hull, in another context, addressed himself to the same hypothesis: "In connection with the Polish-Russian dispute then and later on, and in connection with other questions between us and Russia, a suggestion was advanced from time to time that all we had to do to bring about a settlement was to threaten that we would cut off the Lend-Lease assistance we were sending her. Neither the President nor I seriously entertained this suggestion for a moment. Russia, Britain, and the United States were in the same boat, which would float or sink depending on their abilities in jointly fighting the common enemy. Our Lend-Lease supplies to Russia were helping to pin down or eliminate enemy armed forces on the Eastern Front which otherwise we would have had to fight on the Western Front.

"The very making of such a threat would have engendered bad feeling between Moscow on the one hand and London and Washington on the other. Russia could always argue, moreover, as we ourselves had done, that the sending of aid to her was in our own best interests. If we made the threat and Russia refused to accede to our demands, we would then have faced a dilemma. Would we cut off military aid and thereby hurt ourselves militarily? Or would we continue it, thereby proving that our threat had been an empty one? And if we did cut it off, and let Moscow go its own way, could we then have the slightest hope of reaching a general postwar agreement with the Soviet Government?

"On the other hand, if Stalin bowed to such a threat—and we had not the slightest assurance he would do so—what valid hope could we cherish that an agreement negotiated under a virtual ultimatum would be carried out when the Axis Powers were defeated and Russia no longer needed our military help?" Hull *Memoirs*, II, 1272-73.

42. McNeill, pp. 432-33. The passage continues: "Indeed, the tragedy moved with the inevitability of Greek drama. Poland's fall, like that of Oedipus, came as a result of the defects of Polish virtues. Courage, pride, stubbornness, and impetuosity became folly and recklessness, and brought dire catastrophe. Catastrophe it was, for Russia as much as for Poland, and for the Western Powers as much as for Russia. The failure of Allied policy to achieve a peaceable settlement of the Polish problem in the first seven months of 1944 may well be considered the turning-point in the history of the Grand Alliance. Although a semblance of harmony was reestablished at Yalta in February, 1945, that harmony was never translated from words into deeds. Despite all later efforts to mend the breach between East and West, the bad blood created in Poland in 1944 proved the beginning of the end. . . ."

43. Mikolajczyk (pp. 97-98) poignantly narrates his dialogue with Churchill as follows: " 'How near we got at the beginning of the year!' he said, stalking around the room. 'If you had come to an agreement with the Russians at that time, you would not have today those Lublin people. They are going to be a frightful nuisance. They will build up a rival government and gradually take over authority in Poland.'

"I reminded him again of the Atlantic Charter and other pacts that directly or indirectly pledged sovereign rights to Poland.

" 'I shall tell Parliament that I have agreed with Stalin', Churchill declared flatly. 'Our relations with Russia are much better than they have ever been. I mean to keep them that way'.

"He added, 'I talked to your General Anders the other day, and he seems to entertain the hope that after the defeat of the Germans the Allies will then beat Russia. This is crazy! You cannot defeat the Russians! I beg of you to settle upon the Curzon Line as a frontier. Suppose you do lose the support of some of the Poles? Think what you will gain in return. You will have a country. . . .'

"I shook my head, and it infuriated him that I refused his compromise.

" 'Then I wash my hands of this', he stormed. 'We are not going to wreck the peace of Europe. In your obstinacy you do not see what is at stake. It is not in friendship that we shall part. We shall tell the world how unreasonable you are. You wish to start a war in which twenty-five million lives will be lost!'

" 'You settled our fate at Teheran', I said.

" 'Poland was *saved* at Teheran,' he shouted.

" 'I am not a person whose patriotism is diluted to the point where I would give away half my country', I answered."

According to Ciechanowski (p. 335), when Churchill was asked during the same conversation whether he would accept the cession of British territory if Britain found herself in such a situation, the British leader is supposed to have replied: "I certainly would, and be blessed by future generations. There is no other alternative. Poland is threatened with virtual extinction. . . ."

44. Churchill, *Triumph and Tragedy,* p. 240. One peculiar feature of Mikolajczyk's last conference with Stalin on that occasion was the Soviet leader's answer when the Polish premier bluntly asked him whether he intended to make Poland a Communist state after the war. Stalin is supposed to have replied, "No, absolutely not. Communism does not fit the Poles. They are too individualistic. Poland's future economy should be based on private enterprise. Poland will be a capitalistic state." Mikolajczyk, p. 100.

45. Ciechanowski, p. 347.

46. Ibid., pp. 341-42. On the idea that the world organization would solve the problems left unsolved during the war, George Kennan had commented earlier in a memorandum sent to the State Department from Moscow: "An international organization for the preservation of peace and security cannot take the place of a well-conceived and realistic foreign policy . . . and we are being . . . negli-

gent of the interests of our people if we allow plans for an international organization to be an excuse for failing to occupy ourselves seriously and minutely with the sheer power relationships of the European peoples." (Feis, p. 436).

47. *Stalin Correspondence*, II, 175.

48. Chester Wilmot, *The Struggle for Europe* (London: Collins, 1952), p. 584.

49. Royal Institute of International Affairs, *The Realignment of Europe*, edited by Arnold Toynbee (London: Oxford University Press, 1955), p. 190.

4

Mostly Poland:
Yalta and the Aftermath

At the time of the Yalta Conference, the Red Army was in possession of almost all prewar Poland. In a series of gigantic offensives in January 1945, it had cut across Poland and into Germany all the way to the Oder River and had spearheads only forty miles from Berlin. The Russians had advanced in the north to Danzig and cut off twenty-five German divisions in East Prussia. They were penetrating into Upper Silesia, the only German industrial area untouched by Allied bombing attacks; and in the south, they had advanced from Hungary to within eighty miles of Vienna. Meanwhile, in the west, the Allies had only just regained the line they had been holding six weeks before when the Rundstedt offensive had begun. Except for the Roer River sector, the fortified Siegfried Line was still intact; the Rhine had yet to be forced; and, as Wilmot reports, there was doubt in General Eisenhower's headquarters that a large-scale crossing of the lower Rhine could be carried out soon.[1]

Mostly Poland: Yalta and the Aftermath

This situation was, in large part, the result of Hitler's gamble in the Ardennes, for which he had committed the entire German strategic reserve. Hitler's purpose had been primarily political. By demonstrating to the Western Allies that victory was not certain, he still hoped to persuade them to make a separate peace. He followed with the closest attention every evidence of inter-Allied disagreements. He had exclaimed in December to the assembled generals that "if we can now deliver a few more heavy blows, then at any moment this artificially-bolstered common front may collapse with a gigantic clap of thunder."[2] After the disaster of the Russian offensive had struck him in January, he felt that at any moment a Western offer might come to him to prevent the Russians from advancing further toward the Atlantic.[3] His only hope now was a falling out among his enemies. The purpose of Roosevelt, Churchill, and Stalin was to demonstrate that such a falling out was not to be expected.

The Yalta Conference dealt with many subjects. With regard to the defeat of Germany, it resulted in an agreement to concert the final offensives from East and West. This was clearly in the mutual interest. The Western Allies considered that the crossing of the Rhine would expose their forces to the greatest danger, and they wanted assurances that no German troops could be drawn from the Eastern Front at that critical time. The Russians, on the other hand, were fearful that unless the Americans and British pressed their attacks in the West (and especially in Italy, where operations had quieted down), the Nazis might draw troops from those fronts and throw them to the East.[4] With respect to the Far East, agreement was reached on Russian entry into the war, and the Western leaders paid for this by giving Stalin assurances that Russia would obtain the territories and rights it had enjoyed before it was defeated by the Japanese in 1904, plus the Kurile Islands. The question of Ger-

77

man reparations was extensively discussed and seemed agreed in principle. With regard to the United Nations organization, the West obtained a major concession when Stalin gave up his insistence that disputes involving one of the great powers should not be discussed without its agreement. There was also agreement that only countries that declared war against Germany by March 1 should be admitted to initial United Nations membership. Here it must be noted, since Stalin made a point of it during his second conversation with Hopkins in May (see Chapter 2), that it was understood that Argentina, which had collaborated with the Axis throughout the war, would not be among the initial members of the new world organization.[5]

But by far the greatest amount of time spent by the Conference was on the subject of Poland. In the words of one historian, "the Polish question was a disheveled presence in every conference hour. It was discussed in the private talks which Churchill, Stalin, and Roosevelt had with one another; in the group meetings of the Foreign Ministers; and at all but one of the plenary sessions. It became the testing ground between the West and Communist Russia—between two conceptions of security."[6] The questions were still what would be the boundaries of the future Poland, and how the country was to be governed. To both of these questions, the conference in the end provided ambiguous answers.

The territorial question had meanwhile become further complicated by propaganda claims of the Polish Provisional Government in Warsaw to the effect that the Polish borders in the West should extend not only to the Oder but in its southern part along the Western Neisse river to the Czech border near Goerlitz, adding another sizable chunk of German territory over and above what Churchill thought he had agreed to at Tehran. As for the eastern boundary, Roosevelt pleaded rather than argued.

He referred once more to the six or seven million Poles in the United States and said, "It would make it easier for me at home if the Soviet Government could give something to Poland. I raised the question of giving them Lwow at Tehran. It has now been suggested that the oil lands in the southwest of Lwow might be given them. I am not making a definite statement but I hope that Marshal Stalin can make a gesture in this direction."[7] Churchill said that he stood by his agreement to the Curzon Line, but if Russia were to make a magnanimous concession, the British would heartily acclaim such action.

Stalin responded heatedly and at great length and with the arguments with which we are familiar since Chapter 2 of this study. Molotov followed up this statement with a draft which spoke of digressions from the Curzon Line in some regions "of 5 to 8 kilometers in favor of Poland." Churchill argued against extending the Polish border too far into German territory ("It would be a pity to stuff the Polish goose so full of German food that it got indigestion"). Roosevelt now circulated a written statement that the American government would not object if the Polish eastern frontier were set at the Curzon Line with small changes in Poland's favor as suggested by Molotov, but with regard to the western frontier he saw little justification for extending it up to the Western Neisse River.

The eastern border of Poland was thus settled. At the end of the Conference, since the western border was still not agreed, it was decided that the communique would record agreement among the three heads of government on the Curzon Line with digressions of 5 to 8 kilometers in favor of Poland, while stating that delimitation of the western frontier of Poland would be the subject of discussion with a new Polish government and "should thereafter await the Peace Conference." (As it turned out, the Russians turned over to Poland all the territory up to the Western Neisse, and the Poles soon set about expelling the entire German population, i.e., about three million more than Roosevelt and Churchill had been willing to see expelled. In the east, the frontier remained as already agreed in July 1944 between Russia and its chosen Polish instrument, the Lublin Committee.)

With regard to the future Polish government, both Roosevelt and Churchill recognized that some kind of fusion between the London and Lublin groups would have to take place. The question, although it was never clearly stated, was who would be in the majority. The three leaders agreed on the necessity for early elections, so that their discussion concerned—or seemed to concern—only the composition of a new provisional government (a "Provisional Government of National Unity") that would operate until the time when elections could be held, which according to Stalin might be "in about one month." Churchill put forward the names of three candidates for inclusion in the new Provisional Government—Mikolajczyk, Grabski, and Romer—but Stalin declared that it would be unthinkable for the Big Three themselves to put together a new Polish government. After all, there existed a Provisional Government (the "Lublin" government) in Warsaw, and the point of departure for any solution would have to be a consultation with the leaders of that pro-Soviet group. As it turned out, however, Stalin was unable to reach the leaders of the Lublin group by telephone; so it was agreed that the necessary consultations with the various Polish leaders would take place not in Yalta, but later in Moscow. The discussion thus turned to the terms of reference under which those consultations were to be held.

The matter of wording now becomes important, for the charges and countercharges of bad faith in implementing the Yalta decision regarding Poland turn on the precise phrasing of the agreement and the manner in which it was arrived at. The British proposal of February 8 read: "Having regard to the recent liberation of western Poland by the Soviet armies it was deemed desirable to facilitate *the establishment of a fully representative provisional Polish Government* based upon all the democratic and anti-Fascist forces in Poland and including democratic leaders from the Poles abroad. That Government should be so constituted as to command recognition by the three Allied Governments." (The italics are supplied here to emphasize the most important differences between the principal drafts.) The British draft went on to state that the provisional government should then "as soon as possible hold free and unfettered elections on the basis of universal suffrage and secret ballot, in which all democratic parties should have the right to participate and to promote candidatures, in order to ensure the establishment of a Government truly representative of the will of the Polish people."[8]

The Russians did not like the British draft. Molotov stated that the discussions should deal *not with creation of an entirely new government but with enlargement of the existing Provisional Government* through the addition of other democratic elements from within Poland and abroad. He claimed that the Lublin, or Warsaw, government enjoyed great prestige and popularity and said the Poles would never agree to any solution which would greatly change that Provisional Government. He said, "if we wish to achieve a practical result it should be done on the basis of the enlargement of the present government, but how many and who they should be is the subject we should talk about." He gave an indication of the Russian thinking by suggesting that in the first instance, three members of the Provisional Government and two Poles suggested by President Roosevelt should be invited to consult with a three-power commission to be established in Moscow. He argued that after all the whole matter concerned only an interim government pending the holding of free elections. Churchill immediately argued against this position and in favor of creating a completely new government. An impasse had been reached.[9]

Next day the American delegation came forward with what it thought was a compromise between the Russian and British positions. The relevant passage of the American draft read: "That *the present Polish Provisional Government be reorganized* into a fully representative government based on all democratic forces in Poland and including democratic leaders from Poland abroad, to be termed 'The Provisional Government of National Unity'." The U. S. draft had wording similar to the British draft with respect to the holding of free elections, and ended: "When a 'Provisional Government of National Unity' is satisfactorily formed, the three Governments will then proceed to accord it recognition. The Ambassadors of the three powers in Warsaw following such recognition would be charged with the responsibility of observing and reporting to their respective Governments on the carrying out of the pledge in regard to free and unfettered elections."[10]

The British did not like the American draft. As Eden stated in the Foreign Ministers' meeting on February 9, according to the Page minutes: "As regards the Lublin Provisional Government, it was possible that he might be quite wrong but he thought it was a fact that hardly anyone in Great Britain believed that the Lublin Government was representative of Poland. He should have thought that that view was widely held in the rest of Europe and in the United States of America. It was for that reason that the document which he had put forward the previous day *had avoided all mention of adding to the Lublin Government and had stressed that a new start was nec-*

essary."[11] This statement focused with almost embarrassing clarity on the magnitude of the apparent concession contained in the American draft—although both the British and American governments would later strenuously deny that such a concession had been made.

The Russian proposal made by Molotov at the plenary meeting on February 9 involved only some editing of the first sentence of the American draft, which he wanted reworded as follows: "The present Provisional Government of Poland shall be reorganized on a wider democratic basis with the inclusion of democratic leaders from Poland itself and from those living abroad, and in this connection this government would be called the National Provisional Government of Poland." The Soviet foreign minister also said, however, that the last sentence dealing with the responsibilities of the ambassadors of the three governments in Warsaw to observe and report on the carrying out of the free elections should be eliminated since he "felt certain that it would be offensive to the Poles and would needlessly complicate the discussion."[12]

According to the Bohlen minutes of that meeting, President Roosevelt remarked that after studying Molotov's amendment to the first sentence he thought

we were now very near agreement and it was only a matter of drafting. He said that for those governments which still recognized the London Government the use of the words "Provisional Government" (to describe the Lublin group) was somewhat difficult, and he felt that the first words of Mr. Molotov's amendment might read "The Government now operating in Poland." He said he felt it was very important for him in the U. S. that there be some gesture made for the six million Poles there indicating that the U. S. was in some way involved with the question of freedom of elections, and he therefore felt that the last sentence concerning the reports of the Ambassadors was important. He repeated that he felt, however, that it was only a matter of words and details and the three Foreign Ministers might meet tonight and discuss it.[13]

Churchill bore in more heavily on the question of free elections, for which some kind of international observation was a precondition. He referred to the absence of diplomatic reporting from inside Poland and to disquieting reports about the intention of the Lublin government to try as traitors all members of the Polish Home Army. Archly, he observed that "in Egypt whatever government conducts the elections, wins." He recognized the force of Stalin's argument that as long as the Red Army's lines stretched across Poland, the Russians had legitimate security concerns.[14] Both Churchill and Roosevelt argued that they were concerned not only with principle but also with practical politics.[15] Finally, however, Secretary of State Stettinius on Roosevelt's instruction agreed to drop the clause about the ambassadors "observing and reporting" to which Molotov had objected, although Eden wished it to be understood that he did not agree with the American proposal to drop that clause.[16]

In the end, the Declaration on Poland agreed at the Conference was as indicated on page ix of this study, with a middle paragraph about the mechanics of implementation to the effect that "Mr. Molotov, Mr. Harriman and Sir A. Clark Kerr are authorised as a Commission to consult in the first instance in Moscow with members of the present Provisional Government and with other Polish democratic leaders from within Poland and from abroad, with a view to the reorganisation of the present Government along the above lines." (It will be noted that the Declaration thus speaks not once, but twice, of *"reorganizing* the *present* government.") With respect to the right of ambassadors to observe the carrying out of the agreement, there only remained the innocuous sentence: "When a Polish Provisional Government of National Unity has been properly formed in conformity with the above, the Government of the USSR, which now maintains diplomatic relations with the present Provisional Government of Poland, and the Government of the United Kingdom and the Government of the USA will establish diplomatic relations with the new Polish Provisional Government of National Unity, and will exchange Ambassadors by whose reports the respective Governments will be kept informed about the situation in Poland." As Churchill dryly remarked after reporting his last conversation on the subject with Stalin, "This was the best I could get."[17]

A factor which helped to sweeten the Polish pill for Roosevelt and Churchill was Stalin's acceptance of a Declaration on Liberated Europe. That document had been drawn up in the State Department and was introduced rather late in the Conference. The debate on it was perfunctory, and it was agreed after Molotov watered down the operative clause.[18] (The key passages will be found on page viii above.) In the mind of its drafters, the Declaration was intended to establish the principle of joint tripartite responsibility in eastern Europe, and it was to counteract the idea of spheres of influence, which, as we shall see, had been pursued by both Churchill and Stalin (cf. Chapter 5). Every unilateral act by the Russians in eastern Europe could henceforth be branded as a violation of the Declaration on Liberated Europe. It is worth noting, however, that the operative clause of the Declaration required the Russians only to "consult," and even this could apparently take place only when all three of the Allies judged it necessary.

The Yalta decisions were hailed in Britain and the United States as heartening evidence of Allied harmony not only in bringing the war to a successful conclusion but also in building a better world. There were some misgivings about Poland, but major criticisms of Yalta occurred only later, when it became known that there had been secret agreements with respect to China and to the effect that Russia should have three seats in the United Nations. In the House of Commons, Churchill defended the agreement on Poland as the best that could be obtained, and it was in this spirit that it was approved.[19] Meanwhile, Nazi propaganda claimed that Yalta represented a sellout to Stalin, that it confirmed Russian overlordship in east and southeast Europe and the major part of Germany, and that an "iron curtain" would descend on the middle of Europe if Germany were to lay down its arms.[20]

The scene now shifted to Moscow, where, under the Declaration on Poland, Molotov and the American and British ambassadors were to consult with members of the existing Provisional Government and with other Polish democratic leaders from within Poland and abroad, "with a view to the reorganization of the present Government" on a broader democratic basis. And of course they immediately disagreed on the interpretation of the Yalta agreement. Molotov insisted that only Polish leaders who supported the Yalta decisions should be consulted about reorganizing the Provisional Government. This excluded even Mikolajczyk, who had publicly protested against the decision on Poland's eastern boundary, and in effect limited the field to Communists and their sympathizers. Moreover, the Russians made it clear that any reorganization of the pro-Communist government in Warsaw would in their view consist of merely adding a small minority of non-Communist Poles. It was obvious that if this were done, the chances of non-Communist leaders to rally their followers in preparation for an election would be very slim indeed. A further downgrading of the recent Allied agreements seemed to be implied when the Russians announced that Foreign Minister Molotov would not attend the San Francisco Conference where the United Nations was to be born.

In the dispute over the implementation of the Yalta agreements there now supervened an ugly episode when Stalin believed, or professed to believe, that the Western Allies were double-crossing him by negotiating a separate armistice with the Germans in Italy. Local German commanders there had put out feelers for an armistice, and this was immediately reported by the West to their Russian ally. While preliminary contacts were taking place at Berne, the Russian government complained that "negotiations" were taking place without Russian representation. When it was explained to Molotov that there were no negotiations and that, were they to take place, the Russians would be fully associated with them, the Foreign Minister refused to accept this and stated that "in this instance the Soviet Government sees not a misunderstanding, but something worse."[21]

President Roosevelt in a personal message to Stalin explained that no negotiations had taken place in Switzerland, but Stalin replied complaining that "the Germans have already taken advantage of the talks with the Allied Command to move three divisions from Northern Italy to the Soviet front" and he insisted that Roosevelt was wrong and that negotiations were actually taking place with the Germans in Berne.[22] Roosevelt categorically denied this, but Stalin came back claiming he had better information. (There was a parallel correspondence with Churchill.) "I realize," Stalin wrote, "that there are certain advantages resulting to the Anglo-American troops from the separate negotiations in Berne or in some other place, seeing that the Anglo-American troops are enabled to advance into the

87

heart of Germany almost without resistance; but why conceal this from the Russians. . . ?" Stalin suspected that the reason was that the Western Allies had "promised, in exchange, to ease the armistice terms for the Germans." He even claimed that an agreement along such lines was about to be concluded and might already be in effect.[23]

"I have received with astonishment your message of April 3" (containing the above allegations), Roosevelt replied immediately. He reviewed what had actually happened at Berne and added: "For the advantage of our common war effort against Germany, which today gives excellent promise of an early success in a disintegration of the German Armies, I must continue to assume that you have the same high confidence in my truthfulness and reliability that I have always had in yours." But Stalin would not back down. He still insisted that he was better informed than Roosevelt and argued: "It is hard to agree that the absence of German resistance on the Western Front is due solely to the fact that they have been beaten. The Germans . . . are fighting desperately against the Russians for Zemlenice, an obscure station in Czechoslovakia, which they need just as much as a dead man needs a poultice, but they surrender without any resistance such important towns in the heart of Germany as Osnabrueck, Mannheim and Kassel. You will admit that this behavior on the part of the Germans is more than strange and unaccountable."[24] The episode came to an end because the Germans in Italy never produced actual negotiators. But it marked a low point in the dealings between Stalin on the one hand and Roosevelt and Churchill on the other, in which there were accusations of treachery and expressions of bitter resentment at the very time when victory over Germany was being achieved.

It was in this atomosphere that Roosevelt and Stalin exchanged personal messages about Russia's failure to live up to the Yalta agreement on Poland. Roosevelt's message, sent less than two weeks before his death, also pleaded that the United Nations be not depreciated by having Russia represented by someone other than Molotov. The message ended:

> I wish I could convey to you how important it is for the successful development of our program of international collaboration that this Polish question be settled fairly and speedily. If this is not done all of the difficulties and dangers to Allied unity which we had so much in mind in reaching our decisions at the Crimea will face us in an even more acute form. You are, I am sure, aware that genuine popular support in the U. S. is required to carry out any government policy, foreign or domestic. The American people make up their own mind and no government action can change it. I mention this fact because the last sentence of your message about Mr. Molotov's attendance at San Francisco made me wonder whether you give full weight to this factor.[25]

As to the substance of the disagreement on Poland, Roosevelt addressed himself in two key paragraphs to the question of whether the new Provisional Government was to represent a completely fresh start, and to the question how its members were to be picked. On the first subject, he wrote:

> In the discussions that have taken place so far your Government appears to take the position that the new Polish Provisional Government of National Unity which we agreed should be formed should be little more than a continuation of the present Warsaw Government. I cannot reconcile this either with our agreement or our discussions. While it is true that the Lublin Government is to be reorganized and its members play a prominent role, it is to be done in such a fashion as to bring into being a new government. This point is clearly brought out in several

places in the text of the Agreement. I must make it quite plain to you that any such solution which would result in a thinly disguised continuance of the present Warsaw regime would be unacceptable and would cause the people of the U. S. to regard the Yalta agreements as having failed.

On the matter of picking members for the new government, Roosevelt wrote:

> It is equally apparent that for the same reason the Warsaw Government cannot under the Agreement claim the right to select or reject what Poles are to be brought to Moscow by the Commission for consultation. Can we not agree that it is up to the Commission to select the Polish leaders to come to Moscow to consult in the first instance and invitations be sent out accordingly. . . . We have not and would not bar or veto any candidate for consultation which Mr. Molotov might propose, being confident that he would not suggest any Poles who would be inimical to the intent of the Crimea decision. I feel it is not too much to ask that my Ambassador be accorded the same confidence and that any candidate for consultation presented by any one of the Commission be accepted by the others in good faith. It is obvious to me that if the right of the Commission to select these Poles is limited or shared with the Warsaw Government the very foundation on which our agreement rests would be destroyed.[26]

Roosevelt sent this message at the urging of Churchill, who sent a stronger parallel message to Stalin.[27] There is evidence, not all of it published as yet, that the American President at least at one time had doubts about this controversy over Poland and that he perhaps realized that the principal point had already been given away at Yalta. In a message to Churchill which perhaps predated this exchange with Stalin, he warned that "If we attempt to evade the fact that we placed, as clearly shown by the [Yalta] agreement, somewhat more emphasis on the Lublin Poles than on the other two groups from which the new Government is to be drawn, we expose ourselves to the charge that we are attempting to go back on the Crimea decision."[28] However, Roosevelt did feel that the Western Allies had every right to resist the Lublin group's claim to a veto over what Poles were to be consulted. (As we shall see, President Truman was not sensitive to this differentiated emphasis as between the two contentious questions about the Yalta agreement on Poland.)

Stalin's reply, five days before Roosevelt's death, did nothing to narrow the difference. He claimed that the reason for the impasse over Poland was "that the U. S. and British Ambassadors in Moscow . . . have departed from the instructions of the Crimea Conference." With regard to the nature of the government that was to be formed, he wrote:

> At the Crimea Conference the three of us regarded the Polish Provisional Government as the government now functioning in Poland and subject to reconstruction, as the government that should be the core of the new Government of National Unity. The U. S. and British Ambassadors, however . . . ignore the Polish Provisional Government . . . and at best place individuals in Poland and London on a par with the Provisional Government. Furthermore, they hold that reconstruction of the Provisional Government should be understood in terms of its abolition and the establishment of an entirely new government. . . . Obviously, this thesis cannot but be strongly resented by the Polish Provisional Government. As regards the Soviet Union, it certainly cannot accept a thesis that is tantamount to direct violation of the Crimea Conference decisions.

On the matter of invitations to Poles to appear before the Commission for consultations on the formation of a new government, Stalin took the position that they must be issued not by individual members of the Commission but "by the Commission as a whole, as a body"—in other words, that Russia should have a veto. He went on to say:

> The Soviet Government proceeds from the assumption that, by virtue of the Crimea decisions, those invited for consultation should be in the first instance Polish leaders who recognize the decisions of the Crimea Conference, including the one of the Curzon Line, and, secondly, who actually want friendly relations between Poland and the Soviet Union. The Soviet Government insists on this because the blood of Soviet soldiers, so freely shed in liberating Poland, and the fact that in the past thirty years the territory of Poland has twice been used by an enemy for invading Russia, oblige the Soviet Government to ensure friendly relations between the Soviet Union and Poland.[29]

As an indication of the proportions between cabinet members of the existing Warsaw government and outsiders which Stalin considered appropriate, he suggested using Yugoslavia as a model. There Tito had nominated twenty-one cabinet members and Subasic, the exile leader, had nominated only six. This message of Stalin, his last to Roosevelt, was dated April 7.

Let us pause here to throw a glance at the newspaper headlines of that first week of April 1945: On April 1, the U. S. Tenth Army landed in Okinawa. . . . On April 2, it was announced that the Allied 21st Army Group had pushed to 100 miles north and northeast of the Rhine. . . . On April 3, General Eisenhower made it known that the German Army Group B and part of Army Group H were cut off by Allied encirclement of the Ruhr. . . . On April 4, the French First Army entered Karlsruhe, while the Russians captured Bratislava. . . . On April 5, Molotov informed the Japanese ambassador that the Soviet government desired to denounce the Russian-Japanese Neutrality Act. . . . On April 6, the U. S. fleet off Okinawa was attacked by a strong force of Japanese suicide aircraft. On the same day, the Polish government in London issued a statement reporting that fifteen members of its erstwhile underground, including the deputy prime minister and the last commander of the Polish Home Army, had been invited to meetings with Soviet General Ivanov on March 27 and 28, for which safe conduct was guaranteed, but since those dates no news of any of those Poles had been received. . . . Also on April 6, Secretary Stettinius declared that the United States was doing everything in its power to promote the establishment of a representative Polish government as promised at the Crimea Conference, in time to be represented at the San Francisco Conference. . . . On April 7, the Russians announced that they had reached Vienna.

When President Truman was briefed by the State Department on April 13, the day after Roosevelt's death, the rundown of important pending foreign policy problems included these summary passages: "Since the Yalta Conference the Soviet Government has taken a firm and uncompromising position on nearly every major question that has arisen in our relations. The more important of these are the Polish question, the application of the Crimea agreement on liberated areas, the agreement on the exchange of liberated prisoners of war and civilians, and the San Francisco Conference." Under the heading of Poland, the briefing paper said:

> The present situation relating to Poland is highly unsatisfactory with the Soviet authorities consistently sabotaging Ambassador Harriman's efforts in the Moscow Commission to hasten the implementation of the decisions at the Crimea Conference. Direct appeals to Marshal Stalin have not yet produced any worth-while results. The Soviet Government likewise seeks to complicate the problem by initiating and supporting claims of the Warsaw Provisional Polish Gov-

ernment to represent and speak for Poland in international matters such as the San Francisco Conference. . . . Because of its effects on our relations with the Soviet Union and other United Nations and upon public opinion in this country, the question of the future status of Poland and its government remains one of our most complex and urgent problems both in the international and the domestic field.[30]

One positive development in this bleak picture occurred when Ambassador Harriman conferred with Stalin immediately after the news of Roosevelt's death had been conveyed to him. Stalin voiced his deep sorrow and expressed a willingness to work with the new President as he had with Roosevelt. Harriman, seizing this opening, suggested that the most effective method of assuring the United States and the world of the Soviet desire to continue collaboration would be for Molotov to go to the United States, first to see President Truman, and second to attend the conference at San Francisco. Stalin replied that if such a request came to him from the new President, he would comply with it. And so Molotov came to Washington—but his visit there worsened rather than improved the situation.

Before Molotov arrived in Washington, the situation had become still more tense because of two developments: on April 21, despite protests by the British and U. S. governments, Russia had signed a treaty of mutual assistance with the Polish Provisional Government, thereby lending emphasis to its position that that government was to be merely "reorganized" with the addition of a few outsiders but without any possible change of its basic pro-Soviet policies. On the other hand, Churchill and Truman had sent another message to Stalin in which they had rejected the Russian position and suggested, as a "constructive suggestion," that there be invited to the consultations in Moscow three members of the Warsaw Provisional Government; three members of the London government; and two non-Communist figures from inside Poland—thus making a clear non-Communist majority. The two Western leaders had said that the Warsaw government would unquestionably play a "prominent" part in the "new" provisional government, but they could not admit that it should dominate that government. "The real issue between us," they had said, "is whether or not the Warsaw Government has the right to veto individual candidates for consultation. No such interpretation in our considered opinion can be found in the Crimea decision. . . ." Churchill and Truman had also firmly rejected the applicability of the Yugoslav pattern to Poland.[31]

The dispute became still hotter when President Truman received Molotov at the White House. Upon being briefed on the continued deadlock on the foreign minister level (Stettinius, Eden, and Molotov had met in Washington and got nowhere in their discussion), the new President decided, as he reports in his memoirs, that "it was now obvious that our agreements with the Soviet Union had so far been a one-way street and that this could not continue." He took counsel with Stettinius, Secretary of War Stimson, Navy Secretary Forrestal, Admiral King, General Marshall, Ambassador Harriman, and other advisers. The record of that consultation is exceedingly revealing of the differing viewpoints on what should or could be done.[32] Truman sided with those who counseled toughness, and in very blunt terms he told Molotov that the United States considered that Russia had gone back on the agreement reached at Yalta. He hinted broadly that Russia could give up any hope for American postwar assistance if it did not satisfy American public opinion. And he handed Molotov a note ("For Information of Marshal Stalin") which contained the key phrase: "The U. S. Government cannot be a party to any method of consultation with

95

see note — Stimson was right, Forrestal, Truman wrong — obstinacy worthless in situation where our power limited

Polish leaders which would not result in the establishment of a new Provisional Government of National Unity genuinely representative of the democratic elements of the Polish people."[33]

Molotov remonstrated. He said that in the past the Big Three governments had been able to work out their differences, but now it appeared that two of them were attempting to impose their will on the third. Truman interrupted to say that all the United States was asking was that the Soviet government carry out the Crimea decision on Poland. Molotov said Russia stood by the Crimea decision. "I replied sharply," Truman recalls, "that an agreement had been reached on Poland and that there was only one thing to do and that was for Marshal Stalin to carry out that agreement in accordance with his word." Molotov said Stalin had given his views in the message of April 7, and he could not understand why, if the three governments could reach an agreement on the question of the composition of the Yugoslav government, the same formula could not apply in the case of Poland. "Replying sharply again," Truman recalls, "I said that an agreement had been reached on Poland and that it only required to be carried out by the Soviet Government."

Molotov repeated that his government supported the Crimea decisions but that he could not agree that an "abrogation" of those decisions by others could be considered a violation by the Soviet government. He added that surely the Polish question, involving as it did a neighboring country, was of very great interest to the Soviet Union. "Since Molotov insisted on avoiding the main issue," Truman recalls, "I said what I had said before—that the U. S. Government was prepared to carry out loyally all the agreements reached at Yalta and asked only that the Soviet Government do the same. I expressed once more the desire of the U. S. for friendship with Russia, but I wanted it clearly understood that this could be only on a basis of the

96

mutual observation of agreements and not on the basis of a one-way street. 'I have never been talked to like that in my life,' Molotov said. I told him, 'Carry out your agreements and you won't get talked to like that'."[34] And thus ended a singularly sterile interview.

The President's memorandum was handed to Molotov on April 23. On April 24 Stalin sent his reply to both the memorandum and the Churchill-Truman message. The reply said, among other things:

> [Your] messages indicate that you still regard the Polish Provisional Government, not as the core of a future Polish Government of National Unity, but merely as a group on a par with any other group of Poles. It would be hard to reconcile this concept of the position of the Provisional Government and this attitude towards it with the Crimea decision on Poland. At the Crimea Conference the three of us, including President Roosevelt, based ourselves on the assumption that the Polish Provisional Government, as the Government now functioning in Poland and enjoying the trust and support of the majority of the Polish people, should be the core, that is, the main part of a new, reconstructed Polish Government of National Unity. . . .
>
> Another circumstance that should be borne in mind [Stalin added] is that Poland borders on the Soviet Union, which cannot be said about Great Britain or the U. S. A. Poland is to the security of the Soviet Union what Belgium and Greece are to the security of Great Britain. . . . I do not know whether a genuinely representative Government has been established in Greece, or whether the Belgium Government is a genuinely democratic one. The Soviet Union was not consulted when those Governments were being formed, nor did it claim the right to interfere in those matters, because it realizes how important Belgium and Greece are to the security of Great Britain. . . . I cannot understand why in discussing Poland no attempt is made to consider the interests of the Soviet Union in terms of security as

97

well. One cannot but recognize as unusual a situation in which two Governments—those of the U. S. and Great Britain—reach agreement beforehand on Poland, a country in which the USSR is interested first of all and most of all, and place its representatives in an intolerable position, trying to dictate to it. I say that this situation cannot contribute to agreed settlement of the Polish problem. I am ready to accede to your request and to do all in my power to reach an agreed settlement. But you are asking too much. To put it plainly, you want me to renounce the interests of the security of the Soviet Union; but I cannot proceed against the interests of my country.[35]

The next scene of the drama was played at San Francisco, but it differed from the previous scenes in that it was played before the world public. Up to this point, all the correspondence between the heads of state had of course been secret and most of the other events since Yalta had found only muted and muffled reflection in the public press and had in any event been vastly overshadowed by the spectacular news about the final battles of the war. (On the day the San Francisco Conference opened, April 25, Russian and American troops, having fought their way through Germany from East and West, met on the Elbe River.) At the conference, the Polish issue almost immediately precipitated a violent public quarrel as Molotov demanded that the Provisional Government of Poland be invited to the Conference. Stettinius, seconded by Eden, took the position that until a "new and representative" Polish Provisional Government was created in conformity with the Yalta decision, an invitation to—and thus recognition of—the Lublin government "would be a sordid exhibition of bad faith."[36] Russia was overwhelmingly voted down. Next the admission of Argentina came up, and again Russia was overwhelmingly voted down, although Molotov on his part now cited a Yalta conference decision.[37]

Mostly Poland: Yalta and the Aftermath

At San Francisco, Stettinius, Eden, and Molotov also continued their negotiations on the formation of a new Polish government, but their deadlock continued. Meanwhile, Churchill had sent yet another message to Stalin, the longest he ever wrote to the Russian leader during their wartime correspondence. Churchill insisted that in the new government there should be "a proper balance and a proper distribution of important posts in the government; this result should be reached as we agreed at the Crimea by discussing the matter, with true representatives of all the different Polish elements which are not fundamentally anti-Russian." The British leader closed his message with these prophetic words:

> "There is not much comfort in looking into a future where you and the countries you dominate, plus the Communist parties in many other States, are all drawn up on one side, and those who rally to the English-speaking nations and their Associates or Dominions are on the other. It is quite obvious that their quarrel would tear the world to pieces and that all of us leading men on either side who had anything to do with that would be shamed before history. . . . I hope there is no word or phrase in this outpouring of my heart to you which unwittingly gives offence. If so, let me know. But do not, I beg of you, my friend Stalin, underrate the divergencies which are opening about matters which you may think are small to us but which are symbolic of the way the English-speaking democracies look at life.[38]

On May 3 Molotov revealed at San Francisco that Soviet authorities had indeed arrested sixteen leaders of the Polish underground and that they were charging them with preparing and carrying out subversive activities against the Red Army. Eden and Stettinius thereupon decided to break off the negotiation. On May 5 Stalin sent his reply to Churchill, of which excerpts will be given further below. On May 8 the war in

99

Europe officially ended with the German capitulation at Reims. (The Russians held off their victory announcement until May 9, when the ceremony had to be repeated in Berlin.) On the same day, President Truman signed the order terminating Lend-Lease (see Chapter 6). On May 9 Molotov left San Francisco for Moscow, leaving behind a deadlock not only on the Polish question but also on the question, vital to the very existence of the United Nations, whether a dispute involving one of the Great Powers could be discussed in the Security Council without its consent.[39]

As we are now approaching the end of this chapter, having brought the story almost to the time of the Hopkins-Stalin conversations, it may be helpful to summarize the situation of the two sides with respect to Poland. The issue was basically whether the Communists and their allies, or the essentially anti-Soviet conservatives in Poland, would have a majority in the new government. Historians may argue inconclusively whether the Western leaders had in effect yielded the substance of this point to the Soviets in Yalta—but it is a fact that Churchill and Truman did not think so. They pressed, as had Roosevelt, for a new Polish government genuinely responsive to the will of the people. To Stalin it was obvious that any such government would be hostile to Russia—and from what we have seen in Chapter 3, the majority of patriotic Poles had indeed good reason to be hostile. The Russian dictator came very close to admitting this in his reply to Churchill dated May 4.

> The United Nations are interested in constant and durable friendship between the USSR and Poland [he wrote]. Hence we cannot acquiesce in the attempts that are being made to involve in the forming of the future Polish Government people who, to quote you, "are not fundamentally

100

anti-Russian" or to bar from participation only those who, to quote you, are "extreme people unfriendly to Russia." Neither one nor the other can satisfy us. We insist, and shall continue to insist, that only people who have demonstrated by deeds their friendly attitude to the Soviet Union, who are willing honestly and sincerely to cooperate with the Soviet state, should be consulted on the formation of a future Polish Government.[40]

Clearly, if such qualification were to be accepted, there would be no democracy in Poland as the West understood it. And, as it turned out, that is what happened. *of course not — but here is the point*

The Hopkins mission to Moscow (Chapter 2) resulted in a compromise under which there were to be invited to "consult" on the formation of a new Polish government: four leaders of the Lublin group; three Poles from London (but not from the government-in-exile); and five from Poland. However, one of the three Poles from London was a Lublin Pole, and "three or four" of the five invited from Poland were sympathetic to the Lublin group.[41] When the consultation finally did take place, seven of the twelve Poles invited to Moscow were Communists or pro-Communists, and when the new Provisional Polish Government of National Unity was formed, fourteen of its twenty-one cabinet seats, including the ministries most valuable for the internal control of the country, went to veterans of the Lublin Committee. With the Polish issue settled, Stalin immediately withdrew his objection to the voting formula in the United Nations, Allied administrative arrangements in Germany were regularized, agreement on Allied administration of Austria was reached in the European Advisory Commission (where it had been hung up for months), and the ground was prepared for the Potsdam Conference. Stalin even expressed gratitude for Lend-Lease.[42] But the dispute over Russian control of Poland was not over. Indeed, as we shall see in the next chapter, it broadened into a dispute over Russian control over most of eastern and southeastern Europe.

By the time of the Potsdam Conference in July 1945, the United States and Great Britain had recognized the new Communist-dominated Polish government, though stressing its obligation to "hold free and unfettered elections as soon as possible" in accordance with the Yalta decision (cf. page ix). Both Churchill and Truman pressed Stalin for public assurances that the Polish elections should also be freely observed by the world press, and Truman emphasized the importance of this issue as a factor in American domestic politics. "There are six million Poles in the United States," he said. "A free election in Poland reported to the United States by a free press would make it much easier to deal with these Polish people."[43] Stalin, after some argument, agreed to include in the Potsdam communiqué some words about the observation of free elections.[44] But although the Soviet premier had told Roosevelt at Yalta that elections could take place in Poland one month after the country's liberation,[45] it was actually only two years later, in January 1947, that elections were held—after the non-Communist parties in Poland had been thoroughly terrorized, their news censored, their meetings often banned, and some of their leaders jailed.[46]

i.f.
what we
did in
S Korea

NOTES

1. Chester Wilmot, *The Struggle for Europe* (London: Collins, 1952), p. 631.

2. Ibid., p. 578.

3. Ibid., p. 626. Hitler suggested that, if only the Russians would proclaim a National Government for Germany, the English would "really start to be scared." Then he went on, "I have given orders that a report be played into their hands to the effect that the Russians are organizing 200,000 of our men led by German officers and completely infected with Communism, who will come marching into Germany. . . . That will make them feel as if someone had stuck a needle into them." (*Fuehrer Conferences,* Fragment 24, January 27, 1945, quoted by Wilmot.)

4. Herbert Feis, *Churchill, Roosevelt, Stalin—The War They Waged and the Peace They Sought* (Princeton, N.J.: Princeton University Press, 1957), pp. 498-99; *Yalta Papers* (See chap. 1, note 1), pp. 597 and 646.

5. Argentina declared war on Germany only on March 27, 1945, after the Inter-American Conference at Chapultepec, Mexico City, had called upon it to do so. According to James F. Byrnes, *Speaking Frankly* (New York: Harper, 1947), p. 39, Roosevelt and Stalin agreed at Yalta that with respect to Argentina and Turkey, not only the date of the declaration of war but also their status as associated nations who had helped in the war effort should govern the invitation. In any event, the Argentine declaration of war was after the agreed cut-off date of March 1. (Cf. also *Yalta Papers,* p. 773.) At Chapultepec, however, Stettinius yielded to Latin American pressure and agreed to support Argentina's entry provided it fulfilled certain conditions. It was a moot point, up to the time of the San Francisco Conference, whether all those conditions had been fulfilled. President Truman, who was consulted just before the Conference, was strongly opposed to Argentine adherence to the United Nations Declaration. Later, however, the matter became embroiled with Russia's demand that Poland be invited to the Conference, and in the end Stettinius was given a free hand. Ruth B. Russell, *A History of the United Nations Charter* (Washington: Brookings Institution, 1958), pp. 632, 636-37.

Cordell Hull has said about this episode: "To Secretary Stettinius over the telephone I spoke as strongly as I could against admitting Argentina to the San Francisco Conference. I said that the American delegation had to regain the leadership in the Argentine question that the United States had lost at the Mexico City Conference. . . . I would have voted against the admission of Argentina to the United Nations had I been called upon to vote. I was suddenly informed, however, that our delegation had already voted unanimously to admit her. I also said to Stettinius that if the American delegation were not careful we should get Russia into such a state of mind that she might decide that the United Nations organization was not going to furnish adequate security to her in the future." Hull, although a member of the U.S. delegation, was at the time in a hospital in Washington. *The Memoirs of Cordell Hull* (New York: Macmillan, 1948), II, 1722.

6. Feis, p. 521.

7. *Yalta Papers*, p. 677.

8. Ibid., p. 870.

9. Ibid., pp. 776-78.

10. Ibid., p. 804.

11. Ibid.

12. Ibid., pp. 842-43.

13. Ibid., p. 846.

14. Ibid., pp. 852-53.

15. Churchill (Matthews minutes): "In Parliament I must be able to say that the elections will be held in a fair way. I do not care much about Poles myself." (Ibid., p. 853.) Roosevelt: "I don't want the Poles to be able to question the Polish elections. The matter is not only one of principle but of practical politics." (Ibid., p. 854.)

16. Ibid., p. 872.

17. Churchill, *Triumph and Tragedy* (see chap. 3, note 5), p. 385.

18. The original American proposal (*Yalta Papers*, p. 863) included the phrasing "When, in the opinion of the three governments, conditions in any European liberated state or any former Axis satellite state in Europe make such action necessary, they will immediately *establish appropriate machinery for the carrying out* of the joint responsibilities set forth in this declaration." Molotov objected to this in the Foreign Ministers' meeting of February 10 and proposed that the paragraph, instead of speaking of establishing appropriate machinery, should end "will immediately *take measures for the carrying out of mutual consultation.*" (*Yalta Papers*, p. 873.) This is approximately the language reflected in the final document. In any case, the

words "when, in the opinion of *the three governments*" made it clear that unanimity would be required for this clause to become operative.

Herbert Feis (p. 550) comments on the Declaration for Liberated Europe: "It is hard to judge whether either Soviet or British governments shared the sense of the American formulators that its principles might govern events. Its loose net of phrases allowed easy passage to any determined purpose. The struggle within these countries was not just another chapter in Anglo-Soviet rivalry for influence in Europe. It was part of a world contest between those who looked to Moscow for leadership and those attached to other social ideas and systems. As long as that contest went on, coalition arrangements composed of such mutually hostile elements could be only temporary; and unless it was suspended, the resort to free elections, as the solvent of internal political differences, was certain to be impeded. What would happen if the people of one of the countries on the Soviet frontiers elected a government actively opposed to the Soviet Union? What if one of the countries in the West elected a Communist government? Looked at another way, the question was whether the Anglo-Soviet attempt to limit the struggle by a division of spheres of influence should be discarded for excellent political principles which might, however, in the circumstances, have wayward results."

McNeill comments: "The Americans conceived this Declaration as a sort of antidote to the 'spheres of influence' deal which Churchill and Stalin had concluded in October 1944. Tripartite responsibility and action in all areas of Europe was to be the pattern for the difficult period after the end of hostilities, and special spheres in which one or another of the Allies would have preeminent influence were to be abandoned. Stalin clearly had no such thought in mind when he accepted the Declaration. Perhaps he felt it a harmless piece of rhetoric, soothing to the Americans. After all, three-power action, by the terms of the Declaration, would occur only when all three of the Allies judged it necessary, and any one Power could always find any proposed action unnecessary if its own policies seemed to be called in question. . . ." Royal Institute of International Affairs, *America, Britain, and Russia—Their Cooperation and Conflict, 1941-1946*, by William Hardy McNeill (London: Oxford University Press, 1953), p. 559.

19. Cf. Captain Thorneycroft's speech in the House of Commons

on February 28, 1945, quoted in Norman A. Graebner, *Cold War Diplomacy: American Foreign Policy, 1945-1960* (Princeton, N.J.: Van Nostrand, 1962), Document No. 2, pp. 141-42, from which the following passages: "I concede at once—and this may be embarrassing for the Government—that I do not regard the Polish settlement as an act of justice. It may be right or wrong, it may be wise or foolish, but at any rate it is not justice as I understand the term. It is not the sort of situation in which you get two parties to a dispute putting their case forward in front of a disinterested body and in which the strength and power of one of the parties is never allowed to weigh in the balance. The sooner we recognize that we are a long way from that sort of thing happening the better.

"The Government had two choices only. They could have postponed the issue. . . . They could have said, 'No, we want this submitted to arbitration. We cannot do anything without the consent of the London Polish Government'. No one knows what would happen in those circumstances, but one can safely say that it is unlikely that there would in any circumstance be a free, independent and democratic Poland. The Red Army is in occupation of that country and the Lublin Committee is in control. . . . The second course that they could adopt was to make the best settlement they could and impose it deliberately on the Poles. . . .

"We have encouraged the London Polish Government to negotiate, and have criticized them because they did not negotiate very well. We have told them they must make concessions, and then we have blamed them because they did not make concessions. I do not regard that as a sensible or an honourable course. I do not believe you can ask a Pole to decide to hand over a half of his country. I do not think it is a fair thing to ask any Pole to do. If they agreed to do that, they would divide Poland for a generation, perhaps for all time, into those who thought they were patriots and those who thought they were traitors. This is to perpetuate civil war. Nor could you ask the Poles as an act of policy to take a large slice of their powerful neighboring State. . . . That is a decision which must be taken by more powerful States. I do not believe that you save your honour in this matter by imposing on others the obligation of making a decision which you ought to make yourself."

106

20. Göbbels in *Das Reich* of February 24, 1945: "Should the German people lay down their arms, the agreement between Roosevelt, Churchill and Stalin would allow the Soviets to occupy all East and Southeast Europe, together with the major part of the Reich. An iron curtain would at once descend on this territory which, including the Soviet Union, would be of enormous dimensions. Behind this curtain would begin a mass slaughter of the people, probably with the acclamation from the London and New York Jewish press. . . . The remainder of Europe would be engulfed in chaotic political and social confusion which would only represent a preparatory stage for the coming bolshevization."—Churchill's "iron curtain" speech at Fulton, Missouri, which popularized the term, was given on March 5, 1946. But Churchill had used the term "iron curtain" much earlier, in his message to President Truman of May 12, 1945. There is no evidence that the British leader was aware of Göbbels' earlier use of the term "iron curtain" to describe the division of Europe that was being created in early 1945 by Russian policy and military power.

21. Churchill, *Triumph and Tragedy*, p. 442.

22. *Stalin Correspondence* (see chap. 3, note 19), II, 200.

23. Ibid., II, 206.

24. Ibid., II, 209. The matter was somewhat awkward for the Western Allies because they had notified the Russians prior to sending officers to Berne to contact the German emissary. When the Russians demanded that three Soviet officers be also present at the interview, the Western Allies declined and went ahead with the preliminary contacts on their own, though promising to cut the Russians in as soon as actual negotiations would take place. Two other awkward features in subsequent developments of the affair, which might have come to the attention of Russian agents in Switzerland, were these: the German SS General Wolff, who said he could arrange for the surrender of General Kesselring's forces in Italy, continued to deal with Kesselring even after that general had been transferred from Italy to take command of the German forces on the Western Front. (Allen W. Dulles, who conducted the contacts in Switzerland, has subsequently explained [*The Secret Surrender*, New York: Harper & Row, 1966, p. 124] that Wolff tried to get Kesselring to influence the new commander in Italy, Gen. Vietinghoff.) Further-

more, although Wolff never returned to the subsequent place of contact in Switzerland where Allied officers had awaited him, his go-between (an Italian industrialist, Baron Parilli) made precisely the kind of proposal that Stalin suspected—that the Germans in Italy would not surrender themselves but would be granted the right to withdraw from Italy after the cessation of hostilities. But contrary to what Stalin suspected, that idea was not for a moment entertained by the Western Allies. Neither, however, was it explicitly rejected. Parilli was just told that if the Germans would send someone with full authority to Allied Force Headquarters, the draft copy of the capitulation would be handed to him there. (Cf. *The Italian Campaign, 12 December 1944 to 2nd May 1945: A Report to the Combined Chiefs of Staff by the Supreme Allied Commander Mediterranean, Field Marshall the Viscount Alexander of Tunis*, London, H.M. Stationery Office, 1951.)

25. *Stalin Correspondence*, II, 204. The last sentence of Stalin's message to which Roosevelt referred had responded to Roosevelt's warning that Molotov's absence from San Francisco would be construed all over the world as a lack of comparable interest in the great objectives of that Conference on the part of the Soviet government. Stalin's reply to this had been: "As to the different interpretations, you will appreciate that they cannot determine the decisions to be taken." Ibid., II, 200.

26. Ibid., II, 202-203.

27. *Stalin Correspondence*, I, 309-10. Churchill interpreted the Yalta decision as calling for both a "new" and "reorganized" Polish government. Technically he could point to the fact that the Protocol used the word "new" twice in describing the government that was to be created. When it came to describing *how* it was to be created, however, the Protocol spoke of "reorganizing" the Provisional Government (i.e. the Lublin group) by the "inclusion" of other Poles. Cf. text, p. ix above.

28. Feis, p. 575. The complete text has not yet been published. Mr. Feis had access to official U. S. files in the preparation of his book.

29. *Stalin Correspondence*, II, 211-12. It is interesting to note that the Russian interpretation of this feature of the Yalta Agreement was shared by the bitterly anti-Soviet London Polish government, which considered that the Big Three had accepted domination of the new

Provisional Government by the Lublin group. Cf. Jan Ciechanowski, *Defeat in Victory* (Garden City, N.Y.: Doubleday, 1947), p. 363: "When I told him [Stettinius] that the wording of the Yalta Agreement did not clearly state that an entirely 'new government' was to be formed but implied that a compromise government, dominated by the Lublin communists, had been accepted, Stettinius kept on insisting that this was not the case and that it was clearly understood among the Big Three that there was to be 'an entirely new government and not a reconstructed Lublin government.'"

30. Harry S. Truman, *Memoirs* (Garden City, N.Y.: Doubleday, 1955), I, 15.

31. *Stalin Correspondence*, II, 215-17.

32. Truman *Memoirs*, I, 77-79. Secretary Stimson, Admiral Leahy, and General Marshall counseled against toughness. Secretary Forrestal, Ambassador Harriman and General Deane (who commanded the Military Mission to the Soviet Union) were in favor of laying it on the line. Some excerpts convey the flavor of their positions as recorded by President Truman:

"Mr. Stimson . . . said he would like to know how far the Russian reaction to a strong position on Poland would go. He said he thought that the Russians perhaps were being more realistic than we were in regard to their own security. . . . Admiral Leahy . . . observed that he had left Yalta with the impression that the Soviet government had no intention of permitting a free government to operate in Poland and that he would have been surprised had the Russians behaved differently. In his opinion, the Yalta agreement was susceptible to two interpretations. He added that he felt it was a serious matter to break with the Russians but that he believed we should tell them that we stood for a free and independent Poland. . . . General Marshall said from the military point of view the situation in Europe was secure but that we hoped for Soviet participation in the war against Japan at a time when it would be useful to us. . . . He was inclined to agree with Mr. Stimson that the possibility of a break with Russia was very serious.

"Secretary Forrestal expressed the view that this difficulty over Poland could not be treated as an isolated incident—that there had been many evidences of the Soviet desire to dominate adjacent countries and to disregard the wishes of her allies. It was his belief that for some time the Russians had been under the impression that we would not object if they took over all of Eastern Europe, and he said it was his profound conviction that if the Russians were to be rigid in their attitude we had better have a showdown with them now rather than later. . . . Ambassador Harriman . . . said he felt that when Stalin and Molotov had returned from Moscow after Yalta they had learned more of the situation in Poland and had realized how shaky the provisional government was. On that account they had come to realize that the introduction of any genuine Polish leader such as Mikolajczyk would probably mean the elimination of the Soviet hand-picked crop of leaders. It was his belief, therefore, that the real issue was whether we were to be a party to a program of Soviet domination of Poland. He said obviously we were faced with the possibility of a break with the Russians, but he felt that, properly handled, it might still be avoided. . . . General Deane . . . said he was convinced after his experience in Moscow that if we were afraid of the Russians we would get nowhere, and he felt that we should be firm when we were right."

33. *Stalin Correspondence*, II, 218-19.

34. Truman *Memoirs*, I, 82.

35. *Stalin Correspondence*, II, 219-20.

36. Russell, (see note 5, above), pp. 636-37. The text of the Stettinius statement had been drafted by Senator Arthur H. Vandenberg.

37. Cf. note 5 to this chapter.

38. Churchill, *Triumph and Tragedy*, pp. 494-97.

39. The issue relating to discussion of a dispute in the absence of unanimity among the great powers was subsequently settled during Harry Hopkins' visit to Stalin. During that conversation, on June 6, it appeared that Molotov might not have adequately informed Stalin of the interpretation of the Yalta Agreement on voting procedure which he had defended in San Francisco. Cf. Robert E. Sherwood, *Roosevelt and Hopkins* (New York: Harper, 1948), p. 911.

40. *Stalin Correspondence*, II, 226-27.

41. The record of the fifth conversation between Stalin and Hopkins, in which these arrangements were made, has not yet been

published. Although Mikolajczyk referred to "three or four" of the five Poles from Poland as having been required by Stalin to be "sympathetic to the old Lublin Committee" (Stanislaw Mikolajczyk, *The Rape of Poland—Pattern of Soviet Aggression* [New York: McGraw-Hill, 1948], p. 114), actually only two of them were labeled by him as pro-Communist. However, this was sufficient to give the pro-Communists and their allies a clear majority. Mikolajczyk himself was among the Poles invited from London, as he had meanwhile made a public statement accepting the Yalta decisions on Poland, and he even became a member of the new Polish government; but he was effectively prevented from rallying the forces opposed to the Communists.

42. "These results," wrote McNeill (p. 588), "flowed centrally from the settlement of the Polish issue, and, though Stalin had yielded to the extent of admitting Mikolajczyk and some other non-Communist Poles within the pale, the Western Powers yielded far more. It was perhaps not perfectly clear at the time, but it was proved by subsequent events that Communist domination of the Polish Provisional Government survived the 'reorganization' for which Hopkins' mission had prepared the way; yet it was to prevent such domination that Britain and America had argued so long. Having won a clear path to his appointed goal—a 'friendly' government in Poland—Stalin was willing and anxious to conciliate the West on other issues, and it was doubtless this desire which accounted for the casualness with which he settled the dispute over the veto power on the Security Council. If the West would allow him to dominate Eastern Europe and Manchuria Stalin was willing to cooperate; but he clearly put Soviet interests in these border regions ahead of all other considerations."

43. *Potsdam Papers,* (see chap. 2, note 1), II, 206.

44. Ibid., II, 1123.

45. *Yalta Papers,* p. 781.

46. Cf. Arthur Bliss Lane, *I Saw Poland Betrayed* (New York: Bobbs-Merrill, 1948), Chapter 19.

5

Spheres of Influence

Less than two weeks after the Yalta Conference, the Russians flagrantly violated the spirit of the Declaration on Liberated Europe by forcing a Communist-dominated government upon Rumania. Andrei Vyshinsky, the Soviet deputy commissar for foreign affairs, flew to Bucharest and declared that the Soviet government had to see that order was maintained behind the front; that the government of General Radescu was incapable of maintaining order; and that a new government must be based on "the truly democratic forces of the country."[1] He gave King Michael two hours to inform the public that General Radescu had been dismissed. In leaving the King, Vyshinsky, according to official American reports, "slammed the door so hard that the plaster around the door frame was badly cracked." Vyshinsky next day informed King Michael that the Communist leader, Petru Groza, was the choice of the Soviet government, and he was quoted as saying that unless the King accepted Groza and his team "he would not be responsible for the continuance of Rumania as an independent state."[2]

In order to place this event in perspective, it is necessary to review the background of enemy countries that came under Allied occupation and the arrangements concerning them that had grown up during the war; for the situation in Rumania was totally different, for instance, from the situation in Poland. Poland was a country allied with Great Britain that had been first invaded by Russia and later "liberated" by Russia from the Germans. Rumania, on the other hand, was an ally of Germany, a Fascist-run country whose troops had participated in the invasion of Russia and had, as a matter of fact, shared in the occupation of Yalta and the Crimea until driven out by the Red Army. As we shall see, the situations in Yugoslavia and Hungary were different again. But we must go back quite a bit if we are to see the picture as a whole.

It will be recalled, first of all, that as early as 1942 Russia pressed for Western recognition of the principle that it should regain the boundaries of 1941 after the war; that the British had been inclined to concede this; but that the United States successfully interposed objections (cf. Chapter 3 and its note 10). Stalin's idea, already at that time, had been that Russia should be granted a special sphere of influence in eastern Europe, in return for which he was prepared to recognize British preeminence in the countries to be liberated in the West (cf. Chapter 3). This idea ran completely counter to American policy, which was to agree first on principles of general validity and to apply them to particular cases only when an orderly framework for international collaboration had been established. Spheres of influence, in particular, were abhorrent to Cordell Hull. He recalled in his memoirs: "I could sympathize fully

113

with Stalin's desire to protect his western borders from future attack. But I felt that this security could best be obtained through a strong postwar peace organization."[3]

The first European country to be occupied by the advancing Allied armies was Italy, which capitulated to General Eisenhower's forces on September 3, 1943 under terms that acknowledged the authority of the Allied commander-in-chief to establish military government in Italy. General Smith signed the document, whose terms had been approved by the Russians, "by authority of the Governments of the United States and Great Britain and in the interest of the United Nations." The armistice agreement did not indicate which of the United Nations should take part in the work of supervising and controlling Italian affairs. But the Russian position on this point was indicated even before the armistice was signed. Stalin, on August 22, suggested activation of a "military-political commission" to deal jointly with problems of "various countries falling away from Germany," and he proposed that the commission be located in Sicily.[4] This suggestion was very poorly received by Roosevelt and Churchill, who learned of it while they were consulting in Quebec.[5]

Roosevelt tried to brush off Stalin's suggestion by pretending to misunderstand. He wrote the Soviet dictator: "Why not send an officer to General Eisenhower's headquarters in connection with the commission to sit in Sicily on further settlements with the Italians? He would join the British and Americans who are now working on this very subject."[6] But Stalin was not to be put off: "The despatch of a Soviet officer to General Eisenhower's headquarters," he replied immediately, "can in no way replace the military-political commission, which is required to direct on the spot negotiations with Italy and with the Govern-

114

ments of other countries falling away from Germany."[7] As it was impossible to deny the Russians any role at all, Roosevelt and Churchill agreed to the establishment of the Military-Political Commission—but in Algiers instead of Sicily, and with strictly circumscribed functions which would essentially confine the Russian representative to giving and receiving information.[8] The divergence became obvious when the Russians appointed Vyshinsky himself as their representative, while Roosevelt issued instructions to Eisenhower to set up a separate Control Commission for Italy under his direct command.[9]

The Russians immediately protested the establishment of the (U. S.–British) Control Commission, pointing to the existence of the (tripartite) Military-Political Commission to which they had just appointed a high-ranking representative. In the Russian view, the Commission in Algiers was to have a role in shaping political events in Italy and in guiding the military occupation. In the Western view, its function was purely advisory. In the end it was decided that an "Inter-Allied Advisory Council" should be established for Italy, but the Western Allies successfully insisted that their commander-in-chief must retain full and unrestricted authority. The Russians thus lost in their attempt to obtain an important role in influencing political events in Italy under Allied occupation. Vyshinsky, whose rank was now clearly excessive for an essentially advisory position, soon returned to Russia. Later, when an Allied Control Commission was set up in Rumania, and when the American and British governments asked for a share in determining occupation policies, Vyshinsky denied that request and referred to Italy as a precedent;[10] and the Russian chairman of the commission in Rumania pointed out that since the United States and Britain had made the executive decisions in Italy in the name of all the

– Russians: no participation outside their sphere; limited control within it

– US/British: leading role thruout Europe; possible participation everywhere

what about use of fascist officials in Italy?

United Nations, he felt entitled to do the same in Rumania.[11]

The capitulation of Italy had immediate repercussions in Greece, which had been largely garrisoned by Italian troops. As these troops were withdrawn, their arms found their way into the hands of Greek guerrilla fighters. While the Germans were able to recover control of the main cities and lines of communications in Greece, the war there from the fall of 1943 onward became a triangular affair: the Germans on the one hand, and on the other two Greek guerrilla organizations, ELAS and EDES, which at the same time fought each other. ELAS, the bigger organization, was republican and under strong Communist influence. EDES, although originally also republican, was opposed to the Communists and gradually attracted also conservative and royalist elements. The British in early 1944 tried to promote a truce among the Greek guerrillas. However, in March ELAS and its supporting political organizations, EAM (Greek initials for National Liberation Front), set up a provisional government which implicitly challenged the legitimacy of the Greek government-in-exile in Cairo. This situation had overtones reminiscent of the Polish issue, and it caused special concern to Churchill.

note: 2 guerrilla groupings in Greek govt in exile

Meanwhile, in March 1944 the Red Army had entered Bessarabia, a province of Rumania which had been Russian territory from 1812 to 1917, which Russia had taken back in 1941, and which it now claimed as Russian territory—much in the manner in which it claimed Poland east of the Curzon Line. The Russians also claimed northern Bukovina, an area inhabited by Ukrainians which they had also taken over in 1941. (Perhaps because Rumania was an enemy whose consent was not required, disposition of these territories had not become an important issue in Russia's relations with its Western allies.) As the Russians were now poised on what they considered the true border of Rumania, they issued a public statement on April 2, 1944, disclaiming any intention of annexing Rumanian territory or of "changing the existing social order in Rumania." This statement was apparently designed to influence the Rumanian government to forsake its alliance with Hitler, and to reassure the Western powers about Russia's intentions in eastern Europe.[12] Both the American and British governments praised the Russian avowals.

But Churchill was far from reassured. With great difficulty he had just managed to remodel the Greek and Yugoslav governments-in-exile in such a manner that they seemed to have a chance of coming to acceptable terms with the resistance elements fighting in their countries; and he looked with concern at the prospect of Russian power and influence spreading into the Balkans. He was disquieted, furthermore, by the fact that the Russians in early May had declined to cooperate with him with regard to Greece.[13] He did not feel confident that the United States would support a strong stand in the Balkans, especially in view of President Roosevelt's often expressed distaste at the idea of American involvement in that part of Europe.[14] Although Churchill knew that the idea of spheres of influence was anathema to the American government, which equated it with the kind of power politics that had discredited the peace settlements after World War I, Churchill decided to take an initiative. On May 5 the British government suggested to the Russian ambassador in London an arrangement whereby Rumania would be considered to be in Russia's, and Greece in Britain's sphere of responsibility.

The Russians were willing to accept such a deal, but only if it had the blessing of the United States. This Churchill now tried to obtain.

Such an arrangement [he telegraphed Roosevelt] would be a natural development of the existing military situation, since Rumania falls within the sphere of the Russian armies and Greece within the Allied command under General Wilson in the Mediterranean. . . . I hope you may feel able to give this proposal your blessing. We do not of course wish to carve up the Balkans into spheres of influence, and in agreeing to the arrangement we should make it clear that it applied only to war conditions and did not affect the rights and responsibilities which each of the Great Powers will have to exercise at the peace settlement and afterwards in regard to the whole of Europe.[15]

When these views were presented to him by the British ambassador, Hull was flatly opposed. "It seemed to me," he later wrote, "that any creation of zones of influence would inevitably sow the seeds of future conflict. I felt that zones of influence could not but derogate from the over-all authority of the international security organizations which I expected would come into being."[16]

At first blush [Hull told Halifax] in view of the many charges and counter-charges now rising—and which will certainly rise in the future—about encroachments first by one Government and then by another on the economic, political, military, or other internal affairs of the Balkans and other European countries, it would be a doubtful course to abandon our broad basic declarations of policy, principles, and practice. If these are departed from in one or two important instances, such as you propose, then neither of the two countries parties to such an act will have any precedent to stand on, or any stable rules by which to be governed and to insist that other Governments be governed.[17]

Hull persuaded Roosevelt to reply to Churchill also in this sense.

118

Churchill was convinced that the American position was unrealistic, and he came back with another message to Roosevelt. "Action is paralysed," he wrote, "if everybody is to consult everybody else about everything before it is taken. Events will always outstrip the changing situations in these Balkan regions. Somebody must have the power to plan and act." He referred to a recent mutiny of the Greek forces of the government-in-exile which had been squelched by the British. "If in these difficulties we had had to consult other Powers and a set of triangular or quadrangular telegrams got started the only result would have been chaos or impotence. . . . The Russians are ready to let us take the lead in the Greek business, which means that EAM and all its malice can be controlled by the national forces of Greece. Otherwise civil war and ruin to the land you care about so much. . . ." He pointed out that the Russians were about to invade Rumania and that, "considering that neither you nor we have any troops there at all . . . they will probably do what they like anyhow." He pleaded that the arrangement with Russia be given a trial for three months.[18]

In a separate message to Lord Halifax, which the British ambassador conveyed to Hull, Churchill made some important additional points. First, he said, "it seems reasonable that the Russians should deal with the Rumanians and Bulgarians, upon whom their armies are impinging"—thus indicating that in his view the arrangement should also extend to Bulgaria. He felt, on the other hand, that British primacy with respect to Greece should also extend to Yugoslavia. And he added, archly: "On the other hand, we follow the lead of the United States in South America as far as possible, as long as it is not a question of our beef and mutton. On this we naturally develop strong views on account of the little we get."[19] In other words, Churchill was pointing out that the United States, in effect, had its own sphere

119

indeed

of influence in Latin America. In the end, Roosevelt profited from the temporary absence of Hull from Washington to risk the wrath of his secretary of state by approving the deal on a three-month try-out basis and with the admonition that "we must be careful to make it clear that we are not establishing any post-war spheres of influence."[20]

Although the British told the Russians that they had received a green light from Washington, the Russians decided that they should check directly with the American government to make sure that there was no misunderstanding. By this time, however, Hull was back on the job. With the President's approval he replied confirming that the United States had agreed to the arrangement on a three-month trial basis, but he took the occasion to express the American misgivings about the project at such length and so insistently that Stalin seems to have lost interest in it.[21] In any event, Churchill pleaded in vain with Stalin to give the arrangement a try.[22] But the American note, which had indicated that any British-Russian arrangements "would have neither direct nor indirect validity as affecting the interests of this Government," clearly deprived it of most of its value to the Russians.[23]

The question of spheres thus remained in suspense during the summer of 1944. We have seen that the Russians were poised on the borders of prewar Rumania in April 1944 and that Churchill had managed in May to reorganize the Greek government-in-exile in a manner that seemed to promise the establishment of a truly representative coalition government when Greece would be liberated. In June 1944 the British pressed King Peter of Yugoslavia to appoint a prime minister (Ivan Subasic) who on his part might be able to work with the partisan leader, Tito. The British government clearly was looking for political leaders from eastern and southeastern Europe

120

who would be non-Communist and yet able to work with the Communists on a basis that would make those countries not basically anti-Russian, as they had been before the war. In Greece and Yugoslavia Churchill thought that he had found such a solution. In Czechoslovakia, Beneš seemed to symbolize the same pattern. But in Poland and Rumania it was impossible to work out a compromise.

During the summer months, as the Western Allies broke out of their beachhead in Normandy and the Russian armies mounted their massive offensives in Poland, the Germans moved some of their best divisions out of Rumania. Thereupon, in August, the Red Army finally launched an offensive on that front. The King of Rumania now ousted the Fascist government of the pro-German dictator, Antonescu, and installed a coalition regime of representatives of four parties: the National Peasants, led by the popular conservative, Iuliu Maniu; the Liberals, under Dinu Bratianu; the small Socialist Party; and the even smaller Communist Party. This new government, headed by General Sanatescu, signed an armistice with Russia on September 12 under which it joined the fight against Germany. Contrary to the pattern in Poland, the Russians did not arrive in Rumania with a preformed government of their own but seemed content, at least for the time being, to work with the new coalition government, in which the Communists were clearly in a minority.

The Rumanian armistice also provided that "an Allied Control Commission will be established which will undertake until the conclusion of peace the regulation of and control over the execution of the present terms under the general direction and orders of the Allied (Soviet) High Command acting on behalf of the Allied powers." Molotov made it plain to the United

States and Britain that the Soviet High Command alone would have authority to issue orders to the Rumanian government; that the Soviet member on the Control Commission would exercise executive power for the Commission; and that the functions of the British and American members would be what the Soviet government regarded as analogous to those of the Soviet representatives attached to the Control Commission in Italy. The United States remonstrated for a while, but in the end had to go along with these provisions.[24]

The next country to fall to the Russians was Bulgaria. When Rumania capitulated, the pro-German government in Bulgaria resigned, and its successor at first attempted to follow a policy of neutrality while announcing that it would carry on negotiations with the United States and Great Britain for an armistice and that it would seek "the most sincere relations founded on trust with fraternal Russia." But Russia insisted on more. On September 5 Russia declared war against Bulgaria, and on September 9, after a new government had come into office in Sofia and had declared war against Germany, hostilities by Russia were suspended. The new Bulgarian government was much more heavily weighted in favor of the Communists than the government in Rumania, largely because the Communists had been active as partisans and the Bulgarians in general did not harbor the traditional fears of Russia that existed in Rumania. The preliminary armistice agreement with Bulgaria provided for an Allied Control Commission which clearly lodged action responsibility in the "Allied (Soviet) High Command."[25]

Meanwhile, the British efforts to produce moderate coalition regimes in Greece and Yugoslavia were affected by the Russian advance into the Balkans. In Greece, a Russian military mission to ELAS made its appearance in July 1944.[26] For some reason, however, the Russians seemed to keep to the spirit of the abortive agreement with Great Britain and refrained from lending active support to ELAS. In August Churchill had an interview with the premier of the Greek government-in-exile, Georgios Papandreou, and apparently concluded that he was suited to conciliate the Communist-led resistance movement in Greece without letting it take power in the country. The EAM now decided to join the Papandreou government, and in September an agreement was concluded whereby both the Greek government-in-exile and the two rival undergrounds, EDES and ELAS, recognized the military authority of the Supreme Allied Commander in the Mediterranean, General Wilson, and accepted his appointment of a British general to exercise command in Greece.[27] The stage was set for a British landing in Greece. Would the Communist-led ELAS live up to the agreement and submit to British control? Or would the British have to intervene in a civil war? It seemed to depend, in no small measure, on the position of the Soviet Union.

If Greece was an enemy-occupied country waiting to be liberated, Yugoslavia was a country that in 1944 had very large indigenous forces in the field against the Germans. Marshal Tito, who enjoyed both Russian and British support, was in control of a major part of his country. As in Greece, the future status of the monarchy was a burning political issue. In August Churchill met with Tito in Italy and attempted to effect a reconciliation between him and King Peter. During this period, the Yugoslav partisans were still dependent on the British in Italy for some logistical support, but on September 6 Tito's forces established contact with the advancing Red Army and Britain's bargaining position with Tito correspondingly declined. Later in September Tito flew to Moscow, where, as was much later revealed, Stalin urged him to let King Peter return to Yugoslavia.[28] An agreement was also concluded whereby Tito's National Committee of Liberation would conduct the civil administration of any Yugoslav territory occupied by the Red Army. To Churchill all this again looked most ominous, involving the projection of Russian power into the Mediterranean. The United States was of little help to him because, while it insisted on a policy based on high principles, it refused to get itself involved in eastern European affairs, especially prior to the 1944 elections.[29]

Churchill now decided to go to Moscow and discuss the whole range of problems of east and southeast Europe with Stalin even though Roosevelt, preoccupied with domestic politics, was unable to participate. Churchill arrived in Moscow on October 9 and during his first private meeting with Stalin immediately drove to the heart of the matter. As he recalls: "The moment was apt for business, so I said, 'Let us settle about our affairs in the Balkans. Your armies are in Rumania and Bulgaria. We have interests, missions, and agents there. Don't let us get at cross-purposes in small ways. So far as Britain and Russia are concerned, how would it do for you to have ninety per cent predominance in Rumania, for us to have ninety per cent of the say in Greece, and go fifty-fifty about Yugoslavia?' "[30] While this was being translated, Churchill wrote out on a sheet of paper the proportions he envisaged for Russia and "the others": Rumania 90:10, Greece 10:90, Yugoslavia and Hungary 50:50, Bulgaria 75:25.[31]

"I pushed this across to Stalin, who had by then heard the translation," Churchill recalls. "There was a slight pause. Then he took his blue pencil and made a large tick upon it, and passed it back to us. It was all settled in no more time than it takes to set down. . . . After this there was a long silence. The pencilled paper lay in the centre of the table. At length I said, 'Might it not be thought rather cynical if it seemed we had disposed of these issues, so fateful to millions of people, in such an offhand manner? Let us burn the paper.' 'No, you keep it,' said Stalin."[32]

The deal was made. What was the attitude of the United States toward it? Here, once more, a distinction must be made between the position of President Roosevelt and that of his most important subordinates. Before Churchill went to Moscow, he informed the President in general terms of what he intended to discuss. The President dispatched—or thought he dispatched—a message to Churchill giving his general blessing to the forthcoming talks and suggesting only that Ambassador Harriman be also present. However, when Hopkins learned of that message he feared that it would give the impression that the United States was washing its hands of the Balkans and letting Churchill make commitments also in its name. As reported by Sherwood, "Hopkins immediately investigated and learned that this cable was already going out over the wires of the Map Room. He thereupon took one of the quick and arbitrary actions, far beyond the scope of his own authority, which had gained for him the admiration and affection of Roosevelt ever since the beginnings of the New Deal: he gave orders to the officers on duty in the Map Room that transmission of the President's message to Stalin was to be stopped. . . . Hopkins then went straight to Roosevelt's bed room—the President was shaving at the time—and told what he had done and the reasons why he had done it."[33] He persuaded Roosevelt to send a message to Stalin instead, of a totally different tenor:

"There is in this global war literally no question, either military or political," the message drafted by Hopkins and Bohlen read, "in which the United States is not interested. You will naturally understand this. It is my firm conviction that the solution to still unsolved questions can be found only by the three of us together. Therefore, while I appreciate the necessity for the present meeting, I choose to consider your forthcoming talks with Mr. Churchill merely as preliminary to a conference of the three of us which can take place, so far as I am concerned, any time after our national election." In a separate message to Ambassador Harriman, Roosevelt asked him to bear in mind that there could be "no subjects that I can anticipate that might be discussed between Stalin and the Prime Minister in which I will not be greatly concerned. It is important that I retain complete freedom of action after this conference is over."[34] Still, when the British-Russian deal was made the United States this time did not remonstrate, and Roosevelt even sent a vague greeting to Churchill and Stalin that might have been interpreted as a blessing.[35]

In any event, the deal went into effect and it had immediate favorable consequences for the British position in the Balkans. They were given a free hand in Greece and, as we shall see, used it with determination. With respect to Yugoslavia, Churchill and Stalin announced that they were going to try to bring about a union between the Yugoslav government-in-exile and Tito's National Liberation movement, and they sent a joint message to Tito and Subasic urging them to meet again and work out their problems together. For Bulgaria they completed armistice terms which involved some slight improvements as compared to the situation in Rumania.[36] Most remarkably, Stalin now encouraged Churchill to move British troops into northwestern Yugoslavia and thence in the direction of Vienna.[37] This was a strategy which Churchill had favored at the Tehran conference, where Stalin had discouraged it.[38] Stalin knew that Tito was opposed to such a British landing, and historians are still divided as to why he now approved the idea and even urged it on the British premier.[39] (As it turned out, Churchill was unable—once more—to persuade the American Chiefs of Staff to approve the operation.[40])

British troops arrived in Athens in October, bringing the Papandreou government with them. That government, it will be remembered, was a coalition including representatives of the leftist and republican EAM, the political organization of the increasingly Communist-dominated ELAS underground. But when the Papandreou government now demanded that the guerrilla forces be disbanded, the EAM members resigned, a general strike was called, there were street demonstrations on December 3, and shortly thereafter the ELAS troops began a general insurrection. Churchill immediately ordered the local British commander, General Scobie, to intervene. In a telegram to him, he wrote: "You are responsible for maintaining order in Athens and for neutralizing or destroying all EAM-ELAS bands approaching the city. You may make any regulations you like for the strict control of the streets or for the rounding up of any number of truculent persons. . . . Do not . . . hesitate to act as if you were in a conquered city where a local rebellion is in progress."[41] As Churchill later wrote of this message, he had to admit that it was somewhat strident in tone, but he felt it so necessary to give a strong lead to the military commander that he intentionally worded it in the sharpest terms.[42]

The fighting at first went very badly for the British. The ELAS troops overran most of Athens and in fact overwhelmed their Greek opponents everywhere in the country with the exception of a few square miles in the capital and part of Salonika. There was bitter house-to-house fighting in Athens, and by December 11 Field Marshal Alexander telegraphed, "The British forces are in fact beleaguered in the heart of the city."[43] Massive British reinforcements were brought in from Italy and the Middle East, but Alexander warned that even with those added troops the British would be unable to control all of Greece. To make matters worse, the British action seemed to many in the West as an oppressive and reactionary move against men who had fought bravely against the Germans, and as a stifling of the people's will. Both in Britain and in the United States most of the press condemned the intervention in scathing terms.

Simultaneously, political crises blew up in Italy and Belgium. In Italy the government had fallen and it was proposed to reorganize it with Count Carlo Sforza as foreign minister. Sforza, however, was *persona non grata* with Churchill because of his failure to support the King of Italy at a time (in 1943) when he had promised the British premier to do so. Britain thus vetoed his inclusion in the new government. In Belgium, British troops were called out to prevent a Communist-led demonstration. As in Greece, the question of the future of the monarchy was there mingled with the question of disarming ex-resistance organizations. Thus in three European countries—Greece, Italy, and Belgium—where the British exercised primacy serious political crises broke out, and in each country the British position seemed to be in support of the monarchy and the more conservative elements against republicans and radicals. Churchill's position was made particularly difficult because the American government, in a formal statement by Stettinius, dissociated itself from the British actions in Italy and Greece.[44] Still worse, the prime minister's message to General Scobie leaked out to an American newspaper columnist and seemed to confirm the British action in Greece as high-handed and oppressive.[45]

But Churchill stood his ground. He could afford to conduct a farsighted, though momentarily unpopular, policy because he had charge not only of his party but of a coalition government and needed to fear no elections until after victory had been achieved.[46] Before his Parliament he insisted that Britain was defending not a particular regime but the right of the Greek people to decide freely, under conditions of normal tranquillity, whether their government was to be of the Left or of the Right. He put the question of confidence and was sustained, but by a discouraging margin. On Christmas Day 1944 he flew to Athens and, while he' was unable to bring the warring Greek factions together, he obtained their agreement to the installation of a Regent pending settlement of the constitutional question. (Roosevelt helped by pushing the King to accept this arrangement.) Meanwhile, British troops in Greece were increased to 60,000 and they finally went on the offensive. When Papandreou resigned and General Plastiras, a republican, succeeded him, the British position was also considerably improved. At the same time, a widespread reaction against the terrorism of ELAS in Athens also undermined the power of the insurgents. Finally, on January 14, 1945, a cease-fire was negotiated; and on February 12 a definite peace was arranged whereby ELAS agreed to disband and surrender its arms in return for a guarantee of amnesty.

Throughout this episode, the Russians remained completely quiet. Stalin, as Churchill noted, "adhered strictly and faithfully to our agreement of October, and during all the long weeks of fighting the Communists in the streets of Athens not one word of reproach came from *Pravda* or *Isvestia*."[47] Later, at Yalta, Stalin went out of his way to tell Churchill that "he had no intention of criticizing British policy in Greece."[48] With mock solicitude, he even offered Churchill assurances that a suggested Russian amendment to the Declaration on Liberated Europe, whereby the signatories would have been obligated to "support . . . political leaders of those countries who have taken an active part in the struggle against the German invaders" was not designed to apply to Greece.[49] Churchill on his part said that there had been a rather rough time in Greece and "they were very much obliged to Marshal Stalin for not having taken too great an interest in Greek affairs."[50]

Our narrative has now carried us, though by a different route, again to the Yalta Conference in February 1945. We have already noted that Greece was not a matter of contention there. Neither was Rumania. The British tried to bring up the situation in Bulgaria and Hungary, to make clear that they considered that after the conclusion of hostilities the three Great Powers should have an equal say in the administration of those countries, but time prevented the matter from being discussed.[51] On the other hand, there was some discussion of Yugoslavia, where Britain strove to maintain its 50:50 position of influence. In November 1944 Tito and Subasic had agreed to set up a three-man regency, pending a plebiscite to decide whether King Peter was to come back. However, the two Yugoslav leaders were unable to agree on the composition of that regency council. Moreover, the Yugoslav Communist leader was proclaiming his intention of annexing Trieste and a part of Austria, and Churchill was fearful that this might involve a head-on collision with the British, who were to occupy the disputed areas.

At Yalta Stalin repeated the suggestion which he had made to Churchill in October, that some British troops be transferred from the Italian front to Yugoslavia, whence they should be directed toward Vienna.[52] (Again, the American military leaders refused to entertain the idea.) Churchill proposed some amendments to the Tito-Subasic agreement, and Stalin agreed that those amendments—designed to improve the democratic base of the prospective coalition government—should be jointly urged upon the two Yugoslav leaders by the Big Three. After some hesitation, Roosevelt agreed to go along. The three also

130

agreed to urge Tito and Subasic to get on with implementation of their agreement to form a coalition government. Thus at Yalta there was also no disagreement on Yugoslavia. It is perhaps significant, however, that Stalin claimed he had little influence upon Tito.[53] Churchill questioned this, but subsequent events seem to have shown that Stalin may have been telling the truth.

At the second plenary meeting in Yalta, President Roosevelt also made a remark which Churchill was to label a "momentous statement."[54] He said that he did not believe that American troops would stay in Europe much more than two years after the war. He felt that he could obtain support in Congress and throughout the country for any reasonable measures designed to safeguard the future peace, the President said, but he did not believe that this would extend to the maintenance of an appreciable American force in Europe.[55] It is not recorded what Stalin's reaction to this statement may have been. In any case, it is in this setting and against the background of the Polish issue detailed in Chapters 3 and 4, that the Declaration on Liberated Europe was agreed; and it is against the background of the agreements and disagreements on Rumania, Greece, Bulgaria, Hungary, and Yugoslavia set forth in the present chapter that one must view the violations of the Declaration by the Soviet Union which followed upon Yalta. We have already mentioned the unilateral forceful action taken by the Russians in Rumania. Many other Western grievances accumulated during the period between Yalta and Potsdam.

The Tito-Subasic agreement soon resulted not in a balancing of East and West but in a complete subjection of the Yugoslav conservatives by the Communists. The steps to enlarge the legislative body which had been urged by the Yalta Conference were never taken. "I must also say," wrote Churchill to Stalin

on April 28, when he addressed the Russian dictator in the
Polish matter,

> that the way things have worked out in Yugoslavia certainly
> does not give me the feeling of a fifty-fifty interest as be-
> tween our countries. Marshal Tito has become a complete
> dictator. He has proclaimed that his prime loyalties are to
> the Soviet Union. Although he allowed members of the
> Royal Yugoslav Government to enter his government, they
> only number six as against twenty-five of his own nominees.
> We have the impression that they are not taken into con-
> sultation on matters of high policy and that it is becoming
> a one-party regime. However . . . I do not complain of any
> action you have taken there in spite of my misgivings and
> I hope it will all work out smoothly and make Yugoslavia
> into a prosperous and free people friendly to both Russia
> and ourselves.[56]

Territorial questions, which were supposed to await the peace
settlements, began to bedevil the alliance. As a means of
strengthening the Rumanian Communist Party, the Russians let
it be known in January 1945 that they would return Transyl-
vania to Rumania if the Communist-dominated "National
Democratic Front" came to power; and on March 10, just four
days after Groza took office, they extended Rumanian administration to that area which Hitler had awarded to Hungary. The
unilateral extension of Polish administration to the Western
Neisse has already been mentioned in Chapter 4. But the most
vexing territorial issue concerned the Italian province of Venezia Giulia, where a substantial proportion of the population was
ethnically Yugoslav (Croat and Slovene). Tito's forces swarmed
into this area in April and were eventually confronted by British
troops under General Alexander's command. Another Greece
seemed in the making, and Churchill urged Truman to coop-

erate in forceful action to deny the strategic port of Trieste to the Yugoslavs.

"The great thing is to be there before Tito's guerrillas are in occupation," Churchill wrote the American President. "Therefore it does not seem to me there is a minute to wait. The actual status of Trieste can be determined at leisure. Possession is nine points of the law. I beg you for an early decision."[57] Truman hesitated to allow American troops to be committed, so Churchill authorized Alexander to go ahead using only British divisions. The dispute over Venezia Giulia was to last for many years, but by mid-1945 at least bloodshed between British and Yugoslav troops was avoided by an agreement on June 9. Stalin seemed to support the Yugoslav position, but the dispute between Yugoslavia and the Soviet Union three years later has brought out that Tito was in fact very much displeased by Stalin's failure to back him all the way in Trieste.[58] Churchill's disenchantment with the spheres-of-influence situation in Yugoslavia was recorded in his message to Stalin of June 23: "Our joint idea at the Kremlin in October was that the Yugoslav business should work out around 50-50 Russian and British influence. In fact it is at present more like 90-10, and even in that poor 10 we have been subjected to violent pressure by Marshal Tito."[59] From subsequent evidence, however, it appears that it was perhaps not Stalin who was pushing Tito but the reverse.

We have now accounted for the situation in Rumania, which —like Poland—was a country neighboring upon Russia, a country in which anti-Russian conservatives had predominated, from which Russia took back territory it had previously possessed, and in which Russia installed a completely Communist-dominated government;[60] Bulgaria, where the Communists were given a preponderant position which may initially have been

133

based, at least in part, on friendlier feelings toward Russia and on the anti-German record of Communist guerrillas—a position which the Communists gradually expanded by pressure and terror as 1945 wore on; Greece, where the Communists were beaten down by Britain with the acquiescence of Russia; and Yugoslavia, where British-Russian efforts to bring about a coalition between Communists and middle-class parties resulted only in a government clearly dominated by Tito's national Communist partisans, who had obtained control of their country largely by their own efforts. It remains to say a few words about Hungary and Czechoslovakia to explain why Communist domination there did not become an issue until long after 1945.

When Russian troops crossed into Hungary in October 1944, Admiral Horthy, the "regent" and strong man of Hungary, announced his intention of surrendering to the Red Army—but he was forestalled by a German coup and taken to a German concentration camp. However, a part of the Hungarian army under General Miklos surrendered to the Russians, and based on these elements the Russians installed a Provisional Hungarian Government at Debrecen, in eastern Hungary, in December 1944. The Allies negotiated an armistice with that government, with provisions along the lines of those for Bulgaria, giving the Soviet High Command the control power. The armistice also imposed very substantial reparations on Hungary, but at American insistence the Soviets agreed to scale these down by almost one-half.[61] By November the Red Army reached the outskirts of Budapest, but Hitler sent reinforcements to Hungary which halted the Russian offensive. It was not until April 1945, long after Yalta, that the German army was completely cleared out of the country.

The political organization in the Soviet-controlled part of Hungary, meanwhile, developed completely differently from what had occurred in Rumania, Bulgaria, and Yugoslavia. An underground "Hungarian Front" composed of Communists, Social Democrats, and the conservative Smallholders Party had agreed that those parties would establish a coalition after the war. The Debrecen government with Soviet permission allotted each of the three parties two cabinet posts, with others going to exponents of additional non-Communist groups. During the first months of the coalition the Communists cooperated genuinely with the other parties in preparing and carrying out certain fundamental economic and social changes which were agreed to be long overdue.[62] Most important among these was a land reform in March 1945 by which the huge feudal estates were broken up and over 600,000 peasants received land of their own.[63] The Communist minority position continued long after the Potsdam Conference. Although this takes us beyond the scope of this narrative, it may be noted that surprisingly free elections took place in Hungary under Soviet occupation in November 1945, in which the Smallholders obtained a smashing majority.[64] Nobody knows, of course, whether there was any connection between these free elections and the Churchill-Stalin agreement of 1944 which had assigned to Russia only a 50 per cent interest in Hungary. (The Soviet-engineered Communist take-over of Hungary took place only in 1947.)

If Hungary had been an enemy state, Czechoslovakia was an ally that had maintained a government-in-exile in London throughout the war but one which, in contrast to the Polish government-in-exile, had excellent relations with both Britain and Russia. President Edvard Beneš went to Moscow in December 1943 and there concluded a treaty of mutual assistance with the Soviet Union in which each pledged to act after the war "in accordance with the principles of mutual respect for the independence and sovereignty, as well as of non-interference

135

in the internal affairs, of the other state."[65] It was also agreed that as Russian forces entered Czechoslovakia, they would be accompanied by Czech troops and the liberated areas would be progressively handed over to the Czechoslovak civil administration. When the Red Army entered Czechoslovakia in force, Benes arrived from London via Moscow to establish a provisional government in Slovakia in April 1945. In that government, which arrived in Prague in May, the Communists held seven out of twenty-five cabinet posts. This situation was analogous to that existing in most former German-occupied areas in western Europe[66] and did not give grounds for immediate concern in England and the United States.

Czechoslovakia had a tradition of friendliness and cultural affinity with Russia, which was of course totally absent in Poland and Rumania although it was paralleled to some extent in Bulgaria and Yugoslavia. Friendly feelings toward Russia had been heightened when Great Britain and France had sold out Czechoslovakia at Munich in 1938 over the protests of the Soviet Union. When Russia after the war asked Czechoslovakia to cede its easternmost tip, Ruthenia (also called Carpatho-Russia), which was largely inhabited by Ukrainians, this matter created no issue and the cession was amicably accomplished in June 1945, thereby completing the political unification of all Ukrainian lands within the frontiers of the Soviet Union[67] and giving Russia a common frontier with Hungary. Free elections were held in Czechoslovakia in 1946. (It was not until two years later that the Communists, by terror tactics and aided by Russian pressure, took over the country.)

This, then, completes our account of how the Russians came into eastern and southeastern Europe in the later stages of the war, and how British and Russian policies interacted in those *neglects impact of fascism on Rumania*

areas. We have seen (Chapters 2 and 4) how the West opposed Russian predominance in Poland after Yalta on the basis of the ambiguous compromise that had been reached at that conference. It remains to review, again very briefly, the Western attitude toward Russian predominance in southeastern Europe. This attitude, too, was based on the Yalta agreements, in this case on the Declaration on Liberated Europe (page viii, Chapter 4). Any hope of reversing the process of increasing Russian influence and control depended in mid-1945 on the Western ability to make the Russians facilitate the holding of truly free elections. Any hope of the Soviet Union to maintain its control depended on the avoidance of such elections, especially in Rumania, where, as in Poland, the anti-Russian and anti-Communist sentiment was clearly overwhelming.

"Although I have in mind primarily the difficulties which the Polish negotiations have encountered," Roosevelt wrote Stalin on April 1, 1945, shortly before his death, "I must make a brief mention of our agreement embodied in the Declaration on Liberated Europe. I frankly cannot understand why the recent developments in Rumania should be regarded as not falling within the terms of that agreement. I hope you will find time personally to examine the correspondence between our Governments on this subject."[68] Stalin, on the other hand, pressed Churchill and Truman to extend diplomatic recognition to the Rumanian and Bulgarian governments on the ground that those countries had broken with the Axis and entered the war on the Allied side.[69] Truman's reply was crisp: he was disturbed, he said, to find governments in Rumania and Bulgaria "which do not accord to all democratic elements of the people the rights of free expression and which in their administration are, in my opinion, neither representative of nor responsive to the will of the people."[70] He asked that the U. S. S. R., Britain and the U. S.

concert their policies, i.e., bring about agreed changes in those countries. And there the matter rested until the Potsdam Conference in July 1945.

In President Truman's briefing book, which he studied on the way to Potsdam, was a document which succinctly summarized the situation in eastern Europe as it then existed. The relevant paragraph read:

no, not as you have described it

> The Russians have taken steps to solidify their control over eastern Europe. They have concluded bilateral treaties of alliance with the Lublin Poles (in spite of our objections) and with the Governments of Yugoslavia and Czechoslovakia. They have taken unilateral action with respect to the formation of an Austrian Government, and have acted independently in Rumania, Bulgaria, and Hungary without consultation with the American and British representatives in those countries. An exclusive economic agreement has been concluded with Rumania which makes possible extensive Soviet control over Rumanian industry and which may virtually cut off Rumanian trade with the rest of the world. The Russians have rejected British and American proposals that discussions should take place regarding the political situation in Rumania and elections in Bulgaria. These actions are not in accordance with the Crimea Declaration on Liberated Europe whereby the Big Three were to concert their policies in assisting the liberated peoples to solve their pressing political and economic problems by democratic means. Eastern Europe is, in fact, a Soviet sphere of influence.[71]

...as we did in Italy

At the Potsdam Conference, the United States introduced a document which called attention to the fact that the Yalta Declaration on Liberated Europe had not been carried out; called for reorganization of the Rumanian and Bulgarian governments; and proposed joint supervision ("assistance") of free elections in all the liberated territories.[72] The United States also proposed that the armistice for Italy be eased and that that nation be admitted to the United Nations. Churchill was unenthusiastic about this latter proposal. Stalin first tried to turn Churchill against the American position on Rumania and Bulgaria by privately pointing out to him that he was "not meddling in Greek affairs."[73] When this did not work, the Russians introduced a counter-document which defended the situation in Rumania and Bulgaria and blasted the situation in Greece "where law is not respected, where terrorism rages directed against democratic elements which have borne the principal burden of the fight against German invaders. . . ," etc.[74] This produced quite an uproar, in the course of which the Western representatives pointed out that the Greeks had welcomed supervision of their elections and that the international press was free to observe there, whereas Rumania and Bulgaria were cut off from the world.[75]

Secretary of State Byrnes records in his memoirs how he tried to make Molotov understand that Western insistence on free elections in eastern Europe was not intended to be an infringement of Russian interests: "The United States," he recalls saying to the Soviet commissar,

sincerely desires Russia to have friendly countries on her borders, but we believe they should seek the friendship of the people rather than of any particular government. We, therefore, want the governments to be representative of the people. If elections are held while there are restrictions not only on newspaper and radio correspondents but upon our own governmental representatives as well, the American people will distrust any government established as a result of such an election. We do not wish to become involved in the elections of any country, but, because of the postwar situation, we would join with others in observing elections in Italy, Greece, Hungary, Rumania and Bulgaria.[76]

Beginnings of the Cold War

In the end, although the United States was prepared to substitute the word "observation" for "supervision," Stalin obdurately opposed any decision in the matter of free elections. In a moment of frankness he put the Soviet stand with unusual clarity as well as finality: "A freely elected government in any of these countries," he said, "would be anti-Soviet, and that we cannot allow."[77] When the British complained about the situation in Yugoslavia, the Russians again countered by introducing a paper lambasting Greece. Finally, Foreign Minister Bevin proposed that the papers on both Yugoslavia and Greece be withdrawn, and Stalin agreed with alacrity.[78] As a result, the Potsdam Conference brought no free elections in Rumania or Bulgaria and no change whatever in the division of eastern Europe as it had occurred at the end of the war on the basis of the power relationships as they existed at the time.

NOTES

1. James F. Byrnes, *Speaking Frankly* (New York: Harper, 1947), pp. 51-52.

2. Ibid.

3. *The Memoirs of Cordell Hull* (New York: Macmillan, 1948), II, 1170.

4. *Stalin Correspondence* (see chap. 3, note 19), I, 149.

5. Herbert Feis, *Churchill, Roosevelt, Stalin—The War They Waged and the Peace They Sought* (Princeton, N.J.: Princeton University Press, 1957), p. 172, reports that Roosevelt after receiving Stalin's message "came into the room before dinner saying, 'We are both mad'; and they were. . . . Though Eden and Ismay tried to get [Churchill] to take an easier view of the episode, he would not listen

to any excusing talk. After dinner, talking with Harriman, he remarked gloomily that he foresaw 'bloody consequences in the future' (using the word 'bloody' in its literal sense); and that he thought Stalin an unnatural man—with whom there would be grave trouble."

6. *Stalin Correspondence*, II, 89.

7. Ibid., II, 90.

8. Ibid., I, 154; II, 92. Churchill's description of the terms of reference was somewhat more restrictive than Roosevelt's.

9. "The pattern of Allied control over Italy which thus finally emerged lasted until the end of the war. It was of importance not only for Italy itself, but as a model for other armistice regimes in ex-enemy countries of Eastern Europe. Having excluded Russia from any but nominal participation in Italian affairs, the Western Powers prepared the way for their own exclusion from any but a marginal share in the affairs of Eastern Europe. No other arrangement, of course, conformed to the real distribution of military power and responsibility, or could have been compatible with the mutual distrust which lay close to the surface of Anglo-Russian and, less obviously, in the background of Russo-American relations." Royal Institute of International Affairs, *America, Britain and Russia—Their Cooperation and Conflict, 1941-1946*, by William Hardy McNeill (London: Oxford University Press, 1953), p. 310.

10. Feis, p. 416. Cf. also note 24 to this chapter.

11. Feis, pp. 546-47.

12. The Rumanian government had in fact shown signs of wishing to come to terms with the United Nations, but they were so afraid of the Russians that they insisted that British or American troops be sent into Rumania to counterbalance the Red Army; and this condition had not been accepted. Cf. William D. Leahy, *I Was There* (New York: Whittlesey House, 1950), p. 267.

13. Winston Churchill, *Closing the Ring* (see chap. 3, note 5), p. 551.

14. Hull *Memoirs*, II, 1612.

15. Churchill, *Triumph and Tragedy* (see chap. 3, note 5), pp. 73-74.

16. Hull *Memoirs*, II, 1452.

17. Ibid.

18. Churchill, *Triumph and Tragedy*, pp. 75-76.

19. Ibid., pp. 74-75.

20. Hull learned of the President's approval of the spheres-of-responsibility arrangements only through a telegram from the American ambassador to Greece, who was stationed in Cairo. He described his reaction: "I wrote the President a letter, enclosing a copy of Ambassador MacVeagh's telegram, and asking him whether any changes had been made in our position. The President replied on June 30, simply enclosing paraphrases or extracts of the messages which had been exchanged between himself and Mr. Churchill. These included his message of acceptance of June 12, to which Mr. Churchill had replied two days later expressing his deep gratitude and stating that he had asked Eden to convey the information to Molotov and make clear that the three months' limitation had been agreed to so that there would be no prejudgment of the question of establishing postwar spheres of influence." Hull *Memoirs*, II, 1456.

21. The Russian inquiry was dated July 1, 1944. The U. S. reply, dated July 15, was paraphrased by Hull as follows: "We said it would be unfortunate if any temporary arrangement should be so conceived as to appear to be a departure from the principle adopted by the three Governments at the Moscow Conference definitely rejecting the spheres-of-influence idea. Consequently, this Government hoped that no projected measures would be allowed to prejudice the efforts toward directing the policies of the Allied Governments along lines of collaboration rather than independent action, since any arrangement suggestive of spheres of influence could not but militate against the establishment and effective functioning of a broader system of general security in which all countries would have their part.

"We added that we supposed that the three months' trial period would enable the British and Soviet Governments to determine whether such an arrangement was practicable and efficacious as applying to war conditions only, without in any way affecting the rights and responsibilities which each of the three principal Allied nations would have to exercise during the period of the reestablishment of peace, and afterwards, in regard to the whole of Europe. Finally, we assumed that the arrangement would have neither direct nor indirect validity as affecting the interests of this Government, or

of other Governments associated with the three principal Allies."
Hull *Memoirs*, II, 1458.

22. Churchill, apparently unaware that Hull was dragging his
feet, sent a message to Stalin on July 11 containing the following
paragraph on the Balkan arrangement:

"Some weeks ago it was suggested by Eden to your Ambassador
that the Soviet Government should take the lead in Rumania, and
the British should do the same in Greece. This was only a working arrangement to avoid as much as possible the awful business of
triangular telegrams, which paralyses action. Molotov then suggested
very properly that I should tell the United States, which I did,
and always meant to, and after some discussion the President agreed
to a three-months trial being made. These may be three very important months, Marshal Stalin, July, August, and September. Now
however I see that you find some difficulty in this. I would ask
whether you should not tell us that the plan may be allowed to have
its chance for three months. No one can say it affects the future of
Europe or divides it into spheres. But we can get a clear-headed
policy in each theatre, and we all report to the others what we are
doing. However, if you tell me it is hopeless I shall not take it
amiss." Churchill, *Triumph and Tragedy*, p. 79.

Stalin's reply, dated July 15, read in part as follows: "As regards
the question of Rumania and Greece. . . . One thing is clear to me:
it is that the American Government has some doubts regarding this
question, and that it would be better to revert to this matter when
we receive the American reply to our inquiry. As soon as the observations of the American Government are known, I shall not fail to
write to you further on this question." (Ibid., p. 80.) There is no
evidence of any further written communication from Stalin to
Churchill on this subject.

23. The U. S. reply, in the opinion of one historian, "obviously
deprived the [spheres of responsibility] agreement of much of its
value. If the Americans reserved the right to put a spoke in both the
British and the Russian wheel in any Balkan country, then a division
into operational spheres could have only an insecure foundation."
McNeill, p. 424.

24. Feis, p. 416. "On September 20th, Vishinsky sent Harriman

143

and Clark Kerr a statement of Soviet plans for the organization of
the Allied Control Commission. This provided that the British and
American part in the work of the Commission was to be indeed
subordinate. Each was to be allowed only five officials on the staff;
they were to be permitted to deal with Rumanian officials only
through the top officers of the Commission, all of whom were to be
Russians; and they were to have to ask permission of the chairman
of the Commission before making trips into the country. Vishinsky
also claimed that this corresponded with the position of the Soviet
members of the staff of the Allied Commission in Italy."

Actually, Russia had broken out of its isolation in Italy by ap-
pointing a diplomatic representative there over the objections of the
United States and Great Britain; and Vyshinsky now authorized a
similar direct but powerless representation in Rumania for the United
States and Great Britain, again on the grounds of analogy with
Italy. Ibid.

25. McNeill, p. 472.

26. Ibid., p. 390.

27. Ibid., p. 478-79.

28. Vladimir Dedijer, *Tito* (New York: Simon & Schuster, 1953),
p. 233.

29. The United States was prepared to give Great Britain a free
hand in the Balkans but was not disposed to permit the use of any
American troops in that area. Churchill (*Triumph and Tragedy*, p.
208) indicates that there was a division of primary responsibilities as
between the United States and Britain in the various operational
theatres in Europe. When Churchill became convinced that British
intervention in Greece would become necessary, he secured Roosevelt's consent, which was given on the basis that only British troops
would be used, although American transport planes were to be
made available for the dropping of British parachutists. (Ibid., p.
112.) Throughout the war in the Mediterranean, Churchill pressed
for an Allied invasion either at the juncture of Italy with Yugoslavia
—the Istrian Peninsula—or along the Yugoslav coast; and throughout
the many discussions such plans were rejected by the United States,
though usually on military rather than political grounds. The matter
was also briefly discussed, in the usual inconclusive manner, at the

Quebec Conference between Roosevelt and Churchill in September 1944.

30. Churchill, *Triumph and Tragedy,* p. 227.

31. Ibid. Churchill's own account here differs from that obtained by the State Department through the American embassies at Moscow and Ankara, which spoke of a 75:25 or 80:20 Russian predominance in Rumania, Bulgaria, and Hungary (Hull *Memoirs,* II, 1458). Although Churchill's 50:50 version of the formula for Hungary must be controlling, it is noteworthy that in interpreting the agreement he clearly intended Russia to have a preponderant role in Hungary, as indicated by the last paragraph quoted under note 32 in this chapter.

32. Churchill, *Triumph and Tragedy,* pp. 227-28. This was the same visit as the one described in Chapter 3 in connection with the Polish issue, when Mikolajczyk was summoned to Moscow to negotiate, but refused to make any concession on the Curzon Line.

Churchill's own interpretation of the Balkans deal with Stalin is contained in a message to his cabinet colleagues which he sent from Moscow on October 12, 1944 (ibid., pp. 233-34):

"The system of percentage is not intended to prescribe the numbers sitting on commissions for the different Balkan countries, but rather to express the interest and sentiment with which the British and Soviet Governments approach the problems of these countries, and so that they might reveal their minds to each other in some way that could be comprehended. It is not intended to be more than a guide, and of course in no way commits the United States, nor does it attempt to set up a rigid system of spheres of interest. It may however help the United States to see how their two principal Allies feel about these regions when the picture is presented as a whole.

"Thus it is seen that quite naturally Soviet Russia has vital interests in the countries bordering on the Black Sea, by one of whom, Rumania, she has been most wantonly attacked with twenty-six divisions, and with the other of whom, Bulgaria, she has ancient ties. Great Britain feels it right to show particular respect to Russian views about these two countries, and to the Soviet desire to take the lead in a practical way in guiding them in the name of the common cause.

145

"Similarly Great Britain has a long tradition of friendship with Greece, and a direct interest as a Mediterranean Power in her future. In this war Great Britain lost 30,000 men in trying to resist the German-Italian invasion of Greece, and wishes to play a leading part in guiding Greece out of her present troubles, maintaining that close agreement with the United States which has hitherto characterised Anglo-American policy in this quarter. Here it is understood that Great Britain will take the lead in a military sense and try to help the existing Royal Greek Government to establish itself in Athens upon as broad and united a basis as possible. Soviet Russia would be ready to concede this position and function to Great Britain in the same sort of way as Britain would recognise the intimate relationship between Russia and Rumania. This would prevent in Greece the growth of hostile factions waging civil war upon each other and involving the British and Russian Governments in vexatious arguments and conflict of policy.

"Coming to the case of Yugoslavia, the numerical symbol 50:50 is intended to be the foundation of joint action and an agreed policy between the two powers now closely involved, so as to favour the creation of a united Yugoslavia after all elements there have been joined together to the utmost in driving out the Nazi invaders. It is intended to prevent, for instance, armed strife between Croats and Slovenes on the one side and powerful and numerous elements in Serbia on the other, and also to produce a joint and friendly policy towards Marshal Tito, while ensuring that weapons furnished to him are used against the common Nazi foe rather than for internal purposes. Such a policy, pursued in common by Britain and Soviet Russia, without any thought of special advantages to themselves, would be of real benefit.

"As it is the Soviet armies which are obtaining control of Hungary, it would be natural that a major share of influence should rest with them, subject of course to agreement with Great Britain and probably the United States, who, though not actually operating in Hungary, must view it as a Central European and not a Balkan State."

33. Robert E. Sherwood, *Roosevelt and Hopkins* (New York: Harper, 1948), pp. 833-34; *Stalin Correspondence*, II, 162. Stalin replied: "I was somewhat puzzled by your message of October 5. I

146

had imagined that Mr. Churchill was coming to Moscow in keeping with an agreement reached with you at Quebec. It appears, however, that my supposition is at variance with reality." Ibid., II, 163.

34. Sherwood, p. 834.

35. Feis, p. 450.

36. Ibid., p. 451.

37. McNeill (p. 496) says "Stalin showed no hesitation in agreeing that the operation would be desirable." Feis (p. 445) says Stalin "encouraged" the idea of a British landing on the Istrian Peninsula "and thence across Northwest Yugoslavia and through the Alps; and on to Vienna, there to join up with Soviet forces coming from the east." Feis's account continues:

"Then during the formal military discussion on the 14th, Stalin and General Antonov repeated the suggestion. In accordance with the agreement which Stalin had reached with Tito Russian troops in Yugoslavia were not going to advance farther west than Belgrade; they were going to leave it to Tito's forces to clear the Germans out of the rest of the country. Stalin said he would be glad to see the British move north from Istria, go through the mountains, and join the Soviet columns which would be, he hoped, coming west from Hungary in the neighborhood of Vienna."

38. *Yalta Papers* (see chap. 1, note 1), pp. 494, 545.

39. Dedijer (p. 234) reports that during his talk with Stalin in late September, Tito had said that if the British landed in Yugoslavia, "we should offer determined resistance." Stalin had not replied. "Obviously this answer was not to his liking. Was he at the moment pondering over the arrangements he had made for a division of spheres of influence?"

Feis (p. 445) comments: "It is impossible to resist conjecture why, at this time, and for the first time, Stalin favored such a strategy. Was it only because he wanted this threat at the flank or rear of the German lines in the south, to be sure that they would not be able to shift forces to his central front or Hungary, where it was becoming apparent that the Germans were going to contest every mile? Or was he also displaying his sincere intention to conform to the chart of 'spheres of responsibility' which he and Churchill had marked out a few nights before. . . ? Or was he trying to embroil the British in a clash with Tito, who he knew had grown opposed to having them land in Yugoslavia?"

Wilmot offers another explanation. He says that in the autumn of 1944 the Soviet High Command "was extremely doubtful of its ability to continue the offensive through Poland. It was so concerned on this account that, when Churchill was in Moscow in October, Stalin had strongly advocated that the Allied Armies in Italy should cross the Adriatic and drive north through Yugoslavia in the direction of Vienna. Since Stalin had previously opposed every plan for Allied ground operations in the Balkans, this proposal can only have been dictated by the belief that the intervention of Anglo-American forces in Yugoslavia would tie down the German divisions which were being withdrawn from the Southern Balkans to Hungary, and might even attract reserves from Poland. Stalin would hardly have suggested this move unless he had believed that it would expedite his own advance to Vienna and Berlin." Chester Wilmot, *The Struggle for Europe* (London: Collins, 1952), p. 630.

40. McNeill, p. 496n. Cf. also note 29 to this chapter.

41. Churchill, *Triumph and Tragedy*, p. 289.

42. Ibid.

43. Ibid.

44. The Stettinius statement, dated December 5—the day when the insurrection broke out in Greece—was worded as follows: "The position of this Government has been consistently that the composition of the Italian Government is purely an Italian affair except in the case of appointments where important military factors are concerned. This Government has not in any way intimated to the Italian Government that there would be any opposition on its part to Count Sforza. Since Italy is an area of combined responsibility, we have reaffirmed to both the British and Italian Governments that we expect the Italians to work out their problems of government along democratic lines without influence from outside. This policy would apply to an even more pronounced degree with regard to governments of the United Nations in their liberated territories." Leland M. Goodrich and Marie J. Carroll, eds., *Documents on American Foreign Relations, 1944-1945* (Princeton, N. J.: Princeton University Press, 1947), II, 172. The last sentence clearly applied to Greece, and it especially rankled with Churchill.

45. Churchill, *Triumph and Tragedy*, pp. 298-99.

46. "When we recall what had happened to Poland, to Hungary, and Czechoslovakia in these later years," Churchill later wrote, "we may be grateful to Fortune for giving us at this critical moment the calm, united strength of determined leaders of all parties. . . . There was a strong current of vague opinion, and even passion. . . . Here again any Government which had rested on a less solid foundation than the National Coalition might well have been shaken to pieces." Ibid., p. 293.

With respect to the merits of his action, the former Prime Minister could not repress a feeling of satisfaction that they were subsequently acknowledged: "Now that the free world has learnt so much more than was then understood about the Communist movement in Greece and elsewhere, many readers will be astonished at the vehement attacks to which His Majesty's Government, and I in particular at its head, were subjected. The vast majority of the American press violently condemned our action, which they declared falsified the cause for which they had gone to war. If the editors of all these well-meaning organs will look back at what they wrote then and compare it with what they think now they will, I am sure, be surprised." Ibid., p. 292.

47. Ibid., p. 293.

48. *Yalta Papers*, p. 781.

49. Ibid., p. 849.

50. Ibid., p. 154.

51. The British position paper at Yalta made a distinction in this respect between Bulgaria and Hungary on the one hand, and Rumania on the other. *Yalta Papers*, p. 513-514. The American position paper, on the other hand, lumped Rumania, Bulgaria, and Hungary together. Ibid., p. 568.

52. Churchill, *Triumph and Tragedy*, p. 348.

53. *Yalta Papers*, p. 781.

54. Churchill, *Triumph and Tragedy*, p. 353.

55. *Yalta Papers*, p. 617.

56. *Stalin Correspondence*, I, 340. Churchill used this rather renunciatory statement as an introduction to his categorical rejection of "the Yugoslav model" as a precedent for Poland where in his view a much clearer agreement existed.

It is noteworthy that Churchill refers to his spheres-of-influence deal with Stalin in a letter dated April 28, 1945—in other words, two months after the Yalta Conference—as though it were still supposed to be in effect.

57. Feis, p. 628.

58. Royal Institute of International Affairs, *The Soviet-Yugoslav Dispute* (London, 1948), letter from the Central Committee of Communist Party of Soviet Union to Central Committee of Communist Party of Yugoslavia, dated May 4, 1948:

"In this respect, the speech by Comrade Tito in Ljubljana in May 1945 is very characteristic. He said: 'It is said that this war is a just war and we have considered it as such. However, we seek also a just end; we demand that every one shall be master in his own house; we do not want to pay for others; we do not want to be used as a bribe in international bargaining; we do not want to get involved in any policy of spheres of interest.' This was said in connection with the question of Trieste. As is well known, after a series of territorial concessions for the benefit of Yugoslavia, which the Soviet Union extracted from the Anglo-Americans, the latter, together with the French, rejected the Soviet proposal to hand Trieste over to Yugoslavia and occupied Trieste with their own forces, which were then in Italy. Since all other means were exhausted, the Soviet Union had only one other method left for gaining Trieste for Yugoslavia—to start war with the Anglo-Americans over Trieste and take it by force. The Yugoslav comrades could not fail to realize that after such a hard war the USSR could not enter another."

59. Churchill, *Triumph and Tragedy*, p. 560.

This was the second reference by Churchill to the spheres-of-influence deal (cf. note 56) after the Yalta Conference, where it was supposed to have been superseded, at least in the American view, by the Declaration of Liberated Europe. Cf. also chap. 7, Question 56.

60. Historians have been puzzled by the presence of a few anti-Communists in the Groza government that was installed through Russian intervention. "One of them, Gheorghe Tatarescu, had as Prime Minister in 1936 sentenced Anna Pauker, a leading Communist, to jail. Their inclusion can best be explained as a pious gesture to honour the . . . percentage figure which Stalin and Churchill had fixed in October in Moscow." McNeill, p. 575n.

A specialist on Rumanian affairs wrote in 1951: "Certain events in 1945 are rather difficult to explain on the premises of a fixed intention to sovietize eastern Europe. Why was Hungary permitted to have free elections in 1945, elections which brought in an anti-Communist majority? Even in Rumania, the Soviet presentation to King Michael of its highest award, the Order of Victory, would seem an unnecessarily extravagant gesture if he was to be dethroned at an early date. The inclusion in the Groza Government of such a questionable person as Tatarescu, who was not really needed for his technical competence, whom the local Rumanian Communists regarded with great distaste, and whose presence certainly did not greatly reassure business circles, is perhaps best, if rather weirdly, explained by the Soviet determination to have a 'bourgeois' politician in the new coalition." Henry L. Roberts, *Rumania* (New Haven: Yale University Press, 1951), p. 271.

61. Feis, p. 452.

62. Royal Institute of International Affairs, *The Realignment of Europe*, edited by Arnold Toynbee (London: Oxford University Press, 1955), p. 318.

63. Ibid., pp. 320-21.

64. Ibid., p. 322. The November 4, 1945 election is termed "probably the freest general election ever held in the history of Hungary."

That the outcome was not an accident is suggested by the fact that contrary to obvious Soviet expectations, equally free elections in Budapest during the summer of 1945 had yielded a Smallholder majority; and that anti-Communist agrarian party was known to be stronger in the countryside than in the capital.

65. *Documents on American Foreign Relations, 1943-1944* (Boston: World Peace Foundation, 1945), pp. 642-44.

66. The Communists had minority representations in coalition governments at that time in France, Italy, Belgium, Luxembourg, Norway, and Denmark. In all of those countries the Communists were later evicted from the government when they resorted to subversion and violence. *note bias here*

67. *The Realignment of Europe*, p. 333.

68. *Stalin Correspondence*, II, 202.

69. Ibid., II, 239.

70. Ibid., II, 242.

71. *Potsdam Papers* (see chap. 2, note 1), I, 258-59.

72. Ibid., II, 644.

73. Churchill, *Triumph and Tragedy*, p. 636.

74. *Potsdam Papers*, II, 1044.

75. Ibid., II, 150-51.

76. Byrnes, p. 73.

77. Philip E. Mosely, *Face to Face with Russia* (New York: Foreign Policy Association "Headline Series" No. 70, 1948), p. 23. Also, *The Kremlin in World Politics* (New York: Vintage Books, 1960), p. 214. The quoted sentence does not appear in the official documentation of the Potsdam Conference. Professor Mosely, who speaks fluent Russian, was a member of the U.S. Delegation to that conference, and he told the author that he had himself overheard Stalin utter it.

78. *Potsdam Papers*, II, 525.

6

Gifts, Loans, and Disappointments

On January 3, 1945 Foreign Minister Molotov handed Ambassador Harriman an *aide-mémoire* proposing that the United States grant Russia a $6,000,000,000 credit for postwar reconstruction, at 2¼ per cent interest.[1] Our ambassador commented:

> Molotov made it very plain that the Soviet Government placed high importance on a large postwar credit as a basis for the development of "Soviet-American relations." . . . It is, of course, my very strong and earnest opinion that the question of the credit should be tied into our overall diplomatic relations with the Soviet Union and at the appropriate time the Russians should be given to understand that our willingness to cooperate wholeheartedly with them in their vast reconstruction problems will depend upon their behavior in international matters. I feel, too, that the eventual Lend-Lease settlement should also be borne in mind in this connection.[2]

The ambassador thought that the matter of a postwar credit was likely to come up at the next high-level meeting between

153

Roosevelt and Stalin.[3] However, it was not raised by the Russians at Yalta; nor did the United States use the Russian eagerness for aid to improve its bargaining position at the Crimea Conference.[4]

The published documentation on this aspect of American-Soviet relations during the closing phase of the war is still incomplete. But some indications can be gleaned from sources now publicly available, notably from the Yalta Papers. In that volume there is, for instance, a memorandum from President Roosevelt to the Secretary of State which contains this interesting passage in connection with the problem of the postwar treatment of German industry: "In regard to the Soviet government, it is true that we have no idea as yet what they have in mind, but we have to remember that in their occupied territory they will do more or less what they wish. We cannot afford to get into a position of merely recording protests on our part unless there is some chance of some of the protests being heeded. I do not intend by this to break off or delay negotiations with the Soviet government over lend-lease either on the contract basis or on the proposed Fourth Protocol basis. . . ."[5] The question of what happened to the Soviet application for a credit is indeed so interlocked with the record of the last phase of Lend-Lease and notably with the so-called Fourth Protocol, and also with the question of German reparations, that that background must first be summarized.

Hitler launched the German invasion of the Soviet Union on June 21, 1941. One month later, on July 21, President Roosevelt ordered "immediate and substantial shipments of assistance to the Union of Soviet Socialist Republics." These initial shipments were not gifts but were financed by "advances" from the U.S. Treasury against future Soviet deliveries of gold and strategic materials. In September, the Russian ambassador to the United

States initiated negotiations for military assistance on a repayable credit basis. During the same month, after Hopkins had conferred with Stalin in Moscow and had reported his conviction that Russia would be able to offer prolonged resistance to the invader, a joint British-American mission under Lord Beaverbrook and Ambassador Harriman was dispatched to Moscow to discuss a large military aid program. Meanwhile, President Roosevelt, mindful of possible Catholic opposition to American aid to the Soviet Union, had dispatched Myron C. Taylor, his special ambassador to Pope Pius XII, to Rome to obtain Vatican support for such an aid program.

Myron Taylor's mission to Rome, as reported by Robert Sherwood, was completed at the time when Harriman's mission to Moscow was starting. Taylor "made a supremely tactful and legitimate presentation of the President's case at the Vatican, where he met with a most sympathetic reception. While the results of this mission were given no great amount of publicity, they were reflected in the attitude of the Catholic hierarchy in the United States and no serious issue was raised"[6] when Russia in November 1941 was declared eligible for Lend-Lease assistance. Even so, however, the terms offered by Roosevelt to Stalin on October 30—which the Soviet dictator immediately accepted—did not yet involve the full Lend-Lease treatment. They provided for supplies up to $1 billion in value, to be repaid without interest over a period of ten years starting five years after the war. No such explicit arrangements for repayment of Lend-Lease had been made with Great Britain or other recipients.

Another important difference between Lend-Lease aid to Russia and Lend-Lease to Great Britain lay in the manner in which the items and quantities were determined. In the case of Britain, the United States received and discussed with its ally all information relevant to particular requests such as Britain's own productive capacity, inventories, and the use to which the items were to be put. This resulted in a close intertwining of the American and British economies, paralleling the joint U. S.-British formulation of war plans. No such relationship existed with Russia, which throughout the war regarded its Western allies with utmost suspicion. Were they not, according to the Communist view of the world, basically hostile, capitalist states just like Hitler's Germany? Had they not, in the Communist perspective, tried to direct Nazi expansionism to the East, and did they not hope that Germany and Russia would mutually exhaust each other so that the West could emerge victorious without suffering terrible losses such as Russia was enduring?

To the Russians, the acid test of Western intentions was the establishment of a second front on the continent, and Stalin did not cease to clamor for such a landing that would divert a substantial number of German divisions from the eastern front. As is known, Roosevelt authorized Molotov in May 1942 to inform Stalin that he "expected" that a second front would be created that very year;[7] Churchill persuaded the President to substitute a landing in North Africa for a contemplated diversionary action in France;[8] and Stalin subsequently claimed most vehemently that he had been deceived.[9] (This disagreement became accentuated when the planned major cross-Channel invasion was postponed from 1943 to 1944.) Throughout the war Stalin suspected, or pretended to suspect, that the Western Allies were about to make a separate peace with Germany; and on more than one occasion, especially in 1942, the Western Allies suspected that Russian resistance to the German onslaught might collapse completely—and had not Stalin made a sudden and unexpected deal with Hitler once before?

In any event, the programming of Lend-Lease for Russia was devoid of any of the spirit of cordiality and comradeship which characterized the aid discussions between the United States and Great Britain. The Russians would state their requirements but refuse to explain them or to give any information on the use to which the particular items would be put or what their own production of them was; they rigidly insisted on their own specifications even when this entailed delays and extra costs that must have been harmful to their own purposes; and they refused to permit the kind of inspection of end-item use that was customary as well as helpful elsewhere. Intelligent planning of priorities and assistance in the most efficient use of the material furnished were thus made impossible. General Deane, the head of the wartime U. S. Military Mission to the U. S. S. R., has testified vividly in his book, *Strange Alliance,* to the shortsightedness of the Soviet policy of secretiveness, which prevented American assistance from being as useful as it might have been.[10] At the same time, he attributed Russian failure to substantiate requests to the absence of records comparable to those in use by the Western Allies.[11]

By the middle of 1942, aid to Russia was placed on the same basis as aid to Great Britain in so far as the absence of any quantitative limitation or specific provision for repayment was concerned. The so-called Master Agreement with the Soviet Union stated that the President, pursuant to the Act of Congress of March 11, 1941, had determined the defense of the Soviet Union to be "vital to the defense of the United States" and that the determination of final terms and conditions of extending such aid should be deferred until later. In the preamble, the two governments also declared that they were cooperating in "laying the basis of a just and enduring world peace securing order under law" and referred to their allegiance to the principles embodied in the Atlantic Charter. Under Article III the Soviet government promised not to transfer Lend-Lease materials to other countries, and under Article VII the Soviets, like other recipients, subscribed to American trade policies, notably "the elimination of all forms of discriminatory treatment in international commerce, and . . . the reduction of tariffs and other trade barriers."[12]

This was the framework, but the actual items and quantities to be shipped were determined on an annual basis in the form of the so-called Supply Protocols, which also involved Great Britain and later Canada. The first such protocol had already been negotiated by Beaverbrook and Harriman in 1941. The second protocol was negotiated in 1942, and the third covered the period from mid-1943 to mid-1944. These negotiations were usually prolonged and sometimes acrimonious, but the needs of the eastern front were so urgent that Russia enjoyed an almost absolute priority even while the various Protocols were still under negotiation. (When Molotov was in Washington in May 1942 it was made clear to him that the strain on Allied shipping which this involved had inevitable repercussions on preparations for the second front.[13])

Several reasons have been adduced for the preferential treatment which Russia came to enjoy in the matter of Lend-Lease. First, there is the fact that Russia up to 1944 bore the brunt of the fight against Nazi Germany, suffering enormous losses in men, material, and productive power[14] at a time when the United States was husbanding its manpower and vastly increasing its own productive capacity. Second, the inability of the Western Allies to open a major second front, despite what the Russians could consider commitments to that effect, inevitably placed both the United States and Britain under some moral obligation to give maximum assistance at least in the material field. Thirdly, up to the turning point at Stalingrad in 1943 there was a real and perhaps justified fear that Russia might leave the war. Then later, as we have seen (Chapter 3), there was the need for coordination with the Russian offensives after the cross-Channel invasion was launched. Finally, as stated in Chapter 1, it was felt that Russian military assistance would be required in the Far East even after the defeat of Germany. The basic premise of all aid to Russia was, of course, that it made our own job of defeating the common enemy that much easier. As President Truman has stated: "Every soldier of Russia, England and Australia who had been equipped by Lend-Lease . . . reduced by that much the dangers that faced our young men in winning [the war]. We may never get the money back, but the lives we saved are right here in America."[15]

Total Lend-Lease shipments to the Soviet Union up to September 1945 amounted to $9.5 billion, or 29 per cent of shipments to all countries. In addition to bulk items such as explosives, petroleum products, food and steel, the shipments included 14,700 planes, 7,000 tanks, 52,000 jeeps, 376,000 trucks, 35,000 motorcycles, 2,000 locomotives, 11,000 freight cars, 3,800,000 tires, and over 15 million army boots—all of which clearly contributed to the fighting power and especially the mobility of the Russian armies.[16] According to one authority, American Lend-Lease trucks represented between 10 and 15 per cent of the trucks used on the entire Soviet front.[17] As General Deane has written, "At the Teheran Conference, Stalin told the President and the Prime Minister that his margin of superiority over the Germans was about sixty divisions which could be shifted rapidly from place to place on their extended front in order to provide massed power for a breakthrough in areas of their own choice. It is impossible to conceive how these divisions could have been moved rapidly, or even at all, had they not had American trucks to ride in, American shoes to march in, and American food to sustain them."[18] While this statement is perhaps somewhat exaggerated[19] and tends to over-look the improvement of Russia's own war production by the end of 1943, qualified observers agree that Lend-Lease may well have saved the Russian front from collapse during the early part of the war and obviously contributed appreciably to the later decisive Russian victories on the eastern front.

Approximately one-third of Lend-Lease exports to the U. S. S. R. consisted of industrial materials and products for the expansion and relocation of Soviet industry. Thus the United States furnished a half billion dollars' worth of machine tools as well as electrical furnaces and generators. In addition, entire factories, including a tire plant, aluminum rolling mill, pipe fabricating mills, and petroleum refining equipment were ex-ported to assist the U. S. S. R. in expanding its war production.[20] This was clearly in the American interest as long as the Russian armies were hard pressed and even later when they had started to strike their mortal blows against the retreating Germans. However, when the time came to discuss the Fourth Russian Supply Protocol, covering the fiscal year beginning July 1, 1944, it was found that the proportion of Russian requests for indus-trial equipment and machinery had gone up sharply, amounting to more than $1 billion in value.[21] The question arose whether such items could be delivered before the end of the war and whether, indeed, they were intended to assist Russia in prose-cuting the war or were intended for postwar reconstruction. There was strong sentiment in Congress, where the extension of the Lend-Lease Act was by no means assured,[22] that this instrument of wartime assistance must not be used for the pur-poses of postwar reconstruction. (In April 1945, when the Act came up for its last Congressional renewal, such a limitation was actually written into the law.)

Accordingly, the United States proposed in May 1944 to con-clude a supplementary agreement to the Fourth Protocol providing that any items that would be principally used for post-war reconstruction should be bought by the Russians on credit, at the rate of $2\frac{3}{8}$ per cent and repayable over a period of 25 to 30 years. But the Russians insisted on a rate of 2 per cent, and after prolonged haggling the matter remained in deadlock.[23] Apparently, the Russians calculated that at the end of the war in Europe the United States would find its economy underemployed and that pressure from industry and labor, particularly in factories that stood to gain from pending exports to Russia, would compel the U. S. government to extend credit on more favorable terms.[24] The absence of agreement on the interest rate delayed conclusion of the Fourth Protocol until April 17, 1945. Even then, however, the question of post-Lend-Lease shipments was left in suspense. The Fourth Protocol simply declared that items ineligible for Lend-Lease "may be purchased by the U. S. S. R. if it so elects,"[25] leaving the matter of credits and interest for further discussion. By that time, of course, the Russian request for a $6 billion credit at $2\frac{1}{4}$ per cent interest had been left unanswered for three and a half months.

Why did the United States government insist on concluding a supplementary Lend-Lease agreement with the Soviet Union to provide for payment of interest at the rate of $2\frac{3}{8}$ per cent on postwar shipments when it was confronted with a Russian request for a larger credit at the rate of $2\frac{1}{4}$ per cent? Should not the matter of interest have been negotiable? One answer, certainly, is that new Congressional authority was needed for the credit, whereas the pending orders could have been accommodated under authority of Article 3 (c) of the Lend-Lease Act. It also appears, however, that it had become a matter of principle for the American negotiators that the terms of $2\frac{3}{8}$ per cent, which had been declared to be "final," must not be modified.

When the Treasury Department, for instance, proposed that

the whole business of interest on industrial shipments under Lend-Lease be simply dropped, Assistant Secretary Clayton wrote to Secretary Stettinius: "We told the Soviet negotiators, in full good faith and with definite Treasury concurrence, that the last 3 (c) proposals [for a supplementary agreement] we made to them were our final offer, and that because of legal and other grounds, we could not grant them any better terms. If we should now make the proposals except for the exclusion of interest charges we could not help but give the impression to the Soviet authorities that what we said last summer was not true, and thus we might unwittingly kindle the fire of suspicion which they have had in the past as to our good faith."[26] The idea that an advantageous economic offer to the Soviet Union, at a time when that country was most anxious to secure help for its postwar reconstruction, might "kindle the fires of suspicion" seems strange in retrospect, but it was apparently held with sincerity and certainly with great tenacity by the U. S. negotiators.

Another reason adduced by Assistant Secretary Clayton in the same document related to the U. S. bargaining position on other matters: "By making this new proposal [to waive interest on shipments of industrial goods ordered under Lend-Lease but which were not for war purposes] we would definitely give the impression that we were most anxious, on almost any terms, to make available postwar goods to the Soviet Union. While we are naturally desirous to increase our trade with the Soviet Union to the maximum, and it is in our interest to do so, it would be tactically harmful to deepen the impression they already have that no matter what happens we are going to have to sell goods to the Soviet Union in order to keep our economy going."[27] The Clayton memorandum was written on January 20, 1945, two weeks before the Yalta Conference, where the United

States held a rather weak hand with respect to the issues involving Poland and the countries of southeastern Europe.

President Roosevelt's briefing book for the Yalta Conference included a paper on the "Russian Request for Financing of Acquisitions of Capital Equipment During and After the War" which discussed both the $6 billion credit request and the question of further industrial equipment under Lend-Lease. On the latter subject, the paper told the President that "the Department [of State] proposes to inform the Soviets through Ambassador Harriman that no long-range industrial equipment can be put into production until agreement be reached on the terms of the Lend-Lease 3-C agreement which has been under discussion since May 1944." With respect to the credit request, it was stated that "the Department believes the U. S. S. R. will contract only such credits as it can service. Current Russian gold production of about $200 million a year could service a $6 billion credit on the terms proposed by the Soviets; [or] about $3 billion on usual Export-Import Bank credits." The paper ended with the simple observation: "Postwar credits to the U. S. S. R. can serve as a useful instrument in our overall relations with the U. S. S. R."[28] In a telegram to Harriman a week before Yalta, the State Department reported to him that "the general matter of credits to Russia has been discussed with the President who has displayed a keen interest and believes that it should not be pressed further pending actual discussions between himself and Marshal Stalin and other Soviet officials."[29] However, the matter did not come up between Roosevelt and Stalin in any of their discussions.

The question of credits for Russian reconstruction was not unrelated to the problem of German reparations. Stalin insisted on such reparations at Yalta not only as a matter of just retribution but also to help bind up the terrible wounds that Russia had suffered at the hands of the Nazi invaders. He proposed that the total amount—to be paid in the form of industrial equipment, current production, and forced labor—be fixed at $20 billion, with half of it to go to the Soviet Union. Roosevelt did not oppose this proposal, although he was worried that excessive reparations would result in Germany becoming a burden on the world, and thus on the United States.[30] Churchill, on the other hand, was directly opposed to the fixing of such large reparations, as he foresaw that a starving Germany could become politically unmanageable and that, if Russia took out vast reparations, it might turn out that the West would have to put in compensating aid to the Germans. "The Prime Minister concluded," according to the Bohlen minutes, "that if you wished a horse to pull a wagon you would at least have to give it fodder."[31] Clearly, the question of reparations went to the heart of the kind of Germany there would be after the war, and whether there would be one occupied Germany or separate states in which each occupying power would do what it pleased.

This problem had been foreseen by American diplomats, who had tried to work out a policy for the postwar treatment of Germany in 1944. As reported by one of his former staff members, John G. Winant, the American Ambassador in London, had pointed out to Washington

> that the Russian need for material aid in repairing the vast destruction in the Soviet Union was bound to make the Soviet Government particularly eager to receive reparations deliveries from Germany on a large scale. Since the major part of German industry was located in the western zones, the Allies must try to work out, in advance, a reparations policy which would satisfy a part of the Soviet demands without involving an undue burden for the United

States. . . . He urged that the United States consider ways of helping the recovery of the Soviet economy, such assistance to be linked to the achievement of a satisfactory settlement of the problem of German reparations and of the most important political issues between the two governments.[32]

Winant's pleas, however, were ignored and as a result the United States at the time of Yalta had no clear policy either on reparations or on the question of postwar assistance to the Soviet Union.

In the United States Senate, the question of the $6 billion credit to the Soviet Union came up incidentally when the extension of the Lend-Lease Act was under discussion in the Foreign Relations Committee on March 28, 1945. Foreign Economic Administrator Leo T. Crowley explained the contemplated procedures pursuant to Article 3 (c) of the Lend-Lease Act for "orderly and efficient liquidation of war-supply contracts . . . through the purchase by foreign governments for cash or on credit, of such supplies as may not be produced or delivered in time to be of use in the war." Senator Wiley thereupon asked for elucidation of newspaper reports about a $6 billion credit to Russia under Lend-Lease. Oscar Cox, the deputy administrator, acknowledged that a request for such a credit had been received but said that the Russians had been told it could not be handled under Lend-Lease. Senator Vandenberg next inquired whether the Russians had asked for any Lend-Lease commitments for the period after July 1, 1945 and Cox replied that they had been asked to submit requests for a Fifth Protocol. "Do you expect [such a request]?" Senator Vandenberg asked. "Well," Cox replied, "that depends on what happens in Germany and what the Soviets do in the Japanese war." To which Senator

Vandenberg, who did not seem adverse to some bargaining, replied: "I hope it depends a lot on what happens at San Francisco, too."[33]

By the time the war in Europe ended, in May 1945, the situation with regard to Lend-Lease, reparations, and credits for Russia was as follows. As we have seen, a Fourth Lend-Lease Protocol, confined strictly to war-necessary items, had been signed in April, leaving in suspense the question of items in the "pipeline" which Russia would have to purchase, with the matter of interest rates still in deadlock. The size of reparations to be paid by Germany had not been settled by the Yalta Conference but had been referred to an inter-Allied commission set up in Moscow.[34] That Commission had produced no agreement —in fact, it produced angry acrimony. The Russians claimed that they had been let down by the United States because Roosevelt at Yalta had agreed to the $20 billion figure "as a basis of discussion" whereas the American representatives in Moscow sided with the British in favor of lesser amounts.[35] As for the Russian request for a $6 billion credit, available evidence suggests that the question became tangled up in a legal argument in Washington whether the Export-Import Bank could extend a loan to Russia as long as the Soviet government repudiated the debts contracted in the United States by the Kerensky government during World War I.[36]

Clearly, the United States had lost interest in the idea of a credit for Russian reconstruction in view of all the disagreements with Russia that had arisen since Yalta. The Forrestal Diaries include a message from Ambassador Harriman dated April 11, 1945, in which he had questioned the desirability of giving preferential treatment to Russia in postwar trade and had stated: "Our experience has incontrovertibly proved that it is not possible to bank general good will in Moscow, and I agree with the Department that we should retain current control of these credits in order to be in a position to protect American vital interests in the formulative period immediately following the war."[37] This was one day before the death of President Roosevelt. As we have seen (Chapter 4), when Truman had his angry interview with Molotov with regard to Poland less than two weeks later, the new President only hinted that Russia could expect no postwar assistance from the United States if it did not satisfy American public and Congressional opinion. As far as can be determined from published records, the United States did not make any proposals or counterproposals to the Russian request for a credit until the matter was revived in a different form in 1946 after another Russian request for a loan (made in August 1945) was discovered, having been lost for six months.[38]

As soon as the war in Europe was over, the United States government cut off all Lend-Lease shipments and even ordered some ships en route to Russia and other European nations to turn around and return to American ports for unloading. This produced an outcry, especially from Great Britain, which had been led to believe that Lend-Lease shipments would continue at a rate of approximately $2¼ billion after V-E Day.[39] In Russia, as we have seen from Stalin's complaint to Hopkins (Chapter 2), it was regarded as a hostile blow to bend the Soviet government to the American will on other issues. However, the sudden cessation of Lend-Lease aid was technically in keeping with the letter of the Lend-Lease Act, which, as amended in April 1945, precluded any shipments for postwar relief, rehabilitation, or reconstruction. On the other hand, as Great Britain was still in the war against Japan and as Russia had undertaken to join that war within three months of the end of the war in Europe, the abrupt cessation was unnecessary and,

167

as recognized by President Truman himself, unwise; and he rescinded the order.

President Truman has written frankly about this episode that it taught him a lesson early in his administration—"that I must always know what is in the document I sign. . . . If I had read the order, as I should have, the incident would not have occurred."[40] The document had been submitted to him by the Foreign Economic Administrator and the Acting Secretary of State and he had been under the impression, Truman wrote, that it involved reduction, but not cessation, of American aid. However, the manner in which the order was executed was unfortunate.

> The sudden stoppage of Lend-Lease [Truman wrote] was clearly a case of policy-making on the part of Crowley and Grew. It was perfectly proper and right, of course, to plan for the eventual cutting off of Lend-Lease to Russia and other countries, but it should have been done on a gradual basis which would not have made it appear as if somebody had been deliberately snubbed. After all, we had extracted an agreement from the Russians at Yalta that they would be in the Japanese war three months after the Germans folded up. We were eager for the Russians to get into the war with Japan. . . . With this situation in mind, I clarified the government's attitude.[41]

In a press and radio conference on May 23, the President declared that the order behind Crowley's action was intended to be not a cancellation of shipments but a gradual readjustment to conditions following the collapse of Germany. He also made it clear that all allocations provided for by treaty or protocol would be delivered and that every American commitment would be fulfilled.

This is what Hopkins explained to Stalin in their conversation in Moscow on May 27, 1945. Neither the question of a credit nor the disposition of pending shipments under the abortive 3(c) agreement were discussed on that occasion. The latter subject was subsequently negotiated between the U.S. and Soviet governments and an agreement ("Disposition of Lend-Lease Supplies in Inventory or Procurement in the United States") was concluded in the fall of 1945, providing that "interest on the unpaid balance of the total amount . . . shall be paid by the Government of the Union of Soviet Socialist Republics at a fixed rate of 2⅜ percent per annum"[42]—the rate on which the United States had insisted for one and one-half years. However, three-quarters of the approximately $1 billion in postwar orders which the Russians had tried to include in the Lend-Lease program had never been put into production. As one historian put it: trying to drive a shrewd bargain, the Russians had overreached themselves.[43] At the same time, while America's economic power played such an important role in the wartime military relations with the Soviet Union, it played no role at all in the attempts to work out with Russia a viable and honorable peace.

NOTES

1. *Yalta Papers* (see chap. 1, note 1), pp. 310-11. The Soviet request was couched in terms that made it appear to conform to American as well as Russian wishes: "Having in mind the repeated statements of American public figures concerning the desirability of receiving extensive large Soviet orders for the postwar and transition period, the Soviet Government considers it possible to place orders on the basis of long term credits to the amount of six billion

dollars. Such orders would be for manufactured goods (oil pipes, rails, railroad cars, locomotives and other products) and industrial equipment. . . . The United States Government should grant to the Soviet Union a discount of 20% off the government contracts with firms, of all orders placed before the end of the war and falling under this credit. Prices for orders placed after the end of the war should be left to agreement between the American firms in question and Soviet representatives."

2. Ibid., p. 313. To Molotov, Harriman said, "speaking entirely personally, that I thought the moment entirely favorable for arriving at a final agreement about the Lend Lease orders for the war period and for the opening of preliminary discussions on the question of credits after the war." (Ibid., p. 311.)

3. Ibid.

4. There was one casual reference to the loan request at the luncheon meeting of Foreign Ministers at Yalta on February 5, 1945. According to the Page Minutes (ibid., p. 610), "Mr. Molotov indicated that the Soviet Government expected to receive reparations from Germany in kind and hoped that the United States would furnish the Soviet Union with long term credits. Mr. Stettinius stated that his Government had studied this question and that he personally was ready to discuss it at any time with Mr. Molotov." The matter was not brought up again by either side.

5. Ibid., p. 155. The memorandum was dated September 29, 1944, or three months prior to the Russian loan application. It related, of course, not to the question of offering credits to the Russians but rather to the need for a policy on German industry which would have some appeal to the Russians. The reference to Lend-Lease, however, can be taken as an indication that Roosevelt felt that a punitive policy would be as unlikely to achieve results as "a position of merely recording protests." Secretary of the Treasury Morgenthau in a memorandum to President Roosevelt dated January 1, 1945, or three days before news of the Russian loan application was received, recommended "a plan for comprehensive aid to Russia during her reconstruction period." He said that Harriman had expressed great interest and would like to see the plan advanced. He stated, "I am convinced that if we were to come forward now and present to the

Russians a concrete plan to aid them in the reconstruction period it would contribute a great deal towards ironing out many of the difficulties we have been having with respect to their problems and policies." (Ibid., pp. 309-10.) Morgenthau envisaged credits in the amount of $10 billion (ibid., p. 315.)

6. Robert E. Sherwood, *Roosevelt and Hopkins* (New York: Harper, 1948), pp. 384 and 398.

7. Ibid., p. 563.

8. Churchill was considerably less categorical in giving assurances regarding a cross-Channel invasion in 1942. Churchill, *The Hinge of Fate* (see chap. 3, note 5), p. 342. For his arguments against an invasion of the Continent in 1942, which he advanced in discussions with the United States, cf. ibid., pp. 381-82.

9. Ibid., p. 270.

10. John R. Deane, *Strange Alliance* (New York: Viking, 1947), p. 99.

11. Ibid., p. 98. "It always seemed to me," Deane wrote, "that Mikoyan and his crowd, despite their shrewdness as negotiators, were extremely stupid in not being more cooperative with American representatives in Moscow. I believe that they were incapable of producing facts and figures that would justify any of their requests, because their administrative machinery was not geared to do so. No doubt they conserved considerable manpower by refusing to maintain the statistical records to which we devoted so much time and energy. Nor was careful accounting as essential to them as it was to us. They had only a single front to supply, whereas we had to assess carefully not only the needs of many fronts, but those of many countries. Rather than admit that he could not support his request with facts and figures, Mikoyan took the stand that he need not support them at all. In many cases Averell [Harriman], Sid [Spalding], and I would have been prepared to support the Soviet wishes had they been based on nothing more than a sob story, but even this was not forthcoming—only the haughty statement that 'the Soviet Union requests 50,000 tons of alcohol; therefore she needs it.' "

12. Soviet Master Agreement, Article VII, in *Eighth Quarterly Report to Congress on Lend-Lease Operations,* 78th Congress, 1st Session, House Document No. 129. An identical passage was found

in the British Master Agreement, but it was accepted by the British cabinet only on the understanding that the United Kingdom was not being asked to give up the system of imperial preference in order to obtain Lend-Lease aid. Roosevelt confirmed this understanding in a message to Churchill. (Sherwood, p. 507.)

13. Ibid., p. 574.

14. By November 1941 Russian gross industrial production was less than half what it had been in June 1941. N. A. Voznesensky, *The Economy of the USSR During World War II* (Washington: Public Affairs Press, 1948), p. 24.

15. Harry S. Truman, *Memoirs* (Garden City, N.Y.: Doubleday, 1955), p. 234. Cf. also note 41 to chapter 3, above, on Hull's views.

16. *Twenty-first Report to Congress on Lend-Lease Operations,* for the Period Ended September 30, 1945, p. 25.

17. Ibid.

18. Deane, p. 87.

19. The *Tehran Papers* (see chap. 3, note 30), pp. 490, 500, show that Stalin in the discussion of the military situation referred to his 60-division superiority, but there is no evidence that he said at that time that his troops could be shifted "rapidly" from place to place. On the other hand, Russian superior mobility was clearly a factor in the breakthroughs during the next following year, when German mobility had significantly declined, partly as a result of the western bombing offensive.

20. *Twenty-first Report on Lend Lease Operations,* p. 25.

21. Deane, p. 92.

22. One month before he became President, Harry Truman cast the deciding vote in the extension of the Lend-Lease Act. Truman *Memoirs,* I, 46.

23. Deane, pp. 92-93.

24. Corroboration of this view—that the Russians also expected to obtain shipments remaining from the Lend-Lease program at more favorable prices after the war—is found in the Soviet note of January 3, 1945, where it suggests a "20% discount off the government contracts with firms, of all orders placed before the end of the war and falling under this credit". Cf. above, note 1 to this chapter.

25. *Russian Supply Protocols,* Department of State publication 2759, p. 112.

26. *Yalta Papers,* p. 315.

27. Ibid., p. 318.

28. Ibid., p. 324.

29. Ibid., p. 323.

30. Ibid., pp. 621-22.

31. Ibid., p. 621.

32. Philip E. Mosely, *The Kremlin and World Politics* (New York: Vintage Books, 1960), pp. 176-77.

33. *Hearings Before the Committee on Foreign Relations,* U.S. Senate, 79th Congress, on H. R. 2013, March 28, 1945, pp. 9, 22, and 24.

34. *Yalta Papers,* p. 971.

35. Albert Z. Carr, *Truman, Stalin and Peace* (Garden City, N.Y.: Doubleday, 1950), p. 41. "Although afterward the Russians never ceased to demand that we make good what they called 'Roosevelt's promise' of ten billion of reparations, they certainly sensed at Yalta that there was not much hope for their plan to help revive the Soviet economy at the expense of Germany."

Carr considers that "the question of German reparations may well have been construed by Moscow as a final test of fundamental attitudes in Washington and London. . . . It seems altogether probable that these two matters, an American credit and German reparations, were closely linked in Soviet political thinking, for our attitude toward both questions profoundly affected the rate of Russia's postwar recovery." (Ibid.)

36. The *New York Times* reported that "no answer can be given by the United States to Russia at the present time for two reasons: The Export-Import Bank is limited to loans totalling $700 million, a considerable part of which is already obligated, and again under the terms of the legislation establishing the Bank it is not permissible to lend money to any government which was in default of former payment in April of 1934. There are differences within the Federal Government itself as to whether Russia was in default at that time, some officials arguing that the Soviet Government was obligated to assume the debts acquired in this country by the Kerensky Government and others maintaining that, under law, it wasn't." (January 26, 1945.)

37. *The Forrestal Diaries* (New York: Viking, 1951), p. 41.

38. Ambassador Walter Bedell Smith, in his book, *My Three Years in Moscow* (Philadelphia: Lippincott, 1950), p. 222, recalled that when Secretary of State Marshall saw Stalin on April 15, 1947 and complained about Russian slowness in replying to American communications, Stalin referred to the fate of the January 1945 request for a loan as follows:

" 'With regard to Soviet delays in replying to your representations on various subjects', he [Stalin] continued, 'I would remind Mr. Marshall that more than two years ago the Soviet Government made a request of the United States for a financial credit, and that to date no reply or acknowledgment has ever been received.'

"At this point, I thought it proper to pass to Mr. Molotov a note to remind him that when I came to Moscow I had brought the reply to this request. Mr. Molotov whispered this to Stalin, and received in return a distinct 'family' look. The Generalissimo then corrected his statement accordingly, but remarked that even a year's delay in replying seemed to him to be somewhat excessive."

According to the *New York Times* of March 2, 1946, a Russian request for a $1 billion credit was misplaced "because of errors in transferring the records of the FEA [Foreign Economic Administration] to the custody of the State Department last September" and "turned up only last week." The same paper, on March 3, recalled that "at one point President Truman denied at a press conference, in reply to a question, that the Russians had applied for any credits."

39. *Hearings* on H. R. 2013, March 28, 1945, p. 22.

40. Truman *Memoirs*, p. 228.

41. Ibid., pp. 228-29.

42. Department of State, *Treaties and Other International Acts, Series 3662*, Agreement Between the United States of America and the Union of Soviet Socialist Republics, October 15, 1945, Schedule II, paragraph E.

43. Royal Institute of International Affairs, *America, Britain and Russia—Their Cooperation and Conflict, 1941-1946*, by William Hardy McNeill (London: Oxford University Press, 1953), p. 515.

7

Questions and Answers

QUESTION 1: When the United States and Great Britain defined their war aims in the Atlantic Charter, was the United States at war? ANSWER: No. The Atlantic Charter was signed on August 14, 1941. The United States entered the war on December 7, 1941.

QUESTION 2: Was Russia, which was at war at the time, consulted about this definition of aims? ANSWER: No, Russia was not consulted when the Atlantic Charter was drafted, but it was subsequently asked to adhere.

QUESTION 3: What was the British understanding of the applicability of the Atlantic Charter? ANSWER: Churchill specifically declared that it did not apply to the British Empire. (See note on page x.)

QUESTION 4: When the Soviet Union subscribed to the Atlantic Charter, did it do so without reservation? ANSWER: No. The Soviets entered a reservation that "the practical application of these principles" should be adapted to the "circumstances,

175

needs, and historic peculiarities of particular countries." (See page x.)

QUESTION 5: Did this qualified acceptance of the Atlantic Charter mean that they foreswore the idea of spheres of influence in Europe? ANSWER: No. From the beginning the Russians attempted to get acknowledgment of a privileged position in eastern Europe, for which they were willing in return to acknowledge a privileged British position in western Europe.

QUESTION 6: Was Britain prepared to accept the initial Soviet war aims to the effect that Russia should regain all the territories it had gained as a result of the Nazi-Soviet Pact of 1939? ANSWER: Yes. Churchill considered that this "was the basis on which Russia acceded to the [Atlantic] Charter." (See Chapter 3, note 11.)

QUESTION 7: Why did Britain not give these assurances to the Soviet Union? ANSWER: Because of U. S. objections to any territorial settlement prior to the peace conference. Also, in the U. S. view, such a settlement would not have been in accordance with point two of the Atlantic Charter.

QUESTION 8: After Russia was attacked by Germany in 1941, was the Polish government-in-exile prepared to enter into friendly relations with the Soviet Union? ANSWER: Yes, but only on condition that Russia renounce her war aims and reestablish the Polish state in its pre-1939 boundaries. (See page 41.)

QUESTION 9: Did Russia show any willingness to consider these terms for cooperation with the Polish government-in-exile? ANSWER: No, not even at a time when the Russians were most sorely beset by the invading German armies.

QUESTION 10: What brought about the break between the Soviet Union and the Polish government-in-exile? ANSWER: The discovery by the Germans of the bodies of murdered Polish of-

176

ficers, which led the Poles in London to call for an investigation by the International Red Cross.

QUESTION 11: What was Churchill's reaction to the Polish call for a Red Cross investigation? ANSWER: He thought it a mistake. He said to the premier of the Polish exile government: "If they are dead nothing you can do will bring them back." (Chapter 3, note 18.)

QUESTION 12: What was the opinion of George Kennan on the action of the Polish government-in-exile which brought the break with the Soviet Union? ANSWER: "It is hard, in retrospect, to see how the Poles could have done less."

QUESTION 13: On the basis of all the evidence that has become available since that time, does it look as if the story about the Katyn massacre was a Nazi provocation? ANSWER: The weight of evidence is that the Polish officers in question were killed by the Russians, but there is reason to believe that this was the result of a mistake. (See page 45.) *very poor, flimsy evidence*

QUESTION 14: What, subsequently, was the principal obstacle to reestablishment of relations between the Soviet Union and the Polish government-in-exile? ANSWER: The question of Poland's eastern border. Neither the Soviets nor the Polish exiles were willing to accept, or even discuss, the view of the other side on this question.

QUESTION 15: What was the position of the London Poles with respect to the impending entry into Poland of Russian troops as they were driving the Germans back toward Germany? ANSWER: They threatened to call upon the Polish underground to resist the Russians if they advanced into Poland without a prior agreement with the government-in-exile.

QUESTION 16: What did Russia next propose with respect to the postwar frontiers of Poland? ANSWER: At the Tehran Conference, Stalin proposed that in return for acceptance of the eastern borders of 1939, Poland should be compensated by getting German territory up to the Oder River.

QUESTION 17: What was the American reaction to this proposal? ANSWER: There was no official American reaction to this proposal at the Conference. But Roosevelt privately explained to Stalin that he was worried about the reaction of Americans of Polish extraction.

QUESTION 18: What was the British reaction to this proposal? ANSWER: Churchill agreed with it in general terms, subject to some modifications of Poland's eastern frontier in favor of Poland.

QUESTION 19: How did Churchill attempt to persuade the Polish exile government to accept this new territorial arrangement? ANSWER: He repeatedly urged it upon Mikolajczyk. He said that if the exiles did not act quickly, he "could not be responsible for anything that might take place."

QUESTION 20: By the time the Russians reached the old Polish frontier, would they have been satisfied with an agreement on the territorial question? ANSWER: No, by this time they had started to talk about the need for a "friendly" (i.e., Communist-dominated) Polish government. (See page 53.)

QUESTION 21: By the time the Russian forces were in territory which Russia itself recognized as Polish, what was the Russian position? ANSWER: It had hardened further. Now the Russians asked not only for acceptance of their territorial position, but they set up a puppet organization, the so-called Lublin Committee, which they said must furnish the majority of any Polish government.

QUESTION 22: Why did the U. S. government not take a vigorous and clear-cut position on these issues at that time? ANSWER: Because, as Roosevelt had stated, he was concerned about the Polish-American vote in the 1944 elections; and also, as Hull stated later, because the United States needed Russian military cooperation in view of the forthcoming invasion of western Europe.

QUESTION 23: Who were the leaders of the Polish uprising against the Germans in Warsaw, which the Russians refused to support? ANSWER: They were exponents of the government-in-exile.

QUESTION 24: What is McNeill's opinion about the failure to resolve the Polish question at that time? ANSWER: "The failure of Allied policy to achieve a peaceable settlement of the Polish problem in the first seven months of 1944 may well be considered the turning-point in the history of the Grand Alliance." (Chapter 3, note 42.)   *note – Korea flowing in*

QUESTION 25: Who was in control of Poland at the time of *3/44* the Yalta Conference? ANSWER: The Red Army had occupied almost all of prewar Poland.

QUESTION 26: What was agreed at Yalta with respect to Poland's frontiers? ANSWER: While the United States did not agree on the western frontiers, the eastern frontier was in effect settled substantially along the lines of the original Russian position.

QUESTION 27: What did the West get out of this belated acceptance of the Soviet position on its western border? ANSWER: Nothing. But some Western participants apparently thought that they had obtained Russian agreement to a democratic rump Poland.

QUESTION 28: How about the famous Declaration on Liberated Europe? Was this not a quid pro quo for acceptance of the Soviet border proposal? ANSWER: It was hardly discussed at Yalta and the operative clause was watered down by the Russians so that it provided only for "mutual consultation" instead of the "machinery for the carrying out of the joint responsi-

179

bilities" which the United States had proposed. (See Chapter 4, note 18.) However, the United States attached great imporance to the principles laid down in that document. (See also Questions 55 and 56.)

QUESTION 29: What was agreed at Yalta with respect to the Polish government? ANSWER: It was agreed that the existing (Communist) government would be "reorganized" into a new, fully representative government and that that government should be "pledged to the holding of free and unfettered elections."

QUESTION 30: What was the Russian interpretation of this agreement? ANSWER: It was that only Poles who had agreed to the Yalta territorial decisions could participate in the reorganized government, and that only a few non-Communist Poles could be included in the provisional government.

QUESTION 31: In the ensuing arguments between the Western Allies and Russia, what was the Western position? ANSWER: That the Yalta Agreement called for a completely new Polish government and that a veto on some prospective participants violated the very foundation of the Yalta Agreement.

QUESTION 32: What was Roosevelt's personal view about the position? ANSWER: He had doubts about it, at least on one occasion. As he wrote Churchill, he was aware that under the Yalta agreement "somewhat more emphasis" would be placed on the Lublin (Communist) Poles. (See page 90.)

QUESTION 33: Did the Polish exile leaders agree with the Western position on this matter? ANSWER: Not entirely. Some of them actually felt, like the Russians, that the Yalta Agreement had in effect conceded that the new Polish government would be dominated by the Communists. (See Chapter 4, note 29.)

QUESTION 34: What was President Truman's position on this matter? ANSWER: It was that the Russians were violating the

Yalta Agreement and that the agreement could not be interpreted as involving the establishment of a Communist-dominated provisional Polish government.

QUESTION 35: What was the Russian reaction to this position? ANSWER: It was that it amounted to "abrogation" of the Yalta decisions.

QUESTION 36: How did the Hopkins mission contribute to a solution of this issue? ANSWER: It opened the way for the eventual establishment of a Communist-dominated provisional Polish government. (See Chapter 4, note 41.)

QUESTION 37: Did the Russians live up to their obligation to cause "free and unfettered elections" to be held in Poland? ANSWER: No. Elections were held only in 1947, after the non-Communist parties had been thoroughly terrorized.

QUESTION 38: What was the American position on spheres of influence in Europe? ANSWER: The United States was strongly opposed to them. Secretary of State Hull stated that he felt that Russia's security could be better guaranteed by a "strong postwar peace organization." (See Chapter 5, note 3.)

QUESTION 39: What was the first country liberated or occupied by the Allies (then called United Nations) in the war? ANSWER: Italy, whose surrender was accepted "by authority of the Governments of the United States and Great Britain and in the interest of the United Nations."

QUESTION 40: What was the Russian position on their role in the political direction of the occupation of Italy? ANSWER: They wanted a full role in it.

QUESTION 41: What was the U. S.-British response to this? ANSWER: The request was very poorly received, and the Russians were excluded from the Control Commission. When an "Inter-Allied Advisory Council" was later established, it had no role in determining occupation policies.

QUESTION 42: Did this not imply that the Western Allies in

fact viewed the territories conquered or liberated by them as an exclusive sphere of influence? ANSWER: Yes, at least as far as the wartime period was concerned, but there is no evidence that this was ever explicitly stated as policy.

QUESTION 43: What was the reason for this Western position? ANSWER: The United States and Britain did not wish the Russians to have a role in the occupation of Italy because they were worried that the Russians would support the activities of the Italian Communists; and there is good evidence that that worry was justified.

QUESTION 44: When the United States and Britain later demanded a share in determining occupation policies in Rumania, what was the Russian reaction? ANSWER: The Russians refused, referring to Italy as a precedent.

QUESTION 45: What was the real Russian reason? ANSWER: There is no evidence for this, but quite probably they were afraid that the United States and Britain would support the activities of the anti-Communists.

QUESTION 46: What, then, was the difference between the situation in Italy and in Rumania? ANSWER: In Italy, the Western Allies were pretty sure that in free elections the anti-Communists, whom they favored, would win. In Rumania, the Russians had good reason to fear that in free elections the Communists, whom they favored, would lose.

QUESTION 47: How did the Russians in fact use their predominance in occupied Rumania? ANSWER: They forced a Communist-dominated government on King Michael.

QUESTION 48: When Churchill was prepared, early in 1944, to recognize Russian ("temporary") predominance in Rumania in return for their recognition of similar British predominance in Greece, what was the American reaction? ANSWER: The United States spiked the deal on the ground that it would conflict with the basic declarations of postwar aims and would create a dangerous precedent.

QUESTION 49: When Churchill finally in October 1944 made an agreement with Stalin that in effect established spheres of influence in the Balkans, what was the American reaction? ANSWER: The United States acquiesced in the deal but four months later, at Yalta, it was nullified by the Declaration on Liberated Europe which substituted broad general principles for the pragmatic and temporary arrangement between Churchill and Stalin.

QUESTION 50: What was the immediate effect of the spheres-of-influence arrangement on the British position in Greece? ANSWER: It was most favorable, and Churchill subsequently (at Yalta) expressed his thanks to Stalin for "not having taken too great an interest in Greek affairs."

QUESTION 51: What was the effect of the Churchill-Stalin agreement on the situation in Yugoslavia? ANSWER: Britain and Russia jointly tried to create a coalition government. Stalin encouraged Churchill to move British troops into northwestern Yugoslavia.

QUESTION 52: What was Tito's position with regard to a British military operation in Yugoslavia? ANSWER: He was violently opposed to it. This did not, however, prevent the Russians from reiterating their proposal three months later, at the Yalta Conference.

QUESTION 53: Did the Churchill-Stalin agreement in fact result in a 50:50 division of influence in Yugoslavia? ANSWER: It did not, and Churchill complained about this, albeit rather weakly.

QUESTION 54: What credence should be given to Stalin's statement at Yalta that he had little influence on Tito? ANSWER: From evidence that has become available after Yugoslavia defected from the Soviet bloc, it appears that Tito in any case strongly resented the Churchill-Stalin agreement.

QUESTION 55: Was the Declaration on Liberated Europe which was signed at Yalta put into effect by the Russians? ANSWER: No. The principles of joint assistance to the people of the European liberated states or former Axis satellites, especially as regards the formation of "broadly representative governments" and the facilitating of free elections, were largely ignored.

QUESTION 56: In the opinion of the signatories, did the Declaration on Liberated Europe extinguish the spheres-of-influence deal which Churchill and Stalin had concluded in October 1944? ANSWER: As far as the United States is concerned, the answer is clearly in the affirmative; but we cannot be sure that the Russians felt the same way. The anomalous situation in Hungary after Yalta suggests that the spirit of the October 1944 deal may have lingered on for quite some time.

QUESTION 57: In what respects was the situation in Hungary (where Churchill and Stalin had agreed on a 50:50 division of influence) "anomalous"? ANSWER: Hungary is the only Russian-occupied country where relatively free elections, resulting in a non-Communist majority, were permitted in 1945. (The Soviet-occupied zone of Austria was another such situation.)

QUESTION 58: But was not Hungary taken over by the Communists with Russian military support? ANSWER: Yes, but this took place only in 1947, long after the Cold War had begun. In 1945, the Russians had apparently not yet made up their mind on this matter. Perhaps they might then have been amenable to some bargaining, but this was never explored.

QUESTION 59: What did the United States have available for such bargaining? How about the threat of force? ANSWER: Roosevelt at Yalta said he did not believe American troops would stay in Europe much more than two years after the war.

QUESTION 60: What other bargaining counter might the United States have used in order to exercise a mitigating role at least in such countries as Hungary, Czechoslovakia, and Austria, where Russian predominance had not been accepted by Churchill? ANSWER: Credits, in which the Russians were very interested in view of the devastation they had suffered in the war.

QUESTION 61: Did the Russians have reason to expect that American goods would be available to them on favorable terms after the war? ANSWER: Yes. There was much talk about the expected great American postwar "surplus." The chairman of the U. S. War Production Board and the president of the U. S. Chamber of Commerce ventilated the idea of large postwar credits in their talks with Russian leaders.

QUESTION 62: What was the approximate value of the U. S. "Lend-Lease" aid to Russia during the war? ANSWER: Nine and one-half billion dollars.

QUESTION 63: How was this aid used as leverage during the delicate negotiations with the Russians at the end of the war? ANSWER: It was not used at all. The aid was suddenly cut off in a manner which President Truman (who later rescinded the order) described as one that "made it appear as if somebody had been deliberately snubbed."

QUESTION 64: During the period immediately prior to the Yalta Conference, did Russia apply for a loan for postwar reconstruction? ANSWER: Yes, on January 3, 1945, Russia formally asked for a six billion dollar loan at $2\frac{1}{4}$ per cent interest.

QUESTION 65: Is there evidence that Roosevelt intended to use economic aid as a diplomatic instrument in his negotiations with Stalin? ANSWER: Yes, but it is not conclusive. Apparently he intended to discuss the matter at Yalta. Also, there is a

185

memorandum in which Roosevelt noted that the Russians "in their occupied territories will do more or less what they wish" and went on to say that he did not intend to "break off or delay negotiations" over future Lend-Lease deliveries. (Chapter 6, notes 5 and 29.)

QUESTION 66: Was either the future of Lend-Lease or the Russian request for a six-billion-dollar credit actually used for bargaining purposes at the Yalta Conference? ANSWER: No. Neither of these two matters came up between Roosevelt and Stalin during any of their discussions at Yalta, where the greatest amount of time had to be devoted to Poland.

QUESTION 67: In what other way did the Russians attempt to lay their hands on substantial amounts of capital to help in their reconstruction? ANSWER: Through German reparations, which they wished to fix at $20 billion at Yalta, with half of that amount to go to the Soviet Union.

QUESTION 68: At that time, did the United States have a reparations policy? ANSWER: No. Roosevelt left the lead to Churchill, who opposed such large reparations; but in the end Roosevelt agreed to use the $20 billion figure "as a basis for discussion."

QUESTION 69: Was there contemporary diplomatic opinion that there must have been a link in the Russian mind between their request for exorbitant German reparations and their hope for an American credit? ANSWER: Ambassador Winant "urged at the time that the U. S. consider ways of helping the recovery of the Soviet economy, such assistance to be linked to the achievement of a satisfactory settlement of the problem of German reparations and of the most important political issues between the two Governments." (See page 164.)

QUESTION 70: What other opinion is there available on this

probable link? ANSWER: Carr has stated: "It seems altogether probable that these two matters, an American credit and German reparations, were closely linked in Soviet political thinking, for our attitude toward both questions profoundly affected the rate of Russia's postwar recovery." (Chapter 6, note 35.)

QUESTION 71: Could the Russian loan request have been handled under the heading of Lend-Lease? ANSWER: No, there was strong Congressional sentiment against the use of Lend-Lease for postwar assistance, and a limitation to that effect was actually written into the law in April, 1945. A majority in favor of renewal of the Lend-Lease Act was obtained in the Senate earlier in 1945 only when Vice President Truman broke a tie vote.

QUESTION 72: Why did negotiations for a "Supplementary Agreement" governing credit sales of Lend-Lease equipment to be used for postwar reconstruction fail to bring agreement in the early months of 1945? ANSWER: The Russians insisted on an interest rate of 2 per cent, whereas the U. S. negotiators would not budge from their position that it must be no less than $2\frac{3}{8}$ per cent.

QUESTION 73: What really lay behind that difference in interest rates? ANSWER: Differing views on tactics. The Russians apparently thought that the fear of postwar unemployment would cause the United States to yield. The American negotiators were apparently oblivious of the leverage that might be sought in noneconomic matters, and they only feared that the United States would seem overly eager for postwar trade if it acceded to the Russian terms. (Chapter 6, notes 26 and 27.)

QUESTION 74: What finally caused the Russian loan request to be lost in the Washington bureaucracy? ANSWER: The opinion of legal experts that a loan to Russia would contravene a law which ruled out loans to countries that had defaulted on earlier loans—and the Soviet Union had long ago repudiated the debts of the Kerensky government. (Chapter 6, note 26.)

QUESTION 75: What was the real reason for the failure of interest to develop in the U. S. government for some settlement that might include the loan sought by the Soviets? ANSWER: The growing disillusionment with Russia over the issue of Poland and the other east European occupied territories. Poland was the major issue between Russia and the West when Truman became President.

QUESTION 76: In the absence of any other means of satisfying the urgent Soviet need for capital assets to further their reconstruction, what was the consequence of Allied disagreements over German reparations? ANSWER: The partition of Germany, brought about—among other reasons—by the Soviet desire to plunder that country.

QUESTION 77: But was not the partition of Germany a cause of the Cold War? ANSWER: Under this analysis, it was not a cause but a consequence. By the time of Potsdam (July 1945), it was clear that the Western powers would not accept the de facto Russian sphere of influence in eastern Europe and that they had nothing to offer Russia to make it forgo the establishment of such a sphere also in central Europe.

QUESTION 78: When was the die then cast and the Cold War begun? ANSWER: In the period between Yalta and Potsdam, when the division of Europe was in effect determined by the relationship of military power as it existed at the time, and when the United States failed to throw into the balance its economic power, which was later to play such an important role in the conduct of the Cold War.

8

Comments in Retrospect

McGeorge Bundy:

It is now fashionable in this country to look back at Yalta as a time of wishful thinking, in which American statesmen were outsmarted by Stalin. Critics of Yalta have never shown that Mr. Roosevelt or Mr. Churchill granted anything that they were in a position to withhold (except perhaps the Kurile Islands). The object of the western statesmen at Yalta was to persuade Stalin that the common interest required genuine cooperation on the basis of self-restraint by the Great Powers. It seemed for a moment that he was persuaded. In the event, we have seen that he was not. Perhaps the western statesmen, and the peoples whom, in this, they truly represented, should not have believed peaceful cooperation between Russia and the rest of the world a practical possibilty, but it is hard to deny their central conviction: that such cooperation would have been to the great advantage of all concerned. In any event, they did in fact obtain agreements which, if kept, would have amounted to a pledge of lasting peace. . . .

The men in the Kremlin had three choices after Yalta. One was to accept its principles and to devote themselves to the construction of a sincere peace, based on mutual respect for vital interests, and self-restraint in other areas. The second was to pretend to accept the Yalta principles—in other words, to make an effort to conserve the advantages of the reservoir of good will—while continuing under the surface the great contest for the world ordained by Stalinist theory. It may be that Soviet leaders thought this was in fact the course they were following. But the course that seems most nearly to fit the actual record of Soviet behavior since Yalta is a third one—a policy characterized by an apparent decision to disregard as unimportant the good will of the non-Communist west and to proceed as energetically as possible to expand and consolidate Communist power.

Quoted, by permission, from "The Test of Yalta," *Foreign Affairs,* Vol. 27, No. 4 (July, 1949).

GENERAL PATRICK J. HURLEY:

America was in a position at Yalta to speak the only language the Communists understand, the language of power. The President of the United States at Yalta was in command of the greatest land, navy and air force ever assembled on earth. One quiet sentence to Marshal Stalin in that language could have indicated that America would require him to keep his solemn agreements. That one sentence would have prevented the conquest of all the Balkan states, the conquest of Poland, and the conquest of China. The sentence was not forthcoming. On the contrary, your diplomats and mine surrendered in secret every principle for which we said we were fighting. They talk about Stalin breaking his agreements, gentlemen. He never had to break one. We cowardly surrendered to him everything that he had signed and we did it in secret. President Roosevelt was already a sick man at Yalta.

Hearings before the Committee on Armed Services and the Committee on Foreign Relations, U.S. Senate, *To Conduct an Inquiry Into the Military Situation in the Far East and the Facts Surrounding the Relief of General of the Army Douglas MacArthur from His Assignment in that Area* (June, 1951), p. 2839.

PROFESSOR HANS J. MORGENTHAU:

The Yalta agreements in particular were an attempt, doomed to failure from the outset, to maintain a modicum of Western influence in the nations of Eastern Europe which the Red Army had conquered. That influence was to be maintained through the instrument of free, democratic elections. Yet in view of the fear and hatred with which most of Eastern Europe has traditionally reacted to the colossus from the East, free elections in Eastern Europe could be considered by the Soviet Union only as a weapon with which first to limit, and then to destroy, Soviet control. Thus it was utopian to expect that the Soviet Union would jeopardize its conquests in order to make good on a legal promise to a competitor who had lost his ability to enforce such a promise on the battlefields of the Second World War.

Quoted, by permission, from "The End of an Illusion," *Commentary*, November, 1961.

AMBASSADOR W. AVERELL HARRIMAN:

The most difficult question to answer is why Stalin took so many commitments which he subsequently failed to honor.

Beginnings of the Cold War

There can be no clear answer to this question. I believe that the Kremlin had two approaches to their post-war policies and in my many talks with Stalin I felt that he himself was of two minds. One approach emphasized reconstruction and development of Russia and the other external expansion.

On the one hand they were discussing a possible understanding with us which would lead to peaceful relations and result in increased trade and loans from the West for the reconstruction of the terrible devastation left in the wake of the war. If they had carried out this program they would have had to soft-pedal, for the time at least, the communist designs for world domination—much along the lines of the policies they had pursued between the two wars.

On the other hand, we had constant difficulties with them throughout the war and they treated us with great suspicion. Moreover, there were indications that they would take advantage of the Red Army occupation of neighboring countries to maintain control, and they were supporting Communist parties in other countries to be in a position to take control in the post-war turmoil.

The Kremlin chose the second course. It is my belief that Stalin was influenced by the hostile attitude of the peoples of Eastern Europe toward the Red Army and that he recognized that governments established by free elections would not be "friendly" to the Soviet Union. In addition, I believe he became increasingly aware of the great opportunities for Soviet expansion in the post-war economic chaos. After our rapid demobilization I do not think that he conceived that the United States would take the firm stand that we have taken in the past five years.

Hearings before the Committee on Armed Services and the Committee on Foreign Relations, U. S. Senate, *To Conduct an Inquiry Into the Military Situation in the Far East and the Facts Surrounding*

Comments in Retrospect

EDWARD R. STETTINIUS, JR., former Secretary of State:

From my close association with Franklin D. Roosevelt, I know that he was primarily motivated by the great ideal of friendly cooperation among nations. At the same time he had no illusions about the dangers and difficulties of dealing with the Soviet Union. He emphasized many times that we must keep trying with patience and determination to get the Russians to realize that it was in their own selfish interest to win the confidence of the other countries of the world. . . . It was essential that Prime Minister Churchill and President Roosevelt made an honest attempt at Yalta to work with the Russians. For the peace of the world, they had to make every effort to test the good faith of the Soviet Union. Until agreements were made and tested, the world could not clearly know of the difficulties of securing Russian compliance with agreements.

Quoted, by permission, from *Roosevelt and the Russians—The Yalta Conference* (New York: Doubleday, 1949), pp. 322 and 324.

PROFESSOR PHILIP E. MOSELY:

In hindsight, it is easy to say that the attempt [to cooperate with the Soviet Union] was hopeless and not worth making because the Soviet leadership would never abate its claims to reshape the world in its own image or forego any immediate and material advantage for the sake of retaining the good will of what it regarded as temporary allies. Still, it is to the credit of Western statesmen that they made many efforts to offer postwar cooperation among equals in the hope that Stalin would grant this breathing spell to the sorely tried people of the Soviet Union. To make the cooperation stick, much more should have been done to assure him of assistance in rebuilding the Soviet economy; as it turned out, Stalin and the Soviet people soon felt that their vast sacrifices were forgotten by less war-damaged allies as soon as the fighting was over. That and other policies would have required a much more integrated strategy than American policy-makers seemed capable of achieving during World War II.

Quoted, by permission, from *The Kremlin in World Politics* (New York: Vintage Books, 1960), pp. 155-56.

SENATOR ROBERT A. TAFT:

Power without foresight leads to disaster. Our international relations have been conducted with so little foresight since 1941 that six years after vast military victories in Europe and Asia we face a more dangerous threat than any that has menaced us before. Our soldiers, sailors, marines, and airmen have not failed us. Our political leaders have. By 1941 anyone who was not bamboozled by Soviet psychological warfare knew that the Soviet Government was a predatory totalitarian tyranny intent on establishing Communist dictatorship throughout the world. But our leaders failed to foresee that the Soviet Union would turn against us after the defeat of Germany and Japan. They made no attempt to insure our future against that eventuality. They brought forth no positive policy for the creation of a free and united Europe or for the preservation of the independence of China. They preferred wishful thinking to facts, and convinced themselves that Stalin would co-operate with them to create a free world of permanent peace. So at Teheran, Yalta, and Potsdam they handed Stalin the freedom of Eastern Europe and Manchuria, and prepared our present peril.

Quoted, by permission, from *A Foreign Policy for Americans* (Garden City, N.Y.: Doubleday, 1951), p. 6.

WALTER LIPPMANN:

The terms of the problem were defined at Yalta in the winter of 1945. There, with a victory over Germany in sight, Roosevelt, Churchill, and Stalin made a military settlement which fixed the boundaries where the converging armies were to meet, and were to wait while the governments negotiated the terms of peace which would provide for the withdrawal of the armies. The crucial issue in the world today [1947] is whether the Yalta military boundary, which was intended to be provisional for the period of the armistice, is to become the political boundary of two hostile coalitions.

The Yalta line registered an agreed estimate by Roosevelt, Churchill, and Stalin as to what would be the actual military situation at the close of hostilities. They knew that the Red Army would be in Warsaw, Bucharest, Budapest, Belgrade and Sofia. So Churchill and Roosevelt recognized that the military boundary for the armistice would place eastern Europe within the Soviet sphere. The British, on the other hand, were in Athens; the British-Americans were in Italy; therefore, Stalin recognized that Italy and Greece would be within the British and American sphere. . . .

The British and Americans, of course, could not accept the permanent division of the European continent along the Yalta line. They could not accept a settlement in which Poland, Czechoslovakia, Yugoslavia, Hungary, Rumania and Bulgaria would lose all independence and become incorporated as Soviet

195

republics in the U. S. S. R. They had a debt of honor to the countless patriots in those lands. They realized that if the frontiers of the Soviet system were extended as far west as the middle of Germany and Austria, then not only Germany and Austria but all western Europe might fall within the Russian sphere of influence and be dominated by the Soviet Union.

Thus for the best of reasons and with the best of motives they came to the conclusion that they must wage a diplomatic campaign to prevent Russia from expanding her sphere, to prevent her from consolidating it, and to compel her to contract it. But they failed to see clearly that until the Red Army evacuated eastern Europe and withdrew to the frontiers of the Soviet Union, none of these objectives could be achieved.

Had they seen clearly the significance of the military situation, they would not have committed the United States to anything in eastern Europe while the Soviet government had the power to oppose it, while the United States had no power to enforce it. They would have taken and noted the pledges and promises to respect the independence and the freedom of the nations of eastern Europe which Stalin gave them at Yalta. But they would not have committed the United States to a guarantee that Stalin would keep his pledges while his army was occupying eastern Europe.

For since the United States could not make good this guarantee, the onus of the violation of the pledges was divided between the Russians, who broke them, and the Americans, who had promised to enforce them and did not. It would have been far better to base our policy on the realities of the balance of power, to let Stalin, who made the promises which he alone could fulfill, take the whole responsibility for breaking them; to concentrate our effort on treaties of peace which would end the occupation of Europe.

Comments in Retrospect

Quoted, by permission, from *The Cold War—A Study in U.S. Foreign Policy* (New York: Harper, 1947), pp. 35-37.

ISAAC DON LEVINE:

The road to Teheran, Yalta and Berlin has from its very inception witnessed a race between President Roosevelt's pursuit of Soviet cooperation within the framework of a world organization and Stalin's unrelenting efforts to expand, through seizure and aggrandizement, the Soviet realm. While Roosevelt was busy building the peace of tomorrow, Stalin was preying upon his smaller and weaker neighbors in both Europe and Asia, from Finland to Iran.

This race is the pivot of the history of our days. It is a race between direct action and devious policy. For President Roosevelt never directly challenged the unilateral performance of Moscow. Instead he pressed more and more for the creation of international machinery to checkmate such action. However, the more Roosevelt sought to pin Stalin down through the device of a world organization, the more hurried and frequent became Stalin's overt and covert acts of expansion. Through such procedure Stalin had carved out for himself a vast new domain in Europe while the atmosphere of the great democracies reverberated with the song of international cooperation. By the time the Yalta conference convened, even the blind could see that Soviet unilateral action was making a mockery of world cooperation. President Roosevelt had to go to Yalta. He went determined to win the race against Stalin—by bringing into being his world organization for peace. . . .

In this setting and against this background it was inevitable that out of Yalta would come a high-sounding document serving as a cover for surrender to Stalin on all substantial issues.

Beginnings of the Cold War

Quoted, by permission, from "Yalta Aftermath," *American Affairs,* Vol. 7, No. 3 (July, 1945), National Industrial Conference Board, Inc., New York.

PROFESSOR WILLIAM HARDY McNEILL:

Whatever doubts there must be about Stalin's attitude to European revolution, there were none about his territorial aims. Throughout the war he had asserted that the territories he had annexed in 1939 and 1940 from Poland, Rumania, and Finland were permanently and legally his; and that the countries of Lithuania, Latvia, and Estonia, annexed in 1940, had become member republics of the Soviet Union. Improvement of the military security of Russia's western frontier was no doubt an important consideration which persuaded Stalin to take this position. Prestige was another factor. Stalin was no more than reasserting Russian authority over territories which had long recognized Tsarist rule, and which had been torn away from Russia at the time of her revolutionary weakness after the First World War. Finally, as far as the eastern provinces of pre-war Poland were concerned, Stalin may well have felt the need to pacify Ukranian and White Russian national feeling. At least he said so; and, in view of the rather delicate relationship which had existed between the Ukraine and Great Russia since the days of the Bolshevik Revolution, Stalin may have been speaking honestly.

Unfortunately for Stalin's political programme, there was a potential contradiction between his purposes in Eastern Europe and his hope of remaining on good terms with America and Britain. . . .

What Stalin conceived to be the future role of the Communist parties in the countries neighboring Russia cannot be stated

198

with any certainty. The Soviet Government disclaimed on several occasions any intention of revolutionizing the social order, in Poland or in other adjacent countries. Stalin told Mikolajczyk in October 1944: "Communism does not fit the Poles. They are too individualistic, too nationalistic. . . . Poland will be a capitalist state." . . . It is impossible to be sure that Stalin was frank in making statements such as these; but his day-to-day policy suggests that throughout 1944 he hoped to come to satisfactory terms with non-Communist groups in Poland, Rumania, and other countries similarly situated. . . . Perhaps Stalin hoped that Communist Parties would be sufficiently strong after the war to check by a sort of internal veto any anti-Russian tendencies that might arise in the governments of Europe, and wished no more than that for the immediate future.

If this is a fair statement of Stalin's aims—and in the nature of the case it is highly speculative—he no doubt hoped that they would prove acceptable to the Western Powers. Indeed, Britain and America might well have agreed to Stalin's programme if he had been able to persuade the Poles, Rumanians, and others to accept the role he had assigned to them; but as it turned out he was not able to do so without resort to high-handed intervention and brutal disregard of the niceties of democratic government.

As between the friendship of the Western Powers and a secure politico-military position on his western frontier, Stalin chose the latter. He probably never made the choice in any deliberate and cold-blooded manner. Rather, insisting upon the security of his frontiers, he little by little sacrificed the sympathy of Britain and America. . . .

Quoted, by permission, from *America, Britain and Russia—Their Co-Operation and Conflict, 1941-1946*, Royal Institute of International Affairs (London: Oxford University Press, 1953), pp. 406-408.

Beginnings of the Cold War

AMBASSADOR GEORGE F. KENNAN:

Once we had come into the European war, and granted the heavy military handicaps with which the Western powers were then confronted in that theater, the decisions taken throughout the remainder of the war years were those of harried, over-worked men, operating in the vortex of a series of tremendous pressures, military and otherwise, which we today find it difficult to remember or to imagine. I think that some injustice is being done both to the men in question and to the cause of historical understanding by the latter-day interpretations which regard specific decisions of the wartime years as the source of all our present difficulties. The most vociferous charges of wartime mistakes relate primarily to our dealings with the U. S. S. R. and particularly to the wartime conferences of Moscow, Teheran, and Yalta.

As one who was very unhappy about these conferences at the time they were taking place and very worried lest they lead to false hopes and misunderstandings, I may perhaps be permitted to say that I think their importance has recently been considerably overrated. If it cannot be said that the Western democracies gained very much from these talks with the Russians, it would also be incorrect to say that they gave very much away. The establishment of Soviet military power in eastern Europe and the entry of Soviet forces into Manchuria was not the result of these talks; it was the result of the military operations during the concluding phases of the war. There was nothing the Western democracies could have done to prevent the Russians from entering these areas except to get there first, and this we were not in a position to do. . . .

. . . in all these matters we must bear in mind both the overriding compulsion of military necessity under which our statesmen were working and also the depth of their conviction that one had no choice but to gamble on the possibility that Soviet suspicions might be broken down and Soviet collaboration won for the postwar period, if there were to be any hope of permanent peace. Many of us who were familiar with Russian matters were impatient with this line of thought at the time, because we knew how poor were the chances of success, and we saw no reason why a Western world which kept its nerves, its good humor, and a due measure of military preparedness should not continue indefinitely to live in the same world with the power of the Kremlin without flying to either of the extremes of political intimacy or war.

In the light of what has occurred subsequently, I can see that our view, too, was not fully rounded. We were right about the nature of Soviet power; but we were wrong about the ability of American democracy at this stage in its history to bear for long a situation full of instability, inconvenience, and military danger. Perhaps Harry Hopkins and F. D. R. had more reason than we then supposed to believe that everything depended on the possibility of changing the attitude of the Soviet regime. But, if so, this is then only an indication that the dilemma was crueler than any of us really appreciated. . . .

Quoted, by permission, from *American Diplomacy—1900-1950* (Chicago: University of Chicago Press, 1951), pp. 84-87.

Professor Norman A. Graebner:

Only the most astute observers during the war could see that the United States, in its pursuit of total victory, was helping to create a new balance of power that would prove to be as unacceptable as that created by Hitler. Any return to normalcy required a Russian withdrawal to its prewar boundaries and, in general, its prewar status in world affairs—to be achieved quite automatically through the Soviet acceptance of the principle of self-determination of peoples. Fundamentally, the Atlantic Charter promised a postwar world without permanent victors or permanent losers. For the American people, having suffered no invasion, this was both a feasible and a moral arrangement. . . .

Unfortunately, the well-established facts of international life scarcely warranted the Western expectation of a new world order based on the Wilsonian principles of justice and self-determination. Throughout the war it was clear that Allied interests coincided only on the issue of defeating the common enemy. The United States and Great Britain entered the war as satiated powers, seeking nothing but peace and stability in world affairs. They had written their moral and limited purpose into the Atlantic Charter as early as August, 1941. For the Kremlin this repudiation of the tangible and lasting emoluments of victory was never an acceptable basis of action. Whether Russia eventually signed the Atlantic Charter or not, she would not settle for a world based on the principle of self-determination. Any assumption that she would expected too much denial of that country's historic problems and ambitions.

Quoted, by permission, from *Cold War Diplomacy, 1945-1960* (Princeton, N.J.: Van Nostrand, 1962), pp. 8 and 13.

PROFESSOR JOHN L. SNELL:

The genuine hope of Roosevelt and Churchill for postwar cooperation with the U. S. S. R. proved to be an illusion, but even this hope was virtually imposed by necessity. Knowing that the only alternative to cooperation in the postwar world would be an outright war or lasting and costly vigilance against the U. S. S. R., both of the Western leaders were prepared to make some concessions to obtain Stalin's enduring cooperation. "The only hope for the world," Churchill wrote as late as January, 1945, "is the agreement of the three Great Powers. If they quarrel, our children are undone." . . . If Roosevelt had refused to work for this return to "normalcy" he would have won certain condemnation by the American people. But he could not try for a return to peaceful conditions and at the same time plan for a crusade against Communist Russia.

How deeply Roosevelt really *believed* in the possibility of postwar cooperation with the U. S. S. R. is impossible to know; his saying that he had a "hunch" that Stalin would cooperate is scarcely proof of strong conviction, nor are wartime avowals of his faith in Stalin; Churchill himself once commented that he "felt bound to proclaim his confidence in Soviet good faith in the hope of securing it." Certainly Roosevelt hoped that cooperation would be possible but, hope or no hope, he *had* to work for it, given the expectations of the American people. They would be made willing to assume continuing global responsibilities in peacetime only by the clear demonstration between 1944 and 1947 that Stalin's expansion could be curbed in no other way. It can be left to those who enjoy the Cold War—if there be any—to say that the wartime efforts to cooperate with Stalin should never have been made or should not have been carried as far as they were.

Quoted, by permission, from *Illusion and Necessity: The Diplomacy of Global War 1939-1945* (Boston: Houghton Mifflin, 1963), pp. 212-13.

Principal Sources

(Numbers refer to the notes to the respective chapters, where the full title of each work, its publisher, and date of publication are first stated.)

Wherever possible, I have relied on primary sources, but a number of signposts to the documentary material have been invaluable.

There are two especially useful surveys of the wartime dealings between Russia and the West: William H. McNeill's *America, Britain and Russia—Their Cooperation and Conflict, 1941-1946* (ch.3, n.7) and Herbert Feis's *Churchill, Roosevelt, Stalin—The War They Waged and the Peace They Sought* (ch.1, n.6). Of these, Mc-Neill's book is the more useful for research purposes because it contains more factual information and is painstakingly provided with references to the primary sources. On the other hand, Feis has written much the more readable book. Although I have not had recourse to it, mention should also be made of John L. Snell's compact *Illusion and Necessity—The Diplomacy of Global War, 1939-1945,* which was published subsequently, but from which a perceptive passage is quoted in Chapter 8.

McNeill's volume was published in 1953 under the auspices of the Royal Institute of International Affairs, and the author acknowledges "the scrutiny of a number of individuals familiar with the events narrated, but who must, according to Chatham House policy, remain anonymous." It is an admirable book. Its limitation lies in its publishing date, which was prior to the time when the Yalta and Potsdam volumes, the Stalin correspondence, and even Churchill's last volume (*Triumph and Tragedy*) became available.

It is to Feis that I owe a number of startling discoveries, for instance that Russia, when it initially subscribed to the Atlantic Charter, did so with an important reservation (see the note on p. x); that Churchill told or reminded Roosevelt in 1942 that Russia's acceptance of the Charter had been on the basis that it would regain the enlarged territories it occupied at the time of the German attack (ch.3, n.11); and that Roosevelt recalled to Churchill after Yalta that it had been understood there that the Lublin Poles were to have preponderance over the non-Communists (ch.4, n.28). Feis acknowledged the use of State Department records and of papers in possession of Mr. Harriman that have not yet been published.

With regard to Poland, the books *The Rape of Poland—Pattern of Soviet Conquest* by former Prime Minister Mikolajczyk ch.1, n.11) and *Defeat in Victory* by former Ambassador Ciechanowski (ch.3, n.23) are invaluable, also for information that does not necessarily support the wisdom of the policies of the erstwhile Polish government-in-exile, e.g., the detailed evidence of how persuasively Churchill urged a conciliatory policy toward Russia upon the reluctant Polish leaders (ch.3, n.33, n.43). On the Katyn massacre, the House *Hearings* (ch.1, n.9) are the most useful source because they contain both the Polish and the Russian cases, in addition to material not found in either. A useful summary is also found in Zawodny's *Death in the Forest* (ch.3, n.16). There are some unexplained discrepancies between the original Polish documents, the House *Hearings,* and Zawodny's book as regards the exact composition of the prisoner population of Starobielsk, Kozielsk, and Ostashkov.

Of course, the memoirs of the participants in the various negotiations are prime source material: the Hull *Memoirs* (ch.1, n.8), Churchill's *The Second World War* (ch.3, n.5), the Truman *Memoirs* (ch.4, n.30), also Sherwood's *Roosevelt and Hopkins* (ch.2, n.1)— where many years ago I first came upon the record of the Stalin-Hopkins conversations—and, to a lesser extent, Byrnes's *Speaking Frankly* (ch.1, n.10), Stettinius's *Roosevelt and the Russians—The Yalta Conference* (see p. 193), and the *Forrestal Diaries* (ch.1, n.4), and Leahy's *I Was There* (ch.5, n.12).

Principal Sources

Although both Feis and McNeill provide admirable descriptions and analyses of the Yalta Conference, I have relied primarily on the State Department's volume *The Conferences of Malta and Yalta* (ch.1, n.1). The same is true of the Department's volumes *Conferences of Cairo and Tehran* (ch.3, n.30) and *Conference of Berlin (Potsdam) 1945* (ch.2, n.1.). Chapter 2 is, of course, entirely drawn from the Potsdam volume. In addition, I have occasionally consulted the useful *Documents on American Foreign Relations, 1944-1945* (ch.5, n.44) and the fascinating *Documents on German Foreign Policy* (ch.3, n.1), which were published by the Department of State.

The Russians have "scooped" the West with their official publication of the *Stalin Correspondence* (ch.3, n.19), which contains the texts of all the important wartime messages between Stalin on the one hand and Churchill, Attlee, Roosevelt, and Truman on the other, and thus constitutes important primary source material. I was informed that the texts are authentic. On the other hand, one message from Churchill to Stalin, which is contained in *Triumph and Tragedy* (ch.3, n.5), is not found in the *Stalin Correspondence,* apparently because it was sent after the end of the war in Europe.

For many years I had collected clippings from the *New York Times* on materials related to the beginnings of the Cold War. For this study, I also methodically went through the Department's microfilmed files of the *New York Times* for the period between Yalta and Potsdam, and for part of that period also consulted the records of official radio broadcasts of Russia and Germany. It was while doing this that I came upon the historical oddity of Göbbels's authorship of the term "iron curtain" in February 1945 (ch.4, n.20). On the subject of military operations, I have relied on Wilmot's *The Struggle for Europe* (ch.3, n.48). In the matter of the surrender negotiations in Switzerland, Wilmot's shorter account contains some facts not mentioned by Feis, so I have gone back to the primary source adduced by Wilmot, since Feis's sources are not stated (ch.4, n.24).

On the history of the San Francisco Conference, I have used Ruth Russell's *A History of the United Nations Charter* (ch.4, n.5), also for corroboration of the information on Argentina obtained from the survey volumes. In the same manner I have used, for reference purposes, *The Realignment of Europe* (ch.5, n.62), a companion volume to the excellent one by McNeill, also published under the auspices of the Royal Institute of International Affairs, and also edited by Arnold Toynbee, but of more uneven quality. *Tito* by Vladimir Dedijer (ch.5, n.28), and the angry exchange between the Yugoslav and Soviet Communist Parties, reproduced in *The Soviet-Yugoslav Dispute* (ch.5, n.58), issued by the Royal Institute, were the sources from which my inferences were drawn regarding Stalin's apparent willingness to carve up the Balkans.

Source materials on the history of Russia's request for a $6 billion credit are limited. The *Yalta Papers* (ch.1, n.1) contain some revealing documents on the earliest reactions in the United States government, but more will become available when the 1945 volume of *Foreign Relations of the United States* is published. I have used the President's reports on Lend-Lease as primary sources, but have had to rely on Deane's rather chatty *Strange Alliance* (ch.6, n.10) for some facts that cannot yet be documented. One of the most revealing bits of information came to my attention when General Smith's *My Three Years in Moscow* (ch.6, n.38) was first serialized in the *New York Times,* and his account of a conversation in 1947 disclosed that it had taken us over a year to respond to the January 1945 request. (It appears, however, that Stalin's statement that the request had not even been acknowledged is in error. On this point, we must await more published documentation—also on how it could happen that a renewed Russian request could get "lost" in the United States bureaucracy.) The Senate *Hearings* (ch.6, n.33) and Mosely's excellent essays on the frustrations of United States postwar planners (ch.5, n.77; ch.6, n.32) round out the principal sources of this chapter.

It will not have escaped the reader that I have refrained from making judgments in the narrative, except when it is a matter of evaluating the evidence itself, as in the case of the meaning and wording of the "ambiguous compromise" at Yalta on the formation of a Polish Provisional Government of National Unity. There are, however, some exceedingly interesting judgments of the events contained in Feis and McNeill, and I have placed these in the notes whenever they seemed particularly relevant. For instance, both of these professional historians seem to agree in their evaluation of the Declaration on Liberated Europe as a clear case of misunderstanding, and I have quoted extensively from them in note 18 to Chapter 4 because these comments seem important. Similarly, I have picked up in note 19 extensive quotes from Captain Thorneycroft's speech about the Polish settlement because it seems to contain useful insights that deserve consideration. I owe this quotation to Norman Graebner's interesting documentary study, *Cold War Diplomacy* (ch.4, n.19). Also, McNeill's comment on the importance of Italy as a precedent for the occupation policies in the Balkans (ch.5, n.9) makes explicit a judgment that is perhaps implicitly contained in the historical facts as they have been presented.

Index

Index

Index